THE CRITICAL THINKING TOOLKIT

GALEN A. FORESMAN, PETER S. FOSL, AND JAMIE C. WATSON

THE CRITICAL THINKING TOOLKIT

WILEY Blackwell

This edition first published 2017

Registered Office
John Wiley & Sons Ltd, The Atrium, Southern Gate, Chichester, West Sussex, PO19 8SQ, UK

Editorial Offices
350 Main Street, Malden, MA 02148-5020, USA
9600 Garsington Road, Oxford, OX4 2DQ, UK
The Atrium, Southern Gate, Chichester, West Sussex, PO19 8SQ, UK

For details of our global editorial offices, for customer services, and for information about how to apply for permission to reuse the copyright material in this book please see our website at www.wiley.com/wiley-blackwell.

Library of Congress Cataloging-in-Publication Data

Names: Foresman, Galen A., author.
Title: The critical thinking toolkit / Galen A. Foresman, Peter S. Fosl, and Jamie C. Watson.
Description: Hoboken : Wiley, 2016. | Includes bibliographical references and index.
Identifiers: LCCN 2016006532 (print) | LCCN 2016012956 (ebook) | ISBN 9780470659960 (cloth) | ISBN 9780470658697 (pbk.) | ISBN 9781118982020 (pdf) | ISBN 9781118981993 (epub)
Subjects: LCSH: Reasoning. | Critical thinking. | Logic.
Classification: LCC BC177 .F67 2016 (print) | LCC BC177 (ebook) | DDC 160–dc23
LC record available at http://lccn.loc.gov/2016006532

A catalogue record for this book is available from the British Library.

Cover image: Getty/© Lisa Quarfoth

Set in 10/12pt MinionPro by Aptara Inc., New Delhi, India

1 2017

SKY10027150_051921

To our students and to the Logos

Contents

Acknowledgments

The authors would like to thank in the first place our families for their patience as we labored on this book. Without their support, inspiration, and advice this project would not have come to fruition. In particular, we wish to thank Cate Fosl and Darlena Watson. We are especially grateful to Robert Arp for getting the ball rolling on this project, as well as to editors Jeff Dean and Liam Cooper for making sure it kept rolling.

We thank Julian Baggini, too, for graciously permitting us to extend the Toolkit program to the field of critical thinking and for permitting us to rework material drawn from a number of entries in *The Philosopher's Toolkit* for this text. We thank Nathan Gray and Nathan Eric Dickman (Young Harris College) as well as Robert Bass (University of North Carolina, Pembroke) for valuable insights and examples. We thank Kevin Decker for his close reading and helpful criticisms. One of the greatest critical thinkers we know, Jamie Miller, offered us helpful advice, pedagogical as well as logical. Cate Fosl (University of Louisville) offered important insights on matters of race and feminism. Jack Furlong and Bob Rosenberg (Transylvania University) helped refine sections dealing with the natural sciences. Alexander Dick (University of British Columbia) advised the authors on topics in critical theory.

We are grateful, too, to the institutions that have supported our academic work: North Carolina Agricultural & Technical State University, Transylvania University, and Broward College. We are also grateful, more generally, for the continued existence of institutions of higher education that sustain the cultivation and communication of critical thinking. Our civilization depends deeply upon those efforts and on the support of donors, governments, and students. The professors who introduced us to logic and critical thinking deserve special acknowledgment, as we recognize that it is most immediately and perhaps most crucially through the efforts of fine teachers such as they are that good, clear, and critical thinking is cultivated in our world and passed on to new generations. Outstanding instruction in logic was afforded to us by Professor Frank Wilson at Bucknell University, by Burke Townsend at the University of Montana, Piers Rawling at Florida State University, and by Michael Bradie at Bowling Green State University. They in turn learned from fine and able teachers and inquirers into logic, epistemology, criticism, the sciences, and psychology in a weave of traditions that stretches back to antiquity. We hope in some small way to carry on those traditions in this volume. Any errors or shortcomings it presents are wholly our own.

Wiley deserves our deep gratitude not only for publishing our work but also for advancing and sustaining thoughtful publications at a time when doing so is increasingly complex and difficult. No book produced through a fine publisher is realized without the guidance of its editors, and we have been especially fortunate in the editing provided by Alison Kostka, Liam Cooper, and Sally Cooper. We are grateful for the keen eyes and good judgment of copy editor Fiona Screen and proofreader Helen Kemp, for the talents of the artists who produced the book's cover, as well as for the marketing and distribution teams that have made this text available to readers. We salute you all!

Introduction

The Very Idea of Critical Thinking

Critical thinking sometimes seems as if it needs an apology, or rather it seems itself to be a kind of apology, an apology for the humanities and the liberal arts and sciences generally. Having failed to convince many people that the liberal arts are simply good in themselves or in their own terms, academics sometimes seem as though they have concocted the meretricious idea of "critical thinking" in order to help higher education sell itself to the worlds of commerce, law, and politics. Instead of arguing that the liberal arts comprise some of the very best ways to spend a human life, period (and that we ought, therefore, to support them enthusiastically and share them as widely as possible), academics seem inclined to wave the flag of critical thinking to convince governments, parents, students, and donors that the liberal arts offer something that's "useful" or "profitable" in the "real" world.

Critical thinking also seems to appeal to administrators and the administratively inclined because it poses as something testable, as composed of skills that produce "measurable outcomes" readily subject to "metrics" and "assessment." Yielding measurable, quantifiable outcomes is important not only for demonstrating to those outside the academy the value of critical thinking and the liberal arts but also for "accountability," for oversight, for ranking and managing, and perhaps for policing liberal arts faculties.

There is truth in all this, embarrassingly so. But it's not the whole story about critical thinking (or the liberal arts), not by a long shot. The authors of this book are convinced that the family of practices collected under the rubric of "critical thinking" does indeed include some of the best and most important activities human beings have forged and re-forged, shaped and refined over the last three millennia. It's not too much to say, in our view, that critical thinking distills some of the very best of that inheritance. In the development of our sciences, our political institutions, and our very self-understandings, critical thinking has played a central role, and it's simply

The Critical Thinking Toolkit, First Edition. Galen A. Foresman, Peter S. Fosl, and Jamie C. Watson.

fine and good to pass on that treasure to future generations. What has been true of our history remains true today: strong critical thinking is not only useful for commerce, the law, and technology, it's absolutely crucial to a dynamic and thriving culture, and it defines an essential component of any solid education.

But what is critical thinking? What composes it? In this volume, we've taken a broad, interdisciplinary, and relatively comprehensive approach to critical thinking. While many critical thinking texts focus almost exclusively on logical topics, we've also compiled critical insights and practices that have been cultivated by the natural and social sciences, notably psychology, by literature and literary criticism as well as by the fine arts, and by political and social theories. We treat literature, rhetoric, and the arts not simply as obstructions or distractions that get in the way of clear, analytical, and logical thinking – though they sometimes can do that. We recognize in addition that the visual, literary, and generally rhetorical arts possess distinctive tools to enhance and deepen critical thinking. While the critical tools developed by philosophers, logicians, mathematicians, and empirical scientists are extremely important to good critical thinking, the critical instruments honed by theorists in literary, political, and social theory have been profound. No account of the possible methods of critical thinking available today would be respectable or even roughly complete without them. Arguments are, indeed, terribly important, but they're not by any means the whole story of critical thinking. We encourage readers, therefore, to take a similarly broad, interdisciplinary, and inclusive approach and to consider the diverse ways critical thinking has been cultivated across the spectrum of reflective human thought.

Critical thinking in the formal and empirical sciences

Considering the structure of this book, we begin with logic, since logic is basic and essential to critical thinking. Chapters 1–4 of this ten-chapter volume are accordingly devoted to explaining some of the most important critical tools logicians have crafted, especially for the practices of what they call *deductive* reasoning. These techniques can seem a bit daunting to beginners, but because logic is so important we encourage you to press on through them. Logicians have studied the *formal* qualities of deductive inferences over thousands of years, and they've produced several logical systems that critical thinkers can use to test arguments. Those tests are not only indispensable tools for critical thinking. They also share the virtue of producing definite answers about good and bad reasoning using procedures that are clear, reliable, and not terribly difficult to use.

The oldest of these systems we'll address (Chapter 3) was systematized first by Aristotle in fourth-century BCE Greece. It's come to be called *categorical logic* since it's a logic that's based upon categories of things. We'll map out seven tests for the validity of arguments using categorical logic. Those seven by themselves will provide critical thinkers with a rich and powerful set of tools to interpret and assess vast regions of human reasoning.

Yes, humans seem to possess a natural capacity for recognizing good reasoning even without studying critical thinking in a formal way, but the systems we present are important to master because they make it possible for skilled critical thinkers to build on that natural capacity and employ proven and useful rules in expansive ways – including articulating proper explanations and definitions, determining logical equivalences, and identifying contraries and contradictions, as well as a variety of other logical relationships. We'll explain and demonstrate the use of helpful pictographic tests using Venn diagrams and Gensler stars, and after setting out some basic logical theory we'll show you how to apply a number of simple procedures for reliably identifying valid and invalid arguments almost in a snap.

The second principal kind of formal logic we'll address (Chapter 4) has come to be called *propositional* or *sentential logic* – because, yes, it's the logic of propositions or whole sentences. These sections will present you with additional ways to test arguments, especially through what logicians call truth tables, common forms of valid argument, and tried-and-true rules of inference. Truth tables are attractive to people because they offer a graphical way of testing arguments, and one that's simplicity is perhaps even more exhaustive and direct than Venn diagrams. Learning the formal structures of the most common valid as well as invalid arguments together with what we think is an essential collection of other inference rules will help you sharpen the focus of your reasoning detectors so that the success or failure of arguments becomes much more easily recognizable.

Chapter 5 sets out a substantial list of some of the most common ways people go wrong in their daily reasoning. These common *informal fallacies* aren't failures of the formal or structural dimensions of arguments (the stuff of Chapters 3–4), but rather failures of another kind. Sometimes what goes wrong in reasoning isn't a matter of argument form at all but instead often involves psychological factors that yield quasi-inferences that pose as good reasoning but simply aren't. Sometimes, alternatively, the problem lies with the underlying concepts and assumptions behind a claim. Those concepts and assumptions can be irrelevant, confused, or simply false, and as we'll see they can really mess up your reasoning. Good critical thinking skills of the sort described in Chapter 5 have been designed to detect them, and there are many of them. Because some informal fallacies are particularly related to scientific thinking, we'll broach additional informal fallacies across the remaining text, especially in those chapters devoted more directly to inductive reasoning and the empirical sciences.

There are sadly, then, a lot of ways that reasoning can go wrong. The modern natural and social sciences were born from a struggle to deal with many of these kinds of error while simultaneously trying both to understand the world and to answer the philosophical challenge of *skepticism* – the idea that knowledge itself might not be possible. As a result of those challenges, scientists and philosophers of science developed important ideas regarding what counts in terms of empirical inquiry as good *explanation* and solid *justification*. We'll therefore examine what makes scientific forms of inquiry so strong, and we'll also look at how science can go wrong. Chapters 6–9 will draw lessons in critical thinking from the natural and social sciences as well as from ongoing philosophical confrontations with skepticism. We'll examine how best to confront the epistemological challenges of skepticism, how to think well and critically about causal explanations and statistical claims, how to enlist scientific principles critically, how to think critically even about science itself, and we'll consider what science has learned about why human beings make errors. Critical thinkers should certainly be able to assess non-scientific claims using scientific rationality, but they should also possess some facility with assessing scientific claims themselves.

Critical thinking, critical theory, and critical politics

Human beings are linguistic beings. We communicate, reason, and criticize using language, and the critical theories developed by scholars in fields related to rhetoric, languages, and literature have gone a long way toward explaining not only how communication works but also how it fails to work – that is, how language and our human modes of expression themselves create, even require, the possibility of error, confusion, and misunderstanding. The meanings we wish to express are difficult to express. They're elusive and fragile and complicated. We all know this on some level, but critical thinkers must become especially sensitive to it. Narratives, poetic tropes, voice, and other rhetorical dimensions of texts, however, not only offer opportunities for error and distortion. They also yield indispensable ways of understanding our selves and our world. Chapter 10 is designed therefore to help you consider critically the rhetorical and semiotic dimensions of the world in whatever text you confront – and not just in a theoretical way. Like our other chapters, Chapter 10 offers examples and problems for you to use in putting these tools to work.

Human practices of expression are also tied up with political relations. We are, as Aristotle observed, political animals. Moreover, political theorists, especially across the past few centuries, have come to understand that politics doesn't only exist in the halls of government, in voting booths, on explicitly political Internet web sites, or on clearly political TV or radio talk shows. Politics is, rather, pervasive and infuses our ordinary language, our concepts, our conduct, indeed the very institutions that compose our societies and cultures broadly speaking. Engaging political as well as moral topics critically, therefore, may involve not only thought but also action.

Political action may be a matter of subversion and destabilization, of prising open spaces for new ways of life, and deconstructing what we determine needs to change. It may also, however, be about justifying and stabilizing values, principles, and moral claims – those that already exist and we think it important to keep, to protect, and to secure. In order for readers to engage their own political world more effectively, in addition to questions related to justification and values in Chapters 6–9 we also lay out tools drawn from political theory in Chapter 10. We don't presume the political theories we describe to exhaust the field of political thought, and we don't necessarily endorse them ourselves, but we do think these are among the most important critical approaches today, and it's necessary for able critical thinkers to gain some facility with them.

Strong critical thinkers, in sum, should be able not only to wield the tools of logic and science but also those that illuminate the complexities of language and communication as well as those that help confront, advance, or resist the principal forms of morality and politics at work in the world today. Critical thinking should not only be directed toward improved inquiry into questions of truth and falsehood but also into issues of meaning more generally as well as imperatives and possibilities of moral and political action.

Critical thinking, finitude, and self-understanding

There's something else. We wish to make it clear that critical thinking, like our book as a whole, is about self-understanding. It's part of that ancient project enshrined in the inscription on the temple at Delphi and in the liberal arts and sciences: "know thyself." Using critical thinking we produce critiques not just of arguments, data sets, propositions, and texts in the abstract. We also produce critiques that reveal our limits, our weaknesses, our finitude, and our selves as we actually exist in the world. Thinking about the world, about others, and about ourselves in light of a reflective and critical self-understanding of the human condition may be even more important than winning arguments or unreflectively accumulating facts, wealth, or power. It may, indeed, be the most important critical thinking outcome of all.

Using this book

This volume is not a complete text in logic, cognitive psychology, epistemology, critical theory, or political and social theory. The world of ideas is vast. We have collected what we think are the essentials for a basic grasp of critical thinking, and we have compressed, so far as possible, our entries to provide you with substantial and sophisticated but also concise accounts of the tools we address. You may read the text sequentially since it follows an arc from the positive establishment of claims through the complexities of logical and scientific thinking and reasoning to, finally, a critical *denouement* in rhetoric and politics. But the text may be read in other ways, too. You may start anywhere and either follow your own muses or fork off onto the network of paths we recommend using the suggested "See also" pointers at the close of most entries and chapters.

You will often see us referring in the body of the text to the preceding toolkits in this series: *The Philosopher's Toolkit* and *The Ethics Toolkit*. That's because we understand these books to work together synergistically with ours, and they often offer entries that complement and enrich our own. Some of the entries of this volume overlap with entries in those other toolkits (and we are grateful to Julian Baggini for permission to do that), and so together we think they offer a kind of functional whole of critical and philosophical thinking. But this volume stands on its own, too, very much so; and it offers readers a fine gateway all its own to these powerful, critical tools.

Our book also contains larders of examples and problems for study and exercise. These may be enlisted by instructors in their class preparation or simply by readers for further reflection. As we've not always provided answers to these problems and questions, they're as much matters of provocation as instruction. A list of web sites at the end of the volume suggests additional resources relevant to critical thinking freely available on the Internet.

Know thyself and think critically.

1 Basic Tools for Critical Thinking about Arguments

1.1 Claims

"Listen to reason!" cried Charlotte, exasperated after an hour of argument with Charles. And Charlotte's frustration may have been perfectly justified. What is reason? And why should we listen to it? Most basically, reasoning is about advancing *truth claims* by means of special *logical* procedures of *argument* (see 1.2). One of the most basic elements of critical thinking, then, especially when engaged with issues related to logic and science, is to discern whether claims are actually true and to distinguish them from claims that are not true.

In practice, language is our most fundamental tool in this process. Language allows us to articulate what we judge to be true or false, and it allows us to share and communicate those judgments to others. Ultimately, a good critical thinker must develop an acute grasp of language in order to make clear and precise claims about the truth and to assess how well or badly they function in the logic of an argument. Logicians have technical names for the kind of sentences out of which logical arguments are built. They call them *statements* or *propositions*, and they're simply sentences that can be either true or false (in logical terms, they possess a *truth value*). To really understand statements and their truth values, however, keep the following in mind.

- *Bivalence*. Statements or propositions can *only* have one truth value, and it must only be either true or false. Moreover, statements or propositions can't be both true and false in the same sense under the same circumstances. Logicians call this the principle *the law of bivalence*. (To be sure, there are multi-valued logics with values besides true and false, but again they're the subject of a different, more advanced book.)
- *Excluded middle*. There's no middle ground or gray area between truth values in basic logic – no "truthiness" as the comedian Steven Colbert might say. Statements or propositions can't be "sort of true" and "sort of false." Logicians call this

The Critical Thinking Toolkit, First Edition. Galen A. Foresman, Peter S. Fosl, and Jamie C. Watson.

requirement the *law of excluded middle*. (Yep, there are *fuzzy logics* that accept gray areas, but we won't be dealing with them here.)

- *Non-statements and propositions*. Keep in mind, too, that sentences that aren't (in logic's technical sense) statements or propositions simply don't have truth value. Neither questions ("Where are you going?") nor commands ("Stop that!") nor exclamations ("Wow!!!") are properly speaking true or false; and so they can't be proper parts of arguments, logically understood.

Now, the idea of a *claim*, in the sense we use the term here, adds for the sake of critical thinking just a bit more to what logicians strictly call statements and propositions. In particular, *claims* are statements that indicate a position has been taken. A claim, in other words, is a statement or proposition that in some meaningful sense sincerely belongs to whomever or whatever asserts it. One of the first judgments a good critical thinker must make, then, is to determine in just what way a statement is presented. Perhaps it's meant sincerely and seriously, but perhaps it's just being used hypothetically, ironically, as a joke, an instructive example, a lie, or perhaps in the recitation of some movie script. Or maybe it is simply being used to provoke an audience, to gain attention, to test someone's response, or perhaps for some other reason entirely. There are countless things one can do with words and other forms of expression. So, while most of the material in this and the next four chapters applies to all claims, and not just to statements or propositions, we will use the language of "claims" to keep the question of claim or non-claim in mind.

Here's the upshot. Since it's often the case that critical thinking involves discerning truth and error, a good critical thinker must learn how to identify claims that are true, or most likely seem true, while at the same time recognizing and avoiding claims that are best judged false. What's more, a good critical thinker will recognize and admit when he or she does not know whether a claim is true or false. Critical thinking sometimes requires reserving judgment as to whether or not a claim is true until, if ever, sufficient reason for determining the truth or falsity of that claim is discovered.

Beliefs and opinions

In the 1989 comedy film, *The Big Lebowski*, a competitor scheduled to face the main character, the Dude, in the next round of a bowling tournament declares that his team is going to crush the Dude's. The Dude, at least pretending to be unfazed, responds, now famously, by remarking, "Well, that's just your opinion, man." It's not uncommon for people to distinguish strong truth claims from those that are weaker by calling the weaker claims opinions. People often make claims such as, "The world is round," implying it's something we definitely *know* to be true, that it's a *fact*. When, on the other hand, people make claims such as, "Pele was a better athlete than Gretzky," we deflate the claim by saying that it's just their "opinion."

Beliefs can obviously often be either true or false, but a misleading though nevertheless common misunderstanding about the difference between strong assertions (such as knowledge claims) and mere opinions is that opinions aren't really true or false. As such, they're often thought to be free from the same scrutiny and justification required by claims to *know*. The result of this mistaken view is that many people believe that one's opinions are somehow insulated from dispute or challenge. Opinions are treated as if they stand alone as islands in our thoughts, entirely disconnected from criticism and critical thinking. In reality, however, our opinions are still very much claims open to criticism. They are, after all, claims, and therefore either true or false. (Matters concerned with knowing are described as *epistemic*, and *epistemology* is the study of knowledge. Matters concerned with belief we'll sometimes call *doxastic*.)

In addition, it's important to understand that opinions are often influenced by what we value. This mixing of beliefs and values sometimes makes it difficult or confusing to assess their truth. But a good critical thinker's toolkit provides the tools for tackling this seemingly tricky task (see 5.5, 7.2, 8.2, and 8.5). In the meantime, just keep in mind that opinions often incorporate judgments and emotions about what is valuable, either subjectively, to the person expressing the opinion, or objectively, to everyone in the world.

Simple and complex claims

A *simple* claim is a claim that, logically speaking, isn't divisible into other, more basic claims. This is usually a single subject-predicate formula, for example, "It is a cat," or "That ball is round." A *complex* or *compound* claim is a claim logically composed of two or more claims (or, minimally, a single claim that's negated) connected by special words or ideas logicians call *logical operators* or *connectives*. (Of course, not all devices to connect one sentence with another do so as a matter of logic – as any poet or lyricist will tell you.)

Simple claims, as some logicians have observed, are kind of like atoms, while complex claims are kind of like molecules. The claim that "Earth exists" is a simple claim. If, however, we add to the claim that the Earth exists another claim, "Humans live on Earth," then we will have created the complex or molecular claim: "Earth exists, and humans live on it." Notice that a complex claim may be expressed in lots of ways, and yet still be composed of the same simple claims:

> Humans live on Earth, and Earth exists.
> Humans live on Earth, which exists.
> Earth exists, and humans live on Earth.

Sometimes, two sentences, whether simple or complex, can be said to possess the same *meaning*. Having the "same meaning" can, however, mean a variety of things. In this context, let's just say that sentences having the same meaning can be used interchangeably, and one reason for this may be that the claims have the same *cognitive* or *material content*. (Another reason, as we'll discover in the next three chapters, may be that they have the same *formal* qualities, which means they have the same logical structure.) The cognitive or material content of most claims determines the conditions that make those claims true or false – or what logicians call the *truth conditions.* In other words, the claim that the Earth exists is true if and only if the Earth really exists. The Earth's existing is the condition that must be met in order for the claim "Earth exists" to be true.

The truth conditions of complex claims, however, are a bit more, well, complex than those of simple claims. The truth conditions of complex claims are determined not only by the simple claims from which they are constructed but also by the *logical operators* or *connectives* used to combine the simple claims and sometimes other properties of the complex. Common logical operators are "and," "or," "if," "if and only if," and "not." (The last of these, "not," is unique and extremely powerful. It's not used to combine multiple simple claims, but rather to change the truth value of a claim, whether simple or complex, to its opposite value. If true, a negated claim becomes false; if false, a negated claim becomes true.)

Earth exists.	simple claim
Earth does not exist.	negation (not)
Earth exists, and humans live on it.	conjunction (and)
Earth exists, or humans live on it.	disjunction (or)
Earth exists, if humans live on it.	conditional (if)
Earth exists, if and only if humans live on it.	biconditional (if and only if)

Of course, each of these claims has a different meaning, and those meanings are derived from the cognitive content of the simple claims – "Earth exists" and "Humans live on it" – as well as from the logical operators that are used to combine or modify those simple claims.

Here's a tricky bit. It's important to remember that despite the number of simple claims composing a complex claim, a complex claim can be viewed as one, big single claim. That's because a complex claim is, as a whole, either true or false, just like a simple claim. The simple claims "Earth exists" and "Martians exist" have truth values (the first is true and the second, we presume, is false). But combine them into a complex claim using a connective and the result has its own truth value: the claim "Earth exists *and* Martians exist" is false; the claim "Earth exists *or* Martians exist" is true. You will see exactly why in Chapter 4. For now, just be aware that complex claims are single if not simple claims, and that each has its own single truth value.

Truth functionality

Here's something even a little trickier. The truth value of different kinds of complex claims must be determined in different ways. For some complex claims, the truth or falsehood of the whole is *completely* determined in a logical sense just by the truth values of the component claims that compose it as well as by the way they relate to one another – that is, by (1) the simple claims plus (2) the logical operators that connect and modify them. For other kinds of claims, you can only determine the truth value of the whole claim by considering other features of the claim and perhaps only the claim as a whole.

When the truth or falsehood of the whole is *fully* determined by the truth values of its component simple claims plus their logical relations (the first type), we call the claim a *truth function* or say that the sentence is *truth functional*. There are lots of other simple and complex statements and claims, however (the second type), that don't possess this property. Belief statements, for example, are not truth functional. So, the truth value of the sentence, "Oedipus believes that the husband of Jocasta is not the killer of Laius," does not, tragically for Oedipus, depend upon the truth or falsehood of its component simple claim, "the husband of Jocasta is the killer of Laius." Unfortunately, whether or not we believe a statement is often independent of whether or not it's true. (The distinction between truth functions and non-truth functions may seem a bit arcane at this point, but truth functionality will become especially important later, and we'll elaborate on the concept a bit more when we address propositional logics in Chapter 4.)

SEE ALSO

4.1 Propositional vs. Categorical Logics
8.1 Knowledge: The Basics
9.5 Unfalsifiability and Falsification Resistance

READING

Patrick J. Hurley, *A Concise Introduction to Logic*, 12th edn (2015), Sections 1.1, 2.2, 6.2
Julian Baggini & Peter S. Fosl, *The Philosopher's Toolkit* (2010), Chapters 1–3
Anthony Weston, *A Rulebook for Arguments*, 4th edn (2009), I.1
J. van Benthem, *A Manual of Intensional Logic* (1988), Part I

1.2 Arguments

A well-known Monty Python skit presents two men at an "Argument Clinic," a client and a "professional" arguer. The fun begins when the professional arguer simply contradicts everything the client says ("Yes, I did." "No, you didn't." "Yes, I did." and so on.). Shrewdly, the client isn't impressed: "Look this isn't an argument … It's just contradiction." Okay, so what *does* count as an argument?

For critical thinkers, the term "argument" means something very specific. Briefly put, an *argument* is a special tool that systematically collects and arranges reasons in support of the truth of a claim. As the client of Monty Python's Argument Clinic puts it, "An argument's a collected series of statements to establish a definite proposition!" A bit more specifically, arguments are simply sets of claims in which one or more claims are to provide support or justification or proof for the truth of another claim.

Essential to every argument, then, are at least two components: (1) a single *conclusion* and (2) at least one reason or *premise* for the conclusion to be true. Identifying which is which in a given case can sometimes be confusing, though. That premises are intended somehow to support or seem to support a conclusion indicates that a third element is present in logical argument – (3) an *inference* from the premise(s) to the conclusion. It's in the quality of that inference where things get especially interesting for critical thinkers, as not all inferences are good or strong or legitimate.

Logic vs. eristics

It's common for people to confuse verbal altercations with arguments, since commonly, the term "argument" refers only to a dispute between two or more people, any kind of dispute. It's also common for people to confuse *eristics* (the study of *winning disputes*) with *logic* (the study of *reasoning*). Arguments, however, in the technical, *logical* sense discussed here do not require a dispute, disagreement, or even dialogue, and they certainly don't involve yelling, screaming, fisticuffs, or kerfuffles of any other sort. Furthermore, *debates* are also commonly confused with arguments because they are typically composed of many arguments, and the opposing sides of a debate offer arguments in support of the claims they wish to establish. So, debates include argument, but you needn't have a debate to argue.

Arguments vs. explanations

Moreover, not all sets of sentences that lead to statements claimed to be true are arguments. For that reason, often a critical thinker will find himself or herself trying to determine whether or not a set of claims is, in fact, an argument. For example, *explanations* often seem like arguments. But there is deep difference between the two. Explanations are sets of claims that function to establish *how* or *why* something is the case. Arguments, in contrast, undertake to establish *that* some claim, normally a claim in question, is actually true. It's very different, for example, to explain *how* extraterrestrials have made their way to Earth from arguing *that* extraterrestrials have made their way to Earth – though both might involve presenting a flying saucer.

Arguments show that *something is the case.*
Explanations show how *or* why *something is the case.*

Explanations are easily mistaken for arguments because in many respects the two share stylistic similarities. Much like an argument, an explanation will include a single claim upon which all the other claims bear. In an explanation, this claim is called an *explanandum*, and the remaining claims, called the *explanans*, are used to account for ("explain") the explanandum. Because an explanandum is a claim like any other, it is true or false. But an explanation is in no way concerned with establishing or supporting the truth of the explanandum. Instead, the truth of the explanandum is already accepted or presupposed. Often, explananda are easily identifiable because they're not controversial, or we have no obvious reason to doubt that they are true. Take, for example, the following set of claims:

> The speed limit on this road is 45 mph, except when school is starting or ending, at which time it drops to 25 mph. That's *because* during those times it's especially important to protect the school children.

The truth of the explanandum, "The speed limit on this road is 45 mph, except when school is starting or ending," is not at issue. The explanans merely attempts to make clear why this is so.

SEE ALSO

2.1 Deductive and Inductive Arguments
4.1 Propositional vs. Categorical Logics
6.2 Analogies and Arguments from Analogy

READING

Arthur Schopenhauer with A. C. Grayling, *The Art of Always Being Right* (2012/1831)
Ernest Lepore & Sam Cumming, *Meaning and Argument* (2012)
Miriam Joseph with Marguerite McGlinn, eds., *The Trivium* (2002)
G. B. Kerferd, *The Sophistic Movement* (1981)
Ernest Nagel, *The Structure of Science: Problems in the Logic of Scientific Explanation* (1979)

1.3 Premises

One clear difference between proper argument and mere contradiction (as well as most shouting matches) is that an argument depends for its strength upon *premises* functioning as *reasons* to accept the *conclusion*. Premises give an argument its heft, its strength, the ground upon which the conclusion stands. They work together in exacting ways to prove or demonstrate or justify the conclusion. Some arguments enlist only one premise (and every argument must have at least one premise). That seems obvious, since there must be at least one reason to accept the conclusion in order for a set of claims to count as an argument. But that's just the minimum. It may seem odd, but maximally there is no limit on the total number of premises an argument can enlist. An argument may indeed require volumes of text to complete, containing a staggering number of premises, perhaps (though this is something of a matter of dispute) even an uncountable or infinite number.

Enthymemes

Often, an argument will contain implicit or unspoken premises, usually probable claims already accepted by the audience. Arguments of this sort are called *enthymemes*. Enthymemes, then, are informal arguments that rely on premises not explicitly articulated. (We'll see more of them in Chapter 3 when we consider Aristotelian or categorical arguments.) Since enthymemes are not uncommon, in order to assess the merits of arguments properly, a critical thinker will find it very helpful to look for enthymemes or enthymematic arguments and flush out their implicit or assumed claims. In short, sensitivity to enthymemes helps discern assumptions.

Identifying premises

Identifying the premises of an argument is made a lot easier by first identifying the argument's conclusion. Once the conclusion is identified, any remaining claims that are there to support the truth of the conclusion become easier to discern. There are, however, several caveats of which critical thinkers should be mindful.

First, it's not necessarily the case that all of the claims in any given text are used as premises. Many texts contain lots of pieces of information that play no logical role at all in supporting the truth of the conclusion. For example, some claims merely elaborate, highlight, clarify, or give examples in relation to one of the premises. Some sentences are there just for rhetorical purposes. Sentences of those kinds are not relevant to the logic of the argument, though they may be used to clarify or explain a claim or a term, or they may be used to make the argument flow more smoothly. And so the critical thinker will find it useful to set these aside when analyzing and evaluating the argument.

Second, as we've seen, claims may be complex. So critical thinkers will need to consider whether or not compound claims should be untangled and broken up. A complex claim may be easier to work with if it's broken up into separate claims. But be careful if you do this, because sometimes breaking up a complex claim can change its meaning, especially if you lose the effect of the logical operators.

Thankfully, good writers often set off premises and conclusions with indicators. *Indicators* are either single words or phrases that alert the reader or listener to the logic of an argument. (It's good, for that reason, to use logical indicators while writing or speaking. Your audience will thank you.) While it isn't necessary for an argument to contain these words, they do help to clarify an argument's structure. Words or phrases that are specifically useful to indicate that a premise precedes or follows the indicator word are called *premise indicators*. Here are some of the most common:

since	because
given; given that	for; for the reason that
as; insofar as	due to the fact that
in that	it may be concluded from

For example: *It will likely rain today given that it's the rainy season and because the sky is full of thick, dark clouds.* In this argument, two reasons are given for thinking it will likely rain today, and both are preceded by premise indicators: *given that* and *because*.

Be careful, however, because some premise indicators perform other functions in our languages. The premise indicator word "since," for example, does not always indicate that a premise is nearby, because "since" is also used to indicate that a period of time has passed. ("I've lived in this same house since 1965.") Similarly, the word "because" may indicate a premise, but it may also indicate an explanans in an explanation (just as it does in the previous sentence, and also: "My house collapsed because of termite damage").

To be sure that the claim is a premise, a critical thinker must determine whether or not it functions as a reason to think another claim (the conclusion) is true. In an argument without indicators, a critical thinker must do this anyway, but the indicators make things easier by offering a shortcut to determining whether a given claim is best understood as a premise.

These two formulations of the same argument demonstrate how the presence of indicators clarifies the relationship of the claims in an argument:

1. Riley is a mammal at the National Zoo. Riley is an elephant at the National Zoo.
2. Riley is a mammal at the National Zoo, given that Riley is an elephant at the National Zoo.

In the first formulation of the argument, it is unclear whether the arguer is attempting to *prove that* Riley is a mammal at the National Zoo or instead perhaps just report that Riley is an elephant and a mammal at the zoo. Without the indicator words or phrases, readers can't be sure how the text is being used. Context can help, but sometimes context is insufficient. The presence of the indicator phrase in the second formulation of the argument removes this complication by making it clear that one of the two claims is intended as a premise and the other as a conclusion.

SEE ALSO

1.1 Claims
2.3 Classifying and Comparing Claims
3.4 Formal Deduction with Categories: Immediate Inferences

READING

Dan Cryan, *Introducing Logic: A Graphic Guide* (2004)
Harry J. Gensler, *Introduction to Logic* (2010)
Stan Baronett, *Logic* (2012)

1.4 Conclusions

The *conclusion* of an argument is the claim that the premises are to support or justify. In large part, the conclusion is the main point of the argument. If an argument were like a treasure hunt, the conclusion would be the treasure, and the premises would be directions presented to get you to that destination. Similarly, every argument has one and only one conclusion. While there may be important points that must be made on the way to establishing a conclusion, ultimately all the important points should work together to support one single claim. Even though a single argument could take a book or more to complete, it would still have only one conclusion.

Argument structure

Now, authors do often claim to draw multiple conclusions from their arguments. Sometimes that means that they draw subconclusions on the way to a final conclusion. It's also possible that the premises of the argument support the truth of multiple claims or a complex claim that can be broken into multiple claims.

In even the terribly simple argument below, a single premise supports two different conclusions.

P1. I have three buckets of apples.
C1. Therefore I have three buckets.
C2. Therefore I have apples.

Given the premises provided, the author could have also concluded that he or she has material objects or simply something rather than nothing. When multiple conclusions can be drawn from a single set of premises, it is best to think of each conclusion as the result of a single argument. This is often the best practice because keeping arguments distinct, even when they share premises, can help prevent confusions that lead us to error.

Simple and complex arguments

Arguments come in all shapes and sizes. One way to describe the form of an argument is, as with premises, in terms of *simple* and *complex*. *Complex arguments* are arguments composed of two or more *simple arguments*. In a complex argument, the conclusions of simple component arguments become subconclusions in relation to the whole complex. As subconclusions in the complex argument, they also function as premises for the conclusion of the complex argument.

Identifying conclusions

As there are indicator words and phrases for premises, there are indicator words for conclusions as well. *Conclusion indicators* are words or phrases that alert the reader to the presence of the conclusion. Below is a list of commonly used conclusion indicator words and phrases:

therefore	it follows that; we may conclude that
hence	so; so that
thus	entails
implies	consequently

Conclusion indicators are fairly reliable indicators of conclusions; but just as it was with premise indicators, it's always important to check the claim indicated by the conclusion indicator to see if that claim is, in fact, the logical, final conclusion of the argument. It is not uncommon for conclusion indicators to mark the presence of a subconclusion in a complex argument. Context and the rules of logic will often clarify things, but it's notoriously difficult, especially in highly complex texts, to discern the arguments. In fact, when we get to Chapter 10 (especially in 10.5), to what's called the "semiological problem," we'll see that the very nature of language and interpretation ensures that this work remains difficult. That difficulty, indeed, is one of the reasons academic philosophers and other scholars remain in business!

Exercises and study questions

1. Determine whether the following claims are simple or complex:
   - Monday Night Football is the most widely watched television program in the United States.
   - If you go to the store, then please purchase some milk and eggs.
   - All the cars are vehicles with bad gasoline mileage.
   - Either the weather is going to improve, or we'll need to cancel the picnic.
2. Identify the premises and conclusion in the following arguments:
   - It's important that we respect the choices of others, and it's important that we help look out for the welfare of others. Consequently, we must ensure that the available choices for others are always ones that will benefit their welfare.

- The average age of cars on the road today is around 10 years. Since my car isn't going to last much more than 7 years, its construction is probably inferior to most cars on the road today.
- Most students haven't discovered what they want to do with their lives, and yet many schools want them to declare a major before setting foot on campus. It follows from this that a student's major should be lenient and flexible with the number of required courses, because inevitably students will take classes in a degree field that they may change after a short time.

3. How many conclusions can an argument have?
4. How many premises can an argument have?

SEE ALSO

3.4 Formal Deduction with Categories: Immediate Inferences
3.5 Formal Deduction with Categories: Syllogisms
4.2 Common Deductively Valid Forms
8.6 Justification: The Basics

READING

Merrilee H. Salmon, *Introduction to Logic and Critical Thinking* (2012)
Paul Herrick, *Introduction to Logic* (2012)
Anthony Weston, *A Rulebook for Arguments* (2009)

2 More Tools for Critical Thinking about Arguments

2.1 Deductive and Inductive Arguments

Bridges function properly when they are engineered with (a) strong materials and (b) a supportive structure capable of carrying the loads trucked across them. Arguments, curiously, function in a similar way. It's just that the material out of which arguments are built isn't concrete, steel, or stone. Instead, claims or statements function as materials for creating premises and a conclusion, and so the structure of arguments isn't physical, but logical. Nevertheless, without the right materials and without having them assembled in the right way, an argument will fail just like a poorly built bridge.

All arguments are intended to support the truth of their conclusions, but arguments can be structured in vastly different ways to achieve this goal. Similarly, two bridges built alternatively with concrete and steel may look and work in vastly different ways, like arch bridges and suspension bridges, for example. Regardless of their apparent differences, though, if they're done right, if they have the right structure, they'll still support a road along with the vehicles that drive over it.

For arguments, it's the logical structure that matters, and that structure determines the extent to which the argument will be what philosophers call *truth preserving*—that is, the degree to which reasoning from true premises ensures a true conclusion. It's actually a pretty instructive term, since it captures something of the essence of what makes good arguments work, as well as the essence of what argument is about. In a good argument, true premises are worded and organized in a way that guarantees or makes it very likely that the conclusion is true; truth is *preserved* through the inference.

Another way to think about this is to imagine that the truth of the premises in a good argument flows into the conclusion. The key to this amazing process (and this is important!) is the argument's structure or *form*, and as such, assessing an argument's form is a critical component for evaluating the overall success of the argument.

The Critical Thinking Toolkit, First Edition. Galen A. Foresman, Peter S. Fosl, and Jamie C. Watson.

For this reason, arguments are categorized according to their forms and the extent to which they are truth preserving.

Deduction

Consider this: there are two ways an argument can be poorly engineered: (1) one or more of the premises – the materials out of which the argument is built – is false, or (2) the structure or form of the argument fails to provide adequate support for the conclusion. Of course, arguments whose forms, when functioning properly, are *fully* truth preserving are the strongest sort. They are called *deductive arguments.* When a deductive argument is properly structured, the argument is said to be *deductively valid.* When a deductively valid argument has true premises, it is called a *deductively sound* argument. In a deductively sound argument, the truth of the conclusion will *necessarily* follow from the truth of the premises. The idea has its roots at least as far back as Aristotle, who writes in the *Prior Analytics* (*Prior Analytics*; Book I, Chapter 2, 24b18–20), the fundamental text in the systematic study of deductive reasoning:

> A deduction is speech in which, certain things having been supposed, something different from those that are supposed results *of necessity* because of their being so.
>
> [*Editors' emphasis.*]

There is among philosophers, however, some controversy about what "necessarily" or "of necessity" means in the context of logic. So, one might say instead more cautiously that the conclusion of a valid deductive argument will "definitely follow," "is sure to follow," or "certainly follows." That's just to say, of course, that the truth of the conclusion is entirely supported through the argument's structure and by the truth of the premises. Another common way to put this is to say that a properly structured deductive argument is constructed so that it is *impossible* for the conclusion to be false *if the premises are true* (if the premises aren't all true, all bets are off). That impossibility is central to the way, as we'll see, a lot of critical thinking about reasoning works. Of course, when an argument is not fully truth preserving, when the truth of the premises doesn't entirely guarantee or ensure the truth of the conclusion, the argument is *deductively invalid.*

Deductive reasoning is pervasive in the sciences and in our lives generally. Deductive arguments are common in mathematical reasoning, for example, and they are the kind of arguments that compose the core of computer programming. Generally speaking, however, the arguments people encounter are not usually formulated in the precise, deductively valid forms logicians prefer. Logicians clean things up, but not without some risk. While the practice of carefully recasting an argument so that it is clear and deductively valid can be extremely useful, there is some risk that the result won't quite be relevant to what actually concerns people in a particular context. (We'll address something of what logic can miss or lose when we address matters of rhetoric and poetics in Chapter 10.)

Induction

There are many perfectly good arguments that aren't deductive. These arguments do not guarantee their conclusions, but they do give them enough support that they should be taken seriously. Arguments that are not fully truth preserving but whose conclusions nevertheless follow with a degree of probability are what logicians call *inductive arguments*. The truth of the conclusion of an inductive argument always goes beyond the support of the premises to some extent, and so the extent to which the argument is truth preserving – its *strength* – depends upon the degree to which the premises support the conclusion. *Inductively strong arguments* are arguments structured such that the truth of the premises makes it very *likely* that the conclusion is true. *Inductively weak arguments* are arguments in which the truth of the premises does not lend much support to the conclusion.

Of course, all this is a matter of degree, and so calling an inductive argument "weak" or "strong" may change with context. Normally, calling an inductive argument "weak" just means that, in terms of the case at hand, there is not enough support for the conclusion – in other words, that it would be unreasonable to accept the conclusion based solely on the premises. Most scientists engaged in inductive reasoning require a probability of 95% or more before accepting a conclusion as reasonable. The contexts of civil and criminal law, however, employ different standards of strength. In our day-to-day lives, a better than 50% chance of rain may be enough for us to conclude that we should carry an umbrella with us.

Be careful, though. A deductive argument may contain premises that make probability claims yet still be a deductive argument. Remember that it's not the content of the premises but the way they're related to one another (their structure), the kind of inference they make, that determines whether or not an argument is best understood as deductive. For example, even though the following argument involves claims about what's more or less probable, the structure of the argument is actually a well-established *deductive* form of inference called *modus ponens* (as we'll see in 4.2):

1. If tomorrow's game is a home game that will be played on a sunny day, then our team faces above-average chances of winning.
2. Tomorrow's game is a home game that will be played on a sunny day.
3. Therefore, our team faces above-average chances of winning.

While this may seem a bit confusing, here's the point. When thinking critically about an argument, it's often the case that, after identifying a conclusion and premises, the most pressing order of business is a bit of categorization, beginning with figuring out whether the argument is inductive or deductive. While this can prove tricky at first, as with most things it just requires some practice to get familiar with these categories. Ultimately, once the argument's structure has been figured out, the proper criteria can be used in order to decide whether you're dealing with a *valid* or *invalid deductive argument* or, instead, a *strong* or *weak inductive argument*.

SEE ALSO

1.2 Arguments
1.4 Conclusions
6.1 Inductive vs. Deductive Arguments Again

READING

Merrie Bergmann, James Moore, & Jack Nelson, *The Logic Book* (2013)
David Papineau, *Philosophical Devices: Proofs, Probabilities, Possibilities, and Sets* (2012)
W. V. O. Quine, *Elementary Logic*, revised edn (1980)
Fred R. Berger, *Studying Deductive Logic* (1977)
Aristotle, *Prior Analytics* (fourth century BCE)

2.2 Conditional Claims

When Sammy told her kids that, "If it rains, we'll go to the movies," she was making a conditional claim. A *conditional claim* is a type of complex claim in which the truth of one claim (the *consequent*) somehow depends upon or is contingent upon the truth of another claim (the *antecedent*). You might say that in a conditional claim, the consequent is true when the antecedent is true.

Conditional claims are often articulated in the form "if *p*, then *q*," where *p* and *q* can themselves be either simple or complex claims. For example, "If Barack Obama is president, then the United States has a Democratic president," is a conditional claim composed of two simple claims: (1) Barack Obama is president, and (2) the United States has a Democratic president. In the common "if *p*, then *q*" form, *p* is the antecedent and *q* is the consequent, and so for the current example "Barack Obama is president" is the antecedent, while "the United States has a Democratic president" is the consequent.

You may have noticed that our definition of "conditional claim" is broad. That's intentionally so because for logicians there's a pretty large range of what "depends upon" or is "contingent upon" might mean.

> *In the minimal sort of relationship between antecedent and consequent, a conditional claim asserts simply that when the antecedent is true the consequent is also true.*

Basic logical systems use only that minimal relationship. That means it's possible to accept a conditional statement as true simply when the consequent and antecedent are true as a matter of mere coincidence. For example: "If the Martian moon Phobos is behind the planet Mars, then somewhere on Earth someone is breathing." Since the location of Phobos has nothing to do with the fact that at this point in time people are always breathing on Earth, this conditional statement is true simply as a matter of coincidence. Of course, the connection between the truth of the antecedent and the truth of the consequent may be stronger. There may even be a causal connection: "If you throw that match into that puddle of gasoline, it will catch fire." Alternatively, there may also be a kind of logical connection between an antecedent and its consequent: "If something is red, then it has color" or perhaps "If you add 7 to 5, then the result is 12." There are many relationships that can be captured by a conditional claim.

In fact, a rather important relationship for critical thinkers to remember is the one between premises and conclusion. The relationship between the premises and the conclusion of a deductively valid argument may be expressed through a conditional claim, and among logicians a conditional claim is often used to describe this relationship: "If the premises are true, then the conclusion is true." The relationship here actually has a special name. Valid deductive arguments are conditional claims where the antecedent (the premises) is connected to the consequent (the conclusion) in a particular, logical way called *entailment*. This issue quickly becomes philosophically complex and contested, but as a matter of common usage, it's safe to say that one claim or idea entails another when there is a deep, internal, logical, or conceptual connection between them. (See *The Philosopher's Toolkit* 4.8, "Entailment/Implication.") For example, the claim "Bob is a bachelor" entails the claim "Bob is an unmarried man."

A unique and important feature of conditional statements is that they only proceed in one direction. In the conditional statement "If Barack Obama is president, then the United States has a Democratic president," we know from Barack Obama's being president that the United States has a Democrat as president. You can't, however, run the inference in the other direction. We can't on the basis of this conditional infer from the fact that the president is a Democrat that he is Barack Obama. In "if *p*, then *q*," the truth of *q* follows from the truth of *p*, but the truth of *p* does not follow from the truth of *q*. (Doing so would be what's called the fallacy of "affirming the consequent" or an "illicit conversion." We'll address that and other errors that arise from not understanding conditionals in 3.4 and 4.5.)

Necessary and sufficient conditions

Another way to think about the relationship between the antecedent and consequent of a conditional claim is in terms of *necessary and sufficient conditions.* A *necessary condition* is a state of affairs that must occur for another state of affairs to occur. For example, the presence of breathable oxygen is a necessary condition for humans to live, which means humans must have breathable oxygen in order to live. Written in terms of "if *p*, then *q*," the claim "Breathable oxygen is a necessary condition for humans to live" becomes "If humans are living, then breathable oxygen is present." Therefore:

> *The consequent of an "if… then… " statement is the necessary condition for the antecedent.*

It is common to put the necessary condition mistakenly in the antecedent of the conditional claim, but thinking about the logic of conditionals can help clear things up. In a conditional statement of the form "if *p*, then *q*," we know that the truth of *p* is claimed to correlate with the truth of *q* – that is, a true *p* is claimed to imply that *q* is also true. Keeping this in mind and applying it to the claim, "Breathable oxygen is a necessary condition for humans to live," it should be clear that the presence of breathable oxygen does not result in humans living. Humans need more than just breathable oxygen to live, and so the presence of breathable oxygen alone is not enough to know that humans can live. After all, humans need food, water, and an environment that isn't too hot or too cold as well. There is, for example, breathable oxygen in a hot pizza oven, but that doesn't mean humans can live there. So, while breathable oxygen is necessary for humans to live, it is not the only condition that needs to be met for humans to live.

Necessary conditions are often indicated by the phrase "only if," one of the most powerful phrases, logically speaking, in any language. (Note that there are other ways to indicate necessary conditions, too.) It's quite different for Sammy to say to her children "We'll go to the movies *if* you clean your rooms" from "We'll go to the movies *only if* you clean your rooms." In the first instance, there might be other conditions under which the family goes to the movies – perhaps if the kids persuade her, perhaps if a friend calls and asks, perhaps if it snows or rains. In the second instance, however, the phrase "only if" establishes an exclusive condition that must be met, without which the antecedent won't be true.

> *The component statement designated by the phrase "only if" is the* necessary condition *of a conditional claim.*

Necessary conditions are powerful claims, because they are very strict in their demands. Although, that's not the only way to be logically powerful, as we'll see with another kind of condition.

A *sufficient condition* is a condition that when met is *enough* to know that some other condition has also been met. More strongly put, its truth (in a true conditional) assures that the consequent is also true. In Sammy's first sentence ("We'll go to the movies *if* you clean your rooms"), the children's cleaning their rooms is enough to assure them that they're going to the movies. Sammy's second formulation, however, the one that makes the children's cleaning their rooms nothing more than a necessary condition for going to the movies ("We'll go to the movies *only if* you clean your rooms."), does not give the kids a guarantee that if they clean their rooms they'll go. Meeting a condition stated in the consequent doesn't guarantee the antecedent, and that's because it's merely a necessary and not a sufficient condition.

Here's another example. A blackmailer who says, "I'll not go to the police with the incriminating information I have about you only if you give me the money," has not said that giving him the money will result in his not informing the police. In other words, he has not said, strictly speaking, what will happen *if the money is paid*. The blackmailer has made the much more limited claim that *if the money is not* paid he will inform the police. Paying the blackmailer is necessary for his not going to the police, but it's not sufficient to guarantee it. His threat is consistent with his later demanding still more money or with going to the police anyway. That's one reason blackmail – and cleverly constructed conditionals – can be so maddening.

> *The antecedent of an "if… then… " statement is the* sufficient condition *for the consequent.*

Similarly, the presence of human life in our example is *enough* to know that there is breathable oxygen present. As a result, the presence of human life is a sufficient condition for the presence of breathable oxygen. Of course, this does not mean that human life somehow *causes* the presence of breathable oxygen. The relationship between antecedent and consequent in that example is not causal. Again, conditional claims, simply by being conditional claims, do not imply any particular type of relationship between the antecedent and consequent, causal or otherwise – and so neither do statements of necessary and sufficient conditions.

Biconditional claims

A *biconditional claim* is a complex claim that expresses a relationship of equivalence between two claims. Two claims are considered *equivalent* in this logical sense, when they always have the same truth value (that is, they are both true or both false). The claim, "Suzy will get a raise if and only if she gets a promotion," uses the connective phrase "if and only if" to denote the biconditional relationship between Suzy's getting a raise and Suzy's getting a promotion. When a biconditional is used to connect two claims, it means that one claim will not be true without the other claim also being true – and one claim will not be false without the other claim also being false. In Suzy's case this means four things: (1) if she gets a raise, then she also gets a promotion, *and* it means (2) if she gets a promotion, then she also gets a raise. Moreover, (1) if she doesn't get the promotion, she doesn't get the raise, *and* (2) if she doesn't get the raise, she doesn't get the promotion. The conjoining of these two conditional claims explains why it is called a "biconditional," that is "two" conditionals in one claim.

Like a conditional claim, the biconditional expresses a relationship of implication between two claims, but unlike a conditional claim, the biconditional's implication relationship extends to both of the claims composing the biconditional. Written in terms of claims *p* and *q* the biconditional "*p* if *and* only if *q*" is the same as saying, "if *p*, then *q* *and* if *q*, then *p*," because not only does *p* imply *q* for the biconditional, *q* also implies *p*. Logicians commonly abbreviate this "if and only if" or biconditional relationship with "iff."

In terms of necessary and sufficient conditions, a biconditional claim describes a relationship between two claims such that each individual claim is both necessary and sufficient for the other. For Suzy, this means that getting a raise is both necessary and sufficient for her getting a promotion, and so Suzy can't have one without the other. She will either get a raise and a promotion, or she will get neither. Claims that are both necessary and sufficient come as a package deal, committing whomever advances those claims to accepting both or neither.

Biconditionals are also helpful in critical thinking about concepts, as definitions are often couched as biconditional relationships. For example, a definition of "justice" is a good one if and only if it describes situations that are just or are called "just." If, therefore, we come across a situation that we accept as just but that doesn't fit the definition under scrutiny, then that definition must be somehow inadequate. And if we discern a situation that we identify as unjust but that does fit the definition of justice we're examining, then similarly that definition fails. Philosophers and other critical thinkers often use this strategy to criticize definitions and to clarify concepts.

SEE ALSO

4.5 Common Formal Fallacies
6.3 Fallacies about Causation
9.4 Scientific Method

READING

Michael Woods with David Wiggins, eds., *Conditionals* (2003)
Jonathan Bennett, *A Philosophical Guide to the Logic of Conditionals* (2003)
Julian Baggini & Peter S. Fosl, *The Philosopher's Toolkit* (2010)
Graham Priest, *Logic: A Very Short Introduction* (2000)

2.3 Classifying and Comparing Claims

When thinking critically, it can be helpful to consider the kinds of claims with which one is dealing, especially the way those sentences relate to truth. Logicians have come up with a number of ways of understanding the truth-bearing qualities of claims and other statements both by (a) comparing them and by (b) categorizing them into types.

Comparing claims

Here are four of the principal ways logicians compare statements with one another. (Note that some of them overlap.)

1. *Consistency.* For critical thinking, consistency is one of the most important virtues. So much so, in fact, that those who pride themselves on being good critical thinkers are likely to meet the charge of inconsistency with the utmost indignation. It's a serious charge. The power of consistency in argumentation has a very long history. Socrates (469–399 BCE) in the Platonic dialogues, for example, often ferreted

out inconsistency in the remarks of his interlocutors, much to their chagrin. Even in defending his own life in *The Apology*, Socrates depended on pointing out the inconsistency of his accusers, specifically Meletus. On a far grander scale, in the *Book of Job* from the *Old Testament*, Job questions God's consistency after being allowed to suffer both mental and physical trials for what seemed to Job to be no apparent reason (e.g., Job 10:3). For a devout servant and worshiper of God, Job's suffering seemed inconsistent with what he knew of God's character. While it wasn't an overt accusation of hypocrisy (a logical vice, you might say, when one's actions are inconsistent with one's claims about appropriate actions), Job's remarks were nevertheless an accusation that God did not take lightly.

Very roughly speaking, consistency is about things fitting together in a way that makes sense. Both Socrates and Job were wrestling with situations that did not fit together in ways that made sense to them, and they were both very deeply concerned about it. Of course, their concern with inconsistency was partly a function of how it was about to affect or had affected their lives. Nevertheless, their situations may have been more bearable had they not appeared to be the result of obvious inconsistencies. Good critical thinkers, in any case, are adept at recognizing inconsistencies wherever they may appear; and what's more, they are tenacious about limiting or eliminating them in their own beliefs.

> *In logical terms,* consistency *is a term used to describe a set of claims that can all be true at the same time.*

Inconsistency. This occurs within a set of claims when it is *not possible* for all of the claims to be true at the same time. Maintaining a set of beliefs that is inconsistent means holding onto some beliefs that must, as a matter of logic, be false, which is why a good critical thinker is loath to hold an inconsistent set of beliefs.

2. *Contradiction.* A *contradiction* occurs between two claims when the truth of one necessitates the falsity of another, *and* the falsity of one necessitates the truth of the other. In short, contradictions occur when for logical reasons two claims must have *opposite truth values*, and so one must always be false while the other is true. Contradictory statements can never have the same truth values at the same time. For example, the claim, "All humans are mortal," stands in a contradictory relationship with the claim, "Some humans are not mortal." If "All humans are mortal" is true, then "Some humans are not mortal" must be false. And supposing that "All humans are mortal" is false, then "Some humans are not mortal" must be true.

Note that any set of claims containing a contradiction is inconsistent, since it could never be the case that the contradictory claims could be true at the same time. As a result, the set of claims containing a contradiction will always contain at least one falsehood, which is what makes it impossible for all of the claims to be true at the same time. Contradiction, however, is not the only form of inconsistency, as we'll soon see.

3. *Contrariety.* Contraries are also inconsistent. Contrariety is a relationship between two claims that occurs when at least one of the claims must be false, and

as a result it is impossible for both claims to be true at the same time. In contrast to contradiction, the relationship of contrariety does allow for cases where both claims are false at the same time, since the simple rule of contrariety is just that at least one (and maybe both) of the claims must be false. The claim "Tomorrow is Friday" is contrary to the claim "Tomorrow is Wednesday." Either of these claims might be true, but at least one of them is false, and both are false, for example, if tomorrow is Thursday. Contrariety, of course, makes creating a consistent set of claims impossible, because at least one of the two claims that are contrary to one another must be false. Therefore, a set containing contrariety will always contain at least one false claim, making it inconsistent. So, both contradictions and contraries yield inconsistent sets of statements.

4. *Equivalence.* Equivalence describes a relationship between two claims that always have the *same* truth value. If one claim is true and equivalent to another claim, then the other claim must be true as well. Alternatively, if one of two equivalent claims is false, then the other must be false as well. (The equivalence relationship is, as we saw in 2.2, described by the biconditional.) Common examples of equivalent claims occur when two claims mean the same thing but are expressed in different ways. "Friday is the best day of the week" is equivalent to saying "The day after Thursday is the best day of the week," since, logically speaking, both claims have the same meaning.

Classifying single claims

Here are three useful different categories of claims and other statements logicians have identified in terms of their possibilities of bearing truth.

1. *Contingent statements.* Contingent statements, by far the largest class in natural human languages, are simply statements that can be either true or false. More precisely, they are statements that are possibly true or false. So, the statement, "George W. Bush is president of the United States," can be either true or false, depending upon what year it is. Note that even while Bush was president, the statement remained a contingent truth. This is so because it was possible for Bush to have lost the election that led to his taking office. For a statement to be contingent all that's required is that it is *possible* that in some circumstances it is true and in some other *possible* circumstances it is false. There must be, as metaphysicians like to say, a logically *possible world* in which Bush did not win election to the US presidency. If, for example, Gore had won Florida, things would have turned out differently. One easy way, then, to identify a logically contingent statement is to consider whether its negation is a self-contradiction. No contingent statements have negations that are self-contradictory, because it's logically possible for every contingent statement to possess the opposite truth value from the one it happens to have. Self-contradictions don't work that way.

2. *Self-contradictions.* Self-contradictions are different from contingent statements because under all possible circumstances they always possess the same truth

value – false. Self-contradictions are also always equivalent to one another, of course, because they have the same truth value. It follows from this, if you think about it, that while all self-contradictions are equivalent, none are consistent. In fact, none are consistent with any other statement. That's because, obviously, there can never be a set of self-contradictions or set containing even a single self-contradiction of which all are true – which is what the definition of consistency requires. "This year is 2016, and this year is not 2016" is an example of a self-contradictory statement since no matter what year it is the sentence is false. A typical form of self-contradiction is "*p* and not-*p*."

3. *Tautologies.* There's another class of sentences, *tautologies*, which like self-contradictions always have the same truth value in all possible worlds and, moreover, are always equivalent to one another. In the case of tautologies, however, that's because they're always true. In this sense, tautologies are just the opposite of self-contradictions. "This year is 2016, or this year is not 2016," is an example of a tautology, since no matter what year it is the sentence is true. A common form of tautology is "*p* or not-*p*."

SEE ALSO

3.4 Formal Deduction with Categories: Immediate Inferences
4.3 Equivalences
9.5 Unfalsifiability and Falsification Resistance

READING

David Kelley, *The Art of Reasoning*, 3rd edn (2013)
Deborah J. Bennett, *Logic Made Easy* (2004)
M. J. Cresswell & G. E. Hughes, *A New Introduction to Modal Logic* (1996)

2.4 Claims and Definitions

Some words and ideas seem pretty easy to define. A bachelor is an unmarried man, for example. Some seem a bit harder. A square is a two-dimensional, equilateral, closed, four-sided rectangle. Still others seem all but impossible to define, perhaps because definitions in those cases are in fact impossible. How would you define goodness, or beauty, or justice, or being? Critical thinking, however, often depends upon a sensitivity to the meanings of words and therefore to matters of definition. Claims, as we've discussed, are assertions about what is true or false, but claims would be vacuous if the words that composed them didn't have specific meanings. If you think of all the words you've acquired as books filling the library of your mind, then definitions function like rules for organizing that library by bringing precision and clarity to the concepts related to each word. Definitions tell us what bits of information belong together, and how categories of information relate to one another.

Lexical, stipulative, ostensive, and negative definition

Dictionaries are, of course, relatively good resources for anyone interested in finding out what a word means. Using one set of words to define another word is called a *lexical definition*. But it's important to understand the limits of dictionary definitions. More often than not, a definition in a dictionary requires readers to have a fairly robust understanding of the language already at their disposal. In other words, a dictionary functions in many cases as a cross-reference or translator between words one knows and words that one doesn't yet know. Even the most obscure words in a dictionary, say, for example, "pulchritudinous" or "kalokagathia," must be defined using words that the reader already knows and understands. Otherwise, the dictionary isn't very helpful. Another potential problem with dictionaries is that they often simply report on the way a word is commonly used, which can nevertheless be conceptually problematic and can change significantly over time. Critical thinkers and other inquirers, in contrast, are often interested in more precise, more accurate, and often more enduring definitions; and so sometimes a new or more precise meaning for a term is simply stipulated in what's called, obviously enough, a *stipulative definition*.

The word "friend," for example, is used in many ways and many contexts, but the question as to what is the best definition of "friend" may require moving beyond common usage to a more critical analysis of the concept. Similarly, the word "valid" is often used to describe claims made in common parlance ("You make a valid point."). But as we've discussed in 2.1, the word "valid" in logic has a very specific meaning and applies only to arguments; it does not apply to claims or points. Becoming a good critical thinker, then, requires distinguishing how words are commonly used from the way they are used in more precise contexts.

Sometimes, however, things get even more complex. There seem to be words that may be defined not through other words but only by pointing to something in our experience, through what's called *ostensive definition*. "Red," for example, may be impossible to define without somehow pointing to an instance of red. Individual things may be impossible to define, too, as individuals – though it's certainly possible to *describe* them or *name* them. Could anyone perfectly define you?

In addition, there are *negative definitions*. While it's generally a poor practice to define things negatively, by what they are not rather than by what they are, the medieval Andalusian Jewish philosopher Maimonides (c. 1135–1204) thought that humans could understand God only by articulating what God is not. Positively speaking, according to Maimonides, the human mind just can't apprehend God.

Extension and intension

The *extensional meaning* of a concept is just the set of things objectively picked out by the concept. So, the extension of the concept "dog" would be all those things in the world that are properly picked out by that concept. Refining the definition (as well as the concept of "dog") expands or contracts that extension. Should it include coyotes? Wolves? Hyenas? A good definition should get the extension of a concept just right, not casting it too broadly or too narrowly. It does that by articulating criteria for including or excluding candidates from the term or concept's extension, or from the class or category it designates. We might call devices for determining what is properly included or excluded from a class or group or category *criteria for class membership*. A related idea is *denotation*. What a term *denotes* is its most literal, direct, or apparent meaning. By contrast, the *connotation* of a word, or what it *connotes*, are meanings that are oblique, more figurative, and associated less obviously with it.

The *intensional meaning* of the concept, by contrast, is just what people think or believe or otherwise subjectively take a concept to mean or refer to. In the past, people meant something different by the terms "morning star" and "evening star" in an intensional sense, even though the extension of those terms turned out to be one and the same object – namely, the planet Venus. Good critical thinkers, therefore, should aspire to having the definitions of the substantive terms they use match as closely as possible their true extension. (We know that this can get complicated, but be patient. Its importance will become clearer once we get to Chapters 3 and 4. For a bit of background on this topic, see *The Philosopher's Toolkit* entry, "Sense and Reference.")

Generic similarities and specific differences

Definitions often accomplish their task of setting the proper boundaries among concepts and tailoring terms to their proper extension by situating them among broader but interlocking, containing terms. So, for example, Aristotelians commonly defined human beings as rational animals. "Animal" is a broader term than human, and often called the *genus* term in a definition. "Rational" here establishes what's commonly called the "specific difference" or *differentia*, which indicates what essentially or distinctively sets off humans from other animals. (Of course, this definition of human being has for a long time been rather successfully challenged, but you get the point.) Biologists define organisms in a similar way using a strategy that runs all the way back to Aristotle's *Categories* – that is, by nesting them in an extensive series of increasingly general concepts: kingdom, phylum, class, order, family, genus, and finally species.[1] Now, that's probably a more precise definition than needed for most purposes, but it does exemplify how situating a term or concept among what is more general and more specific, that is, among its similarities and differences in relation to others, can be used to define it.

Definiens and *definiendum*

On a more practical level, in a way analogous to explanations (1.2), every definition has two parts, the *definiendum* and the *definiens*. The definiendum is the word or concept to be defined, and the definiens are the words and statements that identify the genera and differentia for the concept. When definiens fail to articulate criteria for class membership such that it is unclear whether particular examples belong or don't belong to the class or extension, then the definiens are considered *vague* (see 5.13). Clearly, if you'll pardon the pun, a definition should clarify rather than obscure what it's defining.

If, for example, you tried to define coffee cups as "containers from which coffee may be drunk," you might meet some resistance in the face of 20 oz. bottles of coffee. They are, after all, containers from which coffee may be drunk, but it seems wrong to call them coffee cups. The definition seems inadequate because its definiens are too broad. You might also wonder about shoes. Coffee can be sipped from shoes, but certainly they're not cups either. The idea of container just seems too vague.

Concepts with vague or ambiguous definiens should always be clarified if the context of usage isn't sufficient for identifying the intended meaning. This process of clarifying a concept is quite common in the judicial system, where entire court cases hinge on how one defines a concept, like "pornography," "fighting words," "speech," "corporation," "cruel and unusual," "press," "tax," "harassment," "consent," "penalty," etc. To argue effectively and to think clearly, it's crucial to gain facility with the tools of scrutinizing and formulating good definitions.

SEE ALSO

3.4 Formal Deduction with Categories: Immediate Inferences
4.1 Propositional vs. Categorical Logics
10.5 Semiotics: Critically Reading Signs

READING

David Kelley, *The Art of Reasoning*, 3rd edn (2013)
Richard Robinson, *Definition* (1962)
Julian Baggini & Peter S. Fosl, *The Philosopher's Toolkit* (2010)

2.5 The Critical Thinker's "Two Step": Validity and Soundness/Cogency and Strength

Ok, we're on our way. A critical thinker cannot properly evaluate an argument without first identifying the parts of the argument and how they are meant to fit together. We've now acquired the resources to begin doing just that. The process of analysis begins by identifying the premises and conclusion, by clarifying the definitions of terms, as well as by determining whether the argument is deductive or inductive. Only after all that's been accomplished should critical thinkers move on to evaluating the argument – its structure or form and whether it actually does justify some truth claim.

Structure before truth

It's important to understand that the purpose of evaluating any argument is not typically in the first place to assess whether its conclusion is true but rather to determine whether or not the premises provide *adequate support* for the conclusion. Again, what we're after is a process to evaluate the argument taken as a whole, and not merely an attempt to determine whether the conclusion or any individual premise is true by itself. It's crucial to remember this because as strange as it may sound *a flawed argument may still possess a true conclusion.* The process of evaluating the argument may demonstrate that the argument has failed to *support* the truth of that conclusion even while accepting that the conclusion is true. In that case, a better argument must be constructed to demonstrate that there are good reasons for justifying the conclusion as true.

Let's start, then, with a simple two-step procedure for argument analysis. We call this procedure the critical thinker's "two step":

Step #1: Determine whether or not the premises support the conclusion. If they do, go on to Step #2; if they do not, proceed no further.
Step #2: Determine whether or not all of the premises are true.

This procedure shows that there are principally two ways an argument can go wrong: either (1) the structure is wrong and doesn't support the conclusion or (2) one or more of the premises are false. Either or both of these problems might undermine an argument, and all it takes for the argument to run off the rails is for one step to fail. You can see why reasoning well can be so difficult.

To complete the two-step process, the critical thinker will first identify the premises and conclusion. Upon having identified premises and conclusion, the critical thinker will need to determine the support structure of the argument, which is to say, he or she will need to determine whether the argument is best understood to be deductive or inductive. It's the job of the next two chapters to explain some of the principal techniques logicians have developed for deciding whether an argument's structure supports or doesn't support its conclusion.

Be cautious when intellectually dancing our critical two step because the criteria for assessing whether a conclusion has been supported adequately differ between deductive and inductive arguments, and so evaluating inductive arguments by deductive criteria, or vice versa, will result in a misleading assessment of the argument. This is because the premises in a deductive argument are to support the truth of the conclusion completely, whereas inductive arguments have premises that only support the truth of the conclusion to some degree of probability.

For a deductive argument, anything less than a conclusion supported 100% by the premises is failure. Those deductive arguments that meet this criterion during Step #1 are, again, praised as *valid* deductive arguments, and those that fail to meet this criterion are condemned as *invalid* deductive arguments.

Of course, all inductive arguments will fail to meet the criterion of deductive validity, but that's not a problem for them. Inductive arguments, again, aren't to be evaluated by the same criteria as those used for deductive arguments, which is why it would be trivial and perhaps misleading to say that all inductive arguments are invalid. If the inductive argument provides enough support for the truth of the conclusion, such that it is sufficiently probably true, then it is called a *strong* inductive argument. If the inductive argument fails to do this, then it is a *weak* inductive argument.

Many of the sections in the remainder of this book are devoted to showing how critical thinkers can assess various sorts of argument, rhetoric, and claims, though it will require more advanced texts in logic, statistics, mathematics, rhetoric, critical theory, epistemology, and natural science to parse out many of those determinations thoroughly. Suffice it to say for now that once the critical thinker determines that the conclusion is well supported, then he or she proceeds to Step #2 to complete the argument's evaluation – and then perhaps to other forms of criticism we set out. If, however, the argument turns out to be invalid or weak, there may well be no need to proceed to Step #2, since the critical thinker will already know that in a logical sense the premises fail to support the truth of the conclusion. This is one reason logic is so basic to criticism.

Of course, just because an argument has passed Step #1 doesn't mean that its conclusion is true. All you know at that point is that *if* the premises are true, then the conclusion will be true or will likely be true – *and that's a very, very big "if."*

Now, determining whether or not the premises actually are true is the same as figuring out the truth of any other claim, really. Sometimes it's easy, and sometimes it's very difficult. One might say it's commonly a scientific or otherwise a factual issue, rather than a strictly logical question. If in any case a deductive argument is found to be both (1) valid and (2) to enlist all true premises, the conclusion *must* be true as well. When both these conditions are met, and only when both these conditions are met, you've reached the logical gold standard, and the deductive argument can be lauded with the highest praise logic can give by calling it *sound*. More formally:

Deductively valid arguments containing all true premises are called sound *arguments.*

Correlatively:

Inductively strong arguments having all true premises are called cogent *arguments.*

There is, however, an important caveat to cogency that is unlike its deductive counterpart, soundness. Because the truth of the conclusion for all inductive arguments extends beyond the scope of evidence presented in the premises, for an inductive argument to be fully cogent, it cannot be the case that the argument fails to account for or ignores important evidence that would weaken the argument. This is called the *total evidence requirement*, and it is only required for cogent arguments. Not meeting the total evidence requirement risks committing what we'll see is called the fallacy of *suppressed evidence* (see 8.10).

SEE ALSO

2.6 Showing Invalidity by Counterexample
Chapter 3: Tools for Deductive Reasoning with Categories
Chapter 4: Tools for Deductive Reasoning with Claims
Chapter 8: Tools for Critical Thinking about Justification

READING

David Kelley, *The Art of Reasoning*, 3rd edn (2013)
Irving M. Copi, Carl Cohen, & Kenneth McMahon, *Introduction to Logic*, 14th edn (2010)

2.6 Showing Invalidity by Counterexample

One method it will be helpful to master for evaluating deductive arguments is exposing invalid forms by constructing what's called *counterexamples*. This method proves that an argument is flawed by showing that the argument's structure will not guarantee a true conclusion when its premises are true. When successful the test shows that a given argument's structure allows the *possibility* of having true premises but a false conclusion, which in every valid argument must be impossible. For an argument to be valid, it must be logically impossible for all of that argument's premises to be true while the conclusion is false, even if as things stand in the world that's not the case. One of the powerful dimensions of this method is, moreover, that it not only shows a particular argument to be bad, but it also proves that all arguments of the same form are also bad. This can be a very powerful tool for the critical thinker, because it allows for weeding out entire groups of bad arguments that share the same form. Any conclusions depending on these deficient argument forms have not been sufficiently supported.

The first step to showing invalidity by counterexample is *analyzing* the argument to determine its *form*. Suppose you conclude from "all sharks are animals with gills, and all sharks are fish," that "all fish are animals with gills." Is your argument valid? The argument has two premises supporting the conclusion, which can be illustrated more formally as follows:

All sharks are animals with gills.
All sharks are fish.

All fish are animals with gills.

As it turns out, this argument has true premises and a true conclusion. That this happens to be the case, however, does not make it a good argument. It's just lucky. A sound deductive argument must not only have (a) true premises, but also (b) a conclusion that is logically supported by the premises. In this case, it turns out simply to be coincidence, an accident, that all the claims contained in it are true, which is not the case in a valid argument. Here's how to show that.

After deriving the basic structure of the argument, in terms of its premises and conclusion, the next step is to remove what we called in 1.1 the material content from the claims, leaving only the form of the argument. Once that's completed, this particular argument can be rendered in the following form:

All M are P.
All M are S.

All S are P.

For any deductive argument, deriving the argument's form is a process of reducing the argument to its most basic structures by substituting variables for particular content. Doing this is rather like replacing numbers with variables in mathematics to expose the basic mathematical formula of the original math problem. The variables serve as placeholders, and they can be any letter. In this case, "M" is used to take the place of "sharks," "P" takes the place of "animals with gills," and "S" stands in for "fish." (The reason we chose just these letters will be explained in Chapter 3.)

The Next Step (the tough part). After the form of the argument is determined, demonstrating that the form is invalid proceeds by substituting new content for the variables – M, P, and S – but not just any new content. The real skill in using this method is to select just the right substitutions so that the new argument has *true premises* but a *false conclusion*. In this example, if we substitute "dolphins" for M, "animals that live in water" for P, and "mammals" for S, the new argument becomes:

All dolphins are animals that live in water.
All dolphins are mammals.

All mammals are animals that live in water.

This new argument has the same form as the original argument, but as a result of substituting three new terms for M, P, and S, the argument now contains true premises and a false conclusion. That's trouble. Big trouble, in fact, since true premises in a valid deductive argument must by definition invariably lead to a true conclusion. This argument, therefore, simply cannot be valid. This technique takes some imagination and some practice, but refining your skills in this area will bring rewards. The counterexample method of proving invalidity is a very powerful one and well worth your time to master.

Exercises and study questions

1. Determine the antecedent, consequent, necessary condition, and sufficient condition for the following claims:
   - If TyQuana scores a 95% on her final, then she will pass the course.
   - Foods are nutritious if they positively contribute to the overall diet of a person.
   - Water-saving measures are effective means for communities to deal with severe drought only if enough people participate in those measures.
2. Determine whether the following claims are contingent, self-contradictory, or tautologous:
   - Abraham Lincoln was the fifth president of the United States of America.
   - The M1A2 Abrams tank has a top speed of 45 miles per hour, even though it weighs approximately 62 metric tons.
   - Either I have a mouse in my pocket or I don't.
   - Thomas is a bachelor, but he is married to his spouse.
   - If the pie recipe requires 7 apples, then the pie recipe will be followed correctly only if the pie recipe requires 7 apples.
   - I exist!
3. Construct a counterexample to demonstrate that the following arguments are invalid:
   - All dogs are canines.
No cats are dogs.
―――――――――
No cats are canines.
   - If Tom is dead, then he was executed.
Tom was executed.
―――――――――
Tom is dead.
   - Some tools for computation are not solar powered.
All calculators are tools for computation.
―――――――――
Some calculators are not solar powered.
4. Determine whether the following argument is inductive or deductive, then explain why the argument is valid, invalid, strong, or weak.
   - The combined average verbal and math SAT score for incoming freshmen in 2005 was 900. The combined average verbal and math SAT score for incoming freshmen in 2009 was 890. This proves that the combined average SAT score for 2005 was higher than it was in 2009.

- Tony was a male freshman in 2005. In 2005, 40% of incoming freshmen males scored below the average combined SAT score. It's likely that Tony scored below the average combined SAT score.

SEE ALSO

3.4 Formal Deduction with Categories: Immediate Inferences
3.5 Formal Deduction with Categories: Syllogisms
Chapter 4: Tools for Deductive Reasoning with Claims

READING

David R. Morrow & Anthony Weston, *A Workbook for Arguments* (2011)
Anthony Weston, *A Rulebook for Arguments* (2009)
Karen Lambert & Bas van Fraassen, *Derivation and Counterexample* (1972)

NOTE

1. Students learn this series with the mnemonic sentence: Kings Play Chess on Fine Green Silk.

3 Tools for Deductive Reasoning with Categories

3.1 Thinking Categorically

Logic as the formal study of reasoning has been around for thousands of years. Aristotle (384–322 BCE) is commonly credited with having founded the discipline, although less systematic inquiries into reasoning certainly preceded him. Aristotle's principal approach to reasoning was through categories. *Categories* are useful tools for classifying and grouping things based on a shared property or properties. Grouping categorically allows the critical thinker to organize thoughts and concepts in ways that help to define and to delineate relationships clearly among categories as well as among members of categories. For example, to say that my car is blue is to say that my car belongs to a category of things that are blue. In fact, simply saying "my car" assumes a category of things that belong to me, as well as a category of things that are called "cars." The construction of categories is a basic building block of communication, as it would be exceedingly difficult to write or speak about the world without the help of category terms. For the purposes of critical thinking, moreover, possessing clearly defined and related categories is an important component of determining whether claims are true or false.

Types and tokens

To better understand categories, it's helpful to understand the *type–token distinction.* Roughly speaking, *tokens* are particular instances of things in the world, while *types* are general, abstract categories of things. The first US president, George Washington, is a token. He is a particular instance of something in the world. As such, George Washington belongs to many types, like man, human, US president, etc. These categories help critical thinkers distinguish the first US president, George Washington,

The Critical Thinking Toolkit, First Edition. Galen A. Foresman, Peter S. Fosl, and Jamie C. Watson.

from other people who happen to share his name but do not belong to all of the same categories.

Any token can be a member of many categories, and every category to which something belongs tells critical thinkers more about the thing in question. The science and practice of categorizing and classifying things is called *taxonomy*. Taxonomists understand the underlying theory behind the construction of categories, which allows them to put things in their appropriate category. For example, a biologist who has discovered a new organism must understand biological taxonomies to identify properly the new organism's place among similar organisms.

While the real-world consequences of identifying the types to which a token belongs are important for reasoning categorically, these issues typically become important during Step #2 of our Two-Step evaluation process (see 2.5), determining whether the premises are true. Furthermore, you should be aware that a lot of categorical reasoning occurs independently of tokens. For example, to say that all tigers are mammals is to make a categorical claim relating two types (or categories) of things, which does not rely on token examples to be true.

3.2 Categorical Logic

Categorical logic is a type of deductive reasoning that uses categorical claims. This type of deductive reasoning allows critical thinkers to construct valid deductive arguments from claims that relate categories to one another. Categorical logic seems to have been first formalized in a text by Aristotle that's come to be known as *Prior Analytics*. Here are some examples of categorical claims you might encounter in ordinary life.

Every politician takes pride in his or her work.
The mail is always on time.
Boats float on water.
If a Ford automobile is built in the US, then the workers who built it are unionized.
Only French citizens who are 18 years or older are permitted to vote in French elections.
There is a computer in the office.
Nowhere on Earth is free from climate change.

Quantity, quality, and standard form

Colloquially, categorical claims come in lots of forms, and it is often no easy task for critical thinkers to translate their ordinary way of talking about the relation of categories to a standard form that makes those relations clear. Logicians spent centuries developing a powerful system of categorical logic, but to use that system one has to translate ordinary statements into one of four *standard form* categorical sentences, each named after the Latin term associated with their logical meaning. (For more on translating English claims to standard form, see 3.3.) Here's what their general forms look like:

A (from the first vowel in *affirmo*, affirmative):	All S are P.
E (from the first vowel in *nego*, negative):	No S are P.
I (from the second vowel in *affirmo*):	Some S are P.
O (from the second vowel in *nego*):	Some S are not P.

The basic parts: Each of the four standard form categorical claims is composed of a *quantifier*, a *subject term*, a *copula*, and a *predicate term*. In standard form, the *quantifier* is the first word of the categorical claim, and there are only three of them: "All," "No," and "Some." The *quantifier* is immediately followed by the *subject term*, S, which is the category or class being related to the *predicate term*, P, and the category or class that it designates. Linking S and P together is the *copula*, which is denoted by either "are" or "are not."

Quantity

For the critical thinker, categorical claims describe the extent to which the subject term is a member of the predicate term's category, and so the relationship described by these claims is entirely about class membership. (There's clearly, therefore, a lot of overlap here with set theory in mathematics.) The *quantifier* tells the critical thinker the categorical claim's *quantity*, which is the extent or scope of the subject term's category that is being related to the predicate term.

Categorical claims of type A and E are said to be *universal* in their quantity because they relate every member of the subject term's category to the predicate term. Categorical claims I and O, on the other hand, only assert a relationship between at least one member of the subject term's category to the predicate term, and so their quantity is described as *particular*. Note that the quantifier "Some," which is used to indicate the particular, has a very specific meaning for categorical claims. "Some" means "at least one," and allows for the possibility of more. In fact, *some* in this logical sense is consistent with *all* (since if something is true of *all* members of a set, it's certainly true of *some* of them). In common English, however, "some" often means something like "several," in the sense of more than one; and it often suggests *not all*. So it's important for the critical thinker when using categorical claims to keep the technical definition of "at least one and possibly more" in mind and never to assume that the term implies either that there are necessarily more than one or that the claim does not refer to all members of the relevant category.

Categorical claims either relate the entire category denoted by the subject term to the predicate term (logicians call this fully *distributing* the term), or they make the more limited claim of relating at least one member of the subject term's category to the predicate term (i.e., not fully distributing the term).

Quality

Now, having come to terms with quantity, there's a second property of standard form categorical sentences to discern: *quality*. Categorical claims are either *affirmative* or *negative*, depending on whether or not they are asserting class membership or denying class membership, respectively. The A- and I-claims are, as their name (deriving from ***AffIrmo***) suggests, affirmative, while the E- and O-claims are negative (from *n****E****g****O***). Because each type of categorical claim has one of the two properties of quantity and one of each of the two properties of quality, there are only 4 types of categorical claim. The table below shows how quantity and quality apply to each of the four categorical claims.

		Quality	
		Affirmative	*Negative*
Quantity	*Universal*	A-claims	E-claims
	Particular	I-claims	O-claims

Venn diagrams and the meaning of categorical claims

For the critical thinker, using standard form for categorical claims ensures that the meaning of any particular claim is clear. This clarity of meaning allows the critical thinker to make valid deductive inferences from one categorical claim to another (see 3.4), as well as construct valid deductive arguments called categorical *syllogisms* (see 4.5). The nineteenth-century logician John Venn (1834–1923) came up with a visual way of representing these relations. Some of this material can get pretty dry, and visual presentations can help a lot. Boole's technique is called, of course, the *Venn diagram*. The Venn diagrams below illustrate the categorical relationships spelled out by the four central pillars of the categorical system. Each category has its own circle. Here's an A-claim.

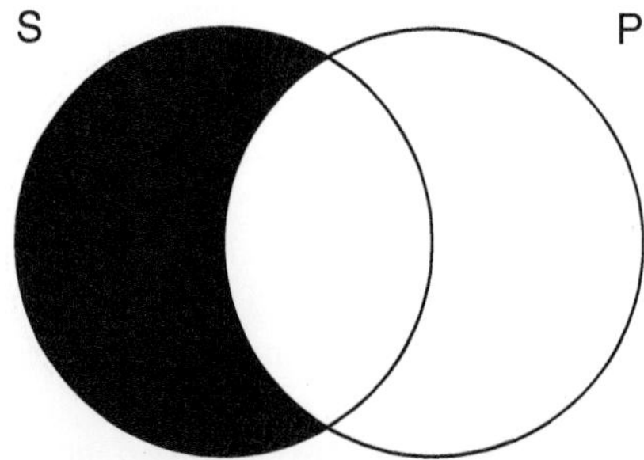

In this A-claim diagram, anything that's an S belongs in the S circle, and anything that's a P belongs in the P circle. The area where the S circle overlaps the P circle contains everything that is both an S and a P. Since the A-claim asserts that every member of class S also belongs to class P, the portion of the S circle that is outside the P circle has been shaded black to indicate that there are no members of S present outside of P. (Shading in is kind of like marking out or erasing.) The shaded area of a Venn diagram will always indicate that there is an absence or void of members, that the claim excludes them from those regions of meaning – hence, the black void.

Below is the Venn diagram for the E-claim; notice that the shaded region is only in the area where the S circle and P circle overlap, since the claim excludes anything from that region.

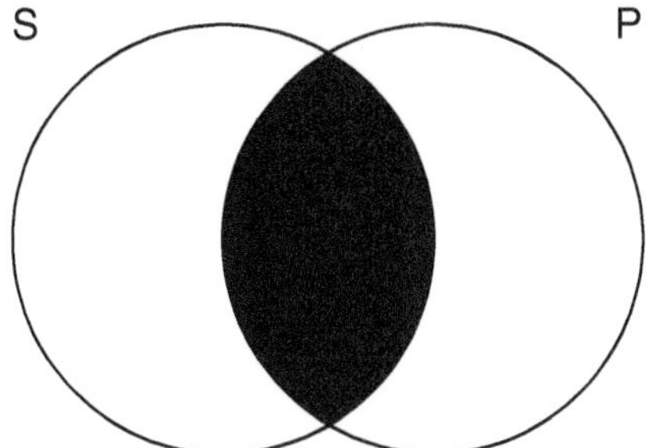

There can be no Ss that are also Ps, which means any members of S must be placed in the unshaded region of the S circle.

When a claim definitely asserts that members of a class (even one) exist in a particular region, the Venn diagram illustrates this with an "X" within that region. The I-claim, for example, asserts that Some S are P, which in terms of the quantity and quality means that at least one thing that is an S is also a P. Since that much is known for sure, the Venn diagram illustrates the information with an "X" placed in the area of overlap between the S and the P circles. Of course, so far as we know from the I-claim, it's possible that there are other Ss outside of P. It's possible too that there aren't. The claim doesn't say, so we just leave those areas blank and open.

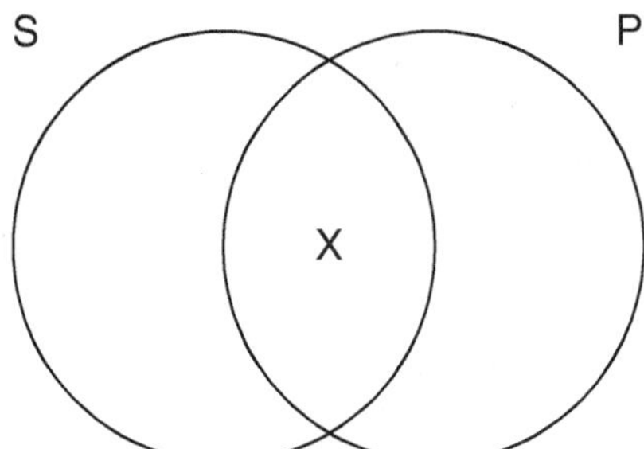

Similarly, the Venn diagram for the O-claim illustrates that at least one member of S is not a member of P by placing an "X" in the S circle *outside* the area circumscribed by the P circle. Again, this O-claim neither implies nor excludes there being Ss inside of P. That's why it's possible for I-claims and O-claims to be both simultaneously true or for just one of them to be true.

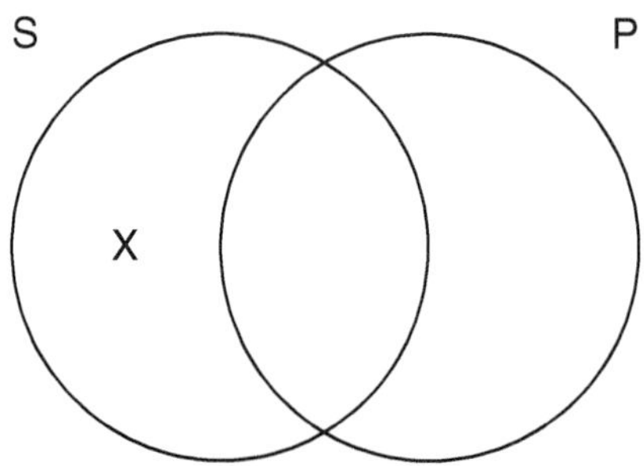

Distribution and its implications

Now, as we've seen, when a categorical statement makes a claim about every member of one of its categories it's said to *distribute* that category. Here we show the distributed categories in each of the four categorical claims. Unsurprisingly, the system covers all the possible combinations.

A: All S are P.	Distributes S only.
E: No S are P.	Distributes both S and P.
I: Some S are P.	Distributes neither S nor P.
O: Some S are not P.	Distributes P only.

For the critical thinker, distribution is useful because it helps us to understand better the implications of a categorical claim. Knowing that both S and P are distributed in an E-claim, for example, alerts the critical thinker to the fact that the E-claim asserts something about the entire category of S and the entire category of P. Again, the critical thinker knows that the entire category of S is outside the category of P, but it turns out that the E-claim also tells him or her that the entire category of P is outside the category of S. In other words, No S are P also means that No P are S. The same sort of symmetry, however, is not to be found with the A-claim.

No terms are distributed in the I-claim, because nothing about either the entire category of S or of P is implied by the fact that Some S are P. For the critical thinker, knowing that Some S are P implies nothing about *all* of S or *all* of P. That's not the case, however, for the O-claim. Some S are not P tells the critical thinker that there's at least one member of S that exists apart from the entire category of P, and so the critical thinker knows something about all of P, namely that it excludes some member of S.

One of the reasons it's useful to know about distribution is that there are five handy rules one can use to detect invalid categorical arguments. We'll address those rules in 3.5 once we get a bit more categorical logic under our belts.

Existential import

Another issue regarding categorical claims about which the critical thinker should be aware occurs with A- and E-claims and their relation to I- and O-claims. It's sometimes assumed that when an A- or E-claim is true there must actually be a member of S that exists. For example, the claim, "All monkeys are marsupials," (A-claim) may appear to imply that at least one monkey exists (a member of S) and that it must be a marsupial.

But philosophers and scientists found that things get sticky when dealing with hypothetical and otherwise imaginary entities. For example, a second Earth-sized planet added to our solar system or unicorns. Is it possible to say anything true about things that do not exist? In other words, do claims about imaginary things have existential import? Or when something does not yet exist but may someday, should we think that categorical claims about those sorts of things have existential import? The following two claims and their existential forms help to illustrate this issue and its solution.

I: Some unicorns are animals with only one horn.
O: Some interstellar spacecraft are not efficient means for picking up groceries.

At first glance, the I- and O-claims seem to assert something true, namely that unicorns are animals with only one horn and that interstellar spacecraft aren't efficient means for picking up groceries. Because I- and O-claims, however, carry existential import, these claims must be false. After all, unicorns and interstellar spacecraft (sadly) don't seem to exist. But for various reasons, one might wish to reason about them.

The problem is solved, however, by handling A- and E-claims differently – namely, by not assuming that they have positive existential import. That would make it possible for the I-claim and O-claim above to be false while nevertheless treating the statements as true in a way that makes no existential commitments. It then becomes possible to reason about such things – perhaps, for example, hypothetically or imaginatively:

A: All unicorns are animals with only one horn.
E: No interstellar spacecraft are efficient means for picking up groceries.

Alternatively, consider:

A: All Wookiees are furry creatures.
E: No Jedi are thoroughly evil beings.

Even though Wookiees and Jedi are both fictional, because A- and E-claims lack existential import, they can remain true even with their fictional subject terms. This approach to interpreting the existential import of universal claims is often credited to George Boole (1815–1864) and is called the "Boolean Standpoint" or "Modern Standpoint." Prior to the Modern Standpoint, logicians sometimes clunked along following Aristotle's interpretation of the universal categorical claims A and E. What's called the "Aristotelian Standpoint" or "Traditional Standpoint," accordingly, assumes that A- and E-claims *do* have existential import. If you like using the Aristotelian system, however, there is another option. Just stipulate the reality, or what's sometimes called the *universe of discourse*, about which you're reasoning and then stick with the Aristotelian system. For example, one might stipulate that one is reasoning about the fictitious universe of J. R. R. Tolkien's 1937 novel, *The Hobbit*, and then restrict existential import of your A- and E-claims to that reality.

3.3 Translating English Claims to Standard Form

Categorical logic offers powerful tools for making reasoning precise as well as for detecting faulty reasoning. But translating English claims into categorical propositions is not a perfect science. Ordinary language is riddled with complexity rarely noticed by those using it. Because of this, the rules for translation in this section are general but imperfect tools to help you with the translation process. They are a lot like measuring sticks, functioning perfectly well to assess the length of most objects, while leaving much to be desired when measuring the circumference of a ball. It is also important to point out that claims are made within particular contexts, and context can influence or even radically change the meaning of sentences. Translation, therefore, requires interpretation, and critical thinkers must be sensitive to the subtleties of language and expression as they go about the business of logical criticism.

A first rule for translating English claims into standard form categorical propositions is that the critical thinker *must have a clear understanding of the meaning of the original English claim.*

A second rule for translating ordinary claims to categorical propositions is that *the subject of the simple sentence determines the quantifier and subject term for the categorical proposition*, while *the predicate determines the predicate term* (though there are unfortunately exceptions).

Implicit quantifiers

Since the quantity of the translated subject term can only be universal or particular, you will need to determine whether or not the original claim refers to an entire class of things or at least one member from a class of things.

Example 1:	Snakes are cold-blooded animals.	All snakes are cold-blooded animals.
Example 2:	Snakes live under that shed.	Some snakes are things that live under that shed.
Example 3:	A few snakes are venomous animals.	Some snakes are venomous animals.

Note how similar Examples 1 and 2 are. It's only because of our mastery of ordinary contexts that we know which quantifier to use (no one who knows about snakes and sheds would think that *all* snakes live under one shed).

Individuals

When the subject refers to *a specific entity*, the quantity becomes *universal* and the subject term is worded to distinguish the individual from a whole category. This creates a class of things that has no more than that one member.

Example 3:	Thomas is a tall person.	All persons identical to Thomas are persons that are tall.
Example 4:	Springfield is the greatest city on Earth.	All places identical to Springfield are places that are identical to the greatest city on Earth.
Example 5:	My snake is a venomous animal.	All things identical to my snake are things that are venomous animals.
Example 6:	Tom's car accident is the worst accident I've seen.	All states of affairs identical to Tom's car accident are states of affairs that are identical to the worst accident I've seen.
Example 7:	Friday is the day after tomorrow.	All times identical to this Friday are times that are the day after tomorrow.

Getting the verb right

Our examples so far have conveniently used forms of the verb "to be," which requires almost no translation. But, of course, many claims in ordinary language don't use the verb "to be," as in "Many birds fly," "The bird smells gross," and "Many carnivorous birds eat worms." So, the next important skill in translating English claims is replacing verbs with the copula "are," and later, "are not."

Many birds fly.	Some birds are things that fly.
The bird smells gross.	All birds identical with that bird are things that smell gross.
Many carnivorous birds eat worms.	Some carnivorous birds are things that eat worms.

All of the examples up to this point have dealt with the affirmative A and I categorical propositions. Let's take a look now at a few E- and O-claims.

Birds do not have gills.	No birds are things that have gills.
Teetotalers never drink beer.	No teetotalers are persons that ever drink beer.
Most of the class won't pass the test.	Some persons in the class are not persons that will pass the test.
None of the baskets have apples.	No baskets are things that have apples.
Nothing can replace his loss.	No things are things that can replace his loss.
Nowhere in the vacuum of space can you find a comfy recliner.	No places in the vacuum of space are places where you can find a comfy recliner.
Chris never drinks alcohol.	No persons identical to Chris are persons that drink alcohol.
I don't disagree with you.	No persons identical to me are persons that disagree with you.

Adverbials

While the critical thinker is familiarizing himself or herself with translating simple ordinary sentences into categorical form, a few special cases may cross his or her path. These special cases occur with adverbial clauses. Here are some examples of claims with adverbial clauses and proper translations for them:

Buy some bread when you get to the store.	All times you go to the store are times you buy some bread.
Whenever kids disappoint their parents they feel guilty.	All times kids disappoint their parents are times they feel guilty.

The keys are where I left them.	All places I left the keys are places the keys are.
Wherever you go there you are.	All places you go are places you are.
My fantasy football team will dominate if my running backs stay healthy.	All times my running backs stay healthy are times my fantasy football team will dominate.
If the Islamic State continues to grow, then the United States will commit ground troops to Iraq.	All times the Islamic State continues to grow are times the United States will commit ground troops to Iraq.

English claims with adverbial clauses that deny class membership can be tricky. Here are some examples of how you might translate them (depending, of course, on the context):

Don't buy bread when you get to the store.	All times you get to the store are times you don't buy bread. *Or* No times you get to the store are times you buy bread.
Whenever kids don't disappoint their parents, they feel acceptable.	All times kids don't disappoint their parents are times they feel acceptable.
The keys aren't where I left them.	All places I left the keys are places the keys aren't. *Or* No places I left the keys are places the keys are.
Wherever you fail to go there you are not.	All places you fail to go are places you are not. *Or* No places you fail to go are places you are.
My fantasy football team won't dominate if my running backs are injured.	All times my running backs are injured are times my fantasy football team won't dominate. *Or* No times my running backs are injured are times my fantasy football team will dominate.

If the Islamic State continues to grow, then the United States won't commit ground troops to Iraq.	All times the Islamic State continues to grow are times the United States won't commit ground troops to Iraq. *Or* No times the Islamic State continues to grow are times the United States will commit ground troops to Iraq.

Trust your instincts

Ultimately, ordinary language is full of unusual sentence structures for expressing claims that won't fit neatly into the patterns set out here. After all, the language has had centuries to evolve and adopt expressions that native speakers understand intuitively, even if they can't identify the subject and predicate of a sentence. The intuitive understanding we develop as masters of a language goes a long way toward constructing an accurate translation, because translation, at its core, is about retaining as much of the meaning of the original claim as possible in the newly translated categorical proposition. If you're a fluent speaker of a language with lots of background experience of how that language uses words, then trust your instincts with translation.

A caveat

Keep in mind, too, that translation into standard logical form doesn't create superior language *per se*. Words have many, perhaps countless, uses, and reasoning is just one of them. A gain in terms of logical clarification may be a loss in terms of poetic or persuasive force or subtle connotation. The tools of categorical logic are powerful, but they should not be thought to be revealing the essential or even necessarily the most important functions of language. Logic's great, but it's not all there is to critical thinking (see Chapter 10).

3.4 Formal Deduction with Categories: Immediate Inferences

If constructing an argument is like building a bridge, then an *immediate inference* is like a bridge with only one support. Under the right conditions, a single support can make for a perfectly good bridge, and similarly, a single premise may be all that is needed to support a conclusion. An *immediate inference* is an argument that proceeds from a single premise immediately to a conclusion. What immediate inferences lack in complexity they make up for in simplicity and elegance.

Equivalences

Anyone who's spent some time with young children knows that, for them, more is always better. Related to this is the sometimes utterly irrational degree to which anything less than absolute and perfect equality implies someone is being treated unfairly. The simple exercise of cutting slices of a child's birthday cake requires surgical precision to ensure perfect equity in the distribution of sweet happiness, lest an injustice make short work of what was an otherwise great party. It can, depending upon the context, be either delightful or frustrating to discover that sometimes for a child five pennies far exceeds the value of a single nickel. Clearly, acquiring even basic concepts of equivalence can dramatically affect one's ability to reason and think critically.

Logicians are concerned principally with two kinds of equivalences, both of which can be precisely defined. *Material equivalences* are different claims that have the same *truth value*. Sometimes it's just by accident that the truth values of sentences coincide, and sometimes it's the result of their logical structure – as we've seen in 2.3. Because it's the logical form or structure of tautologies and self-contradictions that explains the equivalence of their truth values, those of each type are sometimes called *logically equivalent*. (See 4.3 and 4.4 for more on equivalences.)

In categorical logic, statements can be materially and logically equivalent when they make the same categorical claim (i.e., the same claim about what's included or excluded in some category) even if they express that claim with different categorical standard forms. Because of this, equivalent claims can appear to be different, even though they are not, much in the way five pennies can appear importantly different from one nickel for a child. Recognizing categorical equivalences is therefore useful to critical thinkers because it helps in avoiding needless disagreement, as they can be used to show that what may have initially appeared as a significant difference was in fact not so.

Imagine a scenario in which two people are quarreling over how one's faith in God might be evident in good works. The first person claims, "Anyone with faith in God will demonstrate that faith through good works," while the second person adamantly holds, "No one with faith in God will fail to demonstrate that faith through good works." Thankfully, before things get too heated, this dispute can be eliminated altogether simply by showing that the claims are, in fact, equivalent. They say the same thing, categorically speaking. As we're about to see, each claim is just the *obverse* of the other.

Anyone with faith in God will demonstrate that faith through good works.	All persons with faith in God are persons who will demonstrate that faith through their good works.
No one with faith in God will fail to demonstrate that faith through good works.	No persons with faith in God are persons who will fail to demonstrate that faith through their good works.

To understand this equivalence, it is important, however, to notice that the predicate term for the E-claim says, "persons who *fail to* demonstrate ... " as opposed to just, "persons who demonstrate ... ," as it does in the A-claim. Otherwise, these two predicate terms are identical. In categorical logic, as in mathematics, the *complement* of a class or category of things is everything outside that class or category, and so the complement of "persons who demonstrate that faith through their good works" is "persons who do not (or fail to) demonstrate that faith through their good works." Changing the focus of the sentence from the class to the class complement will make it possible for us to transform this sentence into a different but equivalent expression.

There, in fact, are a variety of techniques, often called *transformation operations*, you can use when scrutinizing categorical propositions to transform them into other categorical propositions that have the very same meaning. Doing so can prove extremely helpful not just in ending disputes but also simply in clarifying what a claim means. Here, we will explain three: conversion, contraposition, and obversion.

Conversion

Conversion is a type of transformation that switches the subject and predicate terms in a categorical proposition. In the case of E-claims and I-claims, conversion creates a new claim that is equivalent to the original E- and I-claims. This, however, is not the case for A- and O-claims, and the conversion of an A- or O-claim is not a valid immediate inference. The Venn diagrams below demonstrate why this is the case:

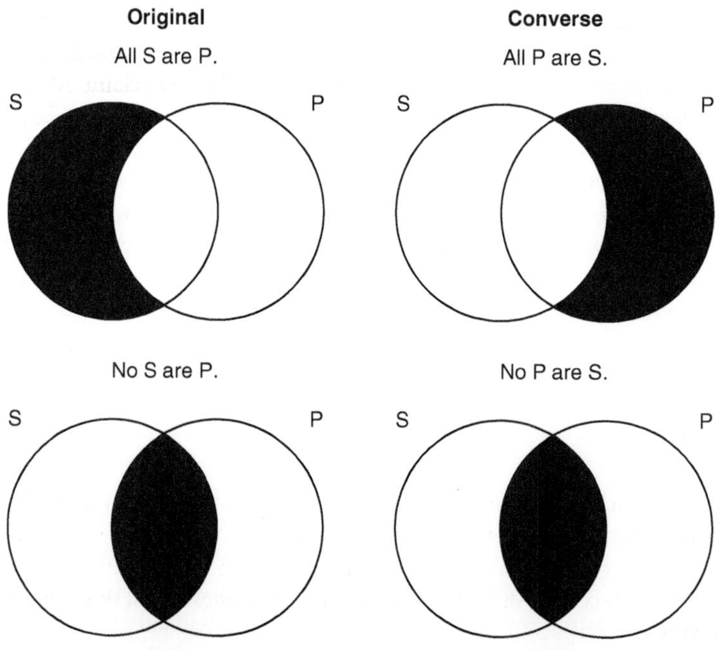

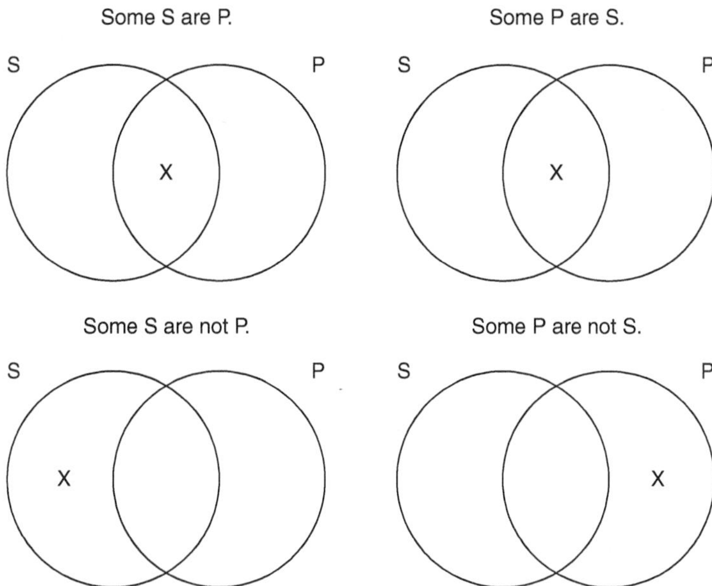

Because the diagrams for the E- and I-claims are the same as their converse, we know that switching the location of the subject and predicate terms does not change the meaning of those claims. The diagrams are symmetrical and rotate around a central axis. A- and O-claims don't have symmetrical diagrams, and switching the subject with the predicate term has the effect of creating a very different claim. After all, a person may be willing to admit that "All clowns are creepy people," but that doesn't mean they think that "All creepy people are clowns." Conversion has a similar effect on the O-claim, which, once transformed, makes a claim about at least one member of P not being a member of S. By failing to recognize that the O-claim and its converse are not equivalent, a person runs the risk of conflating "some tragedies are not murders" with "some murders are not tragedies," a mistake good critical thinkers would be loath to make.

Contraposition

The operation of *contraposition* involves replacing both the subject and predicate terms of a categorical claim with their complements, followed by switching the places of the subject term's complement with the predicate term's complement.

Consider the A-claim: All S are P. We form the *contrapositive* of this claim by taking the following two steps:

Step 1:	Replace the subject and predicate terms with their complements.	All S are P. →	**All non-S are non-P.**
Step 2:	Switch places between the complement of the subject term and the complement of the predicate term.	All non-S are non-P. →	**All non-P are non-S.**

In the case of the A-claim, contraposition creates a claim that is equivalent to the original A-claim. To say that all members of S are members of P, as an A-claim does, is to say that there are no Ss that exist outside the category of P, and so the A-claim's meaning is illustrated with a Venn diagram by shading in the area of the S circle that does not overlap the P circle. (Remember, the shaded area is the area where nothing exists.) For the contrapositive of the A-claim, anything that is not a P is also not an S, and so everything outside the P circle must not be an S. The result of this is that nothing can exist in the area of the S circle that is external to the P circle, which is the same diagram as the original A-claim.

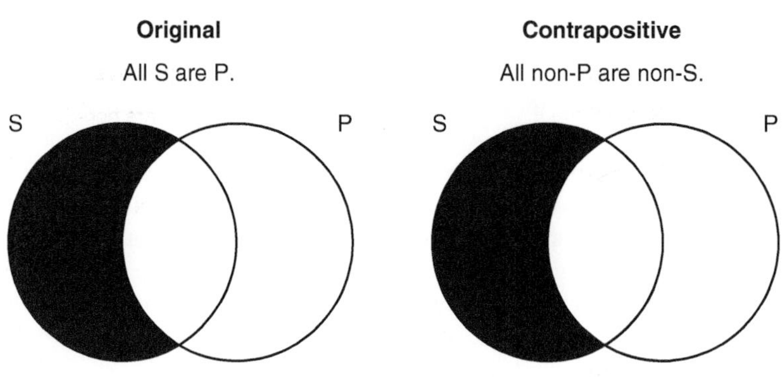

The contrapositive of an E-claim, "No S are P," is "No non-P are non-S," which means that everything that is not a P is also not a non-S. In terms of the Venn diagram, nothing exists outside the P circle or the S circle, because those things would be both non-P and non-S. Hence, the shaded area is outside of both circles, which is obviously different than the original E-claim, and so they are not equivalent.

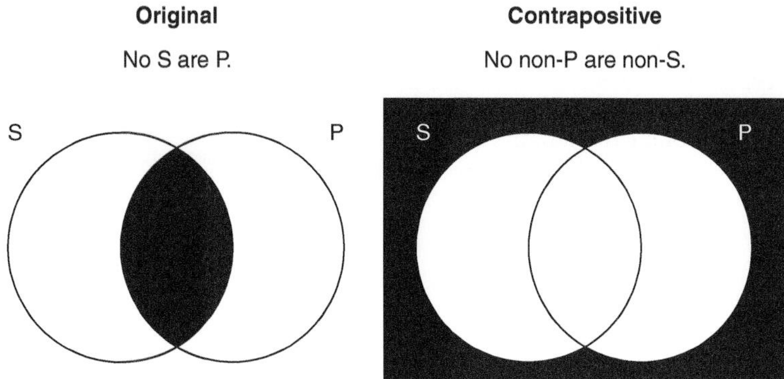

For the contrapositive of an I-claim, "Some non-P are non-S," we know that there exists at least one non-P that is also a non-S. In diagramming this, an X is drawn outside both the P and S circles, since that is the area that is both non-S and non-P. Once again, this Venn diagram is very different from the original I-claim's diagram, wherein the X is drawn in the region of overlap between the S and P circles, indicating that there exists at least one thing that is both S and P. Immediate inferences that contrapose an E- or I-claim are therefore not valid.

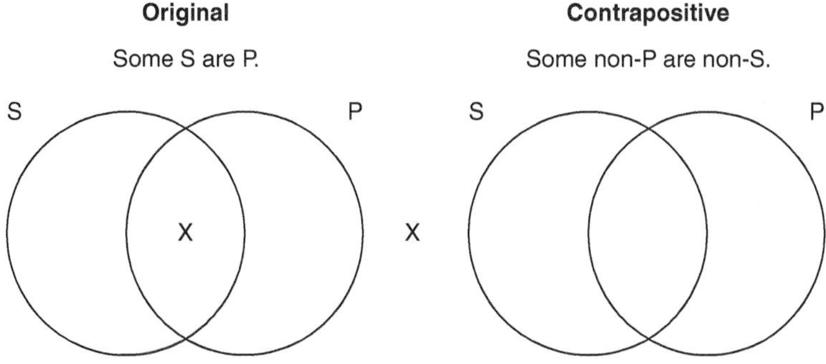

Finally, the contrapositive of the O-claim turns out to be "Some non-P are not non-S." The "not non-S" is a double negative, and it is handled just like any other double negation in the English language by the negatives canceling each other out and leaving just "S." This means that there exists some non-P that is an S, and we diagram this by placing an X outside the P circle (because of non-P), but somewhere in the S circle (because of "not non-S"). The Venn diagram we're left with is identical to the Venn diagram for the original O-claim, and so the contrapositive of the O-claim is equivalent to the original O-claim. Contraposing an A- or O-claim is a valid immediate inference.

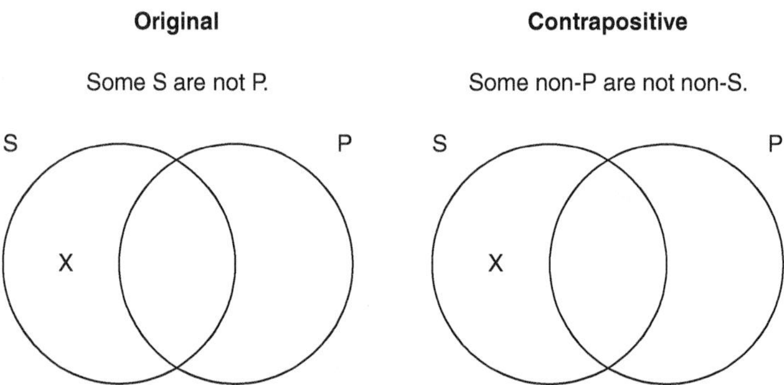

Obversion

Obversion is the most widely useful of the four categorical transformation operations. While *contraposition* is restricted as a form of valid inference to A-claims and O-claims, and while *conversion* is restricted to E-claims and I-claims, *obversion* may be legitimately employed with *all four types* of standard form categorical propositions. An obverted categorical proposition has had its quality switched and its predicate term replaced with its complement. So, the I-claim "Some politicians are honest civil servants" becomes just "Some politicians are not dishonest civil servants." Here's how it works more formally.

"Some politicians are honest civil servants" translates to "Some S are P." To form the obverse, we take the following two steps:

Step 1:	Change the quality of the original claim from negative to affirmative or affirmative to negative.	Some S are P. →	Some S are not P. (The original claim was affirmative, so the new claim is negative.)
Step 2:	Replace the predicate term with its complement.	Some S are not P. →	**Some S are not non-P.**

The Venn diagrams below illustrate how each of the four categorical propositions is equivalent to its obverse.

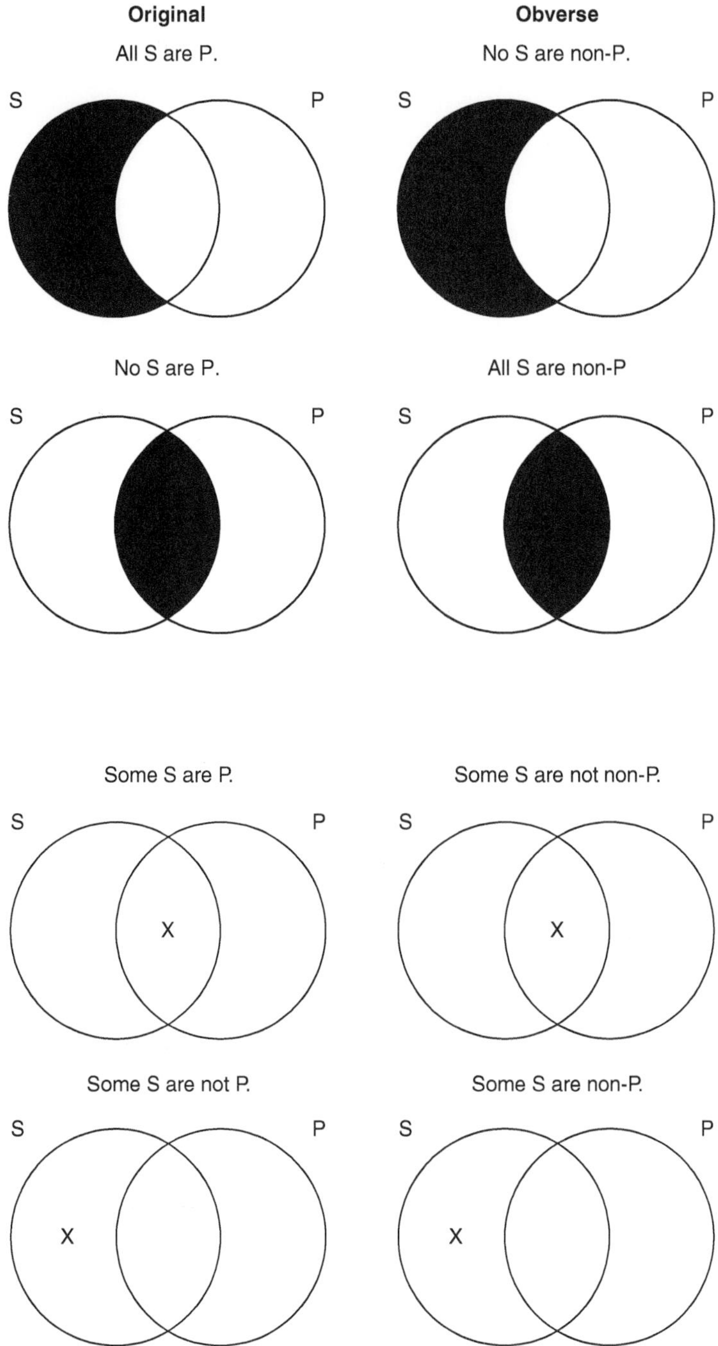
Original
Obverse
All S are P.
No S are non-P.
S
P
S
P
No S are P.
All S are non-P
S
P
S
P
Some S are P.
Some S are not non-P.
S
P
X
S
P
X
Some S are not P.
Some S are non-P.
S
P
X
S
P
X

The Aristotelian and Boolean Squares of Opposition

If someone were to make the claim, "All nuns are compassionate people," perhaps images of women in religious habits helping the poor, sick, and destitute come to mind. Or rather, perhaps fond memories of a certain flying nun or a gospel choir of nuns inspired by Whoopi Goldberg is more familiar. But perhaps someone having attended a Catholic school as a child might recall a strict disciplinarian nun who was quite intolerant of any silly business and hardly the poster-image for compassion. This person might avidly retort, "Some nuns are not compassionate people!" And here we have a clear disagreement. If "Some nuns are not compassionate people," then it is impossible that all of them are. The diagram of the A-claim and O-claim shown below helps to illustrate this.

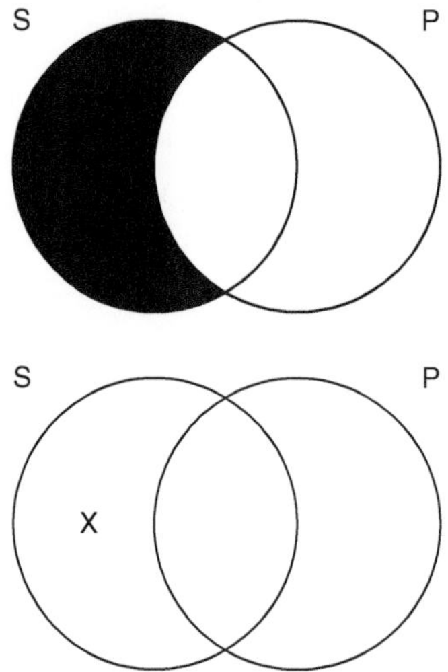

The shaded region of the subject term for an A-claim illustrates that there are no Ss that exist outside the P region, because All S are P for this example, "All nuns are compassionate people." For the O-claim, the X in the S region outside the P circle indicates that there exists an S that is not a P. In other words, there exists at least one nun who is not a compassionate person. As we saw in 2.3, these claims are referred to as *logical contradictions* of one another.

Contradiction

Logical contradictions occur when (1) the truth of one claim necessarily implies the falsehood of another claim – *and*, vice versa, when (2) the falsehood of one implies the truth of the other. If it's true, as the A-claim asserts, that there are no Ss that are not also Ps, then the corresponding O-claim must be false, since it explicitly asserts that there is at least one S that is not a P. Alternatively, if the O-claim is true, then the A-claim must be false, because the fact that there exists an S that is not also a P entails that the region of S external to P is not empty, which is what the A-claim asserts. Moreover, and this is important because it distinguishes contradictions from *contraries*, the falsehood of the A-claim implies the truth of the I-claim. The A-claim is false, after all, just when the shaded area is not empty (as the I-claim holds); and the I-claim is false when the area where it places its X does not contain any Xs (as the A-claim holds).

For categorical propositions, these immediate inferences are often illustrated using what's known as the *Square of Opposition*. There are two versions of the Square of Opposition depending on whether or not one is assuming existential import for the members of the categories – or, more particularly, that at least one of each category exists. The *Boolean Square of Opposition* does not assume existential import, and so it is limited to only two lines of immediate inference for categorical propositions, both of them contradictions, as shown below:

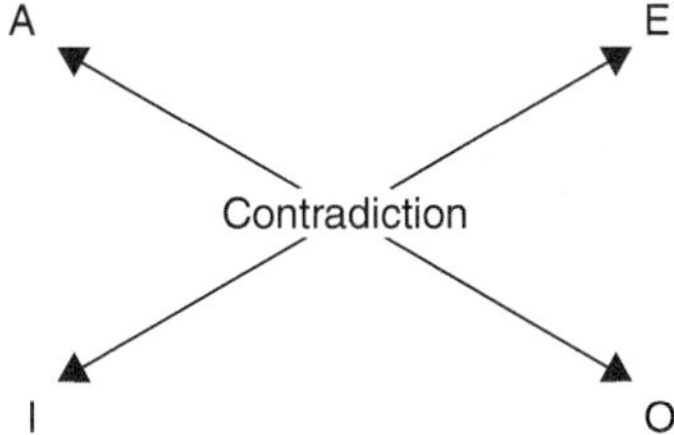

In addition to the logical contradiction between A-claims and O-claims demonstrated in our compassionate nuns example, the Boolean Square of Opposition shows that E-claims and I-claims are logical contradictions, as well. After all, if "No nuns are compassionate people," then it is impossible that "Some nuns are compassionate people," and vice versa.

Now, because it allows existential import, the *Aristotelian Square of Opposition* offers several more immediate inferences than the Boolean Square. Of course, these new relationships are only viable when the terms of the categorical propositions are taken actually to exist. Below, then, is the Aristotelian Square of Opposition (aka the *Traditional Square of Opposition*) with all of its relationships, including logical contradiction (which, you've probably noticed, is a valid inference on both squares).

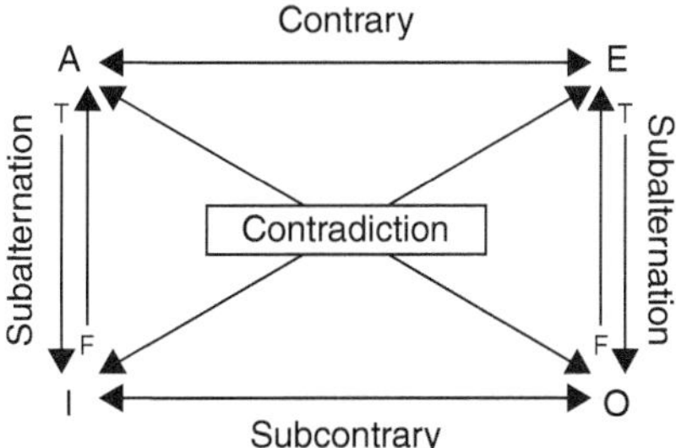

Contrariety

The logical relationship of *contrariety* between A-claims and E-claims for the Aristotelian Square of Opposition holds that an A-claim and its corresponding E-claim cannot both be true at the same time. If an A-claim is true, then we know that the corresponding E-claim must be false, and if an E-claim is true, then the corresponding A-claim must be false. That's true of the contradictories of both A- and E-claims, too. It is, however, unlike with contradictories, possible for both contraries to be false at the same time, and so knowing that an A-claim is false doesn't imply anything about the truth or falsity of the corresponding E-claim, and vice versa. With the logical contrary relationship, there is only an immediate inference when we know that one of the claims is true. The *fallacy*, or error in reasoning, called *illicit contrary* occurs when one infers the truth of an A- or E-claim from the falsity of its corresponding E- or A-claim.

Valid Inference with Contrariety:
All firefighters are courageous people.
Therefore, it's not the case that no firefighters are courageous people.

Illicit Contrary Fallacy:
It's not the case that no dogs are firefighters.
Therefore, all dogs are firefighters.

The reason that the logical contrary relationship holds for A- and E-claims with existing terms can be seen from the diagrams of the A- and E-claims using the Aristotelian model.

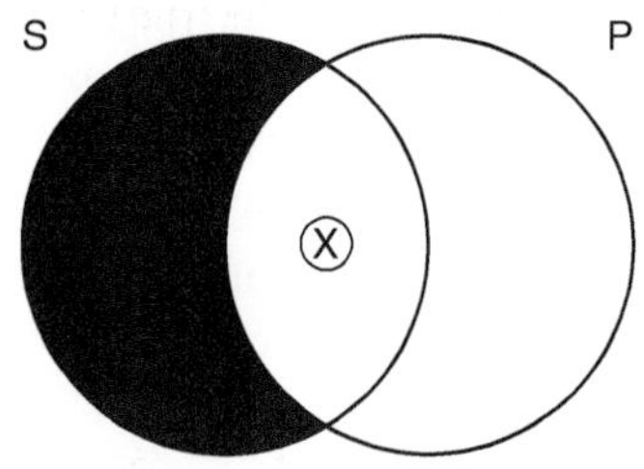

A-Claim (Traditional Model)

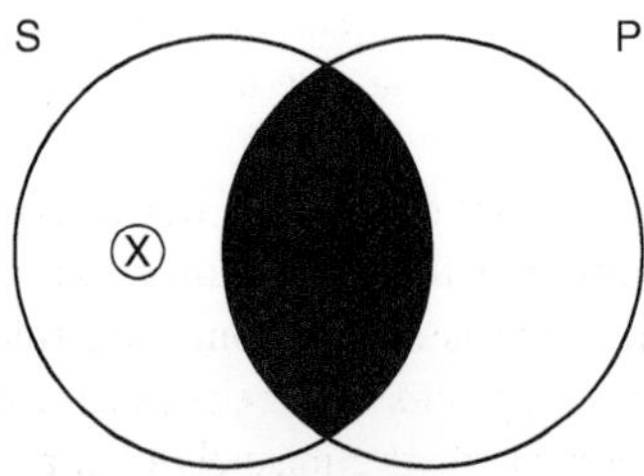

E-Claim (Traditional Model)

If an A-claim is true under the Aristotelian model, then there exists an S that is also a P. Because of this, we know that the corresponding E-claim must be false, since it asserts that there are no Ss that are also Ps. Similarly, when an E-claim is true under the Aristotelian model, we know that there exists an S that is not P, which is indicated with an X inside a circle. The X with the circle around it in the diagram tells the critical thinker that there is at least one thing that exists in that region of the Venn diagram when the claim is true and the S and P terms refer to existing things. If we assume that the E-claim is true and refers to existing things, then the existence of an S that is not a P contradicts the A-claim. Hence, if an E-claim is true, then the A-claim must be false.

It's important to remember with the contrary relationship that when an A-claim or E-claim is false, we can't infer anything about the corresponding E- or A-claim. This is because, as the diagrams indicate, when an A- or E-claim is false on the Traditional model, we do not know whether or not an S term exists. If one were to say, "I know that it is false that all cheeses are things that are aged to perfection," we certainly cannot assume that there exists at least one cheese that is aged to perfection. After all, it may be the case that there are no cheeses that are aged to perfection. We simply do not know one way or the other when an A- or E-claim is false whether or not the corresponding E- or A-claim is true. It may simply be that they're both false.

Subcontrariety

The *subcontrary* relationship on the Aristotelian Square of Opposition is the flip side of contrariety. Whereas contraries can't both be true (but can both be false), subcontraries can't both be false (but can both be true). Alternatively, with contraries at least one (and at most two) is false, while with subcontraries at least one (and at most two) is true. If an I-claim is false, then the corresponding O-claim must be true, and if an O-claim is false, then the corresponding I-claim must be true. If, for example, we know that it is false that some cats are dogs, then we can infer that some cats are not dogs. Once again, it's crucial to making this inference that the categories we're dealing with are not empty, that the S and P terms refer to things understood to exist in the real world, which is fairly easy with an example using cats and dogs.

The reason this immediate inference works may be obvious from ordinary language. After all, it seems clear that when a claim like, "Some dogs are ferocious felines," is made, we know it to be false. We know it is false, because we know that no dogs are felines, ferocious or otherwise. But if we know, "No dogs are ferocious felines," then we also know at least one dog is not a ferocious feline, because existential import on the Aristotelian model assumes that at least one thing exists if the E-claim is true. And if there is at least one dog that is not a feline, then the O-claim must be true. Venn diagrams can help illustrate this chain of logical reasoning. Here's the Venn diagram for the false claim that, "Some dogs are ferocious felines."

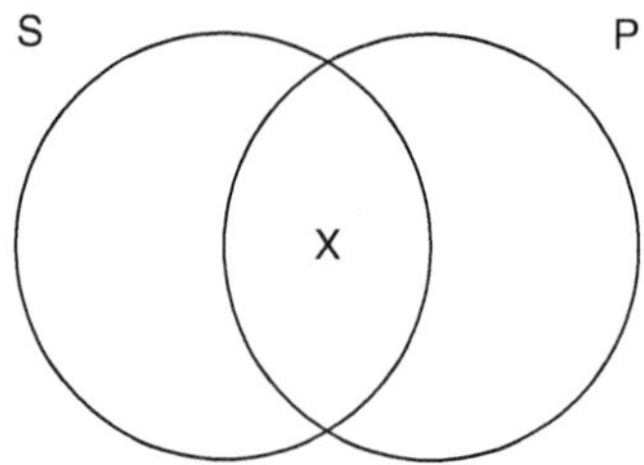

Since we agree that this I-claim is false, it's wrong to assert that something exists where S and P intersect. That "X," in other words, shouldn't be there. Another "X," however, should appear. To see this, remember that "dogs" has existential import in the claim, "No dogs are ferocious felines." And remember, too, that a false I-claim by contradiction implies a true E-claim. Here's the Venn diagram for our E-claim about dogs.

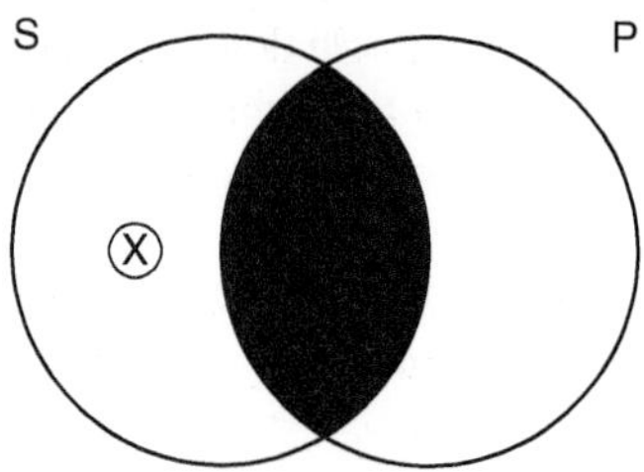

When nothing exists where S and P intersect, we have an E-claim, and because the terms in the Aristotelian system have existential import, S must have at least one occupant. From this true E-claim, then, this follows:

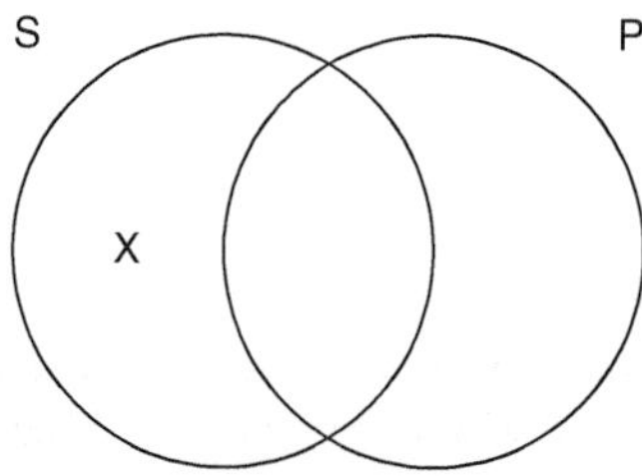

On the Aristotelian model, the E-claim implies that at least one S exists when the S term refers to something that exists in the real world (existential import). And if at least one S exists that is not a P, then the O-claim diagrammed above must be true.

Subalternation

The name for the immediate inference that allows us to infer the truth of an O-claim from the truth of an E-claim is subalternation. The *subalternation relationship* for categorical propositions on the Aristotelian model says that whenever an A- or E-claim is true, the corresponding I- or O-claim is true as well. Furthermore, subalternation also says that whenever an I- or an O-claim is false, the corresponding A- or E-claim is also false. As we have seen, when an E-claim is true on the Aristotelian model, one can assume that at least one thing exists that is not a P, which is why the corresponding O-claim is true. Similarly, if an A-claim is true, then it assumes that at least one S is also a P, which is why the corresponding I-claim is true whenever the A-claim is true. If, however, we begin the inference with an I-claim that is true, such as "Some swans are white things," we cannot jump to the conclusion that "All swans are white things." (That would be a fallacy that we'll see in 6.7 is called "hasty generalization.") Hence, we cannot make an immediate inference from the truth of an I-claim to the truth of an A-claim. If, however, one knows that an I-claim is false, such as "Some dogs are ferocious felines," then this implies that "All dogs are ferocious felines," is false as well. After all, if it's not the case that even a single dog is a ferocious feline, then certainly it must be false that all of them are. Similarly, when an I-claim such as, "Some jellyfish are spineless invertebrates," is false, we can immediately infer that "No jellyfish are spineless invertebrates" is false.

The Aristotelian Square of Opposition allows for more inferences than the Boolean Square, which only allows for the contradictory relationship. But these inferences can't be made when the S term and P term refer to things that do not exist. As much as one might like for the claim "All unicorns are things with only one horn" to imply "Some unicorns are things with only one horn," by way of the subalternation relationship this commits the *existential fallacy*. The *existential fallacy* occurs whenever one uses the contrary, subcontrary, or subalternation relationships with categorical propositions containing terms referring to things that do not exist in the real world.

3.5 Formal Deduction with Categories: Syllogisms

Imagine someone offers the following argument: "Everyone knows that robots are subservient machines, and no subservient machine is self-aware. Hence, it follows that no robots are self-aware. So as long as we keep making robots do our bidding, we needn't fear a future of robot overlords."

Few people worry about a possible future filled with sentient robots, and an argument like the one above can easily be laughed off as mere science fiction. But assuming for the moment that someone felt as though this argument had some credibility, how would they go about demonstrating this?

Categorical syllogisms

Most texts discussing formal deduction with categories begin with an example far less interesting than the sentient robot servant example used here. Perhaps the most common of these examples goes something like this:

> All humans are mortal. Socrates is a human, so Socrates is mortal.

In this example, if the premises are true, the conclusion follows necessarily. It is, therefore, a deductively valid argument. In its current form, it lacks standard form categorical propositions, but that's easily corrected using techniques from Section 3.3 of this chapter. The resulting translated argument would look like this:

P1. All humans are mortal.
P2. All persons identical with Socrates are human.
C. All persons identical with Socrates are mortal.

In logic, all that is needed to illustrate formal deduction with categories is some form of categorical syllogism. Syllogisms, you might say, are classics. They're forms of reasoning that have been used for thousands of years, and they've proven very effective.

Major and minor terms

Loosely speaking, a categorical syllogism is an argument containing three categories and three categorical propositions, i.e., two premises and one conclusion. In standard categorical form, the three categories of a categorical syllogism each occur twice and are given unique names based on where they occur in the categorical syllogism. The subject term of the conclusion is called the *minor term*, and the predicate term of the conclusion is called the *major term*. The third category occurs only in the premises and is called the *middle term*. A standard form categorical syllogism is arranged according to two rules:

1. The *major term* or predicate of the conclusion must be contained in the first premise, which is therefore called the *major premise*.
2. The *minor term* or subject of the conclusion must be contained in the second premise, which is therefore called the *minor premise*.

The Socrates example is already in standard form. "Persons identical with Socrates" is the minor term, since it is contained in the subject of the conclusion, which makes "All persons identical with Socrates are human" the minor premise. "Mortal" is the major term, because it is the predicate of the conclusion, and thus, "All humans are mortal" is the major premise. "Men" is the middle term, since it is contained in both of the premises.

Mood and figure

The primary reason for translating an argument into a standard form categorical syllogism is pragmatic. Logicians have developed methods for evaluating syllogisms, but those methods depend upon arguments being placed in the proper form. As it turns out, there are a finite number of forms that categorical syllogisms can take, and to make things easier, each has been given its own name of sorts. The name of a categorical syllogism depends on what logicians call the syllogism's *mood* and *figure*. The *mood* of a categorical syllogism is determined by the pattern of the four types of categorical propositions that make it up. For the Socrates example, there are three A-claims, and so the mood for that syllogism is AAA. The major premise is listed first and the conclusion last. The Sentient Robot Servant example has a mood of EAE, but to identify the mood correctly, it must be translated into standard form categorical propositions and then a standard form categorical syllogism, shown below:

Major Premise: No subservient machines are things that are self-aware.
Minor Premise: All robots are subservient machines.
Conclusion: No robots are things that are self-aware.

The *figure* for a standard form categorical syllogism is determined by the location of the middle term in each of the premises. There are four possible ways that the middle term can be arranged in two premises:

Figure 1	
M	P
S	**M**

Figure 2	
P	**M**
S	**M**

Figure 3	
M	P
M	S

Figure 4	
P	**M**
M	S

The placement of the middle term in the Socrates example matches Figure 1, so its mood and figure is AAA-1. The Sentient Robot Servant example has the same figure, and so its mood and figure is EAE-1. All the possible forms of categorical syllogisms are identified by this mood-figure combination. In total, there are 64 possible moods, with each having a possible 4 figures, which means there are exactly 256 possible forms for categorical syllogisms. How on Earth, you may be asking, does this make things easy?

Well, while the total number of possible categorical syllogisms is quite high, the number of valid forms actually only makes up about 6% of that on the Boolean model and 9% on the Aristotelian model, which includes the valid forms of the Boolean model. (Because the Aristotelian model allows for existential import, it also allows for more valid forms.) The valid forms for both of these models are listed below, and the term that must exist is noted for the Aristotelian model.

	Boolean	Aristotelian
Figure 1	AAA EAE AII EIO	AAI (S exists) EAO (S exists)
Figure 2	EAE AEE EIO AOO	AEO (S exists) EAO (S exists)
Figure 3	IAI AII OAO EIO	AAI (M exists) EAO (M exists)
Figure 4	AEE IAI EIO	AEO (S exists) EAO (M exists) AAI (P exists)

The Venn diagram test for validity

Here's one of the tests logicians have developed for evaluating categorical syllogisms, and unsurprisingly it involves Venn diagrams. Just like diagramming categorical propositions, each term of the categorical syllogism is represented by a circle, creating three interlocking rings that represent how the terms relate to one another.

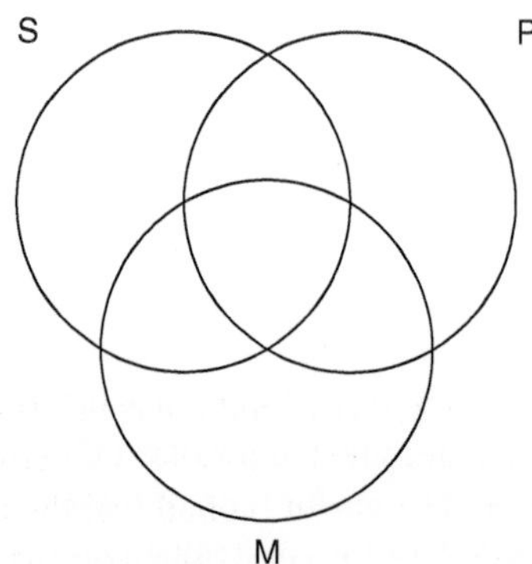

The process for diagramming the syllogism begins with diagramming the major premise. For the Socrates example, which is AAA-1, this means diagramming "All M are P," as shown below:

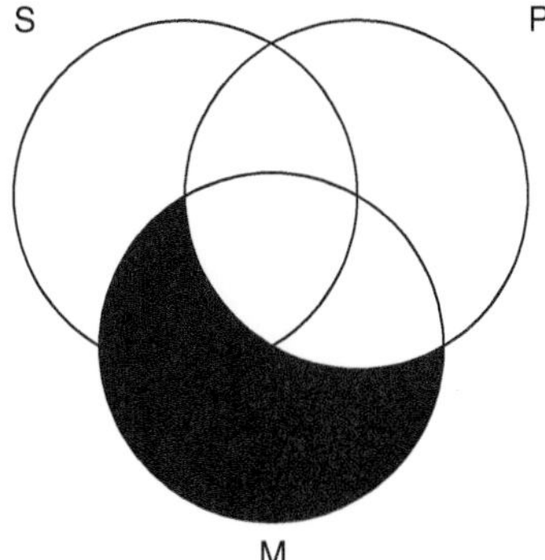

When diagramming premises that are both universal claims, the third term's circle is ignored, and so the shaded region covers a portion of the circle for the S term. After the major premise is diagrammed, the minor premise follows. In the Socrates example, this is "All S are M." In this case, the circle for the P term will be ignored, because the minor premise is universal.

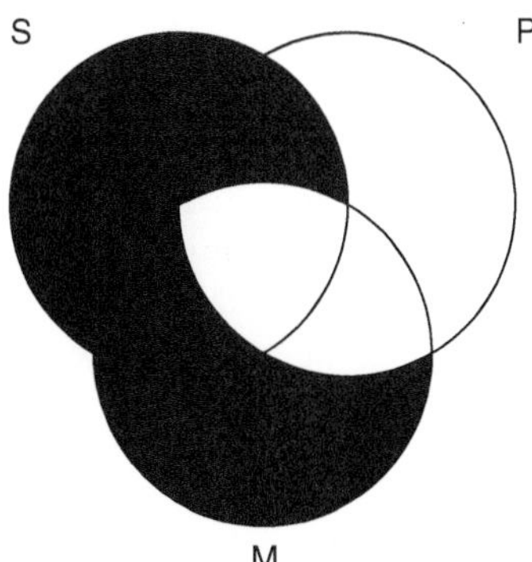

You only have to diagram the premises. After having done so, ask this crucial question:

Is the conclusion already illustrated?

What we're aiming to see is *whether or not the conclusion is already contained in the premises.* In a sense, that's what makes a valid deductive argument, including a valid syllogism, work: the premises already contain all the information expressed by the conclusion. It just has to be drawn out of the premises – precipitated from the premises, if you will. So, in our example, if the conclusion – here, "All S are P" – can be found *already contained in* the diagram of the premises, then the premises are said to *entail* the conclusion, and we know that the argument is deductively valid. In the example at hand, it is clear that the only part of the S circle left unshaded overlaps the P circle, and so it must be the case that "All S are P." The powerful thing about this method is that it shows not only that the particular argument in question is valid but also that *all* arguments of that mood and figure are valid. Therefore, arguments of the form AAA-1, such as the Socrates example, must be deductively valid.

If an argument contains a particular claim in the premises, the process for demonstrating deductive validity with Venn diagrams largely follows the same pattern as before, but it will prove very helpful to diagram the universal premise first. That will make it much easier to locate the proper placement of the X in the particular premise. Take, for example, an argument of the form IAI-3. Graphing the major premise, "Some M are P," looks like this:

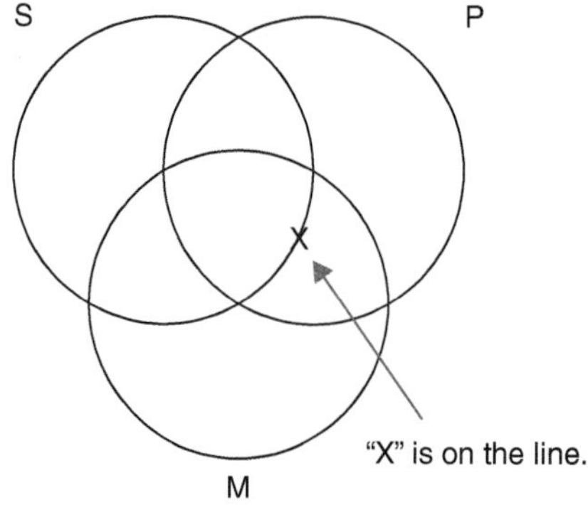

If you try to diagram the major premise first, you encounter an ambiguity, because merely from the premise "Some M are P" we don't yet know whether it belongs inside or outside the S circle. Diagramming the universal premise, here the minor premise "All M are S," makes things a lot clearer. Here's how the premises look having done that:

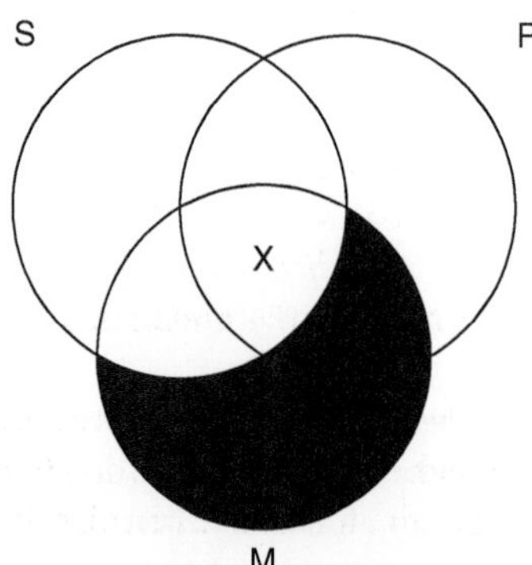

Now that the M circle has been shaded to indicate that all members of M are members of S, there can be no question where the "X" must end up. Since at least one member of M is a P, and all members of M are also members of S, it must be the case that our "X," which represented an M that was also a P, belongs in the region shared by all three terms. As a result, we can see from the diagram of the premises that there exists at least one S that is also a P, which was the conclusion to the AIA-3 categorical syllogism. This demonstrates that arguments of the form AIA-3 are deductively valid.

Five easy rules for evaluating categorical syllogisms

We've covered a lot. So far we've set out five tests for determining the validity of deductive arguments:

1. *Intuition* (relying on our experience and how arguments appear to us)
2. *Two-circle Venn diagrams for immediate inferences*
3. *The Aristotelian Square of Opposition*
4. *The Boolean Square of Opposition*
5. *Three-circle Venn diagrams for categorical syllogisms*

Now that you've got these under your belt, we'd like to share a couple of other tests for the validity of categorical syllogisms. These tests are easier than reading Venn diagrams, even if they don't explain quite as much. The first is a simple rule test – five rules on the Boolean model or four rules if your argument is Aristotelian. If an argument breaks any of these rules, even one, it's invalid. If it passes all these rules, it's valid. We've also listed the names associated with breaking these rules. (Many of these rules depend upon the idea of *distribution*. So, you might want to review 3.2.)

1. *The middle term must be distributed*; if the middle term is not distributed it commits the fallacy of *undistributed middle*.
2. *What's distributed in the conclusion must be distributed in the premises* (though not necessarily the converse – i.e., what's distributed in the premises may or may not be distributed in the conclusion); if the minor term is distributed in the conclusion but not in the premises, the argument commits the fallacy of *illicit minor*; if the major term is distributed in the conclusion but not in the premises, the argument commits the fallacy of *illicit major*.
3. *An argument may not have two negative premises*; if it does it commits the fallacy of *negative premises*.
4. *If the argument has a negative premise, it must have a negative conclusion, and vice versa*; if the argument has either a negative premise but not a negative conclusion or a negative conclusion but not a negative premise, it commits the fallacy of *not conserving negativity*.

5. *N.B. For Boolean arguments only! A particular conclusion may not be derived from universal premises*; if a Boolean argument has a particular conclusion but two universal premises, it commits the *existential fallacy* (this is not a fallacy for arguments made with the Aristotelian condition of no empty sets).

(HINT: This test is made much easier if you simply indicate with an asterisk each term that is distributed when setting out an argument as a standard form categorical syllogism.)

Gensler star test

Here's the second test we'd like to add. For an even easier method of deciding whether or not a standard form categorical syllogism is valid, follow this three-step procedure developed by Harry J. Gensler:

1. Set out the argument in standard categorical form.
2. Mark with an asterisk every categorical term that *is* distributed in the premises.
3. Mark with an asterisk every categorical term that *is not* distributed in the conclusion.

The argument is valid if and only if these two conditions are met:

a. Each categorical term is marked *only once*; and
b. There is *only one* asterisk marked on the right hand side of the argument. In other words, *only one predicate term* in the argument is marked with an asterisk.

Bizarrely easy, we know, but the test actually works. That leaves us then with (so far!) seven tests for determining the validity of deductive arguments. Let's now turn to another system of evaluating arguments. It has ancient and early modern antecedents, but the symbolic methods we're going to explain have been developed only across the last century and a quarter or so. It's come to be called *propositional* or *sentential* logic. Let's take a look.

Exercises and study questions

1. Using immediate inferences, determine whether the following arguments are valid or invalid on both the Traditional and Modern models:
   - *Some automobiles are not things powered by internal combustion.*
     All automobiles are things powered by internal combustion.

- *Some automobiles are things powered by internal combustion.*
  It's not the case that no automobiles are things powered by internal combustion.
- *All bourgeoisie are people in conflict with the proletariat.*
  It's not the case that no bourgeoisie are people in conflict with the proletariat.
- *It's not the case that some overly cooked steaks are tasty.*
  No overly cooked steaks are tasty.

2. Determine whether the following categorical syllogisms are valid or invalid on both the Traditional and Modern models:
   - Some cats are not dogs.
     All felines are cats.
     Some felines are not dogs.
   - All fish are animals with gills.
     All sharks are fish.
     Some sharks are animals with gills.
   - All unicorns are animals with one horn.
     No horses are animals with one horn.
     Some horses are not unicorns.

SEE ALSO

2.1 Deductive and Inductive Arguments
4.1 Propositional vs. Categorical Logics
Chapter 10: Tools from Rhetoric, Critical Theory, and Politics

READING

Patrick J. Hurley, *A Concise Introduction to Logic*, 12th edn (2015)
Harry J. Gensler, *Introduction to Logic* (2010)
Nancy M. Cavender, *Logic and Contemporary Rhetoric* (2010)
Deborah J. Bennett, *Logic Made Easy* (2004)
Aristotle, *The Categories* and *Prior Analytics* (fourth century BCE)

4 Tools for Deductive Reasoning with Claims

4.1 Propositional vs. Categorical Logics

At the outset of this book, in Section 1.2, arguments were defined as sets of claims or other statements in each of which one or more premises provides support for the truth of another, the conclusion. Simple and complex claims alike work together as premises to provide reasons or grounds from which to infer that the conclusion is true. For deductive reasoning, which we began to explore in Chapters 2 and 3, a good argument – more precisely a deductively valid argument – is structured such that the truth of the premises entails in a definite, necessary, or guaranteed way the truth of the conclusion. If the premises are true, then the conclusion must be true.

For categorical arguments, deductive validity depends on the relationships among categories, as defined by the four standard form *categorical* claims. There is, however, another powerful system for analyzing and assessing deductive arguments. Our ordinary language often deals with arguments that are not well translated into categorical terms, especially because doing so masks many of the subtle logical dimensions of those arguments. With these limitations in mind, logicians have turned to whole claims – both simple claims as well as whole complex claims – rather than categories as the basic building blocks for constructing premises, conclusions, and arguments; and they have formulated new ways of expressing those claims. Those new logics have come to be called *propositional* or *sentential* approaches to logic (PL and SL, for short), and precedents to them can be found in the ancient world (e.g., among the stoics) as well as in early modernity (in, e.g., the aspiration of Gottfried Wilhelm von Leibniz to develop a universal language for science). Despite these precedents, however, the real systematic breakthroughs would come late in the nineteenth and early twentieth centuries with thinkers such as Gottlob Frege (1848–1925), Bertrand Russell (1872–1970), and Ludwig Wittgenstein (1889–1951) when logicians actually formulated the systems of propositional logic we will address here.

The Critical Thinking Toolkit, First Edition. Galen A. Foresman, Peter S. Fosl, and Jamie C. Watson.

It can be helpful to think of PL as comprising methods for deriving and evaluating the blueprints for arguments after they have been made. And while it would be far too dangerous and expensive to create and evaluate the structural integrity of blueprints for buildings after we had already constructed them, this is, in effect, what propositional logic does for arguments.

Translating claims into propositional logic

Section 1.1 explains that both simple and complex claims alike are complete units that possess the distinctive quality of being, as complete wholes, either true or false. They are the building blocks of every argument, and when deriving an argument's blueprint, of utmost concern is how the building blocks are arranged. (Whether or not they were good blocks – true claims – to begin with is only handled once it can be shown that the blueprint is structurally valid.) As such, propositional logic begins its analysis of an argument by recasting all of its propositional claims in symbols in a quasi-algebraic and mathematical way. Simple claims are symbolized by capital letters (A, B, C, etc.). While it doesn't matter much which capital letter is used, claims with the same meaning must use the same letter, and it's helpful to use a letter that allows quick identification of the original claim when necessary (often the first letter of a noun in the subject).

Simple Claims	Translation to Propositional Logic
A Smurf is a little blue creature.	S
Tallahassee is the capital of Florida.	T
George Washington was the first president of the United States of America.	G

Complex claims, which are made up of one or more simple claims in combination with logical operators, are symbolized according to specific rules that maintain the essential syntax and semantics of the complex claim. The five most common logical operators are negation, conjunction, disjunction, conditional, and biconditional (see 1.1 and 2.2). These logical operators play central roles in determining a complex claim's truth value, because the truth value of a proper complex claim in propositional logic is a *function* of the truth values of the simple claims comprising the complex claim combined with the logical operator. Ultimately, complex claims and their operators are far less confusing than they may sound, as we will see in a moment. It's first imperative that one becomes familiar with the terms and phrases that often indicate that a logical operator is being used. These indicator words and their associated logical operator are given in the table below:

Name	Indicator Words
Conjunction	**"and," "but," and "although"** It is snowing hard outside, **and** I left my car windows open. I can swim the Atlantic Ocean, **but** I will need a lot of breaks along the way. **Although** we should have stopped for some rest, we drove all night.
Disjunction	**"or" or "unless"** We can go to dinner, **or** we can go to a movie. Tom will drive to Toledo, **unless** his wife goes into labor.
Negation	**"It's not the case that … " or "not" or "no" or *any negation of the main verb by a helping or auxiliary verb*** **It's not the case that** Janice is taller than Dave. Cars **aren't** efficient forms of transportation. Mediterranean jellyfish **have not been** migrating to British waters. **No** unicorns are in my pocket.
Conditional	**"If … , then … ," "only if," "necessary," and "sufficient"** **If** John misses work tomorrow, **then** his wife is in labor. Jackson will take the job **only if** the money is right. Your scoring an A on the final exam is **necessary** for your passing this class. Your apology is **sufficient** for my forgiveness.
Biconditional	**"if and only if" and "necessary and sufficient"** We will go to the beach **if and only if** all the work gets done. Having a ticket is **necessary and sufficient** for your being admitted into the show.

Except for the negations, all of the complex claims above are composed of two simple claims that are combined using a logical operator. In some cases, the simple claims that compose the complex claim aren't immediately obvious, as when using "necessary," "sufficient," and "necessary and sufficient." Often in cases such as these, the subject for the simple claim has been omitted to construct the complex claim. When translating complex claims into propositional logic, each of the logical operators is represented with its own symbol. (The table below contains some very common symbols for translating logical operators, but it's important to note that a variety other symbols are used, depending on which logic book you read.)

Operator	Symbol
Conjunction	$\bullet$
Disjunction	$\vee$
Negation	$\sim$
Conditional	$\supset$
Biconditional	$\equiv$

Symbolizing complex claims with the correct operator begins by identifying each of the simple claims and the logical operator being used. For example:

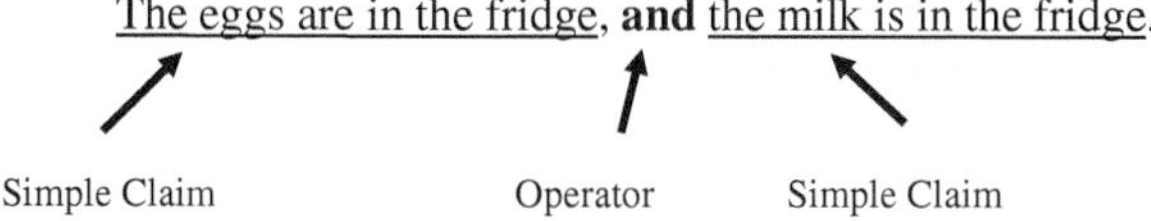

Simple Claim Operator Simple Claim

Next, the simple claims are replaced with capital letters, and the operator is replaced with the appropriate symbol. If "E" is used to replace "The eggs are in the fridge," and "M" is used to replace "The milk is in the fridge," then the resulting symbolized complex claim will look like this:

$$E \bullet M$$

The process for symbolizing a complex claim with multiple logical operators is essentially the same, but often this requires using parentheses to group complex claims that do not contain the main operator of the larger complex claim. (Note: parentheses may only be used to group pairs or groups of two propositions with operators.) For example:

If Sam goes to Washington **and** Sarah goes to California, **then** Elvis will be lonely.

This complex claim is symbolized in this way:

$$(W \bullet C) \supset E$$

Section 1.1 introduced *truth functionality*, the property some sentences have such that the truth of the whole sentence is fully determined by the truth of its component sentences along with the logical operators. It's a terribly important idea in PL, since propositional logicians have taken pains to build a system where, in the interests of clarity, all sentences expressed in the system are truth functional. In truth functional complex claims with multiple operators, the main operator determines the overall truth value for the complex claim, which cannot be determined until the truth values for the component claims are first determined. As a result, when determining the truth value of a complex claim, the truth value of the main operator must be determined last.

Remember that there are complex statements, even claims, that are *not* truth functions, at least not when analyzed into component statements using basic propositional logic. Belief statements, as you may remember from 1.1, resist truth functionality. The truth or falsehood of the statement, "I believe that there are two suns in our solar system," is not fully determined by the truth or falsity of the component claim, "there are two suns in our solar system," and the operator-like phrase, "I believe that." It's an unfortunate reality that you can believe falsehoods, and belief claims such as this one are true or false depending on what you actually believe – not the truth value of the component claims. That's why they're not truth functional claims. The same is the case with statements such as: "*I wonder* whether all deductive arguments with contradictory premises are valid" or "*I hope* that I got that question right on the exam." Even though within them simpler statements may be discerned (e.g., "I got that question right"), the truth or falsehood of those simple statements doesn't fully determine the truth of the whole statement. (Logicians have worked up special logics, sometimes called *intensional logics*, to deal with statements of this sort, but we won't be addressing them here; instead see 1.1 and 2.4.)

Truth tables for claims

One of the most powerful tools in propositional logic is called the *truth table*. The truth table was developed by logicians of the late nineteenth and early twentieth centuries including Frege and Wittgenstein. You can do many things with truth tables, but one of the most helpful is simply defining the truth conditions of propositions. You might say these conditions specify the logical meaning of the statement. For example, take a potentially meaningful claim "*p*." Like any claim, *p* can only be true or false, and we can represent these truth values in a table:

p
T
F

The lower case "*p*" is a *variable*. It acts as a placeholder for both simple and complex claims. (Unlike capital letters, which are *translations* of particular claims in an argument. As a matter of convention lower case letters do not represent specific claims, and so they are not used in translation. Instead, these variables are reserved for defining relationships among claims.) The truth table above illustrates quite elegantly all the possible truth values any claim, *p*, may have. Whether it be simple or complex, every claim can only be true or false.

For complex claims, the logical operator plays a central role in determining the possible truth values any truth functional complex claim may have. While it's still true that a complex claim may only be true or false, exactly when the complex claim is true or false depends on the truth value of the claims that it contains combined with the logical operator. The simplest example is the negation, defined below:

p	$\sim p$
T	F
F	T

The left column of the truth table illustrates the possible truth values that *p* can have, while the right column of the truth table gives all the possible truth values of *p* when it's combined with the logical operator for negation (~).

For all of the other logical operators, a second variable must be added to define the function of the operator. When adding a second variable, the left column of the truth table must be filled out in such a way that *all possible combinations* of true and false are given. This is demonstrated below, along with the truth tables for the other four logical operators:

p	q	$p \bullet q$
T	T	T
T	F	F
F	T	F
F	F	F

p	q	$p \vee q$
T	T	T
T	F	T
F	T	T
F	F	F

p	q	$p \supset q$
T	T	T
T	F	F
F	T	T
F	F	T

p	q	$p \equiv q$
T	T	T
T	F	F
F	T	F
F	F	T

From these truth tables, you can discover four rules governing the logical operators (in a sense, the operators are just rules for relating truth values):

1. *Conjunction.* A conjunction is true only if both of the conjuncts are true.
2. *Disjunction.* A disjunction is sort of the inverse of conjunction: it's false only if both of the disjuncts are false. (Note: this is called an "inclusive or," because both *p* and *q* may be true at the same time. It's different from disjunction in the sense of "either/or but not both"; here it may be both.)
3. *Conditional.* A *material implication* or conditional is false only when both the antecedent is true and the consequent is false.
4. *Biconditional.* A biconditional is true whenever the composing claims both have the same truth value (either both false or both true); it's false when the truth values are different.

In practice, these truth tables allow the critical thinker to determine the truth value of a complex claim when the truth values are known for the claims of which it is composed. So, for example, if we know that the claim, "The eggs are in the fridge" (E), is true and the claim, "The milk is in the fridge" (M), is false, then we know from our rules that the complex claim, "The eggs are in the fridge, and the milk is in the fridge," must be false. In a conjunction, both conjuncts must be true in order for the conjunction to be true. As for "The eggs are in the fridge, or the milk is in the fridge," this complex claim is true, since only one of the disjuncts need be true for a disjunction to be true. The conditional and biconditional claims made up from E and M would also be false.

Testing for validity and invalidity with truth tables

Once the basics of translation and truth tables are understood, truth tables can perform a very powerful and important service – determining whether or not deductive arguments are valid. Since deductively valid arguments are those in which true premises never lead to a false conclusion, a full truth table will demonstrate whether a particular argument's premises *could* ever lead to a false conclusion. For example, suppose someone made the following argument:

> If the Republicans win the next election, then taxes will be lowered. Either the Democrats win the election or the Republicans win the election. But, since it's not the case that the Democrats win the election, we can conclude that taxes will be lowered.

Broken up into premises and a conclusion, the argument looks like this:

P1. If the Republicans win the next election, then taxes will be lowered.
P2. Either the Democrats will win the election, or the Republicans will win the election.
P3. It's not the case that the Democrats will win the election.
C. Taxes will be lowered.

Translated into symbolic propositional logic, the argument looks like this:

P1. $R \supset T$
P2. $D \vee R$
P3. $\sim D$
C. T

Now that the argument has been symbolized, it can be put into a truth table to determine whether or not the premises, when true, ever lead to a false conclusion. To construct the truth table correctly, so that it contains *all* the possible truth value combinations, the total number of rows must be determined using the formula 2^n, where n is the number of simple claims in the argument. Since this argument has three simple claims (D, R, and T), the table will have eight (2^3) rows of truth values. The complete truth table is shown below:

			P1	P2	P3	C	
R	T	D	R ⊃ T	D v R	~D	T	
T	T	T	T	T	F	T	
T	T	F	T	T	T	T	
T	F	T	F	T	F	F	*
T	F	F	F	T	T	F	*
F	T	T	T	T	F	T	
F	T	F	T	F	T	T	
F	F	T	F	T	F	F	*
F	F	F	F	F	T	F	*

The three columns on the left contain all the possible truth value combinations of the three simple claims R, T, and D. The three columns in the middle show the truth values for the premises, determined by the truth value of the three simple claims on each row. The last column contains *all the possible truth values* for the conclusion, given the simple claims on that row. That's where the real power of this technique lies – it covers all the bases, *all the possible* ways the premises can relate to the conclusion given the form of the argument. Whether or not the argument meets the definition of a valid argument becomes, then, utterly clear. Because it's not possible for a valid argument to have all true premises and a false conclusion:

> *The argument is deductively* valid *if and only if there are no rows with all true premises and a false conclusion. If there are any rows with truth premises and a false conclusion, the argument is deductively invalid.*

Hence, any row with a false conclusion, which is indicated here with*, should be examined to see if all the premises are true. For this argument, a false conclusion only occurs when one or more of the premises are false. That's good news for this argument, as it means that it's a deductively valid argument.

Indirect truth tables

While using truth tables correctly will always allow the critical thinker to determine whether or not an argument is valid, it's not often the most efficient way of doing so. If, for example, the argument contains seven simple claims, the truth table would require 128 rows! Now, computers can perform this operation in no time, but for humans constructing such a truth table can be cumbersome and time consuming. Furthermore, unless you're very meticulous in filling out the truth table, this technique is likely to lead to errors. Fortunately, there's a shortcut. To reduce the chances of errors and speed things up, an *indirect truth table* can be used as an accurate and efficient tool for assessing validity and invalidity.

Essentially, an indirect truth table reduces the number of rows contained in a full truth table by trying to construct an invalid row. You begin this process by assuming the conclusion to be false, thereby restricting the possible truth values for those simple claims contained in the conclusion. For example, the translated argument below has a conditional statement, R ⊃ S, for its conclusion, which can only be false when the antecedent is true and the consequent false. Thence, the truth value for two simple claims clearly follows (R=True, S=False), and you apply those values throughout the premises. (Note: the truth value for the main operator of each complex claim here is underlined for clarity.)

	P1			P2				P3			C		
	R	•	M	~	M	v	E	E	⊃	S	R	⊃	S
Step 1:	T									F	T	F	F

Once the truth values for R and S have been applied to the premises, the main operator for each premise is made true in order to *see if it's possible* to construct true premises that entail a false conclusion. Once the main operators are made true, the other simple claims can be deduced according to the definition of each operator. So, for example, R • M is true only if both R and M are true, so M must be true to ensure this premise will be true. As a result, M in the second premise must be true, and the truth table thus far will look like this:

	P1			P2				P3			C		
	R	•	M	~	M	v	E	E	⊃	S	R	⊃	S
Step 2:	T	T	T		T	T			T	F	T	F	F

The second premise is a disjunction, which is only false when both disjuncts are false. Because M is negated (~), the first disjunct of this disjunction is false, and so to make the disjunction true, E must be true. Thus, E in the third premise must be true as well.

	P1			P2				P3			C		
	R	•	M	~	M	v	E	E	⊃	S	R	⊃	S
Step 3:	T	T	T	F	T	T	T	T	T	F	T	F	F

Now, here's the important bit: If E is true in the third premise, then the third premise *cannot possibly* be true, since S must be false, according to the conclusion. Following the definitional rules for each operator has led to a contradiction. S must be true for the third premise to be true, and yet it must be false for the conclusion to be false. When a contradiction like this occurs in an indirect truth table, you know that true premises cannot imply a false conclusion, and so the argument must be valid. That's because if you make all the premises true, the logical operator rules require the conclusion also to be true; and if you make the conclusion false, the rules require that a premise be false, too. You just can't make the premises all be true and the conclusion false while satisfying the rules.

If, however, the argument had been slightly different, as shown below, the third premise would not have created a contradiction. This new argument allows for the *possibility* of true premises and a false conclusion, and so it would be invalid.

	P1				P2				P3				C	
R	•	M	~	M	v	E	E	⊃	~	S	R	⊃	S
T	T	T	F	T	T	T	T	T	T	F	T	F	F

Indirect truth tables can, you should know, include more than one row. New rows are often required whenever it is possible to derive a false conclusion in more than one way. When you encounter a conclusion of that sort, all the possible truth value combinations for that conclusion may need to be explored. Now, of course, for efficiency's sake, you should just check the fewest possible number of rows. Once you find even a single row with true premises and a false conclusion, you can stop – you've proven the argument invalid. As a rule, you'll find such a row, if there is one, most easily if you *focus on the different possible ways that the conclusion can be false*. But note that there are rare occasions where there are actually fewer ways that the premises can all be true than the conclusion be false. In those cases, if you can discern them, just check those rows with all true premises. The overriding consideration here is efficiency: the shorter your table the better.

The indirect truth table below illustrates how you can handle a conclusion that can be false in different ways:

	P1				P2				P3				C	
R	•	M	~	M	v	E	E	⊃	~	S	R	⊃	S
T	T	T	F	T	T	T	T	T	T	F	T	F	F
F	T	Ø			T			T		T	F	F	T
F	T	Ø			T			T		F	F	F	F

Note that this truth table, shortened though it is, covers *all the possible ways* the conclusion can be false. Again, that's what makes this technique work. In the argument above, there are three possible combinations of truth values for R and S that make R • S false. The two combinations contained in rows 2 and 3 quickly lead to a contradiction, which means they are no longer possible examples of how this argument could be invalid. But ultimately, the first row is sufficient to demonstrate that the argument is invalid, and so regardless of how rows 2 and 3 turned out, the argument is invalid. Had premise 1 been just slightly different (a disjunction rather than a conjunction), the indirect truth table might look something like this:

	P1				P2				P3				C	
R	v	M	~	M	v	E	E	$\supset$	~	S	R	$\supset$	S	
T	**T**	T	F	T	**T**	T	T	**T**	T	F	T	**F**	F	
T	**T**	F	T	F	**T**	T	T	**T**	T	F		**F**		
			T	F	**T**	F	F	**T**	T	F		**F**		

In the truth table above, M could be either true or false to make the first premise true. If M is true, then E must be true for the second premise to be true, which ultimately doesn't lead to a contradiction in premise 3, thereby demonstrating that the argument is invalid. Additionally, rows 2 and 3 illustrate how M being false leads to two possible variations of truth values for E in premise 2, both also demonstrating the argument is invalid.

In the end, using indirect truth tables to test for validity can save considerable time. A traditional truth table for any of the arguments in this section would have required 16 rows, and despite the added complication of multiple roots to a single truth value illustrated in these last two indirect truth tables, they're still considerably shorter than the alternative.

Strange validity

Note that there may be no rows with all true premises and a false conclusion because there may simply be no rows with all true premises. Yes, that's possible in some arguments. When it's not possible for the premises to all be true under any circumstances, it means that the argument has inconsistent premises, and arguments with inconsistent premises – for example, contrary or contradictory premises – are, technically speaking, valid. Even an argument with a single but self-contradictory premise is valid on the basis of the definition of validity. It's beyond the scope of this text, but you can, in fact, prove anything validly from a contradiction. (This result has so disturbed some logicians that they've embarked on developing alternative logics, sometimes called *paraconsistent* or *dialetheist* logics, to deal with this problem.)

That seems odd, we know, but remember that arguments with inconsistent premises cannot be *sound*. Sound arguments must have all true premises, and arguments with inconsistent premises can't achieve that. So even if arguments with contradictory or otherwise inconsistent premises are always valid, and even if you can derive anything from a contradiction, these results, while curious, are nevertheless for our purposes trivial.

In a similar way, arguments with tautological conclusions will always be valid, regardless of the truth value of their premises. Because a tautology is always true, arguments with tautologous conclusions can never have true premises and a false conclusion. They're valid just as a matter of definition. Curiously, too, you can prove a tautology from any set of premises, even from true ones. For this reason, this type of argument, while perhaps in some cases not only valid but also sound (valid plus true premises), is generally viewed as uninformative. The premises play no real supporting role in the truth of the conclusion.

4.2 Common Deductively Valid Forms

Determining whether a deductive argument is valid is often a process that begins with an argument that's not fully articulated, leaving to the critical thinker the job of translating it and expressing it more precisely before assessing the merits of the argument's construction. In order to assess the argument, a critical thinker must first analyze it, breaking it down into discrete parts so as to determine whether or not they were originally assembled in an appropriate manner (i.e., in a deductively valid way). Truth tables and indirect truth tables in all their algorithmic glory are the natural end to thinking about and assessing deductive arguments in this analytic manner. But supposing a good critical thinker wanted to construct a deductively valid argument, where would he or she begin?

While methods exist for deriving arguments from truth tables, such methods miss the main point for why one might wish to construct an argument in the first place, which is to provide support, justification, or proof for the truth of a claim. To that end, what's needed is a system of rules for propositional logic that allows the critical thinker to move from one claim to another in a *truth preserving* way. Logicians have developed several techniques for doing this, but it suffices in many cases to have a basic knowledge of the most common deductively valid forms to construct or assess the validity of most arguments. Here are some of the classic valid forms.

Modus ponens

Perhaps the most common form of reasoning – since our brains seem to be hardwired to reason this way – is *modus ponens*, Latin for "way that affirms" or "method of affirming." *Modus ponens* contains two premises, a conditional and an assertion that the antecedent of the conditional is true. From these, one can validly deduce the consequent of the conditional as the conclusion. Below is the structure or form of *modus ponens*:

$$\begin{array}{l} p \supset q \\ \underline{p \qquad\quad} \\ q \end{array}$$

Note that p and q are variables, and any proper claim – simple or complex – can be substituted for them. In the examples that follow, the first uses only simple claims as *substitution instances* for these variables in *modus ponens*, while the second substitutes a conjunction for the antecedent. Lots of substitutions are possible for this form. Regardless of the complexity of the substitution, however, the form remains valid, and so any otherwise properly articulated argument based on the form will be valid.

P1. If it is raining, then I need an umbrella.
P2. It is raining.
C. I need an umbrella.
P1. If the sun has set and the ambient light is low, then the stars in the sky will appear very bright.
P2. The sun has set and the ambient light is low.
C. The stars in the sky will appear very bright.

To demonstrate that *modus ponens* is a valid form, one need only construct an indirect truth table, shown below:

P1			P2	C
p	$\supset$	q	p	q
T	T	F	T	F

When the conclusion of *modus ponens* is false, it's not possible to make the premises all true. If p is true in the second premise (and it must be, if the argument is to be shown to be invalid), then a problem with assigning truth values arises in the first premise. Our shortened truth table method instructs us to try to make the premises true – but remaining consistent with the truth assignments we've already made requires us to assign "true" to p and "false" to q, and a true conditional cannot have a true antecedent and false consequent. Similarly, if after making the conclusion false, P1 is made true by making p true, then a problem arises in the second premise, since to be consistent with the assignments already made and the demands of validity p would have to be both true and false – and that can't be so. Because you can't consistently make its premises true and its conclusion false, the argument form called *modus ponens* is therefore a valid form.

Modus tollens

Like *modus ponens*, *modus tollens* begins with a conditional. But rather than affirming the antecedent in the second premise, *modus tollens* denies the consequent. In Latin, the expression is *modus tollendo tollens*, which means "method that denies by denying," which is essentially what *modus tollens* does. By denying the consequent of the first premise, one can deduce that the antecedent is not true, illustrated below:

$$\frac{\begin{array}{c} p \supset q \\ {\sim}q \end{array}}{{\sim}p}$$

In a conditional statement, *modus ponens* tells us that the truth of the antecedent is sufficient for the truth of the consequent. *Modus tollens* reverses this logic such that a false consequent entails a false antecedent. As with *modus ponens,* and all the valid forms in this chapter, the variables may be substituted with either simple or complex claims. Below are two examples:

P1. If pictures are hanged, then people are hung.
P2. It is not the case that people are hung.
C. It is not the case that pictures are hanged.
P1. If Sam drives to the movies and Kevin drives to Waffle House, then Anton rides with Kevin.
P2. It is not the case that Anton rides with Kevin.
C. It is not the case that Sam drives to the movies and Kevin drives to Waffle House.

The indirect truth table shown below demonstrates that *modus tollens* is a valid form. To make the conclusion false, p must be true, and the second premise is only true if q is false. If, however, p is true and q is false, then the first premise cannot be true. Consequently, a problem in assigning truth values arises in the first premise of the indirect truth table when trying to make the argument invalid, and thus, the argument form is valid.

P1			P2		C	
p	$\supset$	q	~	q	~	p
T	T	F	T	F	F	T

In disputes, the relationship between *modus ponens* and *modus tollens* behaves much like any other argument between siblings. "If Mom hugs me, then she loves me more than you!" To which every astute, critical-thinking sister responds, "Since she doesn't love you more than me, I guess you won't be getting a hug from Mom." Using a conditional claim as a premise allows one to use *modus ponens* to prove a point, but it also opens the door for a complete denial of the consequent, resulting in a denial of the antecedent. And, unless the antecedent is something difficult to deny, the critical thinker must be weary of the sibling wielding *modus tollens.*

Hypothetical syllogism

The valid forms we've seen thus far are useful for deriving a claim or the negation of a claim from a conditional. The hypothetical syllogism combines two conditional claims from the premises to create a new conditional claim.

$$\begin{array}{c} p \supset q \\ q \supset r \\ \hline p \supset r \end{array}$$

Provided the *consequent* of one of the premises, *q*, is the same as the *antecedent* of the other premise, also *q*, the conditional claims are merged into a new conditional composed of the antecedent from the first premise, *p*, and the consequent of the second premise, *r*. This valid form is sometimes known as *the chain rule*, because the premises are linked like a chain with their shared claim, *q*. It also follows very much the same pattern as *transitivity* in mathematics.

The indirect truth table for hypothetical syllogism is shown below:

P1			P2			C		
p	$\supset$	q	q	$\supset$	r	p	$\supset$	r
T	**T**	F	F	**T**	F	T	**F**	F

To make a hypothetical syllogism invalid, *p* and *r* from the conclusion must be true and false, respectively. Having made *r* false in the conclusion, *q* must be false as well in order for the second premise to be true. If *p* is true in the first premise because of the conclusion, and *q* in the first premise is false because of the second premise, then a problem arises once again, thereby proving that the hypothetical syllogism must be a valid form.

Disjunctive syllogism

The disjunctive syllogism is a valid form commonly used in the logical process of elimination. A detective might know, for example, that either Sue committed the murder or Jack committed the murder. Discovering evidence that exonerates Sue from having committed the murder, the detective concludes that Jack committed the murder. In propositional logic, the form of this deduction would be:

$$\begin{array}{c} p \vee q \\ \sim p \\ \hline q \end{array}$$

Given that it must be either *p* or *q* (maybe both) from the first premise, the second premise denies that it is *p*, leaving only *q* as true. The indirect truth table demonstrating this is shown below:

P1			P2		C
p	v	*q*	~	*p*	*q*
F	<u>T</u>	F	<u>T</u>	F	<u>F</u>

When the conclusion is false, *q* from the first premise must be false as well. In order for the second premise to be true, *p* must be false. If, however, *p* and *q* are both false in the first premise, the disjunct cannot be true. As a result, both premises cannot be true while the conclusion is false, and so the argument form must be valid.

Constructive and destructive dilemmas

Constructive and destructive dilemmas are valid forms commonly found in public debate, but they are just as familiar to individuals who are attempting to discern the best course of action to take in their day-to-day lives. Both constructive and destructive dilemmas begin with two conditionals joined by a conjunction, $(p \supset q) \bullet (r \supset s)$. This premise is often referred to as *the horns of the dilemma*, because it puts in sharp relief the consequences of either option in the dilemma. The commonality of this type of thinking is easiest to recognize from the first person perspective, where it could be loosely translated to say something like this:

> If I do *p*, then *q* will result, and if I do *r*, then *s* will result.

So, for example, a student deciding between two universities to attend might consider thusly, "If I attend Mountain University, then I can spend my weekends skiing, but, if I attend Beach State, then I can spend my weekends surfing."

In the *constructive dilemma*, the second premise is *p* v *r*. For the student thinking about colleges this translates, "Either I attend Mountain University or I attend Beach State," which is why these forms are dubbed "dilemmas." There are just two possible options available. This form, in particular, is considered a constructive dilemma, because regardless of whether or not *p* is true or *r* is true or both are true, at least one of the variables must be true, and so something will result, be that *q* or *s* or both. (It works kind of like two *modus ponens*.) With a constructive dilemma, rest assured that this student is either going to spend his or her weekends skiing or surfing, and definitely not at home helping with chores. The form for the constructive dilemma as well as the indirect truth table demonstrating that it's a valid form are found below:

$$\frac{\begin{array}{l}(p \supset q) \bullet (r \supset s) \\ p \vee r\end{array}}{q \vee s}$$

P1							P2			C		
(p	⊃	q)	•	(r	⊃	s)	p	v	r	q	v	s
F	T	F	**T**	F	T	F	F	**T**	F	F	**F**	F

For this indirect truth table, the false disjunction in the conclusion makes q and s false in their respective conditionals in the first premise. Since the main operator for the first premise is a conjunction, it will only be true when both conjuncts are true ($p \supset q$ and $r \supset s$). Having already made q and s false, the antecedent for both conditionals must be false (p and r) so that the respective conditionals are true and the main operator comes out true as well. Once the first premise is determined, a contradiction arises in the second premise from both p and r being false, since at least one must be true to make the disjunction true.

The *destructive dilemma* differs in that the second premise is $\sim q \vee \sim s$, as opposed to $p \vee r$. The result is a disjunction, $\sim p \vee \sim r$, for the conclusion. For the student considering colleges, the second premise translates, "it's either not the case that I can spend my weekend skiing or it's not the case that I can spend my weekend surfing," ($\sim q \vee \sim s$) to the conclusion, "either I do not attend Mountain University or I do not attend Beach State." Furthermore, the student must now be wary that he or she attends neither Mountain University nor Beach State, because as a disjunction, the conclusion allows for the possibility that both disjuncts are true. (It's kind of like two *modus tollens*.) The full form of the destructive dilemma is outlined below:

$$\frac{\begin{array}{l}(p \supset q) \bullet (r \supset s) \\ \sim q \vee \sim s\end{array}}{\sim p \vee \sim r}$$

The indirect truth table for the destructive dilemma, shown below, demonstrates that it is a valid form. The contradiction arises in the second premise, because q and s must be true in order for the first premise to be true, but as a result, the disjuncts of the second premise are both false. Since the second premise cannot be true, given that the first premise is true and the conclusion is false, the destructive dilemma is valid.

P1							P2					C				
(p	⊃	q)	•	(r	⊃	s)	~	q	v	~	s	~	p	v	~	r
T	T	T	**T**	T	T	T	F	T	**T**	F	T	F	T	**F**	F	T

Because constructive and destructive dilemmas are such common valid forms in political debate, it's imperative for the critical thinker to assess them for soundness. If one of the premises turns out to be false, then the argument is unsound and fails, even when it has a valid form. The two approaches for demonstrating that constructive and destructive dilemmas are unsound are the same, since their structures are closely related, both employing *the horns of the dilemma* as the first premise, and the dilemma as the second premise. Because these forms of criticism are so common, they've been named, and so the critical thinker may demonstrate that constructive and destructive dilemmas are unsound either by *grasping by the horns* or *escaping between the horns.* It sounds very dramatic, like a logical bullfight, doesn't it?

Criticizing constructive and destructive dilemmas

To grasp the horns of the dilemma, the critical thinker needs to show that the horns of the dilemma are a false premise. Because the horns of the dilemma are formulated as a conjunction, one need only demonstrate that one of the conditionals in the conjunction is false for the entire premise to be shown to be false. For example, suppose you're confronted with the following constructive dilemma:

P1. If I go to the party, then my academic career is over, but if I stay home to study, then my social life is dead.
P2. Either I go to the party, or I stay home to study.
C. Either my academic career is over, or my social life is dead.

Hopefully, a good, critical-thinking friend would grasp this argument by the horns, pointing out that staying home to study is not tantamount to murdering your social life. Or, perhaps this good, critical-thinking friend might want to diffuse this argument by noting that going to just one party won't end an academic career. Either approach, taken alone, is sufficient to raise doubt about the soundness of the argument, but it's important to note that the astute critical thinker will recognize that undermining one conjunct leaves the other as an open possibility. In other words, the argument's soundness will be sufficiently undermined, while covertly nudging the arguer toward one of the options in the dilemma. After all, if going to one party really isn't all that bad, then why not go?

To escape between the horns of a constructive or destructive dilemma, one need only show that the dilemma presented in the second premise is actually a false one (see 5.12) or that both of the disjuncts are false. To show that the second premise commits the *fallacy of false dilemma*, it suffices to show that there are more than two possible options available. For the previous constructive dilemma, a sharp friend might suggest a third option, incorporating, perhaps, both a social life and studying, like studying with friends at a coffee shop. This third option could successfully avoid both the demise of the academic career and social life. Alternatively, the critical-thinking friend could opt to prove that both disjuncts are false – demonstrating that it's false that the friend goes to the party and that it's false that the friend stays home to study.

4.3 Equivalences

We saw some of the ways categorical logic handles equivalences in 3.4. Here are some of the ways you can investigate equivalences in the propositional system. As with the valid forms from 4.2, too, you'll find that equivalences are useful tools for constructing and analyzing deductively valid arguments. In propositional logic, more precisely, two claims that share the same simple claims are *equivalent* if and only if the truth values for the main operator are identical given identical truth value assignments for all those simple claims. Another way to think of this is that two claims are equivalent if and only if the two claims always have the same truth value given the same set of circumstances. As we'll soon see (in 4.4), equivalences are essential in constructing proofs that show how you can move rationally from premises to conclusions.

In the subsections that follow, we present ten different equivalences. Unlike deductive forms, equivalences aren't easily demonstrated with an indirect truth table because they are not arguments with conclusions. They may be demonstrated with full truth tables, and so it is important to note that in these formal definitions of an equivalence the symbol "::" is used to mean "is equivalent to." An equivalence is fully demonstrated when the truth values for the main operators for each variable are exactly the same on the given truth value assignment. Here's what we mean.

Double negation

Double negation is a lesson often learned when people are young. If one claims, "Pat isn't not going to the mall," then he or she is essentially saying, "Pat is going to the mall." The negation contained in "isn't" cancels out the negation from "not," leaving the positive assertion regarding Pat's activities. Below is the truth table demonstrating the equivalence between p and $\sim\sim p$, followed by a brief explanation.

p	p	::	$\sim$	$\sim$	p
T	<u>T</u>		<u>T</u>	F	T
F	<u>F</u>		<u>F</u>	T	F

On the truth value assignment of true for p, the truth value for the main operator of the first claim (which is simply p, again) is true, and the truth value for main operator of the proposed equivalent claim $\sim\sim p$ is also true. When p is false, once again the truth values for the proposed equivalence are the same, now both false. Because the truth values for these claims are identical on any possible truth value assignment, these claims are equivalent.

Tautology

For logicians, a *tautology* is ordinarily understood as a claim that is always true for any truth value assignment, which can make for some interesting and not so interesting results in arguments (see 4.1, "Strange validity"). More generally, however, tautology also means saying the same thing in two different ways, making it a somewhat redundant title – and yet, still apropos – for the type of equivalence being discussed here. Often, when the same claim is made twice, this is considered redundant and unnecessary, and so the redundancy is eliminated for the sake of clarity and simplicity. Hence, the equivalences of tautology defined below are tools for simplifying redundancies that may occur when deducing the validity of an argument or constructing a deductively valid argument of your own. There are two types of tautology commonly used in this way, and their equivalence is demonstrated below:

p	::	(*p*	v	*p*)	*p*	::	(*p*	•	*p*)
T		T	**T**	T	**T**		T	**T**	T
F		F	**F**	F	**F**		F	**F**	F

(Note that even though *p*, like *p* v *p*, is sometimes false, claims that *p is equivalent to p* v *p* is tautologous or always true. The same goes for *p* and its equivalence with *p* • *p*.)

Commutativity

The equivalence of *commutativity* in propositional logic is the same as that found in mathematics, which allows for changing the order of operands (the object of a mathematical operation) provided this does not change the result. Similarly, in propositional logic, commutativity allows for changing the order of claims provided this does not change the meaning of the complex claim. While this equivalence is typically only defined in terms of the disjunction and conjunction, it also applies to the biconditional. These equivalences and their proofs are shown below:

(*p*	v	*q*)	::	(*q*	v	*p*)	(*p*	•	*q*)	::	(*q*	•	*p*)	(*p*	≡	*q*)	::	(*q*	≡	*p*)
T	**T**	T		T	**T**	T	T	**T**	T		T	**T**	T	T	**T**	T		T	**T**	T
T	**T**	F		F	**T**	T	T	**F**	F		F	**F**	T	T	**F**	F		F	**F**	T
F	**T**	T		T	**T**	F	F	**F**	T		T	**F**	F	F	**F**	T		T	**F**	F
F	**F**	F		F	**F**	F	F	**F**	F		F	**F**	F	F	**T**	F		F	**T**	F

Associativity

The equivalence of *associativity* allows one to regroup claims around different logical operators, so long as the regrouping does not change the meaning of the complex claim. This works with chains of disjunctions, conjunctions, and biconditionals, but not mixtures of the three. The two truth tables below demonstrate that associativity creates an equivalent claim in which the groupings for disjunctions, conjunctions, and biconditionals have been changed.

[*p*	v	(*q*	v	*r*)]	::	[(*p*	v	*q*)	v	*r*]
T	**T**	T	T	T		T	T	T	**T**	T
T	**T**	T	T	F		T	T	T	**T**	F
T	**T**	F	T	T		T	T	F	**T**	T
T	**T**	F	F	F		T	T	F	**T**	F
F	**T**	T	T	T		F	T	T	**T**	T
F	**T**	T	T	F		F	T	T	**T**	F
F	**T**	F	T	T		F	F	F	**T**	T
F	**F**	F	F	F		F	F	F	**F**	F

[*p*	•	(*q*	•	*r*)]	::	[(*p*	•	*q*)	•	*r*]
T	**T**	T	T	T		T	T	T	**T**	T
T	**F**	T	F	F		T	T	T	**F**	F
T	**F**	F	F	T		T	F	F	**F**	T
T	**F**	F	F	F		T	F	F	**F**	F
F	**F**	T	T	T		F	F	T	**F**	T
F	**F**	T	F	F		F	F	T	**F**	F
F	**F**	F	F	T		F	F	F	**F**	T
F	**F**	F	F	F		F	F	F	**F**	F

[*p*	≡	(*q*	≡	*r*)]	::	[(*p*	≡	*q*)	≡	*r*]
T	**T**	T	T	T		T	T	T	**T**	T
T	**F**	T	F	F		T	T	T	**F**	F
T	**F**	F	F	T		T	F	F	**F**	T
T	**T**	F	T	F		T	F	F	**T**	F
F	**F**	T	T	T		F	F	T	**F**	T
F	**T**	T	F	F		F	F	T	**T**	F
F	**T**	F	F	T		F	T	F	**T**	T
F	**F**	F	T	F		F	T	F	**F**	F

Transposition

The equivalence of *transposition* is a combination of the conditional with *modus tollens*. *Modus tollens* shows that with $p \supset q$ if one has $\sim q$, then $\sim p$ can be deduced, which is another way of saying that $p \supset q$ is equivalent to $\sim q \supset \sim p$. It's very much like contraposition, too (see 3.4). Below is the truth table demonstrating this equivalence:

(p	$\supset$	q)	::	($\sim$	q	$\supset$	$\sim$	p)
T	**T**	T		F	T	**T**	F	T
T	**F**	F		T	F	**F**	F	T
F	**T**	T		F	T	**T**	T	F
F	**T**	F		T	F	**T**	T	F

Material implication

In propositional logic, the conditional's truth table is only false when p is true and q is false, and this truth function is often referred to as *material implication.* (For other, stronger forms of implication see *The Philosopher's Toolkit*, "Entailment/implication.") It follows from this that whenever p is false, the conditional is true, or whenever q is true, the conditional is also true. This is summarized in the equivalence of *material implication*, which demonstrates that $\sim p \vee q$ is equivalent to $p \supset q$, shown below:

(p	$\supset$	q)	::	($\sim$	p	v	q)
T	**T**	T		F	T	**T**	T
T	**F**	F		F	T	**F**	F
F	**T**	T		T	F	**T**	T
F	**T**	F		T	F	**T**	F

Material equivalence

When one states that two claims are *equivalent*, this can be understood to mean that whenever one of the claims is true, the other will be true as well, and whenever one of the claims is false, the other claim is also false. The operator for the biconditional is often referred to as *material equivalence*, because while the *forms* of two claims may be very different, the truth values (the matter) of the claims are the same. Unsurprisingly, the truth table for the biconditional illustrates the very relationship expressed when two claims are said to be equivalent. According to the truth table for the biconditional, the biconditional is only true when p and q have the exact same truth value, whether that value is true or false.

Another way to think about this is in terms of conditional claims. If one knows that the truth values will always be the same for two claims, then it's understood that if p is true, then q is true, it is also true that if q is true, then p is true. As a result, the biconditional is equivalent to the conjunction of these two conditionals $p \supset q$ and $q \supset p$, shown in the table below. It's also, by the way, equivalent to the disjunction of $(p \bullet q)$ and $(\sim p \bullet \sim q)$, or more formally: $(p \bullet q) \vee (\sim p \bullet \sim q)$.

If p is true and q is false, the first conjunct will be false, and if q is true and p is false, then the second conjunct will be false. If, however, either both p and q are true or both p and q are false, then the conjunction will be true, and this can be formalized as $[(p \bullet q) \vee (\sim p \bullet \sim q)]$. The tables below illustrate the biconditional's equivalence to the preceding claims:

$(p \equiv q)$ ::	$[(p \supset q) \bullet (q \supset p)]$	$(p \equiv q)$ ::	$[(p \bullet q) \vee (\sim p \bullet \sim q)]$
T **T** T	T T T **T** T T T	T **T** T	T T T **T** F T F F T
T **F** F	T F F **F** F T T	T **F** F	T F F **F** F T F T F
F **F** T	F T T **F** T F F	F **F** T	F F T **F** T F F F T
F **T** F	F T F **T** F T F	F **T** F	F F F **T** T F T T F

Exportation

If a conjunction is the antecedent of a conditional, then that conditional is equivalent to a new conditional containing one of the conjuncts in the antecedent, while the other is made to form the antecedent of a new conditional in the consequent, which has as its consequent the consequent from the original conditional. While that may sound complicated, it's really quite easy to think through. If both p and q must be true for r to be true, then p alone isn't enough for r to be true, but if p is true, then one knows that all that is needed for r to be true is for q to be true. In other words, r is true if q is true provided that p is also true. Or if p is true, then if q is true, so is r, which is symbolized $[p \supset (q \supset r)]$. This equivalence is demonstrated in the table below:

$[(p \bullet q) \supset r]$ ::	$[p \supset (q \supset r)]$
T T T **T** T	T **T** T T T
T T T **F** F	T **F** T F F
T F F **T** T	T **T** F T T
T F F **T** F	T **T** F T F
F F T **T** T	F **T** T T T
F F T **T** F	F **T** T F F
F F F **T** T	F **T** F T T
F F F **T** F	F **T** F T F

Distribution

The equivalence of distribution is a relationship that holds for conjunctions and disjunctions and is similar to the function of distribution in algebra. If one were to make the claim, "Rory went to the store, and either Mary ate the cake or Ralph ate the cake," he or she would be asserting that at least one of two things is true, either Rory went to the store and Mary ate the cake, or Rory went to the store and Ralph ate the cake. This is the equivalence of distribution when the conjunction is the main operator. The disjunction is slightly more complicated. To say, "Rory went to the store, or both Mary ate the cake and Ralph ate the cake," is to assert that at least one of the disjuncts (maybe both) is true. When distributed, the main operator changes to a conjunction of either Rory went to the store or Mary ate the cake, and either Rory went to the store or Ralph ate the cake, symbolized $[(p \vee q) \bullet (p \vee r)]$. From the original claim, we know that if Rory went to the store is true, then the entire disjunction will be true. As for the distributed conjunction, if Rory went to the store is true, then so too will the entire conjunction be true as well. If, however, Rory went to the store is false, then the original disjunction is only true if both Mary ate the cake is true and Ralph ate the cake is true. This holds true for the conjunction that is the distributed equivalence of the original disjunction. Below are the truth tables demonstrating these equivalences:

$[p \bullet (q \vee r)]$ ::	$[(p \bullet q) \vee (p \bullet r)]$	$[p \vee (q \bullet r)]$ ::	$[(p \vee q) \bullet (p \vee r)]$
T **T** T T T	T T T **T** T T T	T **T** T T T	T T T **T** T T T
T **T** T T F	T T T **T** T F F	T **T** T F F	T T T **T** T T F
T **T** F T T	T F F **T** T T T	T **T** F F T	T T F **T** T T T
T **F** F F F	T F F **F** T F F	T **T** F F F	T T F **T** T T F
F **F** T T T	F F T **F** F F T	F **T** T T T	F T T **T** F T T
F **F** T T F	F F T **F** F F F	F **F** T F F	F T T **F** F F F
F **F** F T T	F F F **F** F F T	F **F** F F T	F F F **F** F T T
F **F** F F F	F F F **F** F F F	F **F** F F F	F F F **F** F F F

DeMorgan's Law

DeMorgan's Law was first introduced to formal propositional logic by Augustus DeMorgan (1806–1871). It had been recognized by earlier thinkers like Aristotle and William of Ockham (1287–1347), but DeMorgan is given the credit, since he was fortunate enough to demonstrate the equivalence at the time when propositional logic was being formalized into the logic commonly used today. These two equivalences are essentially a means of distributing a negation across either a conjunction or a disjunction, but they also help to make sense of the meaning behind claims like, "It's not the case that both p and q," and, "It's not the case that either p or q," which are easily confused. In the case of the former, $\sim (p \bullet q)$, this means that both p and q cannot be true at the same time, but either can be true so long as the other is false. In other words, either p must be false or q must be false (maybe both), and hence, this equivalence is symbolized $(\sim p \vee \sim q)$. Alternatively, "It's not the case that either p or q," $\sim (p \vee q)$, means neither p nor q is true. In other words, p is false and q is false, and so the equivalence is symbolized $\sim p \bullet \sim q$. Below are the truth tables demonstrating these equivalences:

$\sim (p \bullet q)$	$:: (\sim p \vee \sim q)$	$\sim (p \vee q)$	$:: (\sim p \bullet \sim q)$
F T T T	F T **F** F T	**F** T T T	F T **F** F T
T T F F	F T **T** T F	**F** T T F	F T **F** T F
T F F T	T F **T** F T	**F** F T T	T F **F** F T
T F F F	T F **T** T F	**T** F F F	T F **T** T F

4.4 Formal Deduction with Forms and Equivalences

Equivalences and deductively valid forms can be used as rules to guide you through a formal deduction. A *formal deduction*, sometimes called a demonstration or derivation, is a process whereby one demonstrates that an argument is deductively valid by proceeding from the premises in a step-by-step manner to derive the conclusion. The steps one takes from premises are only permitted when they are applications of a rule of inference from a deductively valid form or equivalence. They are called, accordingly, *rules of implication* and *rules of equivalence*. With them, each step in the deduction is labeled according to the line(s) from which the form or equivalence has been applied. In this manner, the critical thinker can prove an argument is deductively valid without using a truth table, which may, in even its indirect form, be an unwieldy task.

The example of a completed formal deduction shown below is an illustration of how this method works. The first three rows contain the premises, which are sometimes referred to as "assumptions" for a derivation. The last row in every formal deduction is the conclusion, which is indicated here with the symbol "∴". Rows four through eight, which includes the conclusion, are claims derived from the premises following rules that are completely truth preserving (valid), and so following those rules and assuming the premises are true, anything derived from them is true. For example, the sixth row is the claim S, which was derived from row one, R ⊃ S, and four, R, by means of *modus ponens*. (We'll define the other rules of inference used shortly.)

1	R ⊃ S	Premise
2	T ⊃ D	Premise
3	R • T	Premise
4	R	3 &E (simplification)
5	T	3 &E
6	S	1,4 MP (modus ponens)
7	D	2,5 MP
8	∴ S • D	6,7 &I (conjunction introduction)

The justification for each claim on the rows we infer from the premises is drawn from a set of truth preserving rules. As Section 4.2 of this chapter illustrates, there are deductively valid (i.e., truth preserving) forms common enough to have been named. They have accordingly become well known as rules for formal deduction called *rules of implication*. Similarly, a statement that's equivalent to another maintains the exact same truth value assignment as the claim to which it is equivalent, and so an equivalence rule may be used as a rule in a derivation to substitute a given claim for its logical equivalence. To make things even easier, all of the logical forms and equivalences have been given abbreviations for use in a formal deduction. Different logic texts will give different abbreviations, but the rules are all the same. Here are some of the most common abbreviations.

Rules of Implication	Abbreviation	Rules of Equivalence	Abbreviation
Modus ponens	MP	Commutativity	Com
Modus tollens	MT	Associativity	Assoc
Hypothetical syllogism	HS	Transposition	Trans
Disjunctive syllogism	DS	Material implication	Impl
Constructive dilemma	CD	Material equivalence	Equiv
Destructive dilemma	DD	Exportation	Exp
		Distribution	Dist
		DeMorgan's rule	DM
		Double negation	DN
		Tautology	Taut

Three simple rules

In addition to the forms and equivalences already discussed, there are five vital rules that come from deductively valid forms that have thus far gone unmentioned. That's because they are, for the most part, astonishingly obvious. Since, however, they're critical elements in justifying many steps in derivations, including rows 4 and 5 in the last argument, they're worth mentioning now, beginning with the three simplest.

Conjunction Introduction (&I or Conj)	Conjunction Elimination or Simplification (&E or Simp)	Disjunction Introduction or Addition (vI or Add)
$\dfrac{p \quad q}{p \bullet q}$	$\dfrac{p \bullet q}{p \text{ or } q}$	$\dfrac{p}{p \vee q \text{ or } q \vee p}$

These three rules of implication allow the critical thinker to compose or dismantle conjunctions or disjunctions in truth preserving ways. According to *conjunction introduction*, claims derived in the formal deduction may be joined as a conjunction. If one knows A as well as B, then A • B is justified by conjunction introduction. Alternatively, if one knows A • B from the formal deduction, then A (or B) is derivable by *conjunction elimination* or *simplification*. *Disjunction introduction* or *addition* allows one to introduce a disjunction from a single derivable claim. If one knows D from the formal deduction, then D may be combined with *any* other claim to form a disjunction. From D, one could derive D v P, D v L, or really, D v *anything*. As a result, disjunction introduction allows the critical thinker to introduce claims that have not been previously mentioned in the formal deduction, which is important when the conclusion contains claims not contained in the premises.

Conditional proof and two more simple rules

The difficulty with a disjunction, unlike a conjunction, is that we cannot tell from the disjunction which of the disjuncts is true, and it may be that both are true. As a result, *disjunction elimination* can only be done in a qualified or conditional way, under new assumptions. Eliminating the disjunction requires determining what, if anything, follows regardless of which disjunct is true. If some claim, like S, follows regardless of which disjunct is assumed true, then S can be concluded from the disjunction without the need to show that either of the disjuncts is true by itself. The process of assuming each of the disjuncts is true, separately, in order to derive the same claim from either, introduces an additional feature to formal deductions illustrated in the form of disjunction elimination below. If we assume p without (or having eliminated) q, then some other sentence, r, can be derived; and if that same sentence, r, can be derived from q under the assumption that p has been eliminated, then r follows in any case. Making those assumptions (p without q, and q without p) and then deriving new sentences is called *conditional proof*:

Disjunction elimination (vE)

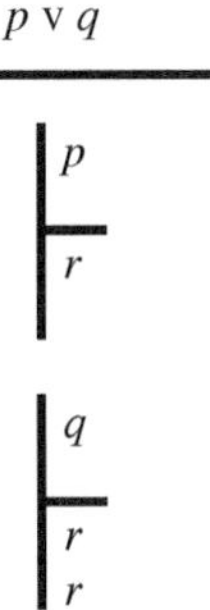

The form of disjunction elimination shown above is not a formal deduction, but it may be demonstrated as a valid form through a formal deduction. Its use of a conditional proof is abbreviated, allowing the critical thinker to skip steps in the process of disjunction elimination. Typically, the conclusion of a conditional proof is a conditional claim, because a conditional proof is basically a sub-derivation within the formal deduction used to introduce conditional claims. This sub-derivation allows for the introduction of new assumptions, which are only conditionally accepted, and because these assumptions are not a part of the original derivation and have not been derived through a truth preserving rule, the conditional proof is offset from the original formal deduction (note the brackets under the derivation line). Once the conditional proof has demonstrated that its conclusion is derivable from the newly introduced assumptions, the conclusion, along with the necessary assumption, may return to the main column of the formal deduction as a conditional claim. The conditionally accepted assumption becomes the antecedent and the derived conclusion claim becomes the consequent. Disjunction elimination allows for skipping all these steps, as well as others, in the process of deriving a single claim from a disjunct.

Below is an illustration of the form for *conditional introduction*, or sometimes just *conditional proof* (CP), which uses the conditional proof format as it's traditionally conceived:

Conditional introduction (⊃I)

| p
|---
| q

$p \supset q$

Here's what disjunction elimination looks like using a fully spelled out conditional proof:

1	A v B	Premise
2	~ A v C	Premise
3	~ B v C	Premise
4	| A	Assumption
5	| C	2,4 DS
6	A ⊃ C	4–5 ⊃I
7	| B	Assumption
8	| C	3,7 DS
9	B ⊃ C	7–8 ⊃I
10	~ A v C	6 Impl
11	~ B v C	9 Impl
12	(~ A v C) • (~ B v C)	10,11 &I
13	C v (~ A • ~ B)	12 Dist
14	C v ~ (A v B)	13 DM
15	C	1,14 DS

While the rule for disjunction elimination and conditional introduction may initially seem complicated in lieu of their use of a conditional proof, they are easy enough to use provided one remembers that these rules are based on valid forms. And, like all the valid forms, their use merely requires that their form be followed in the formal deduction. Below are examples of how disjunction elimination and conditional introduction may be used in formal deductions:

Example 1

1	R ⊃ S	Premise
2	T ⊃ S	Premise
3	R v T	Premise
4	| R	Assumption
5	| S	1,4 MP
6	| T	Assumption
7	| S	2,6 MP
8	∴ S	3,4–7 vE

Example 2

1	~ (R • S) ⊃ P	Premise
2	D ⊃ ~ P	Premise
3	| D	Assumption
4	| ~ P	2,3 MP
5	| (R • S)	1,4 MT
6	∴ D ⊃ (R • S)	3–5 ⊃I

We know that this can get complicated, but be patient. Learning how to employ formal deductions of this sort is a valuable skill for thinking critically. Although getting the hang of all these rules requires quite a bit of practice, the ability to apply an understanding of logical forms and equivalences in a step-by-step manner to show exactly why an argument is valid can be a powerful aid in fixing flawed arguments as well as in constructing new valid arguments. Logicians have accomplished a great deal with these tools, and they've even moved beyond them into new symbolic systems. Beyond the formal deductions in PL, logicians have developed other, more complex and more powerful logics (Predicate Logic, Modal Logic, Deontic Logic) that find their origins in the rules of formal deductions. Each of those systems discloses and clarifies subtle but important new dimensions of reasoning and arguing, dimensions that can invest you with additional strength as a critical thinker. They can certainly help you detect additional fallacies.

4.5 Common Formal Fallacies

A *fallacy*, as we've seen, is just an error in reasoning. Some fallacies are so common they've been given names. A formal fallacy occurs when an invalid argument *form* or structure is taken to be valid. Indeed, a number of invalid forms are easily confused with those that are valid. People do so all the time. In 4.2, we showed how to recognize, construct, and use the valid forms of several important deductive propositional arguments. Here we'll briefly show you how these forms can go wrong.

Affirming the consequent

Recall that *modus ponens* (MP), which affirms the antecedent, has the following form:

1. If *p*, then *q*.
2. *p*.
3. Therefore, *q*.

For instance:

1. If you are thinking of a chair, then you are thinking.
2. You are thinking of a chair.
3. Therefore, you are thinking.

But a subtly deceptive argument form resembles MP but is nonetheless fallacious:

1. If you are thinking of a chair, then you are thinking.
2. You are thinking.
3. Therefore, you are thinking of a chair.

Notice that in the fallacious form we've switched sentences 2 and 3 as they appear in the proper MP, that is, we've taken the *consequent* of the conditional in premise 1 (rather than the antecedent) and *affirmed it* as the second premise. *Modus ponens* means "the way of affirmation," so in short, this fallacy occurs when the wrong component is affirmed:

antecedent → consequent

1. If you are thinking of a chair, then you are thinking.
2. You are thinking.
3. Therefore, you are thinking of a chair.

It certainly doesn't follow that simply because *you are thinking* that *you are thinking of a chair*. The very fact that there are instances where the premises, organized in this way, do not guarantee the conclusion shows that this argument is invalid. Affirming the antecedent of a conditional as a premise is a valid form of inference; affirming the consequent is not.

Consider another example:

1. If it is raining, the sidewalks are wet.
2. It is raining.
3. Therefore, the sidewalks are wet.

If, instead of this argument, someone were to replace premise 2 with the *consequent* of premise 1, a formal fallacy would result, again deceptively similar to the *modus ponens*:

1. If it is raining, the sidewalks are wet.
2. The sidewalks are wet.
3. Therefore, ... ?

Notice that the intuitive (and misleading) conclusion would be, "It is raining." But this doesn't follow. Lots of events could account for the wetness of the sidewalk: a broken sprinkler, snowmelt, or someone washing it with a hose. Just because rain is *sufficient* for making the sidewalk wet doesn't mean that it is the *only* event sufficient for doing so, or that rain is *necessary* for the sidewalk to be wet (see 2.2). Furthermore, even if rain were the culprit, it doesn't follow that it's raining *now*; it might have rained two hours ago. It is not, therefore, valid to infer that it's raining from these premises.

Remember, however, that even if an argument is *formally* fallacious in *deductive* terms, this doesn't mean necessarily that it's a *bad* argument in other terms. It might still be *inductively* cogent. Formally fallacious arguments are simply arguments that are *not valid*, though they are mistakenly treated as though they are.

Examples of affirming the consequent

1. You are guilty of a felony if you fire that gun.
   (This is logically equivalent to: If you fire that gun, then you are guilty of a felony.)

2. You are guilty of a felony.
3. So, you must have fired that gun.

1. If it snows tonight, the barn will collapse in the morning.
2. The barn collapsed this morning
3. Therefore, it must have snowed last night.

1. If you all want a drink, at least one of you does.
2. At least one of you wants a drink.
3. Therefore, all of you do.

1. If you are an executive today, then you can eat in the special dining room.
2. You are eating in the special dining room.
3. So, you must be an executive.

Denying the antecedent

Recall that *modus tollens* (the way of denying, MT) has the following valid form:

1. If *p*, then *q*.
2. It is not the case that *q*.
3. Therefore, it is not the case that *p*.

For instance:

1. If you're thinking of a chair, then you're thinking.
2. You're not thinking.
3. Therefore, you're not thinking of a chair.

A subtly deceptive form of this argument occurs when we deny the wrong bit, in particular the antecedent of the conditional in premise 1. Instead of denying the consequent (which would be valid), the fallacious form denies the antecedent (which is invalid). Here's an example:

1. If you're thinking of a chair, then you're thinking.
2. You're not thinking of a chair.
3. Therefore, you're not thinking.

It doesn't follow from the first premise that, because you're not thinking of a chair, you aren't thinking at all. Perhaps you're thinking of a table, or a unicorn, or a beach ball – or logic. These possibilities show that the argument form is invalid, and therefore, formally fallacious.

Examples of denying the antecedent

1. If you are drinking alcohol, you are of the legal drinking age.
2. You are not drinking alcohol.
3. Therefore, you are not of the legal drinking age.

1. If you are driving faster than the speed limit, you can get a ticket.
2. You are not driving faster than the speed limit.
3. Therefore, you can't get a ticket.

1. You can come back stage only if you have a pass. (This is logically equivalent to, "If you can come back stage, then you have a pass.")
2. You can't come back stage.
3. Therefore, you don't have a pass.

1. You can get married only if you have a license.
2. But you two can't get married.
3. So, you must not have a license.

Affirming a disjunct

Disjunctive syllogisms have the following valid form:

1. Either *p* or *q*.
2. It is not the case that *p*. (Or, it is not the case that *q*.)
3. Therefore, *q*. (Or, therefore, *p*.)

For example:

1. Either the Internet is out, or my router has a problem.
2. The Internet is not out.
3. Therefore, my router has a problem.

A deceptive form of this argument occurs when, instead of denying one of the disjuncts, we affirm it:

1. Either the Internet is out, or my router has a problem.
2. The Internet is out.
3. Therefore, my router does not have a problem.

Remember that, in logic, we assume that a disjunction is "inclusive," which means that, without further evidence, it is possible that both disjuncts are true. Therefore, discovering that it is the case that the Internet is out doesn't imply that it isn't the case that my router doesn't have a problem. Both could be true. But if a disjunction as a whole statement is true, then at a minimum one of the disjuncts is true. So evidence denying one of the disjuncts allows us validly to affirm the other disjunct.

Examples of affirming a disjunct

1. Either we're going to the play or to the game.
2. We're going to the game.
3. Therefore, we're not going to the play.

1. You are either committed to your work or to me.
2. And I know you're committed to your work.
3. So, you must not be committed to me.

1. The car's battery is dead, or the starter's broken.
2. I just tested the battery, and it's definitely dead.
3. So, the starter must be okay.

Exercises and study questions

Using a truth table, determine whether the following arguments are valid or invalid.

1. $$\frac{\begin{array}{l} A \bullet B \\ B \supset C \end{array}}{C}$$

2. $$\frac{\begin{array}{l} A \vee B \\ B \supset C \end{array}}{C}$$

3. $$\frac{\begin{array}{l} \sim (A \vee B) \\ \sim A \supset \sim C \end{array}}{\sim C \bullet \sim B}$$

4. $$\frac{\begin{array}{l} A \equiv B \\ A \supset (B \supset C) \end{array}}{B \supset (A \supset C)}$$

SEE ALSO

2.6 Showing Invalidity by Counterexample
Chapter 5: Tools for Detecting Informal Fallacies
Chapter 7: Tools for Critical Thinking about Experience and Error

READING

Patrick J. Hurley, *A Concise Introduction to Logic*, 12th edn (2015)
Mary Michael Spangler, *Logic: An Aristotelian Approach* (2013)
Deborah J. Bennett, *Logic Made Easy* (2005)
William T. Parry & Edward A. Hacker, *Aristotelian Logic* (1991)
Julian Baggini & Peter S. Fosl, *The Philosopher's Toolkit* (2010)

5 Tools for Detecting Informal Fallacies

5.1 Critical Thinking, Critical Deceiving, and the "Two Step"

By now you've discovered how difficult it is to think critically. There are hundreds of ways that reasoning can go poorly, leading you to false, useless, or unsupported conclusions. As we've seen, in order to manage all these possibilities, logicians have identified categories of bad reasoning called *fallacies*. A fallacy is simply an error in reasoning, often a common error, and understanding fallacies will help you both to avoid making mistakes in your own reasoning and to avoid succumbing to the bad reasoning of others.

There is, however, a dark side to acquiring an understanding of fallacies. Some of you will use the information in this book to reason well, but others, perhaps the more unscrupulous among you, will use fallacies to lead others to reason poorly. Understanding fallacies does confer this power, although rather than critical thinking, leading others to reason poorly is better understood as *critical deceiving*. For instance, you may be a politician aspiring to win an election or an advertiser trying to sell something. You may be a lawyer and find yourself tempted to convince a jury to acquit your client or to prosecute a defendant using whatever means are available – regardless of whether or not those means meet the requirements of good reasoning.

Let's say you're a defense attorney, and your client, Jason, has most definitely committed the crime with which he's been charged. The evidence is stacked solidly against Jason, but as his lawyer, you accept that it's your duty (not to mention livelihood) to defend him to the best of your ability. After learning that Jason's childhood was miserable and that his adulthood has been sad and tragic, you decide to convince the jury that, regardless of whether Jason committed the crime, he should not be held legally responsible for it. You recount to them the litany of Jason's failures, hardships, and frustrations. *Surely*, you tell the jury at the end, with deepest, heartfelt (although perhaps disingenuous) passion, *this man did not commit this crime.*

The Critical Thinking Toolkit, First Edition. Galen A. Foresman, Peter S. Fosl, and Jamie C. Watson.

Now, there are certainly complexities lurking here. There are potentially real and mitigating considerations, for example, concerning the extent to which a history of abuse and deprivation can either *excuse* a criminal act (i.e., accept that it was wrong but should not be punished) or even *justify* it (i.e., show that it was actually not wrong but in these circumstances right). But simply to *appeal to emotions alone* as if they themselves offered reasons or proof for the innocence of your defendant is not to reason properly. After all, the evidence appears to be quite contrary to that conclusion. From a logical point of view, then, critical thinking and critical deceiving rely on the same mechanisms. Understanding, therefore, that there are those willing to misuse those mechanisms makes critical thinking all the more important.

Returning to those logical mechanisms as set out in what we've called the *critical thinking two step*, a solid argument (whether *sound* or *cogent*) must meet two conditions: (1) that the conclusion follows from the premises (either *validly* or *strongly*) and (2) that the premises are true. A fallacy intentionally or unintentionally undermines one of these conditions.

Fallacies are often divided into two broad categories: *formal* and *informal*. In a formal fallacy the argument's appearance leads a potential reader to believe that the argument is deductively valid when it isn't. Fallacies like this are called "formal" because they explicitly fail to achieve the proper structural form of a valid argument (the first step of the two step). Formal fallacies constitute a serious worry in technical writing, especially in the work of philosophers, mathematicians, and scientists. Other fallacies are "informal"; and while they may be expressible in perfectly valid deductive forms, they fail in other ways.

Note that formal and informal fallacies *do not* apply equally to deductive and inductive arguments. Inductive arguments reach conclusions with just different degrees of probability, and so they cannot commit deductive, formal fallacies. Deductive arguments, on the other hand, may commit formal and informal fallacies. Consider our attorney's argument for Jason's case:

1. Jason is pitiful.
2. If Jason is pitiful, then Jason's attorney is right.
3. Therefore, Jason's attorney is right.

You might be surprised to learn that actually this argument is deductively valid (it has the form called *modus ponens*; if its premises are true, the conclusion must be true), and so it does not commit any formal fallacy. Jason's pitiful life, however, has nothing to do with whether his attorney is correct in asserting Jason's innocence. Guilt and innocence are matters of whether Jason is responsible for committing the crime, and arguably his pitiful circumstances are insufficient to determine that. (Students who plead for better grades on the basis of pity would do well to consider this!)

Now, this case is relatively clear, but it's important to notice that informal fallacies are tricky because they don't themselves undermine the first condition of a good argument. In the example here, the conclusion does follow from the premises – validly, even – and yet the argument is a poor one. The problem lies elsewhere, often, as we'll see, in the larger context in which the claims and the argument are made.

> *As a general rule, to avoid informal fallacies, keep a precise and clear focus upon the argument itself and its terms, not on your opponent or on irrelevant features of the context.*

With these definitions and qualifications in mind, then, let's turn to some of the most common and most deceptive informal and quasi-informal fallacies. Getting a firm grasp on these will help you avoid succumbing to the misleading reasoning of the deceptive and the careless.

5.2 Subjectivist Fallacy

"I like vanilla ice cream, so vanilla ice cream is the best ice cream for everyone." The *subjectivist fallacy* is committed when someone appeals to subjectivity inappropriately to justify some conclusion.

Objective truths are true independently of what subjects believe or feel, while subjective truths are only about a subject's beliefs and feelings. In this sense, subjective experiences are those available only to an individual subject having the experience, while objective experiences are those that are available to multiple perceivers whose cognitive faculties are functioning properly. Objective truths, therefore, are true for everyone, but subjective truths may only be true for individual subjects, as in our ice cream example. Nevertheless, the subjectivist fallacy is often tempting for people, and it's tempting for two reasons. In the first place, it's not always so clear what is and what is not a merely subjective truth, and secondly, our subjective experiences are often extremely powerful and intense, so intense that they lead us to think all people must share them.

Some obvious epistemological questions arise here. One worry about sense experience is that we cannot get "outside of our perceptions," so it may be the case that there are no purely objective experiences. But this worry shouldn't lead us to abandon objectivity completely. After all, even if our experiences are all to some extent subjective, they might still represent objective reality in a reasonably adequate way. So, if someone dismisses your argument *solely* on the grounds that you're appealing to subjective evidence, you may point out that she has committed the subjectivist fallacy. On the flip side of that coin, simply pointing out that your conclusion is grounded in your personal subjective experience isn't enough to protect it from the criticism that it's objectively false. The fact that the subjective experience of a colorblind individual doesn't register that an object is red is no proof that it's not red.

> *Typically, we regard those judgments that are consistent and shared to be properly objective and those that are diverse and not shared to be properly subjective.*

Even with this rule of thumb, however, things get tricky. To take our ice cream example, judgments about the flavors of foods have been shown to be diverse enough among healthy, normal people to make objective claims about what flavors are "best" misplaced. But what if everyone or almost everyone agreed about vanilla the way that people agree about foods that taste bitter or sweet? Would that make claims about vanilla more objective? David Hume, in his well-known 1757 essay, "Of the Standard of Taste," suggests that agreement about aesthetic judgments, especially well-informed and well-considered agreement, is a sign of a kind of objectivity. Doesn't the enduring and widespread agreement about the beauty of the Parthenon and the *Iliad* indicate that they are, in fact, beautiful? Landscape paintings are considered beautiful more or less universally around the world.

We can see the problem more clearly with a different example:

Jane: "I saw the car hit you. It was a red Ford."
Frank: "Well, what you saw was just your subjective perception of what happened."

Of course, since seeing is a sensory event, and Jane's conclusion was based on her seeing, her claim *does* rest on a subjective perception. Jane, however, generally finds that her seeing is more than merely subjective. She is healthy and awake and has no reason not to trust her sense of sight and that her knowledge of cars is in some meaningful way shared. What she perceives seems objective; and her past experiences with judgments based on her eyesight have proven reliable and in agreement with others. The important question is not whether her perception is subjective but whether Jane saw a red Ford, that is, whether a red Ford hit Frank. The point is that, just because her perception of seeing the car that hit Frank is subjective, it doesn't follow that there is no objective fact of the matter as to what sort of car hit him or that Jane's perception and testimony isn't relevant evidence about that fact.

Similarly, consider our agreements about what is positioned above and below something else. Stoplights all position the red light on top and the green at the bottom. This makes it possible for even colorblind people to use stoplights. Now, certainly when we see a stoplight we're employing subjective sensory perceptions. But because those subjective perceptions are so universal and consistent we also understand them to reveal objective truths. There may even be a kind of objectivity proper to aesthetic judgments.

The toughest questions related to the subjectivist fallacy are often moral questions. Imagine that person *A* says, "It would be wrong of you to take that. It belongs to someone else," and that person *B* responds, "Well, that's just your subjective opinion of what's right and wrong." Notice that it's trivially true that this accusation is based upon *A*'s opinion. The problem is that, in dismissing *A*'s claim this way, *B* seems to be implying that this is *all* morality is or could be – that there is no objective fact about which to disagree. The difficulty here is that subjectivism about morality is a controversial issue. Some regard all morality as merely subjective. Others do not. Unless the subjectivist claim about morality has been established, doesn't it remain at least possible that *A*'s belief tracks an objective truth?

Indeed, to be sure, it might actually be the case that morality and eyesight are radically subjective to individuals such that we could never effectively argue by appealing to reasons about whether something is properly right or wrong, beautiful or ugly, blue or red, or even above or below. It seems telling, however, that (1) this often is not our experience of the world – that is, in our day-to-day lives we do effectively find agreement in our reasons for making these judgments; and that (2) there may be no other standard than our ordinary agreements in our judgments, which suggests that further skepticism regarding the truth of these claims may rest on an impossibly strict standard for knowing and communicating.

Here's the upshot. When possible and reasonable, the careful critical thinker will press her interlocutor (as well as herself) to *provide reasons* for his claims rather than simply dismissing (or accepting) them as subjective opinions. Be wary of appeals to the merely subjective, and when possible demand reasons.

Legitimate appeals to subjectivism

One qualification should be added here. Not all appeals to purely subjective opinion are fallacious. If someone is genuinely intending to express only a subjective experience, then it is appropriate to appeal to the merely subjective. For instance, imagine if again during an outing to the ice cream shop I were to say, "This vanilla ice cream tastes wonderfully sweet to me." You would be wrong to challenge me with the claim, "You're wrong. It tastes awful." "Tasting sweet *to me*" here implies features to which I have a kind of privileged subjective access (the quale associated with sweetness). Because judgments about mere pleasure or sensation do seem subjective in the sense of being merely relative to individuals, we regard them differently from the way we regard judgments about general sense experience. (See *The Philosopher's Toolkit* 4.14 on the objective/subjective distinction and for more on subjectivity.)

Examples of the subjectivist fallacy

1. Fiona: "As Einstein shows, gravity is not primarily a function of mass, but of the curvature of space-time. Therefore, since your argument depends on the assumption that gravity is a function of mass, you must abandon your conclusion."
   Tara: Well, that's Einstein's *opinion* about gravity." [That is, Einstein's conclusion can be discounted because his theory was also his opinion.]
2. Prosecutor: "Ladies and gentlemen of the jury, you have heard testimony from five witnesses that this defendant punched Mr. Smith at 2:30pm. Therefore, you must convict."
   Defendant: "Ladies and gentlemen, this court is interested in fact, not mere opinion. These witnesses saw what they wanted to see. You cannot base your decision on these subjective experiences." [Implicit conclusion: You should not convict.]

3. Yuki: "Historical evidence shows unequivocally that Jesus of Nazareth was a real person."
Jane: "That may be true for some historians. But why think their subjective views should hold true for everyone?" [Implicit conclusion: It isn't true for everyone.]
4. Clara: "Jack's argument is weak, and the premises are not obviously true."
Jack: "What Clara says about my argument makes me feel sad and angry, so she must be wrong." [Jack's view is that Clara's wrong that his argument is flawed because of his subjective response to her criticism.]

5.3 Genetic Fallacies

The *genetic fallacy* occurs when someone wrongly infers something about a concept, event, or thing based on claims about its origin. It's often formulated as a rejection or dismissal of a claim on the grounds that the claim's cause, origin, or original use or meaning is different from its truth, justification, or contemporary use. For instance, imagine that someone says, "I apologize," after doing something distasteful to you (whether intentionally or unintentionally). Imagine that you then respond by saying, "Well, since the word 'apology' comes from the Greek word for 'defense,' I can only assume you are trying to defend your despicable behavior!" Aside from being difficult, you've committed the genetic fallacy. Just because the word "apology" *originally* meant "defense" doesn't mean it still does or that this person intends it that way.

Similarly, someone may dismiss the truth or significance of religious belief on the grounds that its origins are cultural: "You believe what you believe because your parents did, and then it was encouraged by your culture. If you had been born anywhere else, you wouldn't be a Muslim." Though it may be true that you originally believed because your parents did, it need not be the case now. Instead, you may be a philosopher of religion and find compelling evidence for the truth of your religious tradition. Alternatively, you may now just find it easier to adhere to Islam than any other worldview. Both alternatives are irrelevant to how you originally formed the belief. Because the origins of your beliefs can be unrelated to the reasons for your holding those beliefs now, any dismissal based on their origin commits the genetic fallacy.

Legitimate appeals to origins

Appealing to origin of some thing or event is not fallacious if the origin is *relevant* to the issue at hand. It would be strange, for instance, to complain about someone's appeal to Darwinian evolution if he or she were attempting to explain what a cat is. In other words, it's not fallacious for a person to explain, for example, that, "A cat is a mammal that emerged within the genus *felus* 10–15 million years ago," since in this case the origin of the cat is part of what makes it a cat. Therefore, an appeal to how it came about is relevant and informative.

This sort of explanation is often useful in identifying institutions. The identity of a college, for instance, doesn't depend on which professors or administrators the college has (these change regularly) or on what buildings compose it (they can be torn down and new ones built). Therefore, as part of their identity, members of a college will often cite how old the college is, who founded it, and why it was founded. These features, in addition to its location and functions (mission and goals), help distinguish the institution from others similar to it. Thus, origins can be relevant when attempting to explain or justify claims about something's identity. But we must be careful: institutions, like other things, change. That an institution was founded on a certain set of principles doesn't mean it continues to organize itself according to those principles. A lot of colleges, for instance, were started in order to train women to be teachers but have now become coeducational universities. In this case, appealing to origins may not be helpful for describing what it currently is.

Examples of the genetic fallacy

1. "Christianity now dominates Western culture only because of the significant political power it came to yield through the Roman Empire. Therefore, the tenets of the Christian faith are no more legitimate than any other religious tradition."
2. "The behaviors we now regard as 'moral' and 'immoral' developed through environmental selection pressures to protect the human race. Therefore, they are merely practical rules and have nothing to do with what's really right or wrong."
3. "Comfy Hotels was founded on principles of honesty and charity. It would be wrong to call such a company immoral or greedy today."
4. "The chemist August Kekulé claimed that he got the idea for the molecular structure of benzene from a daydream. Now, what sort of science is that? We shouldn't accept his claims about benzene."
5. "The word 'apology' originally meant 'a legal defense,' so it is inappropriate to use it now to mean 'I'm sorry.'"

5.4 *Ad Hominem* Fallacies: Direct, Circumstantial, and *Tu Quoque*

The *ad hominem* fallacy is a particularly common kind of genetic fallacy, one in which an arguer appeals to a person's character or circumstances or behavior in order to undermine that person's argument or claim. Like the genetic fallacy more generally, *ad hominem* is often categorized as a "fallacy of relevance" because a person's character or circumstances or behavior are *irrelevant* to whether her or his claims are true or their arguments sound. When used intentionally, the *ad hominem* distracts third-party audiences from the relevant line of argument – so, as you can imagine, this strategy is often used in smear campaigns in political races.

For instance, when running for US president, Barack Obama attempted to express his sympathy over the increasing price of food by noting the increasing cost of arugula or rocket lettuce to a group of Iowa farmers. Obama's opponents immediately charged that Obama was elitist and distant from the normal American voter, many of whom do not know what arugula is. The implication was that Obama could not be a good president, because he is too different from the majority of Americans. (Note that the other side of the political spectrum is not immune from this, either. The same charge was made against Mitt Romney when he was photographed jet skiing in New Hampshire.)

Of course, these are fallacious (and absurd) arguments. A presidential contender's food choices, recreational interests, and tax bracket are not obviously relevant to his or her competence to serve as president. If someone, however, thinks they are (and they may be), then an argument needs to be made connecting these dots. Simply to assert that a candidate is different in a personal way and then to infer something about his or her political views is to commit the *ad hominem* fallacy. It's a very common fallacy, and it can be analyzed into three distinct forms: the *ad hominem*, direct; the *ad hominem*, circumstantial; and the *tu quoque*.

Direct

An *ad hominem* that appeals to a person's character is called an "*ad hominem*, direct" fallacy. For example, if I try to convince you that a new policy proposed by your boss is worthless because your boss is loud, obnoxious, and is impatient with his wife, I am committing an *ad hominem*, direct fallacy. The boss's character has nothing to do with whether his policy is worthless.

Some logic texts call this an "*ad hominem*, abusive" fallacy. The implications are the same, but the word "abusive" can be misleading because an *ad hominem* fallacy need not appeal to the negative aspects of a person's character. Politicians often promote not only their candidacies but also their platforms by showing that they are "upstanding members of their communities," or "active churchgoers," or "a loving spouse and parent." All of these facts (if they are facts) may be interesting, but they seem *irrelevant to whether the candidate's platform is a good one for the polity.* The point here is that these are examples of the *ad hominem*, direct fallacy, even though they appeal to the positive aspects of a person's character.

Legitimate appeals to character

An important qualification is worth highlighting here. If the conclusion under consideration is about a person's character, appealing to a person's past character as evidence is not fallacious. For instance, imagine we are defense attorneys vetting a witness for trial and we discover evidence that this person is a liar. This character information is directly relevant to the person's credibility on the witness stand: we want an honest person, and now we have evidence that this person isn't honest. Similarly, if you are choosing an accountant, and you discover evidence that one of your choices has a track record of falsifying tax documents, then you have a reason (albeit a character reason) not to choose that accountant. When character is the issue, evidence about character is *relevant*, and often the burden falls upon the critical thinker to decide whether character really is the issue.

Examples of the ad hominem, *direct fallacy*

1. "Senator Jones is callous and curt. In addition, he is not well read and mostly keeps to himself. Therefore, you should not take his tax policies seriously."
2. "Governor Speak is hard working and kind. She is honest and finishes what she starts. Therefore, she would make a great senator, and you should all vote for Speak!"
3. "You know, your cardiologist is an angry person. He yelled at me when I was in the waiting room and refused to say hello when I walked in. His diagnosis and his recommendation that you'd be healthier if you lost weight, exercised more, and ate less fried food must be mistaken."
4. "She is the flakiest and shallowest person I know: she only ever talks about herself, she is completely indifferent to anything you have to say, and she is obsessed with shoes. She keeps talking about her vegetarianism, too. Surely, her views about that must be wrong."
5. "Aristotle accepted slavery and believed that women are less rational than men, therefore his views on deductive logic are nonsense."
6. "Why are you listening to those people? You don't want to be like them. If I were you, I would reject anything they have to say."
7. "Williams is a crotchety loudmouth with a terrible temper. You can't believe a word he says about women's rights."

Circumstantial

An arguer does not have to focus only on someone's character to commit an *ad hominem* fallacy. You can also commit this fallacy if you focus on a person's *affiliations* or *circumstances*. If you attempt to discredit a person's argument or claim by pointing out that he is affiliated with an unsavory group or that his socio-economic status or standpoint prohibits him from speaking truly or because that person has a vested interest in the claim's truth, you have committed an *ad hominem*, circumstantial fallacy – an *appeal to an arguer's circumstances*.

Some political pundits dismiss the claims of certain politicians with claims like, "It's just another misleading conservative/liberal [take your pick] ploy." Notice, that, at this point, it doesn't matter what the policy is; we can already see that this response is fallacious. This claim does not give you any reason to believe that the "ploy" is misleading *except* that it was attempted by conservatives/liberals. "Ploy" is often used as a derogatory term for a "strategy," for instance, to indicate that it is somehow devious or deceitful or that someone is "trying to get one over on you." But, again, the only reason given for thinking that it's devious or deceitful is that it's attempted by "conservatives" or "liberals," so we'll examine this aspect of the argument.

Is a strategy misleading *just because* it is proposed by conservatives/liberals? Not obviously. This is where the arguer commits an *ad hominem*, circumstantial fallacy. "Misleading-ness" is not entailed by conservatism or liberalism (proponents of either could be honest and right from time to time!), nor is misleading people part of their ideologies. The arguer might point to a long line of deception from conservatives or liberals as support for the claim. There may be grounds for suspicion in that, but a shabby track record wouldn't tell you anything necessarily about the strategy currently in question. Maybe, unlike past positions, the current strategy is not deceptive. Strictly speaking, each claim must be evaluated on its own merits.

The *ad hominem*, circumstantial fallacy is also common in race and gender debates. Consider the following hypothetical interchange where the relevant "circumstance" is gender:

> Melissa: "The evidence shows that women are paid less than men for the same jobs."
> Eric: "Since you're a woman, Melissa, your claim about that must be false."

There are legitimate epistemic issues bearing on claims made by people occupying certain social positions – much like subjective experiences – in that their standpoint may be more or less interested and limited (as we'll see in 7.6). Nevertheless, it's hasty to the point of distortion to exclude from the outset the views of those whose standpoints maybe be suspect simply because of their standpoints. In short, while a good critical thinker may be wise to be cautious of the influence Melissa's gender may have had on her views, that social position ought not to be grounds for concluding that her views are false. Similarly, a person's skin tone, hair, identity, or ethnic background ought not to be considered relevant *per se* to whatever truth claims he, she, or they might make. In other words, a person's circumstances may give us a reason to be suspicious about a claim, but they don't give us grounds for concluding that the claims that person makes are false or that the reasoning supporting them is flawed.

> *Circumstances give grounds for caution, suspicion, and heightened scrutiny but not for concluding that someone's claims are false.*

Perhaps the most common use of *ad hominem*, circumstantial arguments is in cases where the criticized party has a vested interest in the conclusion for which she is arguing. For instance, if a Catholic priest claims that abortion is morally impermissible, it would be fallacious to respond by saying, "Of course, his claim is wrong, and his argument is flawed. He's Catholic and a man!" Perhaps the priest simply thinks there are good, non-religious reasons for objecting to abortion (see, for instance, Don Marquis's "An Argument that Abortion is Wrong," 1989), and perhaps even as a man his reasoning is sound.

Indeed, that he is a male and a Catholic may fully *explain* why the priest personally has adopted that position, at least as a matter of his psychological development. But, still, it's very important to remember that the question of *how* or *why* that person came to adopt a belief or claim is often independent from the question of whether that claim is true or false and whether the reasoning behind it is sound. (Remember from 1.2 that *arguments* are different from *explanations*.) It's true that when dealing with questions about morality, such as abortion, as opposed to, say, scientific matters, things can get tricky. That's because the question of whether moral claims are best thought of as "true" or "false" and how they are best thought of as "right" or "wrong" is philosophically controversial and complex. Nevertheless, as a general principle of critical thinking, we think it best, at least as a matter of first assessment, to consider personal circumstances, such as those of the Catholic priest, irrelevant to whether or not a claim under scrutiny, *as a matter of logic*, is *justified*. (For the same reasons, it would be wrong to say of a woman arguing against the priest that: "Of course, her claims about abortion rights are wrong. After all, she's a woman, a women's studies professor, and a feminist.")

Conceptually speaking, explanations *for someone's holding a position are different from* justifications *for that position.*

As another example of *ad hominem*, circumstantial reasoning, consider someone who owns a relatively large corporation and argues that governments should not impose certain regulations on corporations. It would be fallacious to dismiss that claim by noting that the person making it has a vested interest in corporations. She might have good reasons that are irrelevant to her immediate interests as a business-owner. Perhaps her immediate interests motivated her to study the issue deeply. Perhaps she decided to own her own business (rather than enter public service) precisely because she finds good reasons for allowing people to pursue their private interests independently of governmental restriction. Or her personal interest may indeed have been the motivating cause of her opposition to the regulation. But the motivation behind her personal judgment is not decisive in assessing questions about whether her position is right – and also assessing whether or not the arguments she marshals are cogent or sound. Until you investigate the field of reasons relevant to the question – hers as well as perhaps others she hasn't considered – you can't say whether or not her position is justified. Any dismissal purely on the grounds that she has a vested interest in the conclusion is irrelevant and exemplifies the *ad hominem*, circumstantial fallacy. (This cautionary rule, by the way, also applies to any claims made by a labor leader or a government regulator who supports the regulation.)

Legitimate appeals to circumstances

The same caveat applies here as to *ad hominem*, direct. If the claim in question is about a person's circumstances, evidence about those circumstances may be relevant. Particularly, in cases where there is a *conflict of interests*, a person's circumstances are directly relevant to evaluations about that person's behavior. For instance, if a company manager hires his lazy son to work there just because he wants to give his son a job, it would not be fallacious to claim that the manager is acting inappropriately. It is in his interests to hire a member of his family, but if that family member is not good for the company, then the manager is violating his duty to run the company profitably. Thus, although this is an appeal to the manager's circumstances, since the conclusion is about those circumstances (the manager's circumstance in being the manager commits him to running the company well), this is not a fallacious appeal to circumstance.

Remember, too, that *interests may be complementary* rather than necessarily in conflict, and that the hiring of a family member is not necessarily inappropriate. If the firm is family owned and operated and the person hired competent, the decision may be justifiable. (Compare 5.10 below.)

Examples of the ad hominem, *circumstantial fallacy*

1. "It's not possible that Senator Wilkins's policies can really be good for businesses, because his parents belonged to unions."
2. "Of course, Mr. Perkins holds untenable views about war; he has stock in BAE Systems."
3. "Senator McCain's claims about China must be false. He is a Republican!"
4. "Dr. Craig is wrong when he says that Homer was a real, historical person. Dr. Craig is a classicist. His job security depends on his advancing that claim."

Tu quoque

Have you ever tried to win an argument by pointing out that your opponent is a hypocrite? If so, have you ever thought that that was just too easy? Out loud you might have exclaimed, "Ha! You're a hypocrite. So, you're wrong!" But in the back of your mind you might have been wondering: *Did I really get the best of that interchange? Was that the relevant point to make?* If so, the little voice in your head was on to something. As we've seen over and over, claims must be evaluated on the basis of reasons and evidence, not on how the person advancing them behaves. Someone who tries to win an argument by pointing out that the other person is a hypocrite commits a variation of the *ad hominem* fallacy known as "*tu quoque*," or "you too" (pronounced: *tü-'kwō-kwē*).

The *tu quoque* is fallacious because a person's hypocrisy, while perhaps morally objectionable, has nothing to do with the *truth* of the claim he or she is defending. For instance, someone who is currently cheating on her husband might nevertheless offer a perfectly cogent argument for why adultery is morally wrong. Pointing out her hypocrisy does not affect the likelihood that her claim is true or undermine the possibility that her argument is a good one. When you accuse someone of hypocrisy you're simply pointing out an inconsistency between the accused's actions and assertions. Big deal! What you really want to know is whether what's claimed is *true* – we need some *reasons* to believe or disbelieve *the claim*. Indeed, if our adulterer's argument is good, then we have good reason to conclude that she is acting immorally. But, the fact that she is acting hypocritically cannot help you evaluate whether her claim about adultery is true or false.

In fact, if you point out that she is a hypocrite, she may actually agree with you. She might say, "Yes, that's right, I'm an adulterer. And since I believe that adultery is wrong, I am doing something wrong. But the fact that I'm doing it doesn't change the fact that it's wrong." Thus, rather than pointing out people's hypocrisy, focus on the reasons they offer (or fail to offer).

Legitimate appeals to hypocrisy

Appealing to a person's inconsistency can be reasonable when the issue in question is a matter of character. For instance, if a politician offers a compelling argument for voting on a particular policy, but someone else produces evidence that this politician has never voted in favor of that sort of policy in the past, then this may constitute a warning signal. Since the Affordable Care Act supported by President Obama (aka "Obamacare" or the ACA) was in part modeled on the healthcare program in Massachusetts developed by Gov. Mitt Romney, we might, in the context of an election where Romney is running for office, reasonably wonder about what's behind his criticisms of the ACA. Romney's behavior may not be problematic; people often have good reasons for changing their minds. But if it turns out that there are ulterior and unpalatable motives behind the change or if something illegal is happening, then the circumstances behind his views may be proper to consider. They would be, in other words, circumstances relevant to deciding whether to re-elect this politician. In cases like these, character problems such as hypocrisy may matter.

In addition, keep in mind that there are cases where the legitimacy of a person's position depends in part on a consistency between claims and behaviors. In those cases, hypocrisy can be a problem. For instance, if someone were applying to be a pastor of a church that regards drinking alcohol as a sin, because serving as an example as well as offering arguments is relevant to the work of pastoring such a congregation, no matter how good an argument against drinking the applicant can present, evidence that he or she regularly drinks alcohol remains a good reason to reject the application.

Examples of the tu quoque *fallacy*

1. Officer: "Did you know you were going 20 miles over the speed limit?"
   Driver: "Yes, but officer, you had to go at least that fast to catch me. So, since you would be a hypocrite to give me a ticket, can I assume I'm off the hook?"
2. "Senator MacMillan can't possibly be serious about her proposal for cutting spending. The senator has more personal debt than any other member of Congress."
3. "That doctor smokes and drinks. It is unlikely that he can advise you about a healthy lifestyle."

5.5 Appeal to Emotions or Appeal to the Heart (*argumentum ad passiones*)

The relationship between emotion and reasoning can be a complex one, but in general we counsel avoiding *appeals to the heart.* In an appeal to the heart or *appeal to emotion* or *passions* fallacy, an arguer attempts to use your emotional attitude toward a situation in order to persuade you to accept a truth claim about that situation. The problem with this strategy is that emotions about a situation are often *irrelevant* to truth claims about that situation. For instance, you may feel badly for someone (you may feel he has had an unfortunate life or that he lacks many of the opportunities and benefits of living in a society that others enjoy or that he has been the victim of a tragedy). Or you may feel fondly about someone, love them, admire them, or take pride in their accomplishments. These feelings, however, are irrelevant to whether or not what he or she claims is true. *Your feelings* about people or about anything, really, are not reliably correlated to evidence that might establish the truth or falsity of *claims* by them or about them. Typically, when people inappropriately appeal to emotions rather than evidence or reasons in support of some claim, they reason fallaciously. There are three versions of the appeal to emotion of which to be wary:

Appeal to pity (*argumentum ad misericordiam*)

Many of us, when we feel sorry for someone, have an uncontrollable urge to help or to remedy what leads us to pity. Unfortunately, this urge may take the form of wishing to agree with or support the pitiful figure's claims. But, as we saw in 5.1 with Jason, doing so risks fallacious reasoning. Imagine you are a voter, and a politician's campaign manager attempts to convince you to vote for that politician on the grounds the politician has suffered a great deal in her early life. You are told, in addition, that because the politician's life has been so pitiful in comparison with her opponent's, you should accept her views on the human source of climate change. Is her pitiful life a good reason to accept those views? Clearly not. Even if you do feel sorry for her, this is no indication that her views on the scientific question of the causes of recent climate change are either true or false.

Legitimate appeals to pity?

Although there is a good bit of psychological research showing that emotions play an important function in our reasoning, and although many philosophers (including *moral sentiment* theorists such as David Hume and Adam Smith) have argued that emotions play an important role in moral and aesthetic reasoning, they are often irrelevant, strictly speaking, to assessing truth claims about factual matters. (For an explanation of some of this research, see Antonio Damasio's 1994 book, *Descartes' Error*.) But if we aren't speaking strictly, could an emotion play a substantive role in reasoning?

Aristotle, in his book *Nicomachean Ethics*, argues that living a virtuous life is a matter of having the right sort of response to various emotional experiences. For example, if you experience fear, you can respond by letting it overwhelm you (cowardice), you can be fearless and overconfident about it (rashness), or you can find a balance, or *mean*, between the feelings of fear and confidence (courage). For Aristotle, the emotion is an indicator; it tells you something about yourself to which you can respond. The difficult part is that it doesn't tell you whether the emotion was appropriate to begin with. So, if you experience extreme fear of open spaces (a type of agoraphobia), then it would be courageous of you to overcome this fear. But the fear doesn't indicate whether there is anything to be afraid of in the first place.

Aristotle, however, also says that emotions can be trained and controlled by reason, so that they pick out important details that motivate us to act. If I see a friend in trouble, I shouldn't have to think, "Would it be good to help this friend?" If my emotions are properly attuned, I will just start helping. If I learn about a child who is being abused and starved and my emotions are properly functioning, the pity I feel is accurately placed, and may lead me to take action. Of course, emotions do not tell us which actions to take or which will be effective, but if they are tuned in to the right sorts of circumstances, they can inform us that something is amiss (or not amiss). It takes many years of critical thinking to see clearly when an emotion is fitting or appropriate, and, if Aristotle is right, it takes a whole lifetime to train our emotions properly. The point here is to emphasize that emotions such as pity can be used in good critical thinking, but they are difficult to use well, and they are often more manipulative than informative.

Examples of the appeal to pity fallacy

1. "Look at those big eyes and those floppy ears! How could you possibly suggest that we should euthanize this puppy? We certainly shouldn't euthanize her."

2. "I've worked so hard on this paper, and I will be on academic probation if I don't get an A, and that will make me lose my scholarship, and then my parents will be upset. You see? For all these reasons, my paper totally deserves an A!"
3. "You should select me rather than the other applicants and host my art show. I mean, even if my art isn't all that great, I've been out of work for months just so I could focus on my craft. I'm the poster child for the starving artist!"
4. "Look, I've been oppressed all my life and have suffered unspeakable injustices. So my views on traffic policy are true."
5. "I lost my spouse and child to a horrible murder, therefore I'm the best consultant for your growing steel manufacturing business."
6. "You just have to come to my party! You wouldn't want me to be sad, would you? I'd be hurt for weeks if you don't make it!"

Appeal to fear (*argumentum ad metum*)

In an *appeal to fear*, an arguer uses an unreasonable threat of bad consequences to convince his or her audience to accept a claim. (For that reason, sometimes this fallacy is called argument from adverse consequences.) Now, sometimes fear is relevant to deliberations. So, for example, information about the consequences of smoking might produce a reasonable fear of what might happen if you take up a cigarette habit, and that fear and the *reasons* that motivate it might be relevant in your deliberations about doing so. If, however, I try to convince you to accept a claim simply by instilling in you fear that is unreasonable, then you do possess a reason to accept the conclusion – but not a good reason, and certainly not a reason that *justifies* the *truth* of the claim. See "legitimate appeals to pity" above for more on legitimate appeals to emotion.

Examples of the appeal to fear fallacy

1. "If you don't accept these views on the existence of God, people will shun you."
2. "You know what will happen to you if you don't agree with our dictator's declaration that 2+2=5. So, of course 2+2=5. Right?"
3. "I fear the consequences of acknowledging that my son is a drug dealer, so he is not a drug dealer."
4. "My spouse would be so angry with me if I agreed with your political position, so I have to stand against it."

Appeal to guilt

In the *appeal to guilt* version of the appeal to emotion, an arguer attempts to convince you to believe or act by inciting feelings of guilt in you. Many instances of the appeal to guilt occur in relationships, when one person attempts to use guilt as emotional blackmail. For example, an overly clingy mother who wants her son to drive her to the supermarket might remark under her breath so that her son can hear her, "You would think any good son who loves his mother would drive her to the supermarket." The implication is that the mother–son relationship will somehow be damaged by the son's refusal to drive her, or that the mother's approval of her son will diminish in virtue of this refusal. The mother is trying to incite guilt in the son to motivate him to drive her to the store. But this is a fallacious (and malicious) tactic. There may be no relevant connection between a son's refusing to drive his mother to the supermarket and the strength of his relationship with his mother, as the son may have perfectly legitimate and compelling reasons for refusing that would not affect their relationship in the least. In fact, her appeal to guilt in such a manipulative way may give him a good reason not to drive her to the store.

Legitimate appeals to guilt?

It's important to remember that *doing wrong* and *feeling guilty* are in particular instances independent. You may feel guilty for acts that are perfectly permissible (e.g., drinking alcohol), and you may not feel guilty for acts that are impermissible (e.g., stealing from your neighbor). Remember, too, that guilt might be evaluated in its relationship to conduct in either psychological or logical ways. Taking a certain course of action, for example, may have the psychological effect of relieving guilt, even though it may be unreasonable to do so (e.g., giving up soft drinks to alleviate guilt over having lied to your parents about some serious matter). Feeling guilty may, indeed, be an important and legitimate signal to motivate you to ask, "Hey, is this conduct okay?" That is, it may constitute a good reason to *double-check* whether or not your behavior is morally *justified* – even though it's not *by itself* sufficient to justify the claim that your behavior is immoral. Survivors of disasters where many others are killed often suffer, for example, from *survivor guilt*, the sense that it was wrong for them to have lived while others perished. That guilt is not well grounded. On the other hand, guilt over war crimes, human rights abuses, or other serious crimes might rightly be understood to motivate *reparations* or *restorative* efforts to mend the harm in some way, as far as reasonably possible. Feeling guilty *and* having good reasons for having done wrong can be good grounds for apologies, reparations, or restorative efforts. But without good reasons for understanding the wrong, those gestures may be misplaced.

Examples of the appeal to guilt fallacy

1. "In the next 60 seconds, an animal will be abused or beaten. How could you live with yourself if you don't give money to the Stop the Abuse Foundation!?!" [There may be good reasons to give to this charity, but the threat of feeling guilty if you don't is almost certainly not one of them.]

2. You've been such a lousy spouse, having had that affair years ago. You owe it to me to agree that we should invest our life savings in stock in Enron Corporation." [Enron went bankrupt in 2001.]
3. "I feel so guilty about how I neglected my daughter after my divorce. So, I must agree with her now that astrology is scientifically sound."
4. "You've spent your entire life as the member of a privileged group, pampered and mooching off the hard work of others. I know you feel guilty about that. You should definitely therefore accept my claim that the interior angles of a proper triangle add up to 450 degrees, as well as my other beliefs that up is down and black is white."
5. "You feel guilty about forgetting my birthday, therefore you should help with this river cleanup project."

5.6 Appeal to Force (*argumentum ad baculum*)

The appeal to force or *ad baculum* (appeal to the stick) fallacy overlaps with the appeal to fear, in particular with regard to those fears generated by *threats*. That's because an *ad baculum* argument presents a threat of force as grounds for accepting some claim as true. For example, during periods of the Spanish Inquisition, people who wouldn't convert to Christianity were threatened with expulsion from Spain, or, worse, torture and death. (For similar reasons the appeal to force is sometimes called the *Galileo fallacy* – that is, since Galileo was threatened with torture unless he recanted the Copernican astronomical theories he advanced.) Threats of this sort aren't "arguments" in the technical sense; they are more appropriately thought of as *coercive* declarations. Nevertheless, the employment of a threat is presented often in a way that mimics an argument. A threat, for example, may operate like a premise in argument form such as this one:

1. If you don't accept *p*, I will do *x*.
2. You don't want *x*.
3. Therefore, you should accept *p*.

So, even threats can be evaluated as arguments. The same goes for the fallacious use of feelings of guilt, fear, and pity.

Because of this threats do constitute reasons – often *compelling* ones – to believe or behave in certain ways. But reasons of this sort aren't consistent with good reasoning. In a good argument, the premises give epistemic support (i.e., support *relevant* to *knowing*) for the *truth* of the conclusion. In the case of threats, this is not the case. The "should" in the conclusion refers to a *practical* reason, not an *epistemic* reason.

The practical and the epistemic

We'll see later, in Chapter 6, how reasons that raise the likelihood that a conclusion is *true* are called "epistemic" reasons because of their relationship with knowledge. Practical reasons, on the other hand, can motivate belief or action independently of the truth of a conclusion. For instance, I may have a practical reason to drive on the right side of the road (in the US) when no one is around, namely, so I won't get a ticket. In this case, it is my *dislike* or aversion for tickets that motivates me; there is no set of premises that would support the claim, "It is true (outside of practical considerations) that everyone should drive on the right side of the road." We must be careful here because practical reasons aren't necessarily *bad* reasons. If you only go to church because your mom goes and you want to make her happy, you have good practical reasons for going, even though you haven't thereby proven the truth of anything.

Examples of the ad baculum *fallacy*

1. "You'll agree that the Sun orbits around the Earth, right? You wouldn't want your bones broken, would you?"
2. "Your answer on the exam was wrong. Why? Let's put it this way: disagreeing with me on this could hurt your grade significantly." [Note: even if grading is an appropriate method of evaluation, and even if the teacher is an appropriate authority on right answers in this context, this threat is no answer to the question of why the answer is wrong.]
3. "I'd hate to see your career come to an end because you believe the CEO's plan is not the most efficient or profitable."
4. "You'll agree with me that the Greeks fought the Chinese at the battle of Marathon, or else I'll never speak to you again."
5. If you don't believe in Santa Claus, you won't get any presents.

5.7 Appeal to Ignorance (*argumentum ad ignorantiam*)

"I've looked everywhere in my toolbox, and so I've concluded that my hammer just isn't there." Is there anything wrong with that reasoning? No, but be careful. By itself the absence of evidence is not evidence *for* or *against* anything. In what logicians call an *appeal to ignorance* fallacy, an arguer appeals simply to *a lack of evidence* for or against a claim as proof for the falsity or truth, respectively, of that claim. Having no evidence for a claim does not constitute evidence against its being true. Conversely, having no evidence against a claim does not constitute evidence in favor of its truth. If we have no evidence for or against a claim, then, barring practical reasons for believing, we should suspend judgment about its truth or falsity.

To attempt to justify a claim on the basis of a lack of evidence is to *appeal to ignorance* as evidence. For instance, if someone wanted to defend the truth of the claim: "There is intelligent extra-terrestrial life," he might offer as a reason: "There isn't any evidence against the existence of such life." Even if he were able to substantiate this claim (that is, even if he could show you every news and scientific report since, say, the 1950s and show that not one of them includes any evidence that intelligent aliens *do not* exist), this still wouldn't be sufficient evidence for the claim that intelligent aliens *do* exist. If this is our only evidence, the rational conclusion is to suspend judgment about the existence of extra-terrestrial life.

Similarly, if someone wanted to defend the truth of the claim: "Gremlins don't exist," she might offer as a reason: "There isn't any evidence that gremlins do exist." Again, even if she were to show successfully that there is no evidence that gremlins exist, this wouldn't be sufficient evidence that gremlins don't exist. If this is our only evidence, the rational conclusion, again, is to suspend judgment about the existence of gremlins. (Of course, you might say it's not our only evidence, because we have had experience of the way people make up fictitious beings very much like gremlins. In that sense, they exist merely as characters in human stories and myths.) The point here is subtle, but important. Having *no evidence* is not the same as having *negative evidence*, that is, as having disconfirmed hypotheses.

Negative evidence and no evidence

Imagine a scientific experiment designed to test whether a certain drug, Drug *X*, reduces blood pressure. Let's say that, after the test, the blood pressure readings are identical for people who took the drug and for those who didn't. In this case, the results do not suggest that Drug *X* is effective, but this isn't "no evidence," this is *negative* or *falsifying* evidence, evidence that Drug *X does not* lower blood pressure. We obtained this evidence by formulating a hypothesis: If Drug *X* reduces blood pressure, then, all other things being equal, the blood pressure readings will be lower for those who took Drug *X* than for those who didn't. Since the consequent of this conditional was not true for our test group, we have refuted the hypothesis that Drug *X* lowers blood pressure (recall *modus tollens*, 4.2). In addition to (a) not finding evidence of the hammer's presence in the toolbox, we also know (b) that we've checked the entire box and eliminated *all the possible ways* it could have been in the box. Therefore, we have more than an absence of evidence; we also have positive evidence that the hammer isn't there.

If we take this reasoning and apply it to extra-terrestrial life, we will obtain very different results. We have no idea what sort of hypothesis to form about intelligent extra-terrestrials. We might say: "If there were intelligent extra-terrestrials, they would have contacted us using means we can comprehend." But why believe this? The universe is so incredibly large and the number of possible types of intelligent extra-terrestrial life is so vastly large that it would be difficult to formulate any testable hypothesis about them. It would be practically impossible for us to eliminate all the possible ways and locations in which they might exist. Perhaps they are as ignorant of us as we are of them. Perhaps their technology, despite their intelligence, is vastly inferior to ours, and they couldn't contact us even if they wanted to. Perhaps they live billions upon billions of light years away. Therefore, we actually have no evidence (rather than negative evidence) for the existence of extra-terrestrial life and should suspend judgment.

The conclusion about gremlins is only slightly different. Whether or not the claim, "there isn't any evidence that gremlins do exist," expresses a lack of evidence or, rather, negative evidence depends on context and the arguer's intent. If the arguer actually has a hypothesis in mind that has been disconfirmed by evidence, then she would not have committed a fallacy, and the resulting argument may be good or bad for other reasons. But if she simply cites a lack of any evidence, the argument is fallacious.

Examples of the appeal to ignorance fallacy

1. "Well, you know God doesn't exist, right? There is no evidence that He exists, so clearly, He doesn't."
2. Caller: "Jimmy Hoffa is alive!"
   Journalist: "How do you know that?"
   Caller: "Well, you have no evidence that he isn't."
3. Student: "It has to be true that high fructose corn syrup is safe."
   Professor: "Why is that?"
   Student: "Because scientists don't have any evidence that it isn't safe."
   Professor: "Have scientists studied the effects of high fructose corn syrup?
   Student: "Well, I don't know."
4. "There is no evidence that ghosts don't exist. Therefore, they exist."
5. "There is no evidence that there is not a fault line in this area. So, you should get earthquake insurance just in case."
6. "Our current method works. We know that. We don't know anything about this new method. We have no idea whether it works. Therefore, the current method is probably better than this new method."

5.8 Appeal to Novelty (*argumentum ad novitatem*)

"Have you heard about the new theory that wearing a coprolite necklace protects you from cancer? It's the next, new thing. I'm going with it." (A coprolite is fossilized excrement or feces.) In certain instances, we may be drawn to a claim or action because it is new and exciting. We are often attracted to novelty. But we must beware. The excitement we feel about novelty doesn't constitute evidence or reason to think that any particular claim is true. In the fallacious *appeal to novelty*, an arguer attempts to convince you of a claim simply on the basis of the claim's newness.

The appeal to novelty is common in advertising and political campaigns. The newness of a product is often used to sell it, usually with taglines such as, "Be the first to try *X*" or "Don't miss out on this revolutionary *X*." In addition, any modification of an old product is used as grounds to prefer the modified version: "Get the new version of *X*." Political campaigns, especially for those candidates running for an office for the first time, often appeal to "Change!" as a central reason for voting for that candidate.

But, of course, the fact that a claim is new is not in itself a reason to accept that claim. Newness or novelty itself is not clearly a truth-making feature of claims at all. It could, after all, be a new but also lousy idea. Sometimes newer is not better or truer, and so, as a general rule, the *irrelevance* of the newness to the truth of a claim renders appeals to novelty fallacious.

Legitimate appeals to novelty

Novelty can, in rare circumstances, constitute a reason to *consider* adopting a claim or performing an action. For instance, if you aren't quite satisfied with the current view on some topic, evidence that there is a new alternative may constitute a reason to investigate this alternative. Thus, while an appeal to novelty does not constitute conclusive reasons for adopting a claim as true or right, it can introduce new possibilities to investigate.

Examples of the appeal to novelty fallacy

1. "Be the first to try the new Shiny Mop! It's new, so it must be better!"
2. "New SquashWash! Because it's new, it's much better for washing squash than the old SquashWash."
3. "Tired of the same old politics? Vote for change! Elect John Smith! He's the new guy!"
4. "iPhone 5. The biggest thing to happen to iPhone since iPhone." [An actual advertisement.]
5. Sam: "I just have to have the 2013 Mazda. It must be great." Pat: "But your 2010 is running just fine, and you keep telling me how great it is." Sam: "Yes, but the 2013 is the new model!"

5.9 Appeal to the People (*argumentum ad populum*)

"Come on! Try this new recreational drug! It's perfectly safe. After all, everyone's doing it!" In the *argumentum ad populum* or appeal to the people fallacy (also known as the appeal to popular preference), an arguer misleadingly argues for the acceptance of some claim on the grounds that lots of people accept it.

Bandwagon

When the appeal is simply to the large *quantity* or *number* of people that accept a claim, the error is known as the *bandwagon* fallacy. For instance, someone might argue that you should believe that the Earth is spherical, rather than flat, on the grounds that: "Well, everyone believes it is spherical." Even if it is true that the Earth is spherical (which in fact is not exactly true since it's a bit pear-shaped), the fact that everyone believes it doesn't itself constitute *evidence* that it is true. Beliefs about reality can be mistaken, and a lot of people can share the same mistaken belief. Thus, attempting to justify a claim on the grounds that a lot of people believe it is to appeal to irrelevant information and, therefore, fallacious.

As children, many of us were tempted to appeal to *en masse* belief as a reason for doing something, e.g., "But Mom, everybody's wearing their hair this way!" But our parents were quick to point out the fallacy in such reasoning by asking whether we would follow everyone else in jumping off a bridge if they were all doing it. Of course, the authority that "everyone" exercises on young minds makes this, despite our parents' good advice, a tempting fallacy.

There is a subtle point here that's worth noting. The *ad populum bandwagon* fallacy is an appeal to a large number of people, not specific groups of which you may or may not wish to be a member. If someone tries to convince you to believe or do something by pointing out the affinity of a specific group for this belief or action – for example, "Republicans everywhere believe *X*," or, "The discriminating shopper buys *X*" – the fallacy committed is not properly an *ad populum bandwagon*, but some other variant such as an *appeal to snobbery* or *appeal to vanity*.

Appeal to snobbery

In the fallacious *appeal to snobbery*, an arguer attempts to convince an audience wrongly to accept or reject a claim simply on the grounds that a select or elite group of people accept or reject it. For instance, imagine you happen to mention that you think private citizens should be able to own automatic rifles. If someone were to condemn this belief by saying, "Oh, that's such a Republican belief, and I know you don't agree with *them*," or "That's what those low-class gun-nuts say," he would be committing the appeal to snobbery fallacy. There may be good reasons to disagree with your claim, but the fact that people you don't like also accept it is not one of them. Similarly, an appeal to snobbery might call upon a group thought to be superior.

Appeal to vanity

The related *appeal to vanity* argues for some claim on the grounds that beautiful people accept it. A whisky manufacturer might depict in its advertising wealthy, elite, or extraordinarily beautiful people drinking its product in the hope that those who see it will conclude that the whisky is superior and worth the price. Perhaps not surprisingly, simply raising the price of a product can elicit the same response, even when the product is identical in quality to a cheaper product. The higher price seems to signal that the product is proper to the rich and elite.

The important point to note here is that there are lots of reasons to agree or disagree with some group, but it doesn't follow from their being elite and beautiful, or common and ugly that they are right or wrong about a claim. You may disagree vehemently with anti-abortion activists, or alternatively, with pro-choice groups; nevertheless, the people of both groups probably agree that the Earth is not a disk, that $2 + 2 = 4$, that human life is (in general) valuable. It would seem strange to respond to someone who criticizes the murder of a three-year-old child by saying, "Oh, that's one of those pro-life positions. You don't really believe that, do you?" The relevant question is whether that group is *right* about a belief or behavior, not whether that *group* holds that belief or defends that behavior.

This fallacy is easily confused with a couple of others, and it will be helpful to keep a few distinctions in mind. The appeal to vanity and appeal to snobbery fallacies are easily mistaken for the *ad hominem* fallacy. But recall that the latter appeals to a person's character or circumstances, not the group of which the person is a member. This becomes tricky when a person's circumstances include membership in a controversial group. For instance, if Bill were a Roman Catholic and you have misgivings about the Roman Catholic Church, you may be tempted to disregard Bill's claims on the grounds that he's a member of this institution. This would be an *ad hominem*, circumstantial: you are dismissing *Bill's* claims on the basis of *his* circumstances. On the other hand, let's say Bill is not a Roman Catholic, but you dismiss one of his claims on the grounds that it is the sort of thing that a Roman Catholic would say. This is an appeal to snobbery: you are dismissing Bill's claim on the basis of its association with a *group* you find objectionable. Since both mistakes are fallacious, nothing much hangs on your being able to draw the distinction perfectly; but, for precision, we thought it important to include.

Similarly, the appeal to snobbery is easily confused with the *appeal to celebrity*, since appeals to celebrity attempt to motivate you to be like a certain type of person – a person toward whose categorization as "a celebrity" you may have a snobbish attitude. For instance, if the pop singer Madonna attempted to use her popularity to convince you to vote, this would be a fallacious appeal to celebrity. Who is *she* to tell *you* that you should vote? This appeal is not attempting to attract you to a particular *group* but to the views of a particular celebrity. Because Madonna is not obviously an authority on political processes, the appeal can only be to her status as a celebrity. And the appeal to celebrity is probably better categorized as a species of the appeal to *unqualified (or inappropriate) authority*, which we discuss in the next section.

Examples of the appeal to snobbery and appeal to vanity fallacies

1. "Of course you should accept the truth of atheism. Every sophisticated person is an atheist."
2. "You should definitely buy the $1,000 Manolo Blahniks. Nobody would be caught dead without them this season. Well, nobody who's anybody. It's *de rigueur* for the beautiful people."

3. "You accept Darwinian evolution, right? I mean, only a backward-thinking, religious fundamentalist wouldn't."
4. "Why wouldn't you vote for an increase in taxes? Only a greedy, self-centered jerk wouldn't agree to this tax-increase."
5. "Everybody hip knows that vaccinations aren't safe. So, they're not safe."

Legitimate appeals to the people

There are cases where agreement *en masse* does seem to confer evidence on a claim. According to some philosophers, for example pragmatists such as Richard Rorty (1931–2007), truth is essentially defined by human agreement - agreement about what we perceive, about what perceptions are accurate, about what criteria and standards and methods are appropriate to discern truth, and about even what words mean and how ideas are to be applied to particular situations. But if all knowledge requires intersubjective agreement, wouldn't all knowledge claims be guilty of the *ad populum* fallacy? No. Even if the pragmatists are right that all truth is a matter of agreement, there are still cases where agreement appropriately underwrites truth and cases where it does not. The fallacy of appeal to the people would only refer, then, to those cases where it is not appropriate. How might we discern the difference?

Consider cases where a group of experts in a particular field has reached a consensus on some scientific findings. For instance, if all oncology researchers (scientists who investigate cancer) agree that *X* is the best available method of treating cancer, this would seem to be a good reason to believe that *X* is the best available method. Who would have better information about cancer treatments than people who study cancer treatments? Similarly, if all economists agree that an increase in government spending decreases unemployment but raises inflation, then that seems to be a reason to believe it. Who would have better information about the outcomes of these events than people who study these events?

How much of a consensus must exist among scientists before one of their claims is legitimate? That's a question raised by some who refuse to accept that a scientific consensus exists about anthropogenic climate change and global warming. But even if we can't always tell when there's enough agreement to constitute a reason to accept a group's claims, it's nevertheless true that specialized study confers significant authority on the agreement of experts in a field.

To be sure, this doesn't mean that scientists and economists and other experts are always right. We know that science has a deplorable history of getting at incontrovertible truth: Ptolemy's ideas gave way to Copernicus's ideas, which gave way to Kepler's ideas, which gave way to Newton's ideas, which gave way to Einstein's ... and so on. Nevertheless, people who study particular fields often have a powerful insight into what works in those fields.

In addition to appeals to specialized agreement among experts and to fundamental agreements about human experience, we may have reason to appeal to belief *en masse* simply as a guide to research. Ancient stoics, among others, argued that a deity exists on the basis of what became known as the *consensus gentium* or *consensus of humanity*. Because the *gentium* has proven to be wrong historically about so many things, few today regard human consensus to be convincing as a matter of proof or evidence. The ubiquity of religious belief in divinities remains, however, a provocative fact. That fact may offer a reason to inquire: "Why have all these people believed divine beings exist?" This sort of question has motivated research in sociology, psychology, neurology, and recently, genetics (e.g., is there a "God gene"?). Similarly, marketers may want to know what products people generally agree to buy in order to predict whether a particular advertising campaign will be effective. If a product sells well despite its poor quality, what convinced people to buy so much of it? So, again the fact that lots of people agree that a claim is true is not evidence that it is true, but recognizing widespread belief may help to guide other investigations.

Examples of the appeal to the people fallacy

1. "Ford: America's Best-Selling Pickup." [This is an actual marketing slogan from Ford Motors.]
2. "Reading: Everybody's doing it!" [This is an actual marketing slogan from PBS (Public Broadcasting Service).]
3. "Of course the world is going to end in a great apocalyptic event. We know this because every culture has believed something like it."
4. "That movie is definitely worth seeing. How do I know? Because everyone's seen it. Do *you* know of anyone who hasn't seen it? I don't."
5. "Buy Drek Burgers! Millions and millions have been sold."
6. "It's common knowledge that stress causes ulcers." [It *was* common knowledge until Dr. Barry Marshall proved that bacteria cause them by infecting himself.]

5.10 Appeal to Unqualified Authority (*argumentum ad verecundiam*)

"Steve Jobs said that painting is a great work of art. So it must be." In the *appeal to unqualified authority* fallacy (also known as the appeal to inappropriate authority), an arguer attempts to convince an audience to accept a belief or behavior on the grounds of some kind of authority. Of course, not every appeal to authority is fallacious; the principal reason we rely on textbooks in college is that experts are authorities on the subject of their expertise. Not everyone, however, to whom we appeal as an authority really is an authority. If someone isn't qualified to speak to the truth of a particular claim, then any appeal to that person's endorsement or rejection of that claim as evidence is fallacious.

For instance, your English professor may be incredibly smart – perhaps first in his class – but he may be completely ignorant about economics. So, if you wanted to provide evidence for a claim like, "Increased government spending shortens recessions," it would not help your case to say, "Well, my English professor says it's true." Given his dearth of expertise on economic matters, any appeal to your English professor to support economic claims is fallacious. Similarly, your *economics* professor may have won a Nobel Prize while being deplorably deficient in an understanding of English literature. Thus, any appeal to your economics professor to support an interpretation of Chaucer's *Canterbury Tales* would be fallacious.

Advertisers make widespread use of the appeal to unqualified authority. Commercials that appeal to "9 out of 10 doctors" but do not tell you what sort of doctor, commit the fallacy of appeal to unqualified authority. The word "doctor" derives from the Latin *doct* for learned, but not all doctors are physicians (for example, most English professors are doctors – i.e., hold PhDs), and not all physicians are equally qualified to speak on any health matter. Researchers carry more authority in their areas than clinicians (see 9.6). Oncologists have had more extensive training in cancer research than podiatrists. General practitioners have more extensive experience in treating common illnesses than surgeons. And medical doctors understand human disease better than veterinarians Therefore, the fact that a "doctor" (with no further qualification) endorses a product or idea may not be terribly relevant to whether or not you should accept the product or idea.

Advertisements that include celebrities who have no expertise with respect to the products they are promoting commit this fallacy, too. For instance, Tiger Woods is not (as far as we know) an expert on watches. Therefore, Tiger Woods's endorsement of a particular brand of watch illegitimately positions him as an authority on watches, and is, therefore, fallacious. Using a widely recognized face or name to sell a product or idea may not only be an appeal to unqualified authority but also a fallacious appeal known as the *appeal to celebrity*, a version of the appeal to unqualified authority (compare 5.9, appeal to snobbery, and 5.4 *ad hominem* fallacies, circumstantial).

Could Tiger Woods legitimately advertise golf clubs? After all, he *is* an expert on golf. That depends on how his testimony about the product is being used. To see why, it is helpful to draw a distinction. There are two ways an appeal to authority can be unqualified and inappropriate:

1. *The authority can be irrelevant, or*
2. *The authority can be biased.*

If an authority is *irrelevant*, he or she simply doesn't possess the qualifications to speak on the claim being evaluated. If an authority is biased, he or she may know quite a lot about the topic at hand but nevertheless possess a skewed judgment, perhaps because of a vested interest in particular claims, regardless of whether he or she is an expert on the subject. One might think of this problem as *compromised or corrupted authority*.

The examples given so far are examples of *irrelevant* authorities. Your English professor isn't qualified to speak with authority about economics and your economics professor isn't qualified to speak with authority about medieval literature. The unqualified doctor and celebrity examples suffer the same deficiency. But let's say that a person *is* an expert relevant to the claim or action at issue. Does this automatically render her testimony legitimate? Unfortunately, no.

In many cases, relevant experts are compensated to endorse a product or idea. This doesn't mean that the expert doesn't sincerely endorse the product or idea (he certainly may), and it doesn't mean that the expert doesn't really have good evidence that the claim is true (again, he may very well have such evidence). The fact, however, that he is receiving compensation to endorse something raises a question for the astute critical thinker. There is now a new incentive to say "*X* is true," or "you should buy *X*." If this incentive did not exist, it would be easier to believe that the expert is endorsing the idea or product because he finds it compelling. And so, now we need more information.

Returning to our Tiger Woods case, Woods could certainly speak to the benefits of a certain golf club. But if he is paid to endorse it, we need to know more than *that* he endorses it – we need to know *why*. We need him to explain his reasons for preferring one club over another; that way, we can evaluate the reasons for ourselves ... or at least get a second opinion.

Similarly, at one point in his career the famous astrophysicist Neil deGrasse Tyson began advocating for an increase in public funds for NASA (the National Aeronautics and Space Administration – a publicly funded government agency). Importantly, Tyson is the director of the Hayden Planetarium at the publicly funded American Museum of Natural History, and he receives many other benefits from the government (including prestigious seats on important committees and segments on publically funded television programs). Does any of this mean that Tyson is an *inappropriate* advocate for increased NASA funding? No, of course not. He may be the *most* appropriate person for the job given his expertise and experience. Nevertheless, his vested interest in public funding (his primary source of income and prestige) renders his testimony by itself insufficient. Perhaps NASA is sufficiently funded and Tyson is hoping for a raise. Or perhaps NASA is wasteful with its resources, or it funds projects that serve no public good – perhaps private scientific organizations (e.g., research and development departments in large corporations) are better for the "public" than NASA. What we need from Tyson is not simply his endorsement, but his *rationale* for it.

What these examples show is that the appeal to unqualified authority may be committed even when the authority is an expert in the field. Even experts are subject to biases, and when an expert has a vested interest in a particular claim or behavior it is imperative that we, as critical thinkers, press these experts for evidence beyond their mere testimony. If we do not, we will have succumbed to the fallacious appeal to unqualified (biased) authority.

Before we move on, consider a less obvious case. Imagine that a publication called *The Journal of New Testament Studies* publishes an article claiming that Pontius Pilate never existed. Pilate is certainly mentioned in the New Testament, and it would seem that this journal has a vested interest in such claims. So, is the journal biased? Whether it is an appropriate authority depends on what else you know about the journal. If it is a journal that publishes based on "blind reviews" (the reviewer does not know the author's name) and its editorial board is made up of well-respected scholars who study the New Testament, then it is likely an authoritative source of scholarship on the New Testament. A vested interest in a particular subject matter is not what biases an authority (if so, no expert could be regarded as authoritative by virtue of studying only one field). A commitment, however, to a certain view could bias certain decisions. For instance, if all the editing scholars of this journal are known to have a particular perspective on the New Testament (say, that Pontius Pilate didn't exist) and they only publish scholars who agree with this perspective, then the journal is less respectable as an authority.

Finally, the epistemic standpoints that people occupy in dominant or subordinate strata of society may, according to some analyses, affect the authority (as well as the accuracy) of their claims. We'll address that issue in 7.6.

Examples of the appeal to unqualified authority

1. "Seven out of ten experts prefer Jones's Soap over all the rest!" [Experts in what? Do they have relevant expertise?]
2. "Actress Wanda Sykes says you shouldn't chain your dog." [What makes Sykes's views on animal welfare relevant?]
3. "Paid PETA spokesperson says eating meat is immoral." [May be biased because his income and status is connected to that view. Note that you would commit the *ad hominem*, circumstantial fallacy if you concluded that his view is false or wrong.]
4. "Rock musician Ted Nugent argues that the Second Amendment to the US Constitution guarantees private, individual citizens the right to own automatic weapons. Therefore, the Constitution guarantees that right." [Ted may not possess sufficient expertise to make authoritative judgments about constitutional law.]
5. "The CEO of Chevrolet claims that Chevy trucks are the best. Therefore, there can be absolutely no doubt whatsoever that they are." [Potentially, the claim could be biased because her income and status give her an interest in supporting that view, and so a good critical thinker would do well to be suspicious of her authority in making that claim. But note that you would commit the *ad hominem*, circumstantial fallacy to conclude that her view is false.]
6. "The man at the bus stop says that all Arabs are Muslims. So it must be true."

5.11 Fallacy of Accident

"You can't prosecute me for fraud. The First Amendment to the Constitution grants me the right of free speech, and that includes fraudulent speech." In the *fallacy of accident*, an arguer wrongly applies a principle that holds generally (but not universally) to an obviously abnormal scenario. A general principle may simply be a *heuristic* or *rule of thumb*, and some examples include: It's cold in winter; aspirin cures headaches; birds can fly. There are obvious exceptions to each of these (e.g., sometimes it's warm in winter; some birds are flightless), but, in general, they are true. If someone applies one of these rules of thumb in cases where the generalization doesn't obviously hold, he or she may be committing the fallacy of accident.

For example, if someone were to try to convince you that the death penalty is immoral because "Killing is wrong," that precept may be true in general, but may not be true in this case. Perhaps some people forfeit what we might regard as a right to life by intentionally killing someone else. If this is correct, it is consistent to believe both that it is wrong, in general, to kill, and that the death penalty is not in all cases immoral. Similarly, we might agree that killing is in general wrong, but allow that it is permissible to kill in self-defense. Applying this general rule to these exceptional cases is fallacious, and cannot be done without further rationale for why the rule applies to these well-recognized potential exceptions.

That's true not only of rough rules of thumb but even for legal principles and laws. The First Amendment to the US Constitution guarantees the right of free speech and expression. But it would be wrong to appeal to the First Amendment to defend fraud, blackmail, terroristic threats, and harassment. Moreover, as Justice Oliver Wendell Holmes Jr. famously argued in the 1919 decision to the US Supreme Court case, *Schenck v. the United States*, shouting "Fire!" in a crowded theater (that is, placing others in danger) is not protected speech. The principle of free speech does not apply to all speech, and to misapply the principle is to commit the fallacy of accident.

The fallacy of accident is subtly different from hasty generalizations. In the fallacy of accident, one applies a generalization to a particular case (moving from the general to the particular) wherein it is not obvious that the generalization holds. In a case of hasty generalization, the inference moves in the other direction (from particular to general), as one tries fallaciously to infer a generalization from particular cases. For this reason, hasty generalization is sometimes called *converse accident*.

Examples of the fallacy of accident

1. "Of course felons should be allowed to vote. We live in a democracy, and as a matter of political principle the citizens of a democracy ought all to have the right to vote."
2. "You should not resist an attacker, because as a matter of moral principle it's wrong to hurt people."
3. "There is no such thing as a just war. Why? The commandment says, 'thou shalt not kill.'"
4. "I know it hurts, but don't stop! You know the rule: no pain, no gain!"

5.12 False Dilemma

In the *false dilemma* fallacy (also known as the *fallacy of false alternatives* and the *either/or* fallacy), an arguer presents his audience with two options that either aren't exhaustive of all relevant possibilities or don't exclude each other, and then draws a conclusion from the assumption that they are or do. For instance, imagine someone were to say: "Surely you would rather work for a living than wait to win the lottery. Therefore, you can't support the lottery." Since *working for a living* doesn't exclude *winning the lottery*, as you can do both, the argument constitutes a false dilemma: it assumes you can prefer only one or the other.

Similarly, if someone were to claim, "You should become a member of the conservative party," and were to attempt to justify this by saying, "Well, you're either a conservative or a liberal, and I know you're not a liberal," then this is a false dilemma because there are obviously more options than being conservative or liberal: you could be apolitical, or independent, or libertarian, or socialist, or something else entirely. To try to convince you to become a member of a political party by artificially restricting your options is fallacious.

Dilemmas are genuine (and therefore, not "false") when an arguer can establish that the two options presented are, indeed, the only two available or relevant options and that those options actually do exclude each other. In some cases, there may be only two options available. For instance, "Legally speaking, in the US you can be either married or not married." In other cases, even though there are more than two options, the audience may nevertheless only consider two to be relevant or legitimate. For instance, if two centrists in a Western capitalist country are debating the best form of government, they are likely to regard fascist and anarchist policies as off-limits. Even though anarchist and fascist policies are logically possible, the centrists' assumptions about the best possible policies constrain which options are considered legitimate. If, under these constrained conditions, they are forced to choose between only two options, then arguably no false dilemma has been committed. Context, in other words, matters.

Examples of the false dilemma fallacy

1. "You either support public education, or you don't love children."
2. "You're either a morally lax liberal or a greedy, immoral capitalist."
3. "You either support more taxes to fund social services, or you're not a Christian."
4. "I would rather support my own family than be forced to support someone else's. Therefore, I'm against more taxes for social services."
5. "Either we invade Iraq, or Al Qaeda will take over the US."
6. "The world's population is growing at an unsustainable rate. Executing people is not an option. Therefore, we must begin mandating sterilization."

7. "We need to move to the new education models, otherwise we will get behind other schools. The new models set the pace for contemporary education, and we want to keep up."

5.13 Semantic and Syntactic Fallacies

Natural languages are complex and fluid. Meanings and usage evolve and change, and this subtlety makes poetry, song lyrics, and literature endlessly creative and intriguing. Unfortunately, the complexity and fluidity that allows us to communicate subtly also allows us to obscure meaning and to mislead one another, sometimes in illogical ways. The most common forms of the logical misuse of language of this sort are ambiguity and vagueness.

Ambiguity, two types: lexical and syntactic

A claim can be ambiguous in two ways. On the one hand, *semantically* one of the words in the claim can have two (or more) distinct *meanings*. ("Semantics" refers to the meanings of expressions.) For instance, if someone says, "Meet me at the bank," there may be (without some context) some confusion as to what she means by "bank," whether she means a financial institution, a blood bank, or a river bank. Similarly, if someone says, "She can't find a match," there may be some confusion as to what he means by "match," whether he means a fire-starter, something like a tennis or soccer game, a romantic partner, or a matching sock or glove. In the claim, "She shot him in the temple," it is not clear whether the word *temple* refers to the location of the wound (the front side of the head) or the location of the shooting (a place of religious worship). We call this semantic sort of ambiguity *lexical ambiguity*, the ambiguity of a word or term (note that dictionaries are also called *lexicons*).

To clarify a lexically ambiguous claim, either add a qualifying word (such as "blood" or "river" to bank) or choose a different, unambiguous phrase (instead of, "I'm going to the bank," say something like, "I'm going to deposit a check").

Examples of lexical ambiguity

1. "All this trouble was caused by his shorts." [Does *shorts* mean "short circuits," "short trousers," "men's underwear," or "financial transactions" called shorts?]
2. "The priest married my sister last week." [Does *married* mean "performed the ceremony" or "became the husband of your sister"?]
3. "Jack's in the can downtown." [Following common slang, does *can* mean "jail" or "the restroom"?]
4. "He's a good soldier." [Does *good* mean "competent and effective at being a soldier" or "a morally good person"?]

On the other hand, a claim can be worded in such a way that there are two or more ways to interpret one of its *phrases*. For instance, if someone says, "She agreed to marry him in the woods," it is unclear whether the phrase *in the woods* should be interpreted as the location of the *agreement* (where she agreed) or the location of the *marriage* (where she will marry him). We call this sort of ambiguity *syntactic ambiguity* or *amphiboly*. "Syntax" refers to the rules of grammatically acceptable sentence structure. In a syntactically ambiguous claim, the words are organized in a way that sustains two or more reasonable but contrary interpretations. (Since it's a problem with structure, amphiboly is related to formal fallacies.)

To disambiguate a syntactically ambiguous claim, rearrange the words to avoid the ambiguity ("While they were in the woods, he proposed, and she agreed to marry him") or add qualifying terms ("She agreed to marry him while they were standing in the woods").

Examples of syntactic ambiguity (also known as amphiboly)

1. "We saw them coming with the video camera." [Did they have the camera as they came, or did we use it to see them coming?]
2. "The treasure was found on the shore by the woman with the banana stand." [Did the woman with the banana stand find the treasure, or was it found next to her?]
3. "Joe is a celebrity trainer." [Is Joe a celebrity, or does he train celebrities?]
4. "The CEO canceled his appointment to visit the prime minister." [Did the CEO cancel in order to visit the prime minister or did his original plan to visit the prime minister get canceled?

Vagueness vs. ambiguity

Some words do not readily admit multiple distinct meanings, but their unique meaning can't be distinctly defined. For instance, just precisely when is it appropriate to say that someone is *bald*? Is there a precise number of hairs that establishes, objectively, that someone is bald? Probably not. Similarly, imagine that your son has just grown to six feet in height? Is your son *tall*? Whether he is tall depends on the context. He is probably tall relative to a group of five-year-olds, but not relative to a university basketball team. Thus, baldness and tallness are vague terms; they have clear, but imprecise meanings. You might say their semantic boundaries are *fuzzy*. This makes *vague* language different from *ambiguities*, since the multiple meanings of ambiguities may well be clearly and distinctly apprehensible. The problem with ambiguities is determining which distinct meaning is appropriate. The problem with vagaries is knowing precisely what is meant.

Vagueness, two types: degree and context

These examples highlight two ways in which a word can be vague. On the one hand, a vague word's meaning may be determined in terms of *degrees*. Whether something is bald, dry, clear, or good is a matter of degree – how many hairs, how many water molecules, how distinct, how good. On the other hand, a word's meaning may be determined with relative precision by *context*, so that when context is poorly understood the meaning of words becomes vague. Whether something is tall, big, strong, or overweight depends on what the relevant comparison set is – tall, big, strong, or overweight relative to what or whom?

Some words are vague in both senses. For instance, the term "well-written" is determined partly by context (well-written for a 3rd grader or for a university post-graduate student?) as well as by degree (very well-written? well-written for this group of students? for children of this age?). Similarly, evaluative language regarding athletic ability and musical ability are determined both by degree and context.

To eliminate vagueness, either (1) specify the relevant degree of the term you're using, or (2) specify the context. For instance, instead of saying, "The window is clear," you might say, "The window is clear enough for our purposes." Or, instead of saying, "He's incredibly strong," you might say, "He placed the second strongest in his weight class at this year's Scottish National bench press competition."

Examples of vagueness

1. "Wait until the roads are dry before you start your trip." [*Dry* is vague (but not uninformative in this context).]
2. "He is an excellent pianist." [He is *excellent* relative to whom? Mozart?]
3. "That was a good thing to do." [*Good* is both lexically ambiguous (*practically* good or *morally* good?) and vague (good, as in you-should-have-done-that-anyway or good as in better-than-what-you-could-be-expected-to-do?).]
4. "He has a big truck!" [Big relative to other trucks in its class or big relative to all trucks?]

Equivocation and fallacious amphiboly

Equivocation occurs when two different meanings of the same lexically ambiguous word are used to draw erroneously a conclusion that could not be supported without the ambiguity, commonly a mistaken conclusion. Usually this happens when the meaning of a term is changed over the course of an argument. To see what we mean, consider this silly example:

1. Congress can repeal any law.
2. Gravity is a law.
3. Therefore, Congress can repeal gravity.

Now, no one would offer such an argument seriously, but we can see where this hypothetical argument goes wrong. The word "law" is being used in two different senses: to refer to a *political* law in premise 1 and to refer to a *natural* law in premise 2. Nothing about natural laws follows from the claim that Congress can repeal any political law. So, this arguer has *equivocated* on the meaning of "law."

Fallacious amphibolies similarly occur when one erroneously draws a conclusion that depends upon a syntactic or grammatical ambiguity. For example:

1. Harold: "Seated in the top row of the stadium, the midfielders looked to us no bigger than insects."
2. Maude: "How very odd that the midfielders were up in the stadium seats rather than down on the pitch!"

A more serious example of an equivocation is found in Mary Anne Warren's well-known 1973 paper on abortion.[1] She argues that certain classic arguments against abortion equivocate on the meaning of "human being." Consider her example:

1. It is wrong to kill innocent human beings.
2. Fetuses are innocent human beings.
3. Therefore, it is wrong to kill fetuses.

She argues that premise 1 is obviously true, provided we interpret human beings in a *moral* sense, namely, as referring to all those entities that we regard as having a right not to be killed. Premise 1, however, is not obviously true if we interpret human beings in a *biological* sense – there may be some human organisms that it is permissible to kill, for example convicted killers, battlefield enemies, maybe tumors and fatty tissue. In addition, she argues that premise 2 is obviously true if we interpret the term "human beings" in a *biological* sense, namely, as referring to living matter with human DNA. Premise 2, however, is not obviously true in a *moral* sense – it is not clear whether fetuses are the sort of "human beings" that it is wrong to kill.

She concludes that this argument is successful only if we already accept that premise 2 is true if we interpret human beings in the same moral sense that we do in premise 1. But this is not obvious. The argument, in short, is vulnerable to the charge of equivocating with the term "human being." What philosophers opposed to abortion must do is show not simply that fetuses are human beings but that they are human beings of a specific sort, namely members of what she calls the "moral community."

Note, by the way, that, like amphiboly, equivocation may be thought of as a disguised formal fallacy. Strictly speaking you might say that when the meanings of a term shift in an argument really what's happened is that an entirely new term has been introduced. The confusing thing is merely that the new term looks and sounds just like one of the other terms. Consider this:

1. Brown is my favorite color.
2. Brown is a university in Rhode Island.
3. Therefore, my favorite color is a university in Rhode Island.

In this argument, you might say the word "Brown" actually stands for two different terms, two terms that unfortunately look and sound just like one another. Looked at this way, the argument suffers from a formal problem with its structure, even though it looks merely like a semantic problem with one of its terms.

Examples of equivocation and fallacious amphiboly

1. A famous equivocation is found in Lewis Carroll's *Through the Looking Glass*: "Whom did you pass on the road?" the King went on ... "Nobody," said the messenger. "Quite right," said the King; "this young lady saw him, too. So of course Nobody walks much slower than you." "I do my best," the Messenger said in a sullen tone. "I'm sure nobody walks much faster than I do!" "He can't do that," said the King, "or else he'd have been here first." [Lexical ambiguity: Nobody – a person named "Nobody" or no one at all?]
2. "He stole the money from the bank. And then he buried the money in the bank. Therefore, the money isn't really gone, and he is no thief." [Lexical ambiguity: bank – financial institution in premise 1; riverbank in premise 2]
3. "Political freedom is the freedom to pursue your interests without state persecution. But the poor cannot compete with the rich for the most desirable jobs. To be systematically prevented from pursuing your interests is the very antithesis of freedom. Therefore, the poor have less political freedom than the rich." [Lexical ambiguity: political freedom – freedom from state persecution in premise 1; freedom from market forces in premise 3]
4. Darla: "This morning I had quite a shock when I opened the front door to get the paper and came face to face with my neighbor in my nightgown." Dorrie: "I would have been shocked, too, to encounter my neighbor wearing my night gown." [Amphiboly: it was Darla, not the neighbor, wearing her own nightgown.]
5. "We have to prove that he committed 'disorderly conduct.' Since he did something, it was 'conduct.' He was acting erratically, and 'disorderly' means 'erratic.' Therefore, he committed disorderly conduct." [Lexical ambiguity: "disorderly conduct" is a technical, legal term that differs from the meanings of "disorderly" and "conduct" as they are used in the non-technical contexts that appear in premises 2 and 3. Therefore, the equivocation is on the technical and colloquial meanings of the phrase "disorderly conduct." This was an actual argument made in a Florida trial.]
6. Bernie: "We must condemn racial injustice, which gives our society today a bad reputation abroad." Hillary: "Okay, but I think we should condemn racial injustices even of the sort that aren't noticed abroad." [Amphiboly.]
7. "Priests are 'fathers,' and fathers have children. Therefore, priests have children."
8. "Being 'free' means not being physically restrained. Most government regulations do not physically restrain you. So it's just not true that government regulations limit our freedom."

5.14 Begging the Question (*petitio principii*)

"Spanking is wrong!" Jorge exclaimed to Sonja, just after observing Sonja administer a brief paddling to her unruly son. "What? I don't think so," she responded. "Well, of course, it is," insisted Jorge, "because violence against children is wrong." "Oh, brother," said Sonja, "you're begging the question." Was he?

In the *begging the question* fallacy, an arguer attempts to convince an audience to accept a belief on the basis of premises that already presuppose that the conclusion is true. In this case, Jorge already assumes that spanking counts as violence against children. Or consider, again, if someone were to try to convince you that abortion is wrong by saying: *killing innocent people is wrong, and abortion kills innocent people.* Here, the arguer is assuming in her premises the very claim for which she's arguing in her conclusion. If you already believe that abortion kills innocent people, you might agree with her that abortion is wrong. But this is the very claim that's in question and needs to be proved.

Detecting actual examples of begging the question is difficult because the assumed question-begging claim is often *implied* by one of the premises rather than *explicitly stated* as a premise, just as it was for Jorge. Consider another not-so-subtle example. Imagine that someone says: *God exists, because the Bible says so, and the Bible is the word of God.* In order for the Bible to be the word of God, God must exist. God's existence is implied by the second premise; therefore, this argument assumes what it needs to prove, namely, that God exists. Sometimes this error appears in the form of what's called *circular reasoning* or *arguing in a circle*. Here the Bible is used to prove that God exists, and then, in a circle, the existence of God is used to prove the veracity of the Bible. The seventeenth-century French philosopher René Descartes (1596–1650) has, in fact, been accused of arguing in a circle. Descartes's argument has now become so famous that it's called the *Cartesian Circle*. Descartes is accused, roughly, of arguing that God can be proven to exist on the basis of the clarity and distinctness of our ideas of God – and those features of our ideas of God are legitimate criteria for determining the truth because God guarantees them – the proof of the guarantee is itself proven by the guarantee.

Now, consider a subtler though less famous example. Imagine that someone attempts to argue that some law, Law *X*, is *just* or *fair* because the state properly enacted that law. This premise implies that all laws justly enacted are themselves just. But this is the very claim that needs to be proved!

To avoid confusion, it will be helpful to remember that there are two ways the phrase "begging the question" is used in contemporary English. The way we've been using it is its *logical* usage, meaning to assume what you are trying to prove. Many people, however, use it *rhetorically* to mean *raises the question*. For instance, you may hear a reporter say something like, "This verdict begs the question: What did the jury find so convincing?" The reporter means, "This verdict *raises* the question," and this has become an acceptable use of the phrase *begs the question*. So, when you read or hear the phrase *begs the question*, be sure to note which use is intended, so that you can respond appropriately.

Examples of begging the question

1. "The death penalty is wrong because executing convicted criminals is wrong."
2. "Plato is the best philosopher because all other philosophers are inferior to Plato."
3. "All people are equal because no one is better than anyone else."
4. "This test indicates that Circularity Inc. sells the most reliable products made in this market, and we can be sure it's a reliable test because it was developed by Circularity Inc."
5. "Senator Bates is right that increased government spending leads to inflation. You will see this if you look on page 746 of his Congressional testimony."
6. "The state is obligated to provide welfare services for its citizens because it's government's duty to provide such services."
7. "All lying is immoral because lying violates your absolute obligation to tell the truth!"

5.15 Question-Begging Sentences

In addition to question-begging arguments, there are also question-begging *sentences* (also known as *loaded questions* or *complex questions* when formulated interrogatively). A sentence that presupposes an unsupported claim relevant to the argument at hand is question begging. The most common example takes the form of this question: "Have you stopped smoking?" Whether one answers *yes* or *no*, one admits to smoking. Unless it's already understood that the question has been posed to an established smoker, this question begs the question.

Question-begging sentences are often used in political discourse to corner or stigmatize opponents. Sentences such as, "My opponent continues to harm school children by opposing education funding" and "Do you continue to favor unnecessary spending?" assume that the person referenced really does harm children and favor unnecessary spending – both assumptions yet to be proved in many cases.

A famous example of a question-begging question occurred in 1415 at the Church Council of Constance (Konstanz), Germany. Czech priest and church reformer Jan Hus was on trial for his opposition to the Roman papacy. He was presented with a list of claims he was said to endorse and then asked if he recanted them. Hus, however, hadn't endorsed all of them. So, to recant them would imply that he at one point asserted them, which he didn't. And to refuse to recant them would imply that he still supported them, which he didn't. Hus replied that he could not, in good conscience, recant claims he never held. The Council maintained that the issue of whether he held them was not up for dispute, and Hus was burned at the stake.

Examples of question-begging sentences

1. "Have you stopped using heroin?"
2. "How long have you been unfaithful to me?"
3. "How many times a week do you drink excessively?"

5.16 Missing the Point (*ignoratio elenchi*)

Have you ever seen a dog that is not used to being on a chain or leash run toward something that interests it only to find itself yanked full stop when the tether reaches its end? That's kind of how it feels when you encounter an argument that misses the point.

In a sense every fallacy is what's called a *non sequitur*, which means simply that the conclusion *doesn't follow*. In the most common cases of the fallacy of *missing the point* (also known as the *fallacy of irrelevant conclusion*), a set of reasonable premises is collected that does indeed lead soundly or cogently to a conclusion – just not the conclusion that's in fact been drawn. Having reached a different conclusion from the one the argument is obviously structured to draw, the point has been missed. For example, someone might argue:

1. All humans are mortal.
2. Socrates is human.
3. Therefore, Socrates is not really Greek.

You feel like, "How did *that* conclusion get there?" If you encounter an argument that misses the point, you're likely to find yourself scratching your head and wondering how things went so very wrong. Usually the mistaken conclusion is somehow, more or less, related to the proper conclusion, and that may have led the person who committed the fallacy astray. But a mistaken conclusion, even if related to the right conclusion, is still a mistake.

Another variant called *ignoratio elenchi* (from the Latin for the *refutation's ignorance* of the proper conclusion) occurs when someone offers as a refutation of some point an argument that doesn't actually refute the point at hand. One of the most famous points missed in the history of philosophy is the refutation of George Berkeley's idealism attributed to Samuel Johnson. Berkeley had argued that material substance doesn't really exist, or that the objects of our perception are not actually material entities in the way commonly thought. Rather, they exist only in the perceiving of them. Johnson, who thought this metaphysical theory to be ludicrous, is supposed to have uttered, "I refute it thus!" as he kicked a large rock, a rock that stayed put and resisted the blow he struck. Dramatic though his gesture was, Johnson, however, had missed Berkeley's point, since Berkeley understood full well what we experience when we kick large stones. It's just that, in Berkeley's analysis, all of it – the foot, the stone, the kick, as well as the perhaps subsequent pain in Johnson's toe – are all nothing more than perceptions, the existence of which Berkeley could happily continue to argue could not exist independently of the event of perception.

Examples of missing the point

1. "Every time I park under this tree, my car gets covered in bird droppings. It's happened that way without fail hundreds of times, and it looks like I'm going to have to park under the same tree today. I'm definitely going to start calling my mother more often."
2. "Either the cat or the dog knocked over the vase, and it's quite clear that it could not have been the cat. Therefore, that dog must be put down."
3. "Your claim that increasing interest rates will cause more unemployment is certainly false because the Federal Reserve Bank's manipulating the economy through interest rates is simply un-American."
4. "The findings have been posted in medical journals. Hospitals have now adopted the procedures, and patients testify to its success. This shows just how far the pharmaceutical conspiracy reaches!"

5.17 Fallacy of Composition

The *fallacy of composition* occurs when reasoning about parts and wholes, whether you're thinking about a thing or a set of things. This fallacy is committed when someone infers that, since each member, aspect, or part of a whole (either a thing or a set of things) has a particular feature or property, then the whole must have that same feature or property. The classic example of this fallacy is to reason from the fact that *each human being had a mother* that *the human race (as a whole) had a (single, unique) mother*:

1. Each human being had a mother.
2. Therefore, humanity had a mother.

Of course, although some, such as seventeenth-century poet John Milton (1608–1674), have referred to Eve as the mother of us all, no one should reason from the fact that we have a mother that Eve existed. It's deceptively easy, however, to fall prey to this fallacy.

This fallacy may have been committed by thirteenth-century Dominican philosopher Thomas Aquinas (1225–1274) in the second of his famous Five Ways to God's existence. Thomas begins by noting that everything we perceive in nature has a cause (some event or thing that brings it into existence). By some interpretations, he then infers from this that the whole universe (the totality of everything) must also have had a cause:

> In the world of sense we find there is an order of efficient causes. There is no known case … in which a thing is found to be the efficient cause of itself…. Now, in efficient causes it is not possible to go on to infinity…. But if in efficient causes it is impossible to go on to infinity, neither will there be an ultimate effect, nor any intermediate efficient causes; all of which is plainly false [because, as we noted at the outset, there is an order of efficient causes]. Therefore it is necessary to admit a first efficient cause; and this everyone understands to be God.
>
> *Summa theologiae*, First Part, a, Question 2, Article 3; Ia2.3

There are two ways to read this argument. On the one hand (let's call it Reading 1), Thomas may simply be noting that every event in the universe has a cause, and from this he infers that each causal chain can be *traced to* a single, shared cause. Reading 1 may not be a very good argument (e.g., why not think that causal chains extend back into the past but never converge or derive from a single cause?), but it does not commit the fallacy of composition *per se*. It does not imply that all events *taken as a whole* have one, unique cause.

On the other hand, we may interpret Thomas as noting that *each individual* event in the universe has a cause, and from this, he infers that the universe in which all these causal relations take place *as a whole* must have a cause (Reading 2). In this reading, he *is* committing the fallacy of composition. Thomas is reasoning, on Reading 2 of the passage, from features of *particular* events to a conclusion about the *whole* causal system that they compose, taken as a single thing, and that is indeed the fallacy of composition:

1. Each event in the universe has a cause.
2. Therefore, the whole universe of causal sequences has a cause.

You might also think of composition as "the all-star team" fallacy. Many athletic leagues form "all-star" teams, composed of the league's best players. One thought motivating this might be that an all-star team will be a great team because it is in fact composed of great players. But one risks the fallacy of composition in arguing that because each individual player has an excellent record the team resulting from a composite of them will be excellent. Excellent players may play poorly together, and players' excellence may require the idiosyncratic chemistry of their original teams. In fact, it's confirmation of this to notice that all-star teams are rarely extraordinary.

Examples of the fallacy of composition

1. "All the bricks in that wall are small. Hence, the wall must be small."
2. "All pixels are square, so they couldn't possibly be used to make round objects."
3. "I haven't heard your school's jazz quartet, but I know each of the members, and they're all great musicians. So, I'm sure the quartet is great, too."
4. "Molecules do not exist. This is because molecules are invisible to the naked eye. But if each and every molecule is invisible, then the objects out of which they are made would be invisible to the naked eye, too. Yet, we can see objects with our naked eyes."
5. "The top four graduates from our law school have started their own legal firm. Given their individual successes in our program, we know they will form a highly successful firm."
6. Guest: "Wow, this dish is tasty! How did you know how to make it?"
7. Host: "Well, I knew you liked all the ingredients, so I just put them all together in one dish. You couldn't dislike it, could you?"

5.18 Fallacy of Division

The *fallacy of division* is the inverse of the fallacy of composition. It also occurs when reasoning about parts and wholes and is committed when one infers wrongly that, since a whole thing or set of things has a feature or property, each of its members or parts has that feature or property, too. After all, just because a pie is large doesn't mean that every slice of that pie will be large – a fact often ignored by those who maintain that a growing economy will make everyone working in it better off.

Moreover, when groups of things function in unison, they sometimes produce features or properties that no single part has. For instance, no one would infer that because a team of 6 horses pulls at a strength of 6 horsepower (this is not an accurate description of how horsepower is measured, by the way) each individual horse must pull at 6 horsepower. It is only by working together that the team pulls as hard as it does.

A common example of this fallacy also occurs with music groups. A music group may write songs that are considered very good by people who should know, but each of their members need not be particularly good at playing music. Perhaps the drum or bass line is so simple that practically any beginning student could play it, but the guitarist and singer are advanced in their skills. The result may be a very good band without every member being very good:

1. The Rolling Stones are a phenomenal rock group.
2. We can conclude that their drummer must be phenomenal, as well.

One of the most notorious examples of the fallacy of division has to do with the possibility of dividing mathematical sets. If a line, for example, is only a *finite* length – say, 12 inches – then it seems impossible to imagine that it comprises an *infinite* number of parts. According to geometricians, however, between any two points on a finite line lies another point. If this is right, then a finite line is composed of an infinite number of finite points. You can see this if you divide the line in half, and then divide one of those halves into halves, and then one of those halves into halves, and so on. The result is an infinitely large set of line segments composed of finite segments of the original line: $\frac{1}{2}$, $\frac{1}{4}$, $\frac{1}{8}$, $\frac{1}{16}$, $\frac{1}{32}$, and so on, to infinity. This means that we cannot infer that the number of parts of a single, finite whole is also finite. (You can also see, by the way, how easy it would be to commit a fallacy of composition with this same example: the fact that every member of a set is finite doesn't entail that the whole set is finite. Consider the natural numbers: 0, 1, 2, 3, 4 .... The whole set is infinite, but any particular member fills some finite position in the ordering. If you were trying to count the natural numbers, you would only ever count finite members, such that, for every natural number you count (e.g., 1,743,235), there would be another to count (1,743,236), and then another, and then another. There is no "infinitieth" member, yet the set is infinitely large! Examples like these illustrate why we must:

> *Remember that the properties of wholes may be different from the properties of their parts.*

More particularly for our purposes here, we must be extremely careful about how we reason about their relationship.

Examples of the fallacy of division

1. "This car is an amazing machine. Every part must be finely tuned to perfection."
2. "Your company is a well-oiled machine. You must have hand-picked every member to create such a powerful organization."
3. "Your university's overall GPA is stellar. Every student must be performing at an impeccable level."
4. "You should come to work for our company. The employee's salary pool has been growing. So everyone's salary must be growing, too."

5.19 Is-Ought Fallacy

In the course of an argument about what many are calling the "sixth Extinction," referring to the extraordinary number of species extinctions underway, Dawson declares, "The fact that a species has gone extinct means that it's supposed to be that way. Natural selection is a natural process, and that's just how things are." Darlene responds with the criticism, "Sounds to me as though you're confusing facts with values." What could she mean?

In the *is-ought fallacy*, one wrongly attempts to draw a conclusion about the way something *ought to be* from premises about the way things *are*. In other words, someone illegitimately derives a *normative* claim about reality (the way things ought to be) from a *descriptive* claim about reality (the way things are). The identification of this fallacy is normally attributed to eighteenth-century Scottish philosopher David Hume (1711–1776) and Book 3 of his 1740 *A Treatise of Human Nature* (3.1.1.27, in particular). The conceptual basis for it is often referred to as the *fact/value* distinction. Ethicist G. E. Moore (1873–1958) drew upon the distinction when he argued in his 1903 *Principia ethica* that trying to derive normative claims or ethical properties such as "good" from descriptions of natural properties such as "feels pleasing" lands one in a *naturalistic* fallacy.

In any case, sometimes the inference from facts to values (from *is* to *ought*) seems legitimate: from *the descriptive fact* that I borrow $5 from you, you conclude *the normative fact* that I *ought* to pay you back; from *the descriptive fact that* we agreed that you will work for me at a rate of $10/hr, I can conclude *the normative fact* that I *ought* to give you $20 for working two hours. But notice that in each of these cases, there is an "ought" hidden in the premises. The word "borrow" implies an obligation on my part – a claim on my conduct. Similarly, an employment "agreement" implies obligations on both parties – a claim on the employee to work, and a claim on the employer to pay. But you couldn't reasonably show up at my door and say: "I raked your yard; therefore, you owe me ten dollars." The fact that you worked implies nothing with respect to my behavior – there is no "ought" in that premise, no claim on my behavior.

This fallacy is exceedingly common, and it's called the "naturalistic" fallacy because it often includes an appeal to nature, or the way nature is or tends to work, as a standard for what should be. For instance, people often justify claims about the value of human beings or any of the world's existing species by arguing that natural selection has been progressive and that what is alive today is somehow its culmination. The problem is that there does not seem to be any reason for thinking that natural selection has anything to do with what we should *value*, good or bad. Millions of species of beetles have gone extinct. Is this a morally "bad" thing? Not as a matter of fact. Are modern *homo sapiens* in some moral sense "better" or more valuable than extinct *homo habilis* or the Neanderthals, just because their DNA sequences weren't naturally "selected"? Not as a matter of science. Critical thinkers must therefore be extremely cautious about deriving normative judgments (claims about the way things should be) from *purely* descriptive judgments (claims about the way things are or have been), where by "purely" we mean that there are no "oughts" hidden in the premises.

A notorious example of this fallacy occurs on both sides of the debate over same-sex marriage. Those against same-sex marriage sometimes argue that homosexual behavior is contrary to nature, it is unnatural, and therefore, it should be prohibited. Those in favor of same-sex marriage sometimes argue that homosexuality is a biological fact about people, not a choice, and therefore, it should be permitted. The descriptive facts of the case are clear: there is widespread homosexual behavior among non-human animals (and no marriage arrangements), and there is as-yet no "gay gene," though sexual preference is as likely to be biological as preferences for certain types of food and music. But regardless of these descriptive facts, both arguments are fallacious. Whether homosexuality is "natural" or not, nature implies nothing *by itself* with respect to normative judgments.

To see why, consider a few counterexamples. Many animals eat some or all of their young (and some female spiders kill their mates after insemination). Should we then regard a human mother's eating her own children and killing her mate as morally permissible? Not obviously. Similarly, it may be that the inclination to pedophilia is influenced by genetic makeup, and therefore, in a sense a biological fact about some people. Should we then regard sex with children as morally permissible? Again: not obviously at all. Medicine, air conditioning, and soap are arguably unnatural; and the plague, sweltering heat, and body odor are arguably natural. Nature, it seems pretty clear, offers no simple guide to moral judgments.

Legitimate uses of is-ought inferences

This fallacy is, however, highly contested among philosophers who study moral philosophy. While most agree that, in many instances, nature is no simple guide to morality, there are cases where it seems that a descriptive fact does have moral implications. For example, moral sentimentalists are philosophers who have argued that the very meaning of moral terms and judgments derives from facts about the world, natural and otherwise – in particular, facts related to our feelings and sympathies. Others have argued that moral judgments essentially involve factual matters concerned with flourishing, excellence, perfectibility, and basic human agreement.

We won't get into the details of this debate here. Suffice it to say that, while many philosophers agree that the inference from *is* to *ought* is fallacious, some do not, at least not always. Those who don't agree that is-ought inferences are fallacious, though, do regard some applications as illegitimate and attempt to formulate some means by which to distinguish legitimate from illegitimate applications. We think the examples below are fairly uncontroversial cases where the inference from *is* to *ought* is *illegitimate*.

Examples of the is-ought fallacy

1. "Nature is cruel; therefore, we are also entitled to be cruel." – attributed to Adolf Hitler
2. "You really should let your husband promiscuously have sex with others. Males have an evolutionary disposition to polyamory. It's therefore perfectly permissible."
3. "We must work to root out invasive species! We now have plants from Florida, Spain, and California commingling with the native plants here in the Appalachian Mountains. It is unnatural and therefore must be stopped."

4. "It would be wrong to try to protect a species from extinction caused by our conduct. Humans are part of natural selection, just as other animals. If our way of life eliminates some other species, it only shows that nature prefers us to them."
5. "The human body has a natural inclination to survive. Suicide runs counter to this natural inclination, and is, therefore, immoral."

5.20 Appeal to Tradition

The fallacious *appeal to tradition* is a species of the is-ought fallacy, and it occurs when you attempt to use the descriptive fact that something is traditional as a reason to believe that it shouldn't change or *ought to* stay the same. For instance: "We shouldn't change the color of the carpet. It's always been blue, so it should remain blue." Similarly: "We shouldn't change the policy now. We've always done it this way," and "It was good enough for my father, so it's good enough for me." In these cases, the descriptive facts that "it's always been blue," "we've always done it this way," and "it was good enough for my father," are used as reasons to draw the normative conclusion that things shouldn't change.

To be sure, there may be good reasons to resist change, but these reasons rarely have anything to do with the mere fact that things have always been a certain way. If, in addition, we *prefer* things to stay the same, then tradition could serve as a guide to a *preferred* conclusion. For instance, change the first argument to read: "We shouldn't change the color of the carpet. It's always been blue, and we want to restore this building to its original condition; therefore, the carpet should remain blue." Now we have a *legitimate* reason to resist change. But the simple fact that *X* has always been a certain way doesn't constitute, by itself, a reason not to change *X*.

Legitimate appeals to tradition?

As noted above, tradition can play a guiding role in reasoning. If you're already committed to a tradition as normative, then appealing to that tradition may be a helpful way to make policies and decisions. A church that is affiliated with a particular denomination (e.g., Presbyterian, Episcopal, etc.) and wishes to remain that way would do well not to enact policies that contradict that tradition. (See 10.12 Traditionalist and Historicist Critiques for more about how tradition may ground social-political critical thinking.) Leaders of companies with vision statements must make decisions in accordance with that vision so they don't risk their jobs or shareholders' confidence in the business. But if you place no particular value on a tradition, appeals to tradition (without also offering reasons for thinking that tradition is valuable) are simply fallacious. For instance, it would be inappropriate for someone from Ford Motor Company to appeal to a tradition of management policy of General Motors simply on the grounds that it is a tradition. General Motors' traditions are not (without additional qualification) binding on Ford. On the other hand, if you were to add to the observation of General Motors' tradition the finding that the tradition has proven effective for them, Ford might do well to consider it.

Examples of the tradition fallacy

1. "Bloodletting had been a traditional treatment for cholera and a king's laying hands on a patient had been a traditional therapy for scrofula. Therefore, we should continue to treat these diseases in this way."
2. "Traditionally, marriage has been an exclusively heterosexual institution. Because it's traditionally been that way, it should continue to be that way."
3. "Our company has a long tradition of catering to the needs of the community in this way. Therefore, even though our community might have changed, we shouldn't change our company's goals right now."
4. "Here at Inflexible Management Consulting, we've always prescribed this model of structuring a company. So, no matter how the world has changed, we shouldn't prescribe anything different now."
5. "Our wise forbearers saw fit to bequeath to us a strong culture of blue collar labor and practicality. We have an obligation to stick with their vision, because hiring these upstart college kids is not consistent with the traditions of our culture."
6. "We have a long history of commitment to the divine right of kings. We would trample the insight of our forefathers if we rejected that belief now."
7. "There are many new banks making new promises. Jones Bank has been in business for 60 years. Stay with a tradition. Stay with Jones Bank."

5.21 Quoting Out of Context

The fallacy of *quoting out of context* occurs when an arguer misleadingly uses a single sentence or paragraph of someone else to indicate what that person believes or claims. For instance, Jon might say: "For the sake of argument, let's say it is morally permissible to eat your children." Micah, in response, might take some of Jon's words out of context and use them against him. For example, Micah might later say: "Hey, did you hear how crazy Jon is? He thinks, and I quote: 'it is morally permissible to eat your children.'" Jon did say these words, but he used them in a vastly different way than Micah uses them. Micah takes this quote to indicate Jon's views, even though, when we see it in context (especially following the phrase, "for the sake of argument"), it seems very unlikely Jon would support that idea.

This fallacy occurs commonly when people use historical texts to support claims. For example, it is common to hear people say that Karl Marx disparaged religion on the basis of his claim that, "Religion is the opium of the people" (from the proposed but never completed work, *A Contribution to the Critique of Hegel's Philosophy of Right*). This interpretation is understandable, given Marx's atheism and his belief that the proletariat would eventually rise against the bourgeoisie to overthrow the capitalist economy, as well as his belief that this would require the elimination of any "illusions about their condition," among which he included religion. This is certainly how Lenin uses the quote: "*Religion is opium for the people.* Religion is a sort of spiritual booze, in which the slaves of capital drown their human image, their demand for a life more or less worthy of man" (*Novaya Zhizn* No. 28, December 3, 1905). Marx's claim has also been used to justify the claim that religion is a temporary but needed good: opium was often used, both medicinally and recreationally, to ease suffering. Thus, Marx might have been saying something positive. In context, however, one might also plausibly interpret Marx simply to be making a merely descriptive observation about a particular historical moment: both religion and the critique of religion in that moment are indicators of suffering, and, therefore, substantiate the claim that revolution is inevitable. He writes in *A Contribution to the Critique of Hegel's Philosophy of Right*:

> Religious suffering is, at one and the same time, the expression of real suffering and a protest against real suffering. *Religion is the sigh of the oppressed creature, the heart of a heartless world, and the soul of soulless conditions. It is the opium of the people. ...* The criticism of religion is, therefore, in embryo, the criticism of that vale of tears of which religion is the halo.

Similarly, Socrates is often cited as making the incoherent claim: "All I know is that I know nothing." For being so wise, it sure seems like he missed the mark here: if you know something, then it isn't true that you know nothing; and if you know nothing, then you don't even know that! But when we look at the claim in context, we see that Socrates is speaking with Thrasymachus about the nature of justice and that he's saying he doesn't know anything about justice:

> ... the result of the discussion, as far as I'm concerned, is that I know nothing, for when I don't know what justice is, I'll hardly know whether it is a kind of virtue or not, or whether a person who has it is happy or unhappy
>
> (*Republic*, Book I, 354b–c).

The simplest way to avoid fallacious out-of-context quotes is to know the author and your audience well. Be a careful and open-minded reader. Be able to recognize when a quote accurately represents the author's perspective on the topic.

Legitimate uses of quoting out of context

It is not always illegitimate to use single quotations out of context. When you (1) already have good reasons to believe a quote represents a person's beliefs, or when you (2) are using the quote independently of any reference to the author's views, out-of-context quotations can be useful. For instance, Winston Churchill is well known for having defended democracy, and one of his oft-cited claims is that:

> ... democracy is the worst form of government except all those other forms that have been tried from time to time ....
>
> House of Commons speech (November 11, 1947)

Even though this quote is out of context, most people know enough about Churchill to know that he is not intending to disparage democracy. In fact, Churchill is so well known for his favorable attitude toward democracy that even his criticisms of it are rarely taken as a mark against him:

> The best argument against democracy is a five-minute conversation with the average voter.
>
> Attributed, source unknown

Again, Churchill would not likely have considered this a reason to reject democracy. And if you pressed him about why he still favors democracy, he might refer you to the former quote.

Other examples of *legitimate* out-of-context quotes include this example:

> Achievement of your happiness is the only moral purpose of your life, and that happiness, not pain or mindless self-indulgence, is the proof of your moral integrity, since it is the proof and the result of your loyalty to the achievement of your values.
>
> Ayn Rand, *Atlas Shrugged* (1957)

Ayn Rand is widely known for defending the moral view called "rational egoism," according to which your own happiness is your principal moral duty, and you don't have a duty to make anyone else happy. It would be nice of you to make someone else happy, especially when it contributes to your own happiness. But if helping increase others' happiness conflicts with your own, then helping them is immoral. The quoted selection expresses part of Rand's view, and so it is a legitimate expression of her ideas. Now, consider another example:

> Good philosophy must exist, if for no other reason, because bad philosophy must be answered.
>
> C. S. Lewis, "Learning in War-Time," in *The Weight of Glory* (1965)

C. S. Lewis is widely known for defending Christianity against philosophical objections, a practice called "apologetics" (from the Greek *apologia*, meaning "defense"). His disposition to respond philosophically to those who would disagree with him renders this quote a legitimate expression of his views. Here's another example of a legitimate out-of-context quote from Aristotle:

> One swallow does not make a summer, nor does one day; and so too one day, or a short time, does not make a man blessed and happy.
>
> Aristotle, *Nicomachean Ethics*, Book 1 (1098.a16)

Aristotle defends a moral view that has come to be known as "virtue ethics," according to which your moral character is determined by the extent to which you behave virtuously or viciously over your entire life. This quote expresses an important piece of this view – it isn't one act that makes you good or bad, but how you've lived over time.

Interpreting texts becomes particularly complicated when analyzing the nonfiction writings of authors who write under pseudonyms, such as the nineteenth-century Danish philosopher Søren Kierkegaard (1813–1855) who wrote as "Johannes Climacus" and Benjamin Franklin who wrote as "Silence Dogood" – what a great name! What do these writings reflect about their authors' beliefs and dispositions? Scholars in religious studies tend to refer to Climacus as the author of the pseudonymous works of Kierkegaard, whereas philosophers tend to refer to Kierkegaard. Is one more legitimate than the other?

Regardless of how we might settle these debates, the point is that, in order to attribute out-of-context quotes to a text's author legitimately, we must be able to identify some connection between the quote and his or her ideas. Recall our character Jon, above. If we discover an article in which Jon actually defends eating children, we might have some reason to attribute to him the belief that it is permissible to eat children. Of course, we might also discover that his article was intended as satire (as it was, e.g., for Jonathan Swift in his "A Modest Proposal," 1729).

Examples of fallacious quoting out of context

1. "Plato says people who have gay sex are uneducated. He says so right here in the *Republic*: ' … sexual pleasure mustn't come into it, and the lover and the boy he loves must have no share in it, if they are to love and be loved in the right way … . Otherwise he will be reproached as untrained in music and poetry and lacking in appreciation for what is fine and beautiful' (403a–b)." [In context, we find that it is Plato's representation of Socrates speaking, not Plato himself. In addition, Socrates, it seems, is speaking about one segment of the population (the guardians), not the whole. Further still, even for the guardians, Socrates allows one time of year for them to enjoy sexual pleasure of a variety of sorts, including homosexual intercourse. And even further, Socrates says some pretty shocking things in the *Republic* (e.g., there should be no musical instruments with more than one string; children of the guardian class should be raised communally, without knowing their biological parents), so it might be unwise to use Socrates as he's represented in Plato's *Republic* as an authority figure without looking at the arguments themselves.]

2. "We should definitely get a group together to worship: the Bible says, '… where two or three gather in my name, there I am among them'" (Matthew 18:20). [Despite the fact that God's presence in any situation follows from his (presumed) omnipresence, this verse appeals to the written claim that God promises to be in the presence of two or three who are gathered in his name. And though most take the numbers (two or three) to be hyperbolic (of course God is present with fewer and more people than this), the speaker here places special emphasis on the fact that a "group" is important. But let's ignore that and focus on the implication that God has a special interest in group worship. Without further context, this may seem obvious. But in context, things are quite different. Verses 15–19 of Matthew are about how to handle conflict in a congregation, and verse 16 says, "… if he [who is causing the conflict] does not listen, take one or two others along with you, that every charge may be established by the evidence of two or three witnesses." This suggests that this passage is about Jewish law rather than about worship, and that is exactly what we find: "Only on the evidence of two witnesses or of three witnesses shall a charge be established" (Deuteronomy 19:15). Therefore, to use this passage to support a claim about worship may be to quote out of context.
3. John Kerry (Candidate for US president, September 30, 2004): "No President, through all of American history, has ever ceded, and nor would I, the right to preempt in any way necessary to protect the United States of America. But if and when you do it … you have to do it in a way that passes the test, that passes the global test where your countrymen, your people understand fully why you're doing what you're doing and you can prove to the world that you did it for legitimate reasons." George W. Bush (Incumbent US president, October 2, 2004): "When our country's in danger the President's job is not to take an international poll. The President's job is to defend America." [Note that Bush interprets Kerry's commitment to a "global test" as implying that the president should get permission from other world leaders to protect his own country. Of course, in the previous stanza, Kerry explicitly says this is not what he thinks. The "global test" seems here only to imply that any action can be publicly defended. If this is right, Bush has inappropriately used Kerry's phrase out of context.]
4. Consider "the Pyrrhonian suspension of judgment, the idea that nothing is certain: it is plain that, beginning with itself, it first invalidates itself. It either grants that something is true, that you are not to suspend your judgment on all things; or it objects in saying that there is nothing true. And it is evident that first it will not be true. For it either affirms what is true or it does not affirm what is true. But if the former, it concedes … that something is true. If the latter, it leaves true what it wished to do away with [that is, the idea itself is false]." – Clement of Alexandria from *Stoicorum veterum fragmenta*, II, 121 (Leipzig, 1905–1924, trans. J. von Arim) [This one is more sophisticated, but just focus on part of the first sentence, "the idea that nothing is certain." The type of skepticism mentioned here (Pyrrhonian) recommends suspending belief about all claims. But the *idea* that nothing is certain can be interpreted in more than one way: it can be the *claim* that nothing is certain (which is the way Clement interprets it) or it can be the *attitude* or

disposition or *practice* of not believing anything. The latter is not susceptible to Clement's criticism, and Clement is wrong to interpret it in the former sense. But this is only clear *in the context* of the skeptics' writings. For example, one skeptic explains, "Skepticism is an ability, or mental attitude ... " (Sextus Empiricus, *Outlines of Pyrrhonism*, Book 1, Chapter 4, line 8). This is very different from a claim.]

5. "I realize that Lenin was a Marxist, but he wrote in *What is to be Done?* (Chapter 1) that the dominant political view 'must change from a party of social revolution into a democratic part of social reforms.' Therefore, Lenin believed in democracy!" [Hint: In fact, Lenin argued against this "change."]

5.22 Red Herring

In the *red herring* fallacy, an arguer attempts to distract his or her audience from the topic at hand by introducing attention-getting, yet irrelevant premises. The name of this fallacy is thought to derive from an ancient hunting practice that involves dragging dead fish across a scent trail that hunting dogs are supposed to follow. If the dogs ignore the fish smell and stay on the trail, they are well trained. If, instead, they follow the red herring scent, they need more training.

Political rhetoric is the classic domain of the red herring. Suppose a political leader is accused of using illegal drugs, just as had former Washington, DC, mayor Marion Barry when he was videotaped in 1990 apparently smoking crack cocaine. Suppose at a subsequent press conference, when asked whether or not he or she had ever used illegal drugs, the official responded along these lines: "While I've held office, garbage pick-up has improved, crime rates have fallen, the economy has thrived, and SAT scores for college applicants have risen." It's an answer that might help the official hold office, since these accomplishments, if true, may be satisfying to voters, but the answer utterly dodges the reporter's question. Instead it aims to draw his audience away from a vulnerability exposed by the original question.

Legitimate uses of red herrings?

By definition, there is no epistemically legitimate use of a red herring. Their purpose is to lead astray, to distract. Therefore, unless you're intentionally using them pragmatically to lead others away from some topic, their use is questionable.

Examples of the red herring fallacy

1. Jim: "Our animal shelter's media campaign is offensive to many people, and something needs to be done to correct that."

Sue: "Jim, you don't seem to realize that our shelter has saved thousands of animals and protected the health of the general public for decades. Moreover, I notice that the department that employs you has been accused of misusing postage stamps."

2. Sarah: "Government bailouts for which Shoshone voted are likely to increase inflation."
   Shoshone: "People during my tenure in office are living longer, they have more channels to watch on television, and early reports suggest they suffer less tooth decay."
3. Omar: "Environmental action is meaningless without some indication of how much 'action' is needed. How much of a reduction in carbon emissions do we need to stop or slow global warming? An effective international treaty must specify clearly defined limits on exactly how much carbon may be released."
   Keishaun: "The environmental movement is responsible for our majestic national parks and for cleaning up our nation's waterways as well as for saving scores of species from extinction. Don't you remember how the Cuyahoga River caught fire in 1969?"
4. Vladimir: (to board of trustees) "The budget is overflowing. We cannot afford one more project. Therefore, I urge you to vote against this proposal."
   Leslie: (to board of trustees) "Vlad, we've been at work on this budget for months, and a lot of energy has gone into this proposal. Moreover, our university has been getting a lot of attention recently for the influential publications of our faculty. Our web site has more hits than ever."
5. "The current senator wants to put more emphasis on reducing crime. And he has offered a detailed plan for how he will accomplish this goal. But his plan is flawed in important ways. It ignores the deeper problem that we have with education in this community. Our teachers are vastly underpaid and their healthcare plan is deplorable. Therefore, you should not vote to re-elect the senator."

5.23 Straw Man and Fidelity

If you ever got into a fight with a straw man dressed up to look like Muhammad Ali or Wladimir Klitschko you probably won, and if you claimed afterwards to have beaten up the heavyweight champion of the world, you'd be rightly criticized.

Like the red herring, the *straw man* (or sometime *straw house*) fallacy is an attempt to distract from the relevant aspects of an argument by offering up a caricatured version of it to knock down. In the straw man fallacy, one person rewords or reframes an argument in such a way that (1) the new version does not accurately reflect the original argument, and (2) the new version is easy to criticize or defeat. A straw man, if you think about it, might look like a real man from a distance, but not close up. Moreover, the *Wizard of Oz* aside, a straw man is much easier to fight than the real thing. In more theoretical terms, the straw man fallacy violates what good critical thinkers often call the *principle of fidelity*.

Principle of Fidelity: Faithfully represent arguments you are scrutinizing or criticizing in the most accurate way you can. Don't distort them to serve your purposes.

Consider a case where Manisha says, "It's probably healthier to eat a diet composed primarily of fruits and vegetables than a diet composed primarily of meat, because recent scientific research has found that diets heavy in meat in comparison with vegetarian diets exhibit higher rates of heart disease." Finding the conclusion to this argument distasteful (pun intended), Mark might "straw man" it by saying: "Manisha thinks eating vegetables is *better* than eating meat. And so she thinks vegetarians are better people than carnivores!" Note the subtle play on "better." Manisha says "healthier," which implies "better for your health," but Mark recasts "healthier" as "better" in a moral sense – it's better in a morally significant way. But, of course, it isn't clear that Manisha thinks this at all.

The straw man fallacy occurs in a lot of political discourse as candidates try to entrench voters against a particular party, opponent, or policy. For instance, Eli might argue that substantially enlarging the money supply through what bankers call "quantitative easing" may be a wrong-headed way to remedy a recession because it creates conditions that are likely to increase inflation. In response, Erin might say: "Eli thinks we should not pursue a policy of quantitative easing because it would cause the collapse of our financial institutions." Note that Eli said nothing about a financial collapse. He only made the much more guarded claim that quantitative easing would create conditions that are likely to increase inflation. He said nothing about how likely, how much inflation would result, or what the specific consequences of that would be.

Legitimate uses of straw men/houses?

The straw man is a deceptive strategy, so it is unlikely that philosophers will say that it is ever justified. It is often useful when attempting to *persuade* an audience (irrespective of the truth), perhaps in a courtroom or political campaign or in a lover's quarrel, but it is not an intellectually responsible principle of reasoning. As you'll recall, the first of the three little pigs learned the hard way that a straw house is no proper house at all.

Examples of the straw man fallacy

1. Lynne: "I think it might be a good idea for me to take a few days off, so that I'm fresh before starting on that new project."
   Her boss, Herman: "So, you think the best way to accomplish things is by not working at all?"

2. Karl: "I think our garden would do well if we planted a few tomatoes over here along with some beans to restore nitrogen to our soil."
   Faisa: "So you're saying that we'll only have a proper garden if we fill the yard with tomatoes and chemicals."
3. Prya: "When I was a child, my mother told you never to talk to strangers on my walks home from school."
   Sidney: "Your mother's advice was silly. After all, how could you ever make friends if you weren't allowed to talk to anyone?!"
4. "The Board of Trustees has rejected our proposal to fund our children's program on the grounds that its cost exceeds the institution's resources. In effect, they're claiming it's not worth spending money to help children."
5. In a debate: Politician 1: "We have to be responsible with our budget and cut non-essential funding. I plan to cut $\frac{1}{4}$ of the money used to pay high school coaches."
   Politician 2: "My opponent is asking you to cut $\frac{1}{4}$ of the school budget! This is a direct attack on education, and you should not put up with it."

5.24 Hasty Fallacization

It is very easy to discover fallacies. They can be found in music, advertisements, news reports, the guy next to you at the bar, and even scientific journals. Once people are armed with the ability to recognize fallacious arguments, they often use it liberally and indiscriminately. After college, where their children first learn a handful of fallacies, parents quickly realize that they were right to be skeptical of taking that philosophy class. One of our colleagues recently pointed out how obsessed some people become with fallacies and how this overshadows the original motive for learning to identify them. He suggests adding one additional fallacy to our list – the fallacy of *hastily attributing a fallacy*, or, to coin a phrase: *hasty fallacization.*

Hasty fallacization occurs when someone is more concerned to point out the flaws in others' arguments than with thinking carefully about the subject matter. In other words, someone committing this fallacy is more interested in proving others wrong than in solving a problem or gaining a better understanding of the issues at hand. In many cases, people make claims without intending any substantive or universally generalizable point about reality. Someone who, frustrated at just being cut off in traffic, utters, "Ugh! I hate people!" does not expect to be challenged to defend the claim that, "For all X, if X is a person, then X is something I hate." Neither is the person expecting to be asked for a conceptual analysis of the term "person" or the appropriate application conditions and moral implications of the attitude "hate." She is simply expressing frustration. Similarly, someone who commits a fallacy may have not yet thought completely through an argument and is just trying out an idea or a definition; she may be suggesting something she's heard other people say or simply toying with an explanation. Therefore, be responsible, not over-zealous, with your newfound fallacy fighting skills.

5.25 A Brief Argument Clinic

So far in this book, you have been exposed to a host of argument strategies to use and fallacies to avoid. With all these intellectual tools, it's important not to lose track of the fact that arguments take place among *humans*. Humans are not logic machines, infallible, and always cool headed. We are often insecure, emotion driven, and thoughtless. We often make mistakes, even when we're trying very hard. Therefore, it's important to be aware of and guard against dismissiveness, arrogance, and carelessness. To help with this, here are three questions to answer when deciding whether and how to approach someone with whom you wish to discuss an idea or argument.

Context

Is this the right time and place to have this discussion? A church service is not an appropriate place to start a debate over the existence of God, and a funeral is not an appropriate place to discuss the merits of the philosophical problem of suffering or to tell jokes about the disease that killed the deceased. When someone is agitated or defensive, or may easily become so (for instance, if challenged in a place that feels unsafe), then it's much easier for both parties to commit fallacies. Make sure your interlocutor is in a mental place where he or she can maintain a cool-headed discussion about a topic. Otherwise, you may end up "arguing with a barking dog" (someone who is speaking out of emotion or frustration rather than reason) and ruining a friendship or a working relationship.

Charity

Am I taking the other person's perspective seriously? It's sometimes easy to think that people who disagree with you are stupid or careless – too easy. But remember, there was a time before you began thinking carefully and rationally, too, perhaps about the topic at issue; and it is unlikely that, back then, you would have responded positively to someone who aggressively attacked every flaw in your belief system – even if you recognized them as flaws! Remember also that, even if you're very smart and very good at reasoning, you can still be wrong. The fact that you reject some claims and worldviews on philosophical grounds doesn't mean that you have all the answers, or that you have considered every argument or piece of evidence that supports a view you reject. Carelessness with someone else's view can easily lead to straw men and red herrings. If you abide by the *principle of fidelity*, listen carefully, and respond respectfully, you may discover that someone has an argument you've never considered. And if not, listening carefully to someone's reasons for holding a view you reject may help you to formulate an objection that's more powerful than you might otherwise have produced. It's therefore fruitful for everyone involved to take opposing points of view seriously. It's often a good idea to go beyond the principle of fidelity, which requires only accurate representation. Unless you have compelling reasons for not doing so, go a bit further and exercise what's called the *principle of charity* (from the Latin *caritas* for love).

> *Principle of Charity: Interpret others' remarks in the best possible way – the way that makes their arguments most sound or cogent, that offers them the most veracity, the most coherence, and the most common sense.*

Doing so will lead to stronger reasoning all around. After all, if you can refute the strongest possible version of an opponent's argument, you can certainly refute all of the weaker versions.

Productivity

Is this line of argument getting to the point? Sometimes, a line of argument leads to an overemphasis on tangential or secondary topics. In some cases, this is necessary (e.g., "Let's first agree on what we mean by *X*"). But in others, arguments lead to questions that are not productive for resolving the original disagreement or solving a problem. When arguments go off-topic (especially into areas where neither party is very competent), fallacious arguments are easier to commit and relationships easier to destroy. If you begin to notice this happening, start looking for a way to redirect the conversation back to the issue at the heart of your dispute.

Exercises and study questions[2]

Name the fallacies committed in the inferences that follow.

1. I really feel strongly that Steven Avery's guilty, so he must be.
2. Hume's theory of causation must be flawed because he was a racist.
3. Ideals of equality were developed for cynical reasons in a political contest by a corrupt culture. Therefore, they have no value of legitimacy.
4. We'll beat you unconscious unless you accept as true our ideas on police misconduct.
5. Accepting this theory makes me less afraid of terrorism and global warming, so it must be true.
6. You can't prove that a secret conspiracy of elites doesn't rule the world, so they do.
7. We've got a new ruling party in power now, so things are definitely improving.
8. This nutritional supplement is very popular among people I think are cool, so it must be safe and effective.
9. The high priest of Weehawken told me that there is a twin Earth precisely like ours in a distant galaxy, and on that planet lives a doppelganger for each one of us. So, it must be true.

10. I can harass and slander and defraud you all I want; after all we enjoy free speech in this country.
11. Either we bomb them, or we perish.
12. God is love, love is blind; therefore God is blind.
13. Torture is wrong because inflicting pain and suffering on people to extract something from them is wrong.
14. All cats are mammals, and all mammals are warm-blooded, so therefore we need a strong nuclear deterrent as part of our foreign policy.
15. Every atom is smaller than a grain of sand, and the Earth is composed of atoms, therefore the Earth is smaller than a grain of sand.
16. Society is unjust; therefore it ought to be that way.
17. There has been a long tradition of magical treatment of disease; therefore magical medical theories are true.
18. I have founded a profitable company, employing thousands of people, paying millions in taxes, and generating untold wealth for our shareholders. I am also a famous television personality. I therefore am innocent of the charge of driving while intoxicated.
19. The conduct of our company has been lawful; therefore the conduct of each of our employees has been lawful.
20. With nearly every system failing, Catherine piloted the *Hesperus* to harbor. Clearly, Catherine was truly heroic to pilot a ship while so ill.

SEE ALSO

2.1 Deductive and Inductive Arguments
2.5 The Critical Thinker's "Two Step"
Chapter 10: Tools from Rhetoric, Critical Theory, and Politics
Chapter 7: Tools for Critical Thinking about Experience and Error

READING

Daniel Kahneman, *Thinking, Fast and Slow* (2011)
Dan Ariely, *Predictably Irrational* (2008)
Madsen Pirie, *How to Win Every Argument: The Use and Abuse of Logic* (2008)
Robert Gula, *Nonsense: Red Herrings, Straw Men, and Sacred Cows: How We Abuse Logic in our Everyday Language* (2007)
Jamie Whyte, *Crimes Against Logic: Exposing the Bogus Arguments of Politicians, Priests, Journalists, and Other Serial Offenders* (2004)
Douglas Walton, *The Place of Emotion in Argument* (1992)
Linda Alcoff & Elizabeth Potter, eds., *Feminist Epistemologies* (1992)
Antonio Damasio, *Descartes's Error: Emotion, Reason, and the Human Brain* (1994)

NOTES

1. "On the Moral and Legal Status of Abortion," *Monist* 57.1 (1973): 43–61.
2. Answers to Chapter 5 exercises and study questions: (1) subjectivist fallacy, (2) *ad hominem*, direct, (3) genetic fallacy, (4) *ad baculum*, (5) *ad metum*, (6) *ad ignorantiam*, (7) *ad novitatem*, (8) *ad populum*, (9) *ad verecundiam*, (10) accident, (11) false dilemma, (12) equivocation, (13) *petitio principii*, (14) missing the point, (15) composition, (16) is-ought fallacy, (17) appeal to tradition, (18) red herring, (19) division, (20) amphiboly.

6 Tools for Critical Thinking about Induction

6.1 Inductive vs. Deductive Arguments Again

You'll remember from Chapter 3 that in well-formed deductive arguments the conclusion follows from the premises in a way that's fully truth preserving. That is, the truth of the premises supports or guarantees the truth of the conclusion in a way that's described variously as definite, certain, necessary, or simply always the case. In well-formed inductive reasoning, by contrast, conclusions are accepted even though the premises do not fully warrant them. Conclusions follow, that is, in good inductive arguments with strong probability but not definitely or always.

One of the most important areas of life in which inductive reasoning is common is in reasoning about causes and their effects. Most of our claims about the causal order of nature are justified by inductive inferences made from empirical data. Because, however, there's always more data to collect, because our cognitive and technical instruments sometimes fail, and because, as the eighteenth-century philosopher David Hume (1711–1776) observed, we can't be one hundred percent sure what tomorrow will bring, inferences about the causal order cannot be absolutely certain. Tomorrow someone might discover new data that confounds and contradicts our conclusions. Our instruments may have been flawed, and we may have made mistakes in using them. And so, our conclusions about the facts of the world might turn out to be wrong.

Science, however, isn't only an inductive enterprise. Scientists also use deduction and other forms of thinking all the time. Scientists often use imagination to formulate hypotheses to test and analyze. And whenever scientists use arithmetic or other forms of mathematical reasoning, they're typically engaged in deductive reasoning. Moreover, once natural laws are established inductively (even before they're established), scientists can use deduction to draw out additional hypotheses to test as well as to apply those laws in the contexts of technology, industry, and commerce. So, for example, even though Robert Boyle may have formulated his gas law ($P_1V_1 = P_2V_2$) in

The Critical Thinking Toolkit, First Edition. Galen A. Foresman, Peter S. Fosl, and Jamie C. Watson.

1662 after engaging in imaginative speculation and *inductive* inference, he and others subsequently have been able to reason *deductively* using the law to reach conclusions about volume and pressure.

- Since speculating *imaginatively* and then confirming *inductively* that for any given quantity of gas: $P_1V_1 = P_2V_2$
- If we cut the volume of 10 liters of gas at 1 atmosphere in half (so that V_2 is half of V_1 or 5 liters),
- We can therefore infer *deductively* that P_2 must be twice P_1 or 2 atm. (As a matter of deduction, the product of both sides of the equation must be equal, or here 10.)

So, science is a mixture of lots of different kinds of reasoning and thinking.

Central to scientific thinking is reasoning about what causes what. Yet reasoning about causes is pervasive not only in the sciences but also in the law, in commerce, in politics, in moral reflection, and in ordinary life. Reasoning about causes isn't easy, though; not surprisingly logicians and critical thinkers have identified many different types of error in causal reasoning. Thankfully, philosophers and theorists of scientific reasoning have also developed a number of techniques that can help us avoid these errors and reason better about causes. Strong critical thinkers will do well to become familiar with the typical mistakes made in causal reasoning, as they are very, very common indeed. Knowing the techniques for properly identifying causes, too, can help you both detect poor causal reasoning and sustain strong causal reasoning. In particular, we'll take a look at the techniques for identifying causes and effects developed by nineteenth-century philosopher John Stuart Mill (1806–1873). In this chapter, then, we'll look more closely at causal reasoning as well as other types of inductive reasoning. Together with what we set out here with the book's early chapters about deduction and the informal ways things go wrong, this chapter will give you a solid foundation for thinking critically about logical matters. You might call all this the *basic logic* of critical thinking. Later chapters will both build on this foundation and add nuance to it.

6.2 Analogies and Arguments from Analogy

In Section 2.1, we compared arguments to bridges, arguing that you might think of the content of premises as if it were like the materials out of which bridges are made and the relations among the premises as somehow similar to the way a bridge is structured. When we did that, we were drawing an analogy between the two. Analogies are, in fact, ubiquitous in human reasoning, and they're important in critical thinking.

One way that analogies function is in clarifying the world. People often interpret something they don't understand by drawing analogies with things they already do understand. If, for example, you've ever learned about electrical theory, you've probably encountered analogies, such as water flowing through a pipe. Voltage can be understood as the pressure of the flow; amperage may be grasped by analogy with the volume of the flow. Analogies like this help illuminate the transmission of electricity through a wire.

Analogies are often also used in argument, usually as a special kind of inductive argument. Arguing that the financial collapse of 2008 was analogous to the collapse of 1929, some economists concluded that similar remedies should be administered to help the economy recover. Political analysts have compared the struggle Western Europe has faced with Russia over the Ukraine with the Cold War, arguing that Cold War strategies, such as fortifying NATO and besieging the Russian economy, are the best way to handle the situation. Others draw analogies between the rise of Islamic theocracies such as ISIL and Boko Haram-controlled territories with attempts to establish new caliphates in, variously, the eighteenth- and nineteenth-century Barbary States, the medieval Andalusian principalities, and even with the Ottoman Empire. A version of what's often called the "argument from design" in the philosophy of religion turns upon the analogy between the universe and human artifacts, perhaps most famously the analogy between a watch and living things set out by William Paley in his 1802 book, *Natural Theology*. (Another version of the argument had been criticized earlier by David Hume in his 1779 *Dialogues Concerning Natural Religion.*)

Legal reasoning centrally employs analogies by comparing current cases with past cases – that is by citing precedents (preceding verdicts and decisions). Judges and lawyers do this both to *understand* the case at hand better and also to *justify* or *argue for* some decision. For instance, cases of unjust discrimination with regard to race may be cited to justify arguments about the justice or injustice of other forms of discrimination, for example gender or disability discrimination. If the precedent cases are closely analogous to the present case in important ways, attorneys can argue that the court should reach a decision in the present case similar to the decisions reached in the precedents. One might think of the reasoning like this (where X and Y are things or events, where S and D are similarities and differences):

$$X = S_1, S_2, S_3, S_4, D_1, D_2, D_3, \textit{and some property or feature said to be } S_5$$
$$Y = S_1, S_2, S_3, S_4, D_1, D_2, D_3, \textit{therefore } S_5$$

In words: since *X* has similarities 1, 2, 3, and 4 with *Y*, *Y* must also share similarity 5 with *X*; and that's true even though *X* and *Y* are different in ways 1, 2, and 3.

Criticizing analogies

But that's just where things get tricky. Opposing attorneys are likely to argue that the precedent case cited by their adversary is *not* analogous to the present case or that some other precedent case, where a different verdict was reached, constitutes an even *stronger* analogue to the present case. And so, back and forth arguments from analogy go. To deal with the many analogies and dis-analogies encountered in life, effective critical thinkers will do well to acquire some sense of what makes for strong and weak analogies.

A lot depends upon assessing the similarities and differences among analogues. You see, no two cases are entirely the same, but for many purposes the differences just don't matter. *Strong analogies*, you might say, are roughly those where the similarities are sufficient to serve the purpose of the analogy, whereas *weak analogies* are cases where they aren't. With a bit more detail:

1. *Quantity.* All other things being equal, as a matter of sheer quantity, *the more similarities and the fewer differences, the stronger the analogy.*
2. *Relevance.* Quantity by itself, however, isn't enough. *The similarities and differences considered in evaluating an analogy must be relevant to the use to which an analogy is put.* If one were to draw an analogy between Vietnam and Iraq in arguing for some kind of military policy, the similar bedtime stories parents read to their children in each country is not likely to be relevant to the strength of the analogy.
3. *Weight.* Relevance is only the beginning, however, among the relevant similarities and differences. Some will be more weighty or important than others, so much so that a single but crucial relevant difference might trump a large number of relevant similarities. In other words, in a stronger analogy *the weight of the relevant similarities must outweigh the weight of the relevant differences,* no matter what their number.

These principles give critical thinkers three different approaches to criticism of an analogy. You might, that is: criticize (1) the number of similarities and differences, pointing out that there are far more of one than the other; (2) you might argue on grounds of relevance that the similarities and differences thought to be relevant in an analogy aren't really so; and (3) that the importance of some relevant factors outweighs (or doesn't outweigh) others. Here's an example.

You might argue (using the first principle) that the vast number of differences between the ancient battle of Cannae between Roman and Carthage during the Second Punic War and the battle of Gettysburg during the US Civil War makes any analogy between them weak. On the other hand, you might argue (using the second principle) that most of those differences are irrelevant to, say, questions of troop formation and strength. Still, upon further reflection, you might conclude (on the basis of the third principle) that even if it's true that most of the differences between the two battles are irrelevant, there remains one decisive difference between the two cases: artillery.

SEE ALSO

7.5 Misleading Language
8.5 Justifying Values
10.1 Meta-Narratives
10.2 Governing Tropes

READING

David Kelley, *The Art of Reasoning: An Introduction to Logic and Critical Thinking* (2014)
Anthony Weston, *A Rulebook for Arguments* (2009)
Keith J. Holyoak & Paul Thagard, *Mental Leaps: Analogy in Creative Thought* (1996)
Cass Sunstein, "On Analogical Reasoning," *Harvard Law Review* 106 (1993): 741–791
Stella Vosniadou & Andrew Ortony, *Similarity and Analogical Reasoning* (1989)

6.3 Fallacies about Causation

Human releases of various compounds into the atmosphere are causing the world's climates to change. Allowing the banks to fail will cause the economy to crash. HIV causes AIDS. Fracking for natural gas causes earthquakes. Sloth is the cause of poverty. Mobile phones cause brain cancer. Indulgent parenting causes obesity. A strong US military and resolute foreign policy was the cause of the collapse of the Soviet Union.

Our world is rife with causal claims, many of them as controversial as they are important. Sometimes we are tempted to describe certain events as *causes* when we shouldn't (e.g., "the football team lost because I wasn't wearing my lucky scarf"), and many causal claims are just sloppy and even erroneous. It is in fact very difficult to establish true causal relationships, especially in matters of social science and politics. Causal networks are complex, and often one causal system interrupts or confounds or exaggerates the effects of others. Specious forms of causal thinking are often persuasive to people, and rigorous causal inquiry can be just that – difficult and time consuming. Good critical thinkers will understand this and will be alive to the many ways reasoning about causation can go wrong. In what follows, then, we'll investigate a few of the most common forms of error. When scrutinizing causal claims, good critical thinkers will keep these errors in mind while carefully weighing the reasoning that's been proposed to justify the claims under scrutiny. By simply asserting that someone has got a causal claim wrong you are identifying a Questionable Cause fallacy, *non causa pro causa*, or just *non causa* (roughly, "that's not the cause"), but there are lots of more specific and common ways people go wrong in causal reasoning. Let's take a look at some.

Post hoc ergo propter hoc

It means in Latin: "after this, therefore, because of this." By whatever name, however, this form of faulty causal reasoning is one of the most common. One billiard ball strikes another, and in doing so, causes the second to move; you touch a paint-filled brush to canvas, and in doing so, a mark of that color appears on the canvas; you hammer a nail into wood, and be*cause* of this, the nail sinks into the wood. Because causation works this way, it's tempting to conclude of every successively occurring pair of events that the first causes the second. But sometimes events regularly succeed others even though they're not causally related to one another. For example, day regularly follows night, but day doesn't *cause* night. Similarly, feeling better follows the passing of a cold, but the *cold* doesn't *cause* you to feel better.

Suppose Jim has the habit of saying "green" every time he approaches a red traffic light in the hope that it will turn. On occasion the light actually does turn green when he says the word. Does that mean that on those occasions his uttering the word "green" actually causes the light to turn green? Of course not. Just because some event happens after another event, it doesn't follow that the first event caused the following event. While every cause must happen before its effect (a principle that militates against the possibility of time travel into the past, by the way), causes aren't the only things that precede events. Some events just accidentally precede others and bear no causal relationship to what follows. This isn't just true of individual or occasional events; it can be true of consistent correlations. Reporter Leonard Koppett once joked that there is a strong correlation between the Super Bowl's being won by a team that was part of the NFL before its 1966 merger with the AFL and the stock market's closing higher at that Super Bowl year's end. It's an interesting correlation, but it's unlikely that the formula describes a causal relationship (though, apparently, some people took him seriously). Remember that correlation doesn't necessarily signal causation (even if sometimes it does). If we were to be coy, we might say: correlation does not itself perfectly correlate with causation.

Correlation is not always causation

In two phenomena that appear associated with one another there are four logical possibilities, causally speaking: X may cause Y; Y may cause X; X and Y may both be the result of another, shared common cause Z; or the two may bear no causal relationship and simply be accidentally correlated. Correlations are insufficient by themselves to determine causation, but that doesn't mean it's easy to figure out when one has encountered merely an accidental correlation and when it's a case of real causation. The Scottish philosopher David Hume argues in his 1739 *A Treatise of Human Nature* (and also in his 1748 *Enquiry Concerning Human Understanding*, Sections 4–7) that all we really observe in those things we judge to be causally related are constant conjunctions (correlations) and not a "causal power" or a "necessary connection" between them. Nevertheless, he also prescribes (in Book 1, Part 3, Section 15 of the *Treatise* and elsewhere) various rules for separating those properly and improperly judged to be causally related.

Controversy remains about how to untangle causes from correlations, but here are some principles critical thinkers will do well to keep in mind in distinguishing causal from merely accidental events:

- *In general, those events causally related must always be so, unless some confounding factor interferes with their connection. They are, in some causally relevant sense of necessity, necessarily related. So, the same cause must always produce the same effect.*

The contrapositive holds, too: if the effect does not occur, the cause has not taken place. Although correlation is not always causation, causation is always correlation.

- *As a rule, causes cannot operate at a distance from their effects; more precisely, (a) causes must immediately precede their effects with no lag, and (b) they must be spatially contiguous or in contact. Spatial distance and temporal lags must be explained by some set of interposed events causally related to both the cause and effect.*
- *A causal judgment can be strengthened if we explain by means of some theory how the cause and effect are related, that is, what mechanism leads necessarily from the one to the other.*
- *Every causal judgment must be logically consistent with every other causal judgment.*

Let's go on, then, exploring fallacies related to causation.

Cum hoc ergo propter hoc

Like the *post hoc* fallacy, the *cum hoc ergo propter hoc* ("with this, therefore because of this") variant has to do with erroneously judging accidentally related events to bear a causal connection, in this case, events that coincide. A runny nose coincides with sneezing, but runny noses don't cause sneezing. A famous study once found that increases in men's tie width correlated with increases in the value of equities in the stock markets. Though some argue that size matters in other contexts, Tatu Westling of the University of Helsinki seems only to have found a mere coincidence when he discovered a correlation between strong national economic performance and average (as opposed to extra long or extra short) penis length among a nation's male citizens. Again, instances of correlation are not necessarily instances of causation.

Neglecting a common cause

Often, *cum hoc* errors are the result of neglecting to consider a *common cause* of two events that are erroneously thought to be related as cause and effect. An arguer neglects a common cause when she infers that one event causes another from evidence that they regularly occur together – when event *A* is present, so is *B*; when event *A* is absent, so is *B*. So, while a runny nose does not cause a fever, both may be the result of a common cause, a cold or other illness.

In some places, fish become more active when the water temperature drops. You might be tempted to conclude from this that lower water temperatures cause fish to become more active, and you might be right. But there are a number of alternative explanations that may be just as plausible. For instance, it's possible that fish become active when sunlight decreases after the summer solstice, and that the diminished light may also cause a decrease in water temperature. In this case, the water temperature's decrease does not cause the fish to become active; but, rather, both the falling water temperature and the increased piscine activity are caused by the seasonal change in sunlight.

Smoking often accompanies alcoholism, but while smoking doesn't cause alcoholism, both may be simply the result of something more basic that causes them both – for instance, depression. In some cases, depression may be characterized as what is sometimes called (by those concerned with scientific method) a *confounding variable* ("con-found" means "found with"); and the false causal relationship between alcoholism and smoking is called a *spurious relationship*. If a confounding variable or common cause has been overlooked or neglected as a cause, it is often called a *lurking variable*.

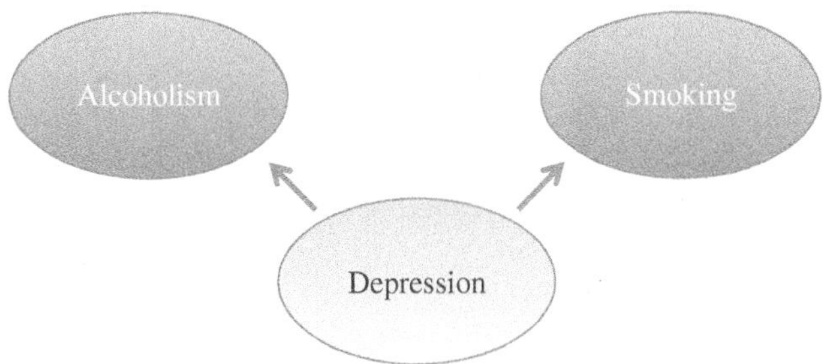

Sometimes the confounding variable isn't lurking at all but is hiding out in the open and just hasn't been understood to be a common cause. The history of reasoning about AIDS offers a good example of this. AIDS is a syndrome. That means it's a cluster of afflictions rather than merely a single illness. Because HIV appears as one among many in that cluster of illnesses, researchers trying to determine the cause of AIDS initially overlooked HIV infection as its cause. They thought HIV was just one of the other afflictions that strike people with AIDS, such as lymphadenopathy, a special kind of pneumonia called *pneumocystis carinii* or (PCP), and Karposi's sarcoma. Sometimes, however, one of the apparently concurrent effects is instead the underlying cause of the whole, and so it turned out to be with HIV. Careful testing and reasoning by scientists including Robert Gallo and Luc Montagnier showed that HIV isn't just one of the many illnesses that people with Acquired Immune Deficiency Syndrome (AIDS) suffer, but instead the cause of all of them collected together.

Sometimes, however, causes are hidden. One way they're hidden is by the ways data are assembled. The University of California at Berkeley was sued on the basis of data from its 1973 graduate admissions that appeared to show unfair discrimination against female candidates: about 44% of males but only 35% of females were admitted. But once the data were distinguished among departments, just the opposite effect appeared. No discrimination against women was evident, and many of the departments even showed a slightly higher admission rate for female than male applicants. The distortion occurred in the combined data set because women had applied to the most competitive departments in proportionally greater numbers, which resulted in higher quantities of women rejected overall but not at greater rates within each department. Consider this hypothetical example to see what happened.

- If 100 women and 10 men applied to a department with an unbiased 90% rejection rate for both genders, it would produce 90 rejected women and 9 rejected men.
- If 10 women and 100 men applied to a department with an unbiased 10% rejection rate for both genders, it would result in 1 rejected woman and 10 rejected men.
- Combine the data from the two non-biased departments and apparent bias appears: 220 applicants (110 men and 110 women), of which women are rejected at a rate of 41% (91 women) while men are rejected at a rate of only 7% (or 19 men).

When combining or separating data sets reverses an apparent causal relationship, the effect is called *Simpson's Paradox* or *Simpson's Effect*.

Oversimplified and contributing causes

Sometimes poor causal reasoning appears in the form of what's called the "single cause" or "complex cause" fallacy. US president Ronald Reagan provoked a storm of criticism when he remarked that: "There are no easy answers, but there are simple answers." That may sometimes be so, but it's also true that sometimes the world is just complex and that phenomena are produced by complex interactions among sets of causes. In the face of complexity it can be tempting, even necessary, to simplify; but it can also be distorting to the point of error to oversimplify the causal background of events. So, whereas violent computer games may contribute to more violence in society, you would commit the fallacy of oversimplified cause to attribute violent crime entirely to that cause. While poor adult earnings, similarly, may be in some cases the result of family dysfunction, it would be an oversimplification to explain poverty generally as a result of poor family values. Social phenomena such as crime and poverty are often the result of highly complex social, psychological, economic, and political factors, and it's a distortion to pretend otherwise.

Higher energy prices, to take another example, may not be good for an economy, but it may be a gross oversimplification to blame economic woes entirely on that factor. The economy is a vast and complicated network of factors – including interest rates, government outlays, debt ratios, consumer expectations, labor unrest, transportation, taxes, unemployment levels, trade balances, etc. – and it's often misleading to explain the behavior of that complex whole on the basis of a single causal factor. When a number of causes act together to produce an effect, they're understood to be *contributing causes*, and taking one of the contributing causes to be the only cause can result in fallacious thinking.

Researchers get around the oversimplification fallacy through what's called a *ceteris paribus* ("all other things being equal") qualification. So, as an economist might say, all other things being equal, rising interest rates will produce higher unemployment. The thing is, of course, outside the laboratory, all other things rarely do remain equal.

Proximate, remote, and intervening causes

The thing about causes is that they come in sequences. One might even metaphorically say that they come in chains. That being so, distinguishing the order of links in the chain leading up to any given effect can produce confusion. The most immediate cause to a given effect is called the *proximate cause*. Causes that are less proximate are called *remote causes*.

Consider this example: Terry died unfortunately when a utility pole crashed down on him as he walked beneath it on a windy day. So, the proximate cause of his death was the trauma from the blow he received from the falling pole. The wind, one might say, was the next most proximate cause. The pole had been weakened, however, by a car that had bumped into it some weeks ago, as well as by the rot and weathering that had taken hold of the pole's wood over the years it stood there. Utility poles, for that reason, are replaced periodically. This one, however, had not been replaced on schedule because of the negligence of the managers of the utility company whose responsibility it is to maintain the poles. We might say, then, that while the proximate cause of Terry's death was internal bleeding and tissue damage, the company who did not replace the pole on schedule bears ultimate, although remote, responsibility. In a similar though more direct way, a mob boss who orders a hit is guilty of murder even if he does not himself pull the trigger. In the example of Terry's death, however, we might also attribute some causal (and perhaps moral and even legal) responsibility to the driver of the car who weakened the pole by striking it, especially if she were intoxicated at the time.

If we think of the damage to the pole caused by the car as something other than what occurs in the normal life of a pole, we might call it, as people often do with this sort of extraordinary event, an *intervening cause*. Intervening causes sometimes magnify or contribute to the effects of existing causal sequences (as the car does in the case of Terry's death), but they can also interrupt and even thwart a causal sequence, such as when aspirin intervenes to lower the body temperature of someone with an infection that would otherwise cause a fever. The universe is chock full of causal sequences intervening, reinforcing, and thwarting one another, which is one reason untangling the complexity and interaction of causal networks takes such time and effort. As a result, good science as well as sound inquiries of all kinds require capable critical thinking.

Exercises and study questions

Explain how each of the following can be understood to be an example of the neglected common cause or *cum hoc* fallacies.

1. "Since we instituted this policy prohibiting drug *X*, drug *X* use in our nation has dropped 20% per year. This shows that the policy is effective." [*For*

example: This reasoning is fallacious because we don't know the drop rate independent of the policy. For instance, if drug X use had already been dropping at 20% per year prior to the policy's being instituted, we couldn't conclude that the policy had any causal effect on drug X usage. In other words, given that prior drop rate, the coincidence of the policy and drug X's usage dropping 20% per year was probably not caused by the policy. In this scenario, both the policy and the drop in national usage were motivated by a pre-existing public concern about X, the common cause of both.]

2. "Ice cream sales have tripled in the last three months, and crime rates have fallen substantially. We obviously need to keep selling lots of ice cream so that crime rates will drop."
3. "Every time it storms, the barometer drops. Storms must have a powerful effect on barometers."
4. "The economy has been in a recession ever since the president took office. He's clearly doing a terrible job."

Explain how each of these can be understood to be an example of the *post hoc* fallacy.

1. "Every time I wear my Flyers jersey, the Flyers win. So, of course I'm wearing my Flyers jersey at tonight's game, and they're going to win!"
2. "If you leave meat out long enough, maggots will appear. So, meat produces maggots."
3. "Whenever I drink coffee before an exam, I do well. So you should drink coffee before our final this morning."
4. "Just after every flash of lightning, we hear thunder. You wouldn't think light could cause sound that way, but it happens every time, so it must be true."

SEE ALSO

2.1 Deductive and Inductive Arguments
6.4 Inductive Statistical Reasoning
8.6 Justification: The Basics

READING

Stephen Mumford & Rani Lill Anjum, *Causation: A Very Short Introduction* (2014)

Carlo Berzuini, Philip Dawid, Luisa Bernardinelli, eds., *Causality: Statistical Perspectives and Applications* (2012)

Judea Pearl, *Causality: Models, Reasoning and Inference* (2009)

David Lewis, "Causation," *The Journal of Philosophy* 70.17 (1973): 556–567

Bertrand Russell, "On the Notion of Cause," *Proceedings of the Aristotelian Society* 13 (1912–1913): 1–26

6.4 Inductive Statistical Reasoning

There's a 30% chance of rain tomorrow. The Republican candidate for governor is just 2 percentage points ahead, well within the margin of error. Las Vegas odds give Man o' War a 5 to 1 chance of winning the Kentucky Derby. Eating half a cup of blueberries everyday cuts your chance of getting cancer by 15%. Ebola carries a 70% mortality rate.

Our lives are awash in statistical claims as well as arguments that depend on them. It's important, therefore, for us as critical thinkers to have a sense of some of the principal errors people make in statistical reasoning. Statistics is an enormous field of its own, and the issues can become terribly complex, but nevertheless, a few central ideas can cut through a lot in our world that's not only difficult but also misleading.

Sampling: random and biased

Determining probabilities is often a deductive process (e.g., determining the probability of pulling two white marbles in a row from a bag of five, only three of which are white). The kinds of statistical reasoning that are, however, typically most interesting and most fraught for people are *inductive generalizations* about entire populations (the *target population*) on the basis of subsets (the *samples*) drawn from those populations or from related *sampled populations*. So, a study might draw inferences about a *target* population of all Scottish voters on the basis of a *sample* of surveys of just a few hundred people drawn from a *sample population* of those listed in the telephone directory. Perhaps the most important dimension of this kind of inquiry is the quality of the sample.

Qualitatively, samples ought as far as possible to *represent* the target populations about which they're to provide information. That is, in order to be *representative*, a sample ought to have the same relevant qualities as the target population. If 65% of the entire target population votes for the Labor Party, and voting patterns are the relevant property, then in order to be representative, 65% of the sample must also vote Labor.

When samples are not representative, they're said to be *biased*, and biased samples are perhaps responsible for most errors in statistical inferences. Researchers try not to acquire biased samples in a variety of ways. Perhaps the most common method is randomizing the sampling process in order to produce a *random sample* from the sampled population. But how does one "randomize"? There are computer programs that generate something approximating random numbers, which can be indexed to, say, entries in the phone book (though that method misses people not in the directories), or the numbers may be assigned to other sample set elements. But no computer program is really random (since program algorithms are composed of definite rules). And, therefore, the process of randomizing often attracts critical scrutiny. Researcher Shere Hite assembled a well-known report on human sexual conduct (*The Hite Report*; 1976), but some of her methods for assembling data drew criticism. For example, Hite had drawn data from survey forms placed in soft pornographic magazines, among other sources; but are the readers of that sort of publication representative of the general population? Are any data sets collected purely from voluntary participants average or normal, since the study then reports only on the kind of person who answers surveys? And is the average person who answers surveys about personal matters different from people on average?

Stratification

Even a truly random sample may not represent a population when the target population is unevenly distributed in some way. For example, suppose one wanted to study what percentage of drivers on a certain highway are on average under the influence of alcohol. Checking simply a random sample of drivers over a 24-hour period would not produce a representative sample, since more drivers are on the road at certain times of day – e.g., hypothetically, 75% of drivers during rush hours between 7–9am and 4:30–6:30pm. Similarly, if 90% of Conservative Party voters are densely clustered in a few postal codes in Scotland, it won't do to sample voters randomly and uniformly across all postal codes.

To deal with biases introduced by uneven distributions, researchers employ a strategy called *stratification.* Data sets are stratified so that the percentages of relevant subpopulations in the sample match that of the target population. So, in the study of drunk drivers, a researcher might be sure to take 75% of his or her otherwise randomized sample during the rush hours and then take the rest randomly from the remaining 20-hour period.

Data sets are often stratified in the social sciences by gender, by age, by geography, and by other factors that are thought to be relevant to studies. Note that assessing whether or not a sample is representative depends upon what characteristics are *relevant.* Sinistrality, or left-handedness, hair color, average weight of pets, and whether or not subjects' surnames have odd or even numbers of letters are unlikely to be relevant to an inquiry about voting preferences. Noting relevant qualities upon which to stratify and assess representation is, however, very important. A sample of only or mainly middle-aged American males will hardly yield results that tell us about all people across the globe or across history. Just this sort of error has characterized some medical research. Ruth Hubbard, a feminist philosopher of science, rightly criticized the important 1989 Physicians Health Study on the effects of daily aspirin on heart disease. Hubbard found that nearly all of the 22,000 subjects of the study were men. Other studies were found to be based upon similarly biased data sets. Unsurprisingly, subsequent research has found that heart disease occurs with different dynamics in women, and so therapies must be designed in light of sex as a relevant factor. Until the 1990s the FDA (the US Food and Drug Administration) routinely only tested new drug therapies on men, while research on women was largely restricted to reproductive issues. That bias may clearly have distorted scientific findings.

The gambler's fallacy

Gamblers can often be heard saying things like, "A seven is due to come up on those dice"; "That roulette wheel has landed on red the last five spins, so the next spin is likely to be black." But that sort of thinking, as ought to be well known, is fallacious, partly an effect of magical or *wishful thinking*. Spins of the roulette wheel, throws of dice, and flips of coins are what statisticians call *independent events*, meaning that past instances of those events have no bearing upon future instances. The past flips of a coin do not somehow reach out from the past and influence present and future flips. Each flip happens on its own, and each flip of a normal coin carries a probability of roughly 50/50 heads or tails. Even if a coin has landed heads the last one hundred flips, on the next flip (assuming it truly is a normal coin) we still face under normal circumstances just a 50/50 chance of landing on tails. If that seems strange, think of it this way: sure, flipping 101 heads in a row is highly improbable, but having already flipped 100 heads, most of that extraordinary event has already occurred. The bit that's left is just a 50/50 event.

Now, of course, some difficulty may arise in figuring out whether or not events are *independent* or *dependent* in relation to one another. If the question involves bags of marbles, as it often does in statistical examples, what matters may be as simple as whether the marbles withdrawn are replaced. In a bag of 10 marbles, 5 of which are white and 5 black, there is a 50% or 5/10 chance of drawing a black marble. But if that black marble is not replaced, there remains then only a 4/9 chance of picking a black marble on the next draw.

With people, things get trickier and more psychological. If a team has lost five games in a row, those past losses may indeed be relevant to the team's next performance simply because athletes, unlike coins, remember and are affected by the past. The team may be demoralized after the string of losses and therefore play even less well than they have in the past. Or they may have become motivated by their recent defeats and may have gained extra determination to win the next game, thereby improving their chances. That's why blinding is so important in medical research, and why consumer expectations are so important in economics. People are historical beings, and they're influenced by their understanding of not only what is presently happening to them but also what has happened to them and to others in the past, as well as by what they believe will happen in the future.

Averages: mean, median, and mode

People are sometimes tempted to commit an error akin to the fallacy of division because of how some statistics are presented, especially averages. When the average American household is said to have "2.3 children," no one thinks, "Wow, I wonder what three-tenths of a child looks like?" But when someone says, "The average income of this neighborhood is $83,000/year," it is tempting to think that each household in that neighborhood makes about $83,000/year. This inference is fallacious. Consider the following four neighborhoods, each with seven households. Each has an average income of $83,000/year, but notice the vast differences in each household income and each neighborhood:

East Neighborhood	West Neighborhood	North Neighborhood	South Neighborhood
1. $83,000	1. $18,000	1. $50,000	1. $35,000
2. $82,000	2. $12,000	2. $60,000	2. $88,000
3. $84,000	3. $10,000	3. $70,000	3. $40,000
4. $82,000	4. $83,000	4. $60,000	4. $40,000
5. $84,000	5. $42,000	5. $95,000	5. $45,000
6. $82,000	6. $391,000	6. $83,000	6. $278,000
7. $84,000	7. $25,000	7. $163,000	7. $55,000

Average annual income of each neighborhood: $83,000

Different kinds of "average." One way to avoid this error – or detect it – is to keep vigilant about the difference between different kinds of averages. Principally, there are three kinds to consider when thinking critically about claims involving "averages." The *mean* is the result of the simple arithmetic process of adding up the relevant quantities and dividing by the number of them. It's sometimes called the *expected value*. Our example above of neighborhood income gives mean averages – each column of seven incomes is summed and divided, of course, by seven to reach an average of $83,000. A second kind of average is the *median*. You might think of the median as that element of the data that stands in the middle, so to speak, such that there are an equal number of data points above and below it. So, in our example above, the median income of East Neighborhood coincides with the mean at $83,000, whereas in West the median is just $25,000, less than one third of the mean. A third kind of average is the *mode*. The mode is just the most frequent or common element. So, in the North Neighborhood the mean is $83k; the median is $70k, and the mode is $60k. When drawn out as a curve, the top of the bump illustrates the mode (or multiple bumps in multi-modal distributions).

Distributions

In what's called a *normal distribution* the mean, median, and mode all coincide – it's the perfect "bell" curve. Curves where the mode is less than the mean will tilt toward the left; where the mode is greater than the mean, they'll tilt rightward. Note, however, that curves can be more or less broad, depending upon how broadly the data are distributed. So, the East Neighborhood will present a high graphical curve, without much spread, as all its data points are clustered around $83,000. East Neighborhood, however, presents a bimodal distribution, where there are three households at $82k and $84k, while only one draws $83k. That means the curve for East Neighborhood will not only be a high, narrow curve; it will also have two bumps of equal height (three households each) with a dip in between them (illustrating the one household that corresponds to the mean and median). South Neighborhood, in contrast, will be much flatter. It will rise quickly to its mode at $40k and then slope more gradually downward stretching way, way out to that one outlying household at $278k.

The *standard deviation* and *variance* describe the distribution or spread of a data set by giving metrics for distance of data from the mean. (Variance of the sample is mathematically defined in several ways depending upon the different kinds of variable involved, but a good general definition is the *mean average of the squared distance of each data point from the sample mean*. Standard deviation is the square root of the variance.) Roughly, the larger the standard deviation or variance, the broader the distribution. If all the data are the same, variance and standard deviation will be zero. In a normal distribution, one standard deviation captures about two-thirds of the data, two standard deviations about 95% of the data, and three standard deviations 99.7% of the data. (Non-normal distributions don't show this pattern.) Obviously, a wide distribution of data will exhibit a larger standard deviation or variance.

All this suggests a few important lessons. When scrutinizing statistical claims about averages, strong critical thinkers will consider how the data might present different averages – that is, different means, medians, and modes. Strong critical thinkers will also consider how broadly or narrowly the data behind any statistical claim are distributed. Highly unequal economic orders might share the same mean wealth with those that are relatively egalitarian, but the median and variance in wealth will be substantially different.

Exercises and study questions

1. Determine the mean, median, and mode for each of the data sets in the neighborhood income table in this section. Draw a graph or curve illustrating each data set. In a few paragraphs, compare and contrast the data and reflect upon what social and political implications one might draw from them.
2. How might one gather a representative sample of illicit drug use or private sexual conduct? How might doing so be different from gathering data about bird behavior or human residential patterns? Write a short essay to explain.
3. "This just in: 65% of Americans approve of the president's performance. (This data was gathered from a survey of 900 registered voters, by calls made between 7pm and 9pm, Monday through Friday.)"

SEE ALSO

Chapter 5: Tools for Detecting Informal Fallacies
6.1 Inductive vs. Deductive Arguments Again
6.3 Fallacies about Causation

READING

Sherri L. Jackson, *Research Methods and Statistics: A Critical Thinking Approach*, 5th edn (2015)
Charles Whelan, *Naked Statistics* (2013)
Timothy C. Urdan, *Statistics in Plain English*, 3rd edn (2011)
David J. Hand, *Statistics: A Very Short Introduction* (2008)
Joel Best, *Damned Lies and Statistics: Untangling Numbers from the Media, Politicians, and Activists* (2001)
Darrell Huff, *How to Lie With Statistics* (1993)

6.5 Base Rate Fallacy

In the base rate fallacy, someone draws an unjustified conclusion about an event, often in causal terms, because he or she ignores (intentionally or unintentionally) the rate at which that event normally occurs. For example, someone might say: "When I exercise strenuously, I get sore. But when I drink water immediately after strenuous exercise, my soreness goes away in a couple of days. So, if you're afraid you'll be sore, you should try drinking water." The speaker here is inferring a causal relationship between *drinking water immediately after working out* and *the waning of soreness*. But the careful thinker (and experienced athlete) will recognize that, whether you drink water or not, soreness will wane in a couple of days. Even if every time you drink water soreness wanes, since soreness still wanes 100% of the time *regardless of whether you drink water*, this successive relationship (*A*, then *B*) is not sufficient for concluding that *A* is the cause of *B*.

Similarly, physicians will often say, "You have a cold. I can prescribe a medication, and it will last about two weeks. Or we can just leave it alone, and it will last about 14 days." This is because physicians understand the base rate duration of a cold, and that, since colds are viral, medical treatments have no causal effect on that rate.

Other examples are more interesting. Consider someone who takes a medical test that is 99% reliable and she is told that she has tested positive. What is the likelihood that she actually has the disease? It is tempting to think 99%, but this is misleading. The probability that she actually has the disease depends on *both* how reliable the test is *and* on how likely it is that anyone ever gets the disease. Let's say you also learn that only 1 person in 100,000,000 ever gets this disease (that's about 3 people in the entire United States). Even if your *test* is really good (99% reliable), the likelihood that you actually have the disease is low (just over 0.0001% or about one in a million).[1] Ignoring the base rate of the disease can lead to gross miscalculations, and therefore, unjustified beliefs.

This mistake is common when people try to evaluate the effects of a change after the change has already been made. For example, if your throat is sore, you might start looking at it in the mirror and thinking it looks pretty bad. But if you don't often look at your throat when you're well, how could you tell? What does your throat *normally* look like?

Similarly, if we pass a law to decrease the rate at which a social problem occurs, and the rate does, in fact, decrease, it might seem that the law was successful. But that conclusion follows only if the reduction was not already occurring, that is, if the base rate of the reduction was changed by the law. For example, in 1974, a federal speed limit of 55 miles per hour was set on interstate highways in order to reduce the number of automobile deaths. From 1973 to 1980, the rate of interstate deaths dropped 17 percent. It might seem that the law was successful. But as it turns out, in the seven years prior to the law (1966–1973), the rate dropped 26 percent. And the greatest drop occurred between 1934 and 1949, when there were virtually no safety regulations on interstate travel at all. When you calculate the rate at which interstate deaths decreased from 1934 to 1980, the 55 mile per hour speed law does not seem to have played a causal role in that decrease. In part as a recognition of this, in 1987 Congress began allowing individual states the option to increase speed limits on rural interstate highways.

Legitimate reasons to ignore base rates?

Base rates are not relevant to all probability calculations – for instance, determining the reliability of a test (false positive and false negative rates) or determining the probability of drawing an ace of spades from a deck of 52 cards. In addition, in some cases, we have good reasons to prefer other information to base rates. Very low probability events do occur, and base rates do not always help determine when they have.

Consider the case of miracles (supernatural suspensions of natural operations). Some have argued that we have good reason to disbelieve that any miracles occur because this is not "the way the world works." In other words, the base rate of the occurrence of miracles is practically zero (even if there were one or two in the history of the world, the base rate is extremely low). On the other hand, weird things do happen in nature at a calculable rate. For example, spontaneous remission of many types of cancer occurs at a base rate of just under 1%. That makes remission unlikely, but possible. But since we don't have anything like this for miracles, it may seem that remission is always more likely than that a miracle has occurred.

But now consider, alternatively, the evolution of consciousness (of the sort we humans seem to have). Assuming that it's in some sense unique, consciousness of a human sort has occurred only once in all of evolutionary history: in other words, the base rate at which evolution has produced human consciousness independently of humans is zero. Should we then believe that evolution is not responsible for consciousness? Note that this is the same reasoning strategy that was applied to miracles. (Be careful not to fall prey to the *ad ignorantiam* fallacy (5.7) here, though; not having reasons or evidence for disbelief is not the same as having reasons or evidence for belief.)

Someone might object that, unlike miracles, we know evolution produces unique, new things, such as photosynthetic processes and echolocation. But notice this reply introduces new information, something else we know about evolution. The miracle-defender can make a similar move: *if* a divine being exists, there is no obstacle to its suspending the laws of nature that it created. In both cases, other information about the nature of the putative cause (whether natural selection produces new things; whether God exists) is more important than base rates in evaluating whether the cause has been accurately identified. What these examples suggest is not that we should ignore base rates, but that, in some cases, we need to know much more than base rates in order to form a rational belief about the cause of an event.

Examples of the base rate fallacy

1. "Ever since I bought this bear repellent, I haven't seen a bear. It must really work."
2. "My cold goes away after I take echinacea. I'm telling you, it really works."
3. "Every time I wash my car, it rains. Why me!?"
4. "I read my horoscope every morning, and nothing too bad ever happens to me. Therefore, if you want your life to go well, you should start reading your horoscope."

SEE ALSO

6.3 Fallacies about Causation
6.4 Inductive Statistical Reasoning
8.10 Evidence: Weak and Strong

READING

Rolf Dobelli, *The Art of Thinking Clearly* (2014)
Lawrence Shapiro, "A drop in the sea: What are the odds that Jesus rose or that Moses parted the waves? Even with the best witnesses, vanishingly small," *Aeon Magazine* (2013)
Daniel Kahneman, *Thinking, Fast and Slow* (2011)

6.6 Slippery Slope and *Reductio ad Absurdum*

In the slippery slope fallacy, an arguer attempts to refute a proposed claim or behavior on the grounds that believing the claim or performing the act initiates a causal chain leading to dire, unacceptable, or unwanted consequences. In doing so, however, the arguer fails to justify one or more of the causal links. The slippery slope fallacy is related to the *post hoc* fallacy in that it attributes causal relationships where there may be none. For instance, in response to a policy that eliminates a tax for certain parts of an education budget, someone might say:

> If we eliminate this tax, our schools will be operating on a shoestring budget. Our school system will cease to function effectively on such a budget, and a school system that is not effective will lead to hoodlums in the streets! Hoodlums in the streets could lead to being robbed and murdered. No one wants to be robbed and murdered. Surely, you cannot approve this policy!

Notice that this arguer has moved from a fairly reasonable conclusion (eliminating this tax will reduce the resources available for our budget) to a conclusion that is not at all obviously true given these premises (eliminating this tax will result, eventually, in our being robbed and murdered). The implication is that eliminating the tax will somehow *bring about* or *cause* the unwanted consequence of hoodlums robbing and murdering in the streets. This argument is more complicated than a mere false cause – the arguer has identified a string of causal relations leading to the extreme consequence. And without additional information about the amount by which the budget is reduced, its causal effect on the school's efficacy, and the latter's causal effect on hoodlums in the streets, this argument is fallacious. Here's another example:

> Author to editor: "You can't change my wording in this article. That's censorship! If we let censorship happen once, we will let it happen again. Eventually, there will be widespread censorship, and people will become afraid to speak their minds. This opens the door to a totalitarian state!"

In this case, the author calls the editor's changing of his work "censorship." It's important to note that this is not a correct use of this term (i.e., it's a subtle *malapropism*) – censorship refers to restrictions on expression imposed by an organization with a monopoly on the use of force (a state or federal government, or political party or group with police or police-like power). It is no more censorship for the editor of a *private* publisher to refuse to print some articles on the basis of their content than it is for someone to ask you to refrain from using certain words in front of her children when you're in her home. But let's imagine this *is* a case of censorship – e.g., imagine the editor is a member of the Pentagon and is imposing a restriction on what the *New York Times* can publish. This one case of censorship *might or might not* lead to others – it almost certainly won't *cause* others. If, for instance, the author wants to publish national secrets amounting to treason, then censorship may be the appropriate course of action for the Pentagon to take, even if it isn't appropriate in any other case. From this one act of censorship we can infer nothing definite with respect to later censorship behavior. In addition, multiple cases of censorship do not obviously (that is, without further evidence) or necessarily lead to widespread censorship, nor do the latter necessarily lead to totalitarian dictatorships – though such cases may indeed be grounds for serious concern. (In the US, the Federal Communications Commission has arguably been censoring the content broadcast across radio and television since its inception in 1934, and yet few would say that the US has become a totalitarian dictatorship.) Each step in the causal chain must be established by argument and evidence. It's not enough *simply to state* that one thing will follow from another.

Reductio ad absurdum and legitimate uses of the slippery slope

If every step in the arguer's chain of inference can be established with evidence, then it is legitimate to point to a "slippery slope." That is, some slopes are in fact slippery. For instance, imagine our friend Jon says:

> I would never text and drive. That's because there are studies showing that your reaction time when texting is similar to your reaction time when you're drunk. And when you're drunk, we know you increase the likelihood of crashing. And if I crash, I could seriously hurt someone. So texting while driving may cause me to seriously hurt someone, and I'm not willing to take that chance.

Notice that each step in this causal chain has been (or we have some reason to believe it has been) supported with evidence. There doesn't seem to be any fallacy here. (There could, however, be a fallacy depending on how strongly Jon thinks "texting while driving" is correlated with "being seriously hurt" and how strong the analogy is between driving while texting and driving while drunk. Each step in this causal chain involves a probability, and each additional probability lowers the overall probability of the link between the events in the causal chain.)

The legitimate slippery slope has affinities with the reasoning strategy known as "*reductio ad absurdum*" (reduction to absurdity). The *reductio ad absurdum* is a formal rule of logic: if you can show that a claim leads to a logically or even morally absurd conclusion (e.g., a contradiction), then you have a reason to believe that claim to be false. In short, you criticize a claim or position by showing that it logically leads to an absurdity. It's often useful for undermining claims or definitions that are too broad or sweeping. For example, imagine someone tells you that any discussion of sex in a workplace amounts to sexual harassment. You might respond by saying, "Let's assume that's true for the sake of argument and see what follows":

1. Let's assume what you say, that as our first premise any mention of sex in a workplace is sexual harassment. (Claim to be criticized)
2. Victims of sexual assault testifying in court against their assailants discuss sex in a workplace.
3. The testimony of victims in courtrooms is not sexual harassment.
4. The claims of premises 1 and 3 contradict one another, and moreover if you were to hold fast to 1 and reject 3 you'd be stuck with the absurd conclusion that victims of sexual assault testifying against their assailants in court are guilty of sexual harassment.

5. Therefore, the claim that any discussion of sex in the workplace is sexual harassment is false.

Similarly, informally speaking, in a *reductio*-like fashion, a critical thinker can show that a claim, *p*, should be rejected simply because its consequences or implications are *unacceptable* or *unwanted* even if not exactly logical contradictions. Legitimate slippery slope arguments fit into this category. No logical contradiction results from asserting that texting increases your chance of serious injury, but its consequences are profoundly undesirable to most people. Therefore, we have a reason to reject the practice.

Examples of the slippery slope fallacy and reductio arguments

1. "Tax rates have increased again! If we don't stop big government, we will be taxed until we're like Norway."
2. "Never forgive anyone. If you forgive one person, then another will expect it. Pretty soon, people will walk all over you."
3. "The conservative platform has already imposed its values into marriage and into what we can watch on television through the FCC. Pretty soon it will be in our bedrooms and in what we can see on the Internet. We are heading for a fundamentalist theocracy!"
4. "If we allow people to marry irrespective of sex, people will demand to be married irrespective of species! Is that what we want? Do we want people to be able to marry their farm animals? Therefore, we must not legalize same-sex marriages."
5. "Your claim that ginger-haired people can read others' minds must be false. If ginger-haired people could read others' minds, they would never accept lies as truths. But ginger-haired people do sometimes accept lies as truths."

SEE ALSO

5.12 False Dilemma
6.2 Analogies and Arguments from Analogy
6.3 Fallacies about Causation

READING

Ali Almossawi, *An Illustrated Book of Bad Arguments* (2014)
S. Morris Engel, *With Good Reason: An Introduction to Informal Fallacies* (2014)
Jacob E. Van Vleet, *Informal Logical Fallacies: A Brief Guide* (2010)

6.7 Hasty Generalization

In the hasty generalization fallacy, an arguer attempts to convince an audience to accept a belief or behavior on the basis of a weak or biased generalization. A generalization is an inference *about every member* of a category of things or events derived *from evidence about a few members* of that category. For instance, if we interviewed 75% of your high school class, and every single person said that Ari was the best athlete of your class, we might *generalize* to the conclusion, "Probably, every member of your high school class believes that Ari was the best athlete." Is this a good generalization? That depends on what makes for a good generalization.

The goal of a generalization is to gather enough information about the members of a category of things or events (a set called the *sample*) that we have good reason to believe that the whole category (a set called the *population*) is *relevantly similar* to these members. As we saw in 6.4, when a sample is relevantly similar to its population, we say it is representative. When a sample is not representative, it's said to be *biased.* If we had interviewed everyone from your high school class, and all of them had said that Ari was the best athlete, then of course we could conclude that everyone believed this – the population is identical with the sample; the sample is *representative* of the population because it *is* the population. But if we only interviewed 75%, our sample would be smaller than the population. So, how do we know whether a population is relevantly similar to (representative of) a sample?

The *number* of members matters, especially because people seem to have an inclination to generalize from just a few, perhaps even one, experience. If we had interviewed only 10% of your class, our generalization about the whole class's beliefs about Ari would be too weak to be justifiable; we wouldn't know whether it is representative. This is one example of a hasty generalization – we don't yet have enough information to know whether the population looks like the sample because the sample is too small. So, how many members are enough? It's difficult to say. Many polls and surveys include very small sample sizes relative to their populations. More is always better. How much more? Unfortunately, there is no determinate percentage. In some cases, you have to decide how many you are *willing* to regard as sufficient. If the sampling strategies we examined in 6.4 are followed (e.g., randomizing and stratifying), sample sizes can be remarkably small. But the science of this is complex. Whenever someone jumps to a general conclusion on the basis of what is clearly too small a sample size, you are warranted in criticizing that inference as a hasty generalization.

Examples of hasty generalization

1. "I had one philosophy class in college, and it was full of nonsense. Therefore, philosophy is all nonsense."
2. "Man, I hate Ford trucks. I know two people who bought Ford F-150 trucks, and both of them had constant problems."
3. "No one I know likes the governor's new policy. I bet most people are against it."

SEE ALSO

2.1 Deductive and Inductive Arguments
5.11 Fallacy of Accident
6.4 Inductive Statistical Reasoning

READING

Ali Almossawi, *An Illustrated Book of Bad Arguments* (2014)
S. Morris Engel, *With Good Reason: An Introduction to Informal Fallacies* (2014)
Douglas Walton, *Informal Logic: A Pragmatic Approach* (2008)

6.8 Mill's Five Methods

Because true causal relationships produce coincidences of events just like those identified by fallacious causal reasoning, some appeals to coincidence must be legitimate. The question is how to determine *legitimate* causal relationships from *mere* correlations. One test for legitimate coincidence is found in a set of five methods for testing causal claims known as "Mill's Methods," as they are set out in John Stuart Mill's 1843 magnum opus about reasoning, *A System of Logic*. These tests or "canons," as Mill called them, may not be as strong as controlled clinical trials (9.6), but for many purposes in life they can be very helpful. In situations such as the social sciences where clinical trials aren't possible and extensive data aren't available, they're often the best that can be done. Let's have a look.

1. Method of Concomitant Variation

Mill calls one of his tests "Concomitant Variation." If one phenomenon changes together in the same degree with another phenomenon while all other phenomena remain fixed, then the first event probably causes the second. For instance, if my ability to stop my car decreases as the level of my brake fluid decreases, and nothing else changes about my car, then losing brake fluid probably causes my decreased ability to stop my car. We can test this hypothesis by comparing the stopping power of my brakes at different levels of brake fluid. If my stopping power increases or decreases concomitantly with an increase or decrease in brake fluid, then we can legitimately identify brake fluid as a relevant causal factor in stopping ability.

> If X varies in regular ways with Y, while all else is constant, then X is the cause or effect of Y.

Similarly, suppose someone suggests that the practice of yoga cures cancer. We can test this by comparing the rates at which samples of people practice yoga with cancer rates in those people. (As we'll see in 9.6, we can strengthen this comparison by comparing cancer rates in people who don't practice yoga as a *control.*) If it turns out that as rates of yoga practice increase cancer rates concomitantly decrease (while nothing else changes), then there is some reason to believe that yoga decreases the likelihood of cancer. Alternatively, if there is no concomitant variation – if cancer rates change irrespective of changes in rates of yoga practice, then we don't have a reason to believe yoga has an effect on cancer. So, the key to determining a legitimate cause is to gather more and better information, often through extensive and careful scientific testing.

2. Method of Agreement

Mill described another method for identifying causal relationships by searching out what is common between correlated phenomena – in other words, that in which they directly *agree.* Paraphrasing Mill:

> *If two or more instances of the phenomenon under investigation have only one factor in common, the factor in which alone all the instances agree, is the cause (or effect) of the given phenomenon.*

So, if some of those who attended a party come down with food poisoning, it can be an effective strategy to look for the foods that were consumed *in common* by those who fell sick, especially if that same food was eaten by *all* those who fell sick. Let's assume there were five foods served at the party (salsa, salmon, carrots, ranch dressing, and tortilla chips), but the only food eaten in *common by all* those who fell sick was the salmon. Consuming the salmon is, to recall 2.2, in this case, a *necessary* condition for becoming sick. In more formal terms:

> *If a party-goer became sick, the party-goer ate the salmon.*

Or by transposition: *If a party-goer did not eat salmon, then the party-goer did not become sick.* In categorical terms: *All party-goers who became sick are party-goers who ate the salmon.* And by contraposition: *All party-goers who did not eat the salmon are party-goers who did not become sick.*

We have grounds, then, according to the Method of Agreement, for inferring that the salmon (perhaps spoiled) was the cause of the illness. Note, however, that we haven't considered whether there were any salmon eaters who didn't come down sick. After all, if you remember the logic of conditionals from 2.2, 3.4, and 4.3, just because salmon eating was a *necessary* condition for coming down sick, it doesn't follow that it was also a *sufficient* condition. In other words, just because *only* those who ate the salmon came down sick, it doesn't follow that *all* those who ate the salmon came down sick. Were there any people who ate the salmon but didn't fall ill? More investigation may be warranted using another of Mill's methods.

3. Method of Difference

Besides considering concomitant variations and agreements, sometimes you can spot causes by examining the differences among things, especially the absence of a relevant factor or property. In a way, this method reasons by means of the converse of the Method of Agreement. Mill's relevant test may be stated like this:

> *If an instance in which the phenomenon under investigation occurs, and an instance in which it does not occur, have every relevant factor except one in common, that one occurring only when the phenomenon occurs; the factor in which alone the two instances differ, is the cause (or effect) or a necessary part of the cause of the phenomenon.*

So, suppose we examined our group of party-goers and discovered that the only factor absent among *all* those who did *not* fall ill, in comparison with those who did become ill, was that those who didn't fall ill did *not* eat the salmon. Mill's Method of Difference, then, would allow us to see that eating salmon was a sufficient condition for becoming ill and therefore the likely cause of the illness. That single consistent *difference* between those who became ill and those who did not points, again, though by a different test, to the salmon as the culprit. It may help clarify things to look at our observation more formally:

> *If a party-goer did not become sick, then that party-goer did not eat the salmon.*

Or by transposition: *If a party-goer ate the salmon, then the party-goer became sick* (which is the converse of the observation we formulated using the Method of Agreement.) Alternatively, in categorical terms (3.2): *All party-goers who did not become ill were party-goers who did not eat the salmon.* And, by transposition or contraposition (3.4 and 4.3): *All party-goers who ate the salmon were party-goers who became ill.* (In fact, really to sort this out, you might compare all these formulations to the way we stated things when we explored the Method of Agreement.)

4. Joint Method of Agreement and Difference

As our salmon example suggests, to really pin down the cause of an event, you can combine the methods of agreement and difference. Doing so will show you both that (a) all occurrences of the effect correlate with occurrences of the cause; and also that (b) all occurrences of the cause correlate with occurrences of the effect. So, if we take another look at our unfortunate party (and you may have already noticed this), we'll find both *jointly* that (a) all those who came down sick ate the salmon; and that (b) all those who did not come down sick did not eat the salmon. More formally:

> *A party-goer became sick if and only if (iff) the party-goer ate the salmon.*

In other words: *If a party-goer became sick, then that party-goer ate the salmon; AND if a party-goer ate the salmon, then that party-goer became sick.* Both conditionals are important, because together they show that eating the salmon was both a sufficient *and* a necessary condition (2.2) for becoming sick. That's important because:

> *Showing both the sufficient and necessary conditions for an event is logically one of the strongest ways of demonstrating what is the true cause of an event.*

There's still one more method for exposing causes, however, that Mill developed.

5. Method of Residues

You might think of Mill's fifth and last method as comprising a process of elimination – even as a *disjunctive syllogism* (4.2). Suppose you face a complex set of phenomena to explain. And suppose you've identified a set of several factors you think may be the causes of another set of several effects. If you remove one effect along with its causes, according to Mill the remaining effects can be understood to be the result of the remaining causes. It's kind of like subtracting causes from a complex in order to isolate their effects. Paraphrasing Mill, again:

> *Subtract from any phenomenon that part already determined to be the effect of certain antecedents, and the residue of the phenomenon is the effect of the remaining other antecedents.*

So, if some poor sod from our disastrous party were to arrive at a hospital showing all the same symptoms exhibited by the rest of those afflicted with food poisoning, plus in addition a high fever, chills, swollen lymph nodes in the neck, and a bright red, highly inflamed throat, you could subtract the food poisoning and the symptoms it produced and then infer that some other cause or causes remain to produce the remaining symptoms – perhaps here a strep infection. As with all of Mill's methods, more testing (in this case perhaps examining the microbes drawn from a throat swipe) may be required to tell for sure.

Exercise and study question

The Method of Difference has proven especially useful in social science research. So, let's look at another example showing how it may be used there. In order to determine what causes some particular country (call it Country X) to go to war against countries that have not first directly attacked it, one might accept what Country X's government officials cite as its reasons – or one might look for a telling *difference*. Suppose the government of Country X declares that, outside of defense in response to a direct attack, it only goes to war to stop serious human rights abuses. Indeed, as it turns out, whenever Country X went to war against another country, that country was a serious human rights abuser. (That is, Country X went to war with a country *only if* that country was a serious human rights abuser.) Human rights abuse then, seems to be a *necessary condition* for Country X to launch a war.

We discover, however, that things are more complicated when we apply Mill's Method of Difference. By scrutinizing the historical record, we observe that there are many other countries in the world that have exhibited serious human rights violations with which Country X has *not* gone to war. Many of the violators are even allies of Country X. While it may be a necessary condition, stopping serious human rights abuses, then, is not a sufficient condition for war in County X. Is there a sufficient condition? Here's where differences are helpful. Closer scrutiny reveals that over the last century the only relevant factor *absent* among *all* countries against which Country X did *not* go to war was obstruction of access to oil. As it turns out, all those against which Country X did *not* go to war were either not oil producers or offered Country X unfettered access to petroleum. In other words,

> *If Country X did not go to war against another country, then that other country did not obstruct Country X's access to oil.*

Even more clearly, by transposition: *If a country obstructed Country X's access to oil, then Country X went to war against that country*. Obstructing access to oil, therefore, is a *sufficient condition* leading Country X to go to war. How might the Method of Agreement and the Joint Method of Agreement and Difference be used to reinforce this conclusion, especially if additional investigation discovered that all those countries against which Country X went to war had obstructed its access to oil?

SEE ALSO

6.3 Fallacies about Causation
9.4 Scientific Method
9.5 Unfalsifiability and Falsification Resistance

READING

Patrick J. Hurley, *A Concise Introduction to Logic*, 12th edn (2014)
Peter Lipton, *Inference to the Best Explanation* (2004)
John Stuart Mill, *A System of Logic, Ratiocinative and Inductive*, 8th edn (1882)

NOTE

1. The formula for calculating this is complicated. It requires applying a formula known as Bayes's Theorem to the probabilities noted. For those interested, it looks like this:

$$P(A|B) = \frac{P(B|A) \times P(A)}{P(B)}$$

Substituting, we get:

$$P(\text{Disease}|\text{Positive test result}) = \frac{P(\text{Positive test result}|\text{Disease}) \times P(\text{Disease})}{P(\text{Positive test result})}$$

The probability of a positive result if you have the disease is 99% and the probability of having the disease is 1 in 100,000,000 or 0.000000001. What's the probability of a positive test result, period? We can treat it as the frequency with which a positive result will come up in a population of 300,000,000, which includes those who have the disease and those who don't. The test will catch 99% of disease instances in the three with the disease or 2.97 cases. In the remaining 299,999,997 people, it will produce false positives one percent of the time, or 2,999,999.97. Add those together and you get 3,000,002.94 out of 300,000,000, which is a shade over 1% (0.0100000098).

$$P(\text{Disease}|\text{Positive test result}) = \frac{0.99 \times 0.00000001}{0.0100000098}$$

$$P(\text{Disease}|\text{Positive test result}) = \frac{0.0000000099}{0.0100000098}$$

$$P(\text{Disease}|\text{Positive test result}) = 9.89999 \times 10^{-7}$$

$$P(\text{Disease}|\text{Positive test result}) = 1 \text{ chance in } 1{,}010{,}102$$

Bottom line: If the test says you have the disease, it is very likely that you don't. Unless you calibrate your risk-taking to a finer grain than about one chance in a million, the test provides no useful information.

7 Tools for Critical Thinking about Experience and Error

7.1 Error Theory

Suppose Maria's spouse asks her where she put her keys, and she replies that they're hanging on a hook in the kitchen. But imagine he doesn't find them there; instead, a search of the house reveals that they are still in the front door lock. Maria could swear that she had hung them in the kitchen, and even seems to remember doing so. How could that be? How could she be mistaken? Of course, mistakes are common; they are so common that we have come to expect them. This doesn't make them less troublesome. In the past, some people mistakenly believed that others were witches and put them to death for it. Still others believed that salamanders spring from fire, that the dead return from the grave to drink the blood of the living, and that the Earth is the center of the universe. Today these ideas seem preposterous. The noun "error" and verb "to err" are related to the idea of wandering, in this case wandering from the truth. How is it so easy to get off track?

Critical thinking isn't only about figuring out *whether* or not ideas, propositions, and theories are wrong and *what* has gone wrong, but *why* and *how* they've gone wrong. To explain how error occurs is to give an epistemic "error theory" for it. Most people who make mistakes are ordinary, normal human beings just like you and me; their cognitive faculties function well most of the time. Still, sometimes they go wrong. In some cases, the consequences are grave, as historical witch hunt executions demonstrate. Among the last words recorded of the pilot of the 2015 TransAsia Airways flight 235 just seconds before it crashed, killing himself and 42 other people, were, "Wow, pulled back the wrong side throttle." A study using 1990 data by Ohio State University estimated that, in the US, perhaps as many as 10,000 innocent people are wrongly convicted of serious crimes each year (a false conviction rate, conservatively, of 0.5 percent).

So, error theories are helpful in at least two ways: they explain whether and why things went wrong, and they suggest ways we can avoid errors in the future. If we

The Critical Thinking Toolkit, First Edition. Galen A. Foresman, Peter S. Fosl, and Jamie C. Watson.

possess a sensible account of why an error was made when we conclude that some claim is erroneous, our conviction is rightly strengthened that an error was actually made. On the other hand, if we find it difficult to account reasonably for the apparent error, it may be a good idea to consider that perhaps no error has been made at all, that perhaps it's other beliefs that are wrong. On January 13, 1920, the now-famous rocket scientist Robert H. Goddard was criticized in the *New York Times* for supposedly basic errors in physics when he published a book arguing that a rocket might one day travel to the Moon. (It took 89 years(!) for the *NYT* to print a correction – on July 20, 2009.)

Of course, in many cases, errors really have been made. Thomas Jefferson erroneously questioned the honesty of a scientist who claimed to have recovered a rock that fell from the sky (what we now commonly call a meteorite). Ignaz Semmelweis (1818–1865) concluded (before the germ theory of disease had been accepted) that physicians in the obstetrics ward of Vienna's General Hospital were transmitting fatal illness to new mothers by not washing their hands (after dissecting cadavers in the morgue!) before delivering babies or treating the mothers. For his efforts to convince his colleagues that they and their filthy practices were the carriers of devastating disease, he was erroneously locked up in a mental institution where he died. Today, hand washing among medical caregivers is mandatory.

So, how do we explain and avoid errors in reasoning? We've already examined common errors in logic called "fallacies." In this chapter, we'll consider some other sources of error. In particular, we'll be looking at errors caused by our cognitive faculties themselves – the way our senses, our memory, our nervous systems, and psychological architecture set us up to err. We'll also consider, however, environment. Our cognitive faculties don't operate in isolation. They are influenced by the world around us, sometimes adversely.

In Reginald Rose's 1954 courtroom play, *Twelve Angry Men*, the legal case comes down to whether a witness's eyesight is reliable. In the climax, the 12-man jury discovers that the key witness for the prosecution had observed the crime not only at night, through the windows of a passing train, while immersed in the train's roar, but also just after having woken up and while not wearing her prescription glasses. Throughout the play, other witnesses and jury members discover biasing factors in their own perceptions and memories, including racial and class prejudice, economic interests, psychological history, and emotional need.

In 1620, Francis Bacon, one of the founders of modern science, described in his *Novum Organum* what he called four "idols" (*idolas*) or sources of error in scientific thinking. He described them as: (1) "Idols of the Tribe," or weaknesses inherent in human nature generally, for example in our general capacity to remember; (2) "Idols of the Cave," flaws in each of us individually, such as near-sightedness; (3) "Idols of the Theater," or errors that are conveyed to us by our society, our customary beliefs, by theology, ideology, prejudice, and superstition; and, finally, (4) "Idols of the Marketplace," errors that are produced by our language itself, that our very forms of speaking, thinking, and communicating encourage us to make. The material we survey in this chapter will cover each of Bacon's idols, too.

SEE ALSO

4.5 Common Formal Fallacies
Chapter 5: Tools for Detecting Informal Fallacies
6.3 Fallacies about Causation

READING

Kathryn Schulz, *Being Wrong: Adventures in the Margin of Error* (2010)
Joseph T. Hallinan, *Why We Make Mistakes* (2009)
Carol Tavris & Elliot Aronson, *Mistakes Were Made (But Not By Me): Why We Justify Foolish Beliefs, Bad Decisions, and Hurtful Acts* (2007)
Barry Scheck, Peter Neufeld, Jim Dwyer, *Actual Innocence* (2000)
James Reason, *Human Error* (1990)

7.2 Cognitive Errors

As we move through our lives, we typically take it for granted that our cognitive faculties present the world to us as it truly is. But the scrutiny of philosophers, psychologists, neurologists, and other inquirers has found that real questions arise about the accuracy and reliability of human cognition, especially under certain conditions. Distortion and error are not only possible for us; they are to be expected. Because the grounds for error are built into the very apparatus of our sensing and thinking, error is, for us, systematic and predictable.

Perceptual error

The plot of the 1992 comedy film *My Cousin Vinny* centers around two innocent men from New York City being tried in Alabama for robbery and murder. The defendants are exonerated through the efforts of their working-class cousin and attorney, Vinny Gambini, along with his brassy and capable girlfriend, Mona Lisa Vito. The plot's resolution and happy ending precipitates as Vinny casts doubt on the testimony of the prosecution's witnesses, one after another, largely by raising questions about the reliability of their perceptual abilities. For example, one of the key witnesses turns out to be profoundly near-sighted. Another only observed the crime through muddied windows.

Constructive perception

One may, indeed, be inclined to think of the way we observe the world as if it were through a simple lens, an old school mechanical camera, or a clear or open window.

But perhaps a more accurate analogy is to understand that just as modern digital cameras contain small computers that process and adjust the image, so, too, our brains and nervous systems are programmed with software to work in conjunction with the lenses and optics of our eyes, as well as the mechanisms of our ears, skin, noses, and tongues. Our senses and cognition don't simply take in the data of the world but process it, shape it, and alter it.

The human eye, for example, contains rods and cones that can detect color only in the center, but normal human beings perceive a complete field of colors, both in the center of their visual fields and at the peripheries. That means, then, that peripheral colors are in some sense projected or painted in by our minds. It's a matter of some controversy, but some thinkers have held that color itself is in a sense subjective, or at least that it emerges in our minds only through the interaction of light with our bodies. If light exists outside our bodies only in differently shaped waves with different frequencies, it's difficult to imagine what it would mean to say that objects themselves are colored. And if that's true, then one might argue that because color is the product of our interaction with the rest of the world, it is in part our construction. So it may be with all the objects and all the dimensions of our perception.

The constructive dimensions of perception have been found to produce a variety of interesting phenomena. One of them is *closure*. People shown a card briefly with the word "THE" but where the "E" lacks a middle bar, nevertheless report seeing the bar there. A phenomenon called *pareidolia* inclines humans to see faces – not only on human heads but also in rust marks on oil tanks, in burnt toast, in clouds, and, perhaps most famously, in the Moon. In a totally darkened room, a single, small stationary light source appears to bounce around (which may explain sightings of UFOs); the movement is really just our eyes shifting around, and it's an illusion called the *autokinetic effect*. It's been shown that our minds adjust our visual perceptions for continuity, so that our minds compensate for changes in brightness, color, and movement in the things we perceive so that our perception seems smooth and continuous.

Selective perception

Perception has not only been found to be constructive but also *selective*. Often we focus on what's *central* and ignore the periphery. We are subject, too, to *wishful thinking* (see 9.6), in which we sometimes actually do see what we wish to see. So, wishing that our planned outing to the beach will happen, we experience the weather improving, the rain abating, by exaggerating the promising signs and discounting the foreboding. Nineteenth-century astronomers, including Giovanni Schiaparelli and Charles E. Burton, claimed to have observed canals on Mars through their telescopes. Other astronomers confirmed their observations – perhaps seeing what they wished to see, too. British historian Hugh Trevor-Roper in 1983 authenticated what were then presented to Germany's *Stern* magazine and an excited world as Hitler's diaries. They were later revealed to be forgeries. In 1912 bone fragments were "discovered" of a prehistoric hominid that seemed to be the missing link between humans and apes. It convinced many physical anthropologists, perhaps because of their wishful thinking, for decades, until in 1953 tests showed that the skull was from a modern human and that the ape teeth had been filed down.

In related phenomena, sometimes called the *angel effects* and *devil effects*, we perceive those we dislike as less capable, immoral, worse in their performance, and ill-intentioned; while, on the other hand, we perceive those we like, or love, or admire to be capable, virtuous, highly productive, and good-willed. We selectively highlight the traits of conduct that reflect better on those to whom we're favorably disposed, and we discount, downplay, or even ignore the positive traits of those to whom we're negatively disposed. That's one reason why the members of political parties or movements often perceive their own candidates and officials much more highly than those of the opposition. Selective perception and wishful thinking also explain why attorneys are reluctant to seat jury members who have already been informed and perhaps formed initial judgments about the case they'll hear. It's also one reason not to allow the parents of figure skaters to sit on the panel of judges scoring them.

On a more troubling note, selective perception also goes a long way to explain what's pernicious about prejudice and stereotypes. In a 2001–2002 study Marianne Bertrand, an associate professor at the University of Chicago Graduate School of Business, and Sendhil Mullainathan of the Massachusetts Institute of Technology, sent approximately 5,000 fictitious résumés to 1,300 help-wanted ads in the *Boston Globe* and *Chicago Tribune*. The résumés presented similar credentials, but racially suggestive names were randomly assigned to them – some white sounding, some African American. The experimenters found that job applicants with white-sounding names were about 50% more likely to be called for an initial interview than applicants with African American sounding names.

Memory

Present perception, of course, is not simply present but involves memory of the immediate past, and this introduces all kinds of sources of error. Memory, both of what's immediate as well as the more distant past, is very different from a physical photograph. Memory is, instead, malleable, revisable, and frequently shifting. Indeed, the complexities of memory and perception explain the surprising fact that erroneous eyewitness testimony is the single biggest cause of false conviction in the US.

Selective memory

Like present perception, memory, too, can be selective. The victims of armed crimes have been found to experience what's called *weapon focus*, a form of tunnel vision, where they find their memory of the crime limited because during the event their attention focuses intensely on the weapon rather than anything else, including the person wielding it. A victim may be able subsequently to describe in great detail the threatening gun that was used but not be able to give as much information about the rest of the crime as witnesses do in cases of nearly identical crimes where no weapon is present. Critical thinkers should, therefore, consider that people's interests or focus of attention may have led them to ignore or downplay otherwise important elements of their experience or their memories.

Post-event information

Information, when acquired after an event, can compromise memory, too. It's a phenomenon upon which the Hollywood film *Inception* is built. If told that there was a poodle at the party, people may well remember a poodle at the party. People will quite unconsciously take new information and use it to re-write their memories of events past. A man perceived sporting a beard today but not ten years ago might find his friends and family surprised when examining old photographs that he wasn't wearing a beard at that family reunion a decade ago. Sometimes the re-write reverts back, and original memories emerge. Other times the revised memory becomes established and people start to remember not the original event but their altered memories of the original event. Stephen Ramirez and his colleague Xu Liu at MIT have, successfully, it seems, implanted the memory of having been shocked into a mouse. Some have speculated that one day the premise of the film *Total Recall* may come true, and rather than actually take a vacation, people will be able to purchase the memories of having gone on one. Critical thinkers, in any case, will be careful to consider the influence that post-event information or other influences may have had upon people's memories.

Closure, continuity, and compromising for consistency

Our tendencies for *closure* and *continuity* affect memory as well as immediate perception. But besides these factors, the distortions through post-event influences can be explained, in part, by people's desires for agreement and avoiding conflict. If two people observe a bank robbery getaway, and one perceives the getaway car as blue while the other sees it as green, their sharing stories with one another is likely to result with one or both re-describing and even re-remembering the car as blue-green, or greenish blue. This being the case, careful investigators will often separate witnesses to a crime in order to keep them from interfering not only with one another's stories but also with their own memories. It is, therefore, important for the police, the investigators of childhood abuse, and even historians to take special care not to embed or feed information to those whom they interview when, instead, their task is to draw information out of them. Careful critical thinkers will be attentive to potential distortions people may have introduced into their reports or their memories in order to achieve closure, continuity, and consistency with others.

Duration between event and memory

Over time, of course, there is more and more chance for memories to be altered by post-event information and modifying remembrances. We all know, too, that over time some memories simply fade away and become confounded. Almost no one can remember what it was like to be an infant or toddler, and many of our childhood memories have fallen into oblivion. This can make historical investigation tricky, and it raises real questions about witnesses testifying to events that happened decades ago. This is not to say that long-term memory is always distorted or that it's always less reliable than short-term memory, but in cases where one is scrutinizing the remembrance of events long past, it's even more important to corroborate those memories with artifacts, physical evidence, or the memories of others.

Issues about long-term memories have troubled the prosecution of Nazi war criminals some arrested decades after the end of World War II. Frank Walus, for example, was fifty-four years old and living on Chicago's west side in 1977 when he was accused of murdering women and children as a Gestapo agent in Poland more than thirty years earlier. Jewish survivors of the Nazi genocide, in fact, testified in open court that they had actually witnessed him commit those crimes. Walus was stripped of his US citizenship, received threatening letters and phone calls, was ruined financially by legal fees, was called "Gestapo" and "Nazi," and had stones thrown at him by his own neighbors. He was facing deportation when officials acknowledged evidence that he had been elsewhere, in Germany working on labor farms, during the time the crimes of which he was accused were committed. Such are the travails of human memory, and critical thinkers will consider the potential distortions that the time between the experience and the memory may have introduced.

Transferred memories

We can even transfer information within and across memories. A dress worn at one party might be remembered as having been worn at another. Innocent victims and by-standers may be remembered as perpetrators. Our memory has the capacity to, as it were, cut-and-paste content from one memory into another. In what's sometimes called the *law of recency*, a phenomenon related to the influence of post-event information, we not only remember best what we've experienced most recently, but we also sometimes transfer the content of recent memories into older ones. For example, you might remember someone you saw recently with glasses as wearing glasses in the past, even though in the past your acquaintance wore contact lenses. Again, good critical thinkers should look where possible for corroboration of memory by others and for physical evidence as an important safeguard against this effect.

Stress and trauma

Stress and trauma can, unsurprisingly, affect both perception and memory. Psychologists Robert M. Yerkes and John Dillingham Dodson produced findings that led to the formulation of what's become known as the *Yerkes-Dodson Law*. Although the shape of the curve described by the law differs in different contexts and for different people, the basic import for our purposes is Yerkes and Dodson's finding that as physical and psychological demands increase, performance also initially increases. You might say that at first there is a positive relationship between demands upon us and performance. But at a certain point, the demands upon us become excessively stressful, and the relationship changes and becomes negative. That is, after a certain point, more stress results in worse performance – including the performance of our cognitive equipment. This means that in extremely stressful situations, we're less likely to perceive well or to remember accurately.

Psychological trauma, or intense and damaging stress, can affect us not only while they occur, but they can also affect both future perceptions and memories of the trauma. The memories of traumatic events are sometimes suppressed in what's called *psychogenic amnesia*, so that trauma victims sometimes lose memories related to the stressful events to the point of forgetting those events altogether. Sometimes the victims of childhood sexual abuse repress for years memories of the events they suffered, only to have them emerge decades later. Are they, however, accurate when they re-emerge? Trauma can also affect future perceptions insofar as triggering events can evoke emotions or physical reactions, such as trembling or anxiety, related to the initial trauma; and they can emotionally color present experience, even in the absence of conscious memories. Sometimes, of course, triggers can evoke vivid memories of the trauma itself, often in exaggerated or extremely intense ways – such as, for example, in nightmares of war. Critical thinkers must consider, therefore, the distortions stress and trauma may have introduced into memory and experience.

Projection

Have you ever thought that someone loved or hated you only to have discovered later that you were mistaken? Freudian psychoanalytic theory may have, at least in some cases, discerned an answer to the question of how this happens in what they call *projection*. It turns out that the mind not only paints in the colors of our peripheral vision, brings closure, stability, and continuity to our experience, and sometimes amends our memories. The mind also projects our emotions and beliefs onto others and onto the world, sometimes unconsciously, and sometimes because we wish to avoid or repudiate those feelings within ourselves. So, through projection the fact that Juan desires his boss Roberto makes Juan uncomfortable with those feelings. Yet, Juan comes to see Roberto's conduct as indicating amorous feelings toward him, even though Roberto has no feelings of the sort. That Mona hates her father may be unbearable to her, and so she projects onto her father hostile feelings toward herself.

Similarly, though in a socially less complicated and more conscious way, we've all heard people describe a stormy sky as angry or a rough sea as raging; we've all heard a clear, sunny, and windless day characterized as calm. These descriptions may be projections (though, they're most likely metaphors). Seas don't rage, storms aren't angry, and air or water that's still isn't emotionally calm (though see 10.2). But it seems simply to be part of normal human psychology to project those feelings onto the world. Victorian art critic John Ruskin called doing so, especially in art that relies on it, from a logical point of view the *pathetic fallacy*, and it's also known as the *sentimental fallacy*.

Transference

A hackneyed old trope has a man coming home from a hard day at the office only to kick the dog. Sometimes it's difficult to express the feelings we hold toward a particular person, perhaps because doing so may generate some sort of highly negative or undesirable reaction. In order to avoid that, Sigmund Freud (1856–1939) suggested that we might transfer those feelings to a different, safer object. The dog kicker isn't really angry with his dog, but because his boss or clients have power over him or might react by taking their business elsewhere, the man transfers his anger to some behavior of the dog's that normally would not provoke a reaction. In assessing people's reports about their emotional experiences, good critical thinkers should be alive to the possibility that the emotions they encounter – in themselves as well as others – have been inflected by transference as well as projection.

Confirmation bias

In games such as *Trivial Pursuit*, players progress and win by answering questions about the world correctly. We are rewarded in school for answering right on exams and in class. Getting it right we normally experience positively, and that positive experience is not all about the external rewards we receive. Let's face it; people just like to be right and don't like to be wrong. It pleases us when our opinions, speculations, hypotheses, guesses, and hunches are confirmed. It's in general emotionally less pleasing, and often downright unpleasant, when they turn out to be partial, or flawed, or simply wrong. That being the case, people have a tendency to notice and to exaggerate evidence that confirms their beliefs or suspicions. There's a name for this phenomenon: *confirmation bias*. You might say it's a variant of *wishful thinking*.

Confirmation bias occurs when our *desire* for a certain outcome affects our abilities to evaluate that outcome accurately. For instance, when a medical researcher hypothesizes that a certain new drug cures a well-known disease, she may want her hypothesis to be right so badly that she misinterprets the strengths of her findings. If, for example, the result she wants would bring her an academic promotion or a certain fame, she may unwittingly regard a small degree of confirmation as much more significant than statistics would warrant.

Those inclined to the political right tend to see in the news stories and information that confirm their views of the world. For those inclined to the political left, it's just the same. Racists notice information that confirms their racialist views; and so do anti-racists. We all do. Interestingly, confirmation bias is so strong that even researchers who are aware of this tendency (even researchers who study confirmation bias!) are subject to it. That's not to say that all our observations of the world are distorted by confirmation bias, but good critical thinkers will consider whether reports they receive and even their own judgments about the world have been affected in this way.

Denial

In 9.5 we will consider the logical flip side of confirmation bias, namely *falsification resistance* and *unfalsifiability*, but here, in our discussion of constructive perception, it makes more sense to consider another psychological phenomenon – *denial*. Denial, as an old joke goes, ain't just a river in Egypt; it's a powerful psychological phenomenon that inclines us to downplay, deny, or even ignore entirely things we don't like about the world and about ourselves – even in the face of compelling evidence. Rather than face a problem, sometimes it's psychologically easier just to deny it or ignore it. Informed about the criminality or death of a beloved child, a parent may react simply by denying that it is so. "You've made a mistake. It must be someone else's child you're talking about. There's been some kind of terrible mix up."

It can be particularly hard to accept negative judgments about yourself and information that seems to lead to them. Confronted with evidence of problems related to, say, consuming too much alcohol, an alcoholic is likely (at first) simply to try to deflate the evidence or to deny that he or she has a problem altogether. The refusal to accept that one has done something wrong or illegal is an instance of a way of thinking sometimes called the *not-me fallacy*. In general, people don't wish to think, for example, that they are immoral, that their family, their nation, their religion, their political party, their school, or even their company – anything in which they are emotionally invested – is bad or has conducted itself improperly, even when it is so. When it somehow serves them to think this way, people will conclude that generalizations don't apply to them, that they are exceptional. Good critical thinkers, therefore, will be sensitive to this trait in human psychology and will be attentive to the many ways that denial may affect people's judgment, including the critical thinker's own.

Not only can our selective perception lead us to ignore information and our capacity for denial to refuse it; we are also plagued by our ignorance. Our interests, our affections, our repulsions, and our epistemic finitude create *blind spots*. There are, that is, to paraphrase former US secretary of defense Donald Rumsfeld, who became famous for this kind of word play, things *we don't know that we don't know*, as well as things *we won't know*, not to mention things *we know that we don't know*, and things *we know but refuse to acknowledge*. Whew!

A little bit of knowledge ...

Sometimes our blind spots are even masked by our knowledge. You may have heard the old adage, "A little bit of knowledge can be a dangerous thing." One reason that can be true is that possessing a little bit of knowledge can give us a false sense of epistemic superiority, an *epistemic delusion* of thinking we know more than we actually know, of thinking we know more than others. You might be a world-famous expert in, for example, the biology of gall wasps. But it doesn't follow from knowing a lot about gall wasps that you know anything about any other topic – moral philosophy, Roman history, climate science, or currency markets, for example. Knowing what is not known, knowing the scope of our ignorance, can be as important to critical thinking as figuring out what is known.

The fallacy of false consensus

If the *ad populum fallacy* (see 5.9) is a fallacy because it's poor reasoning to think that just because lots of people accept a proposition it's therefore true, then the *appeal to* a *false consensus* represents an error in *ad populum*'s very premise. That is, an appeal to a false consensus is an appeal to a consensus or widespread agreement on a proposition that doesn't even exist in the first place. People often imagine they think they know what most experts on some topic have concluded without actually knowing whether or not that's so. They imagine the consensus in order to reinforce their beliefs by placing themselves in imaginary agreement with others. So, you might hear someone say, "most psychologists would say that … " or "ask any twelve military experts, and they'll tell you that's a dumb strategy" or "most NFL coaches would never call for that play under those circumstances." Assuming that those advancing these claims are deeply familiar with neither professional psychologists, nor military strategists, nor professional football coaches, a good critical thinker would do well to call out those appeals as imaginary or at least merely assumed. (See 9.5 and the "No True Scotsman" fallacy for a related error.)

Naïve realism

Philosophers commonly refer to the view that our cognitive faculties present the world to us pretty much exactly as it is with the slightly pejorative term *naïve realism*. That's not to say, of course, that our sensory capabilities are utterly incompetent and can never be trusted. Thomas Reid (1710–1796) and other "Common Sense" philosophers perhaps justly criticized David Hume for excessive skepticism about our perceptions. Still, in light of the findings of psychology, cognitive science, and philosophy, critical thinkers will do well to understand that our perceptions are at least sometimes erroneous and misleading. To be critical about our cognition and perception vaccinates us against being naïve.

SEE ALSO

5.2 Subjectivist Fallacy
8.3 Skepticism and Sensory Experience
8.10 Evidence: Weak and Strong

READING

Mark H. Ashcraft & Gabriel A. Radvansky, *Cognition*, 6th edn (2013)
Kathryn Schulz, *Being Wrong: Adventures in the Margin of Error* (2010)
James Reason, *Human Error* (1999)
Raymond S. Nickerson, "Confirmation Bias: A Ubiquitous Phenomenon in Many Guises," *Review of General Psychology* 2.2 (1998): 175–220

7.3 Environment and Error

On August 23, 1927, Nicola Sacco and Bartolomeo Vanzetti were electrocuted at Charlestown State Prison in Boston, Massachusetts for the murder of two men in the course of a robbery in the nearby town of Braintree seven years earlier. Many have believed the conviction was in error, not least of all because of a number of suspicious aspects of the witness testimony that was marshaled against the pair. The suspicion largely involved matters of environment. As in the fictional *Twelve Angry Men*, these real witnesses made their observations at night, from various distances, and the figures they observed through a car window were in motion. Environment is, indeed, one of the most common causes of error in witness observations and otherwise. Let's look analytically at the environmental factors that most commonly cause trouble.

Obstruction and distraction

Think about the difference between observing something that's motionless and fairly close on a bright, sunny day, in a quiet location, and with no obstructions compared with observing something moving hundreds of yards away on a foggy night, during a downpour in a thunder storm, with loud sirens going off, in a canyon known for its echoes, immersed in a churning crowd of panicked, shrieking people, all the while looking through dirty glasses with outdated prescription lenses. All these elements of this complex environment can divide your attention and obstruct your perception, and so the physical environment of atmosphere, sound, light, and obstructive material can play havoc with your capacity to make accurate observations. Observations may be compromised when made, for example, while your child is screaming with pain or simply for attention. Observations about peripheral matters made in the midst of activities requiring intense focus – perhaps landing an aircraft or walking a tight rope or dodging a sniper's bullets – are likely to be less reliable.

Good critical thinkers will ask questions and take note of the physical conditions under which observations have been made. Could those conditions have led well-intentioned and sincere people to err? Could they have produced distortions or illusions that may have led observers astray? Does the conviction with which a witness asserts claims seem warranted given the difficult circumstances of observation? Might an incongruity between the certainty of a witness's assertions and the doubtful circumstances of observation suggest unreliability, even mendacity, in the testimony? In the case of Sacco and Vanzetti, that observations were made at night, from a substantial distance, and through a moving automobile window certainly raises questions, if not reasonable doubt.

Duration

Have you ever thought you saw an old friend, a family member in a momentary glimpse across a room or in a crowd only to be disappointed upon catching up to her and finding it to have been a complete stranger? The length of time involved in an observation is relevant to the functioning of our cognitive capacities and therefore to assessing their reliability in any particular observation. One of the witnesses who identified Sacco and Vanzetti accused the defendant after only seeing the perpetrator for an instant in the getaway car. Think about how different a good long look at something is from a momentary glance or a flash. The observation might have been momentary because the light source or sound or touch was just a flash or an instant, because an obstruction suddenly blocked or unblocked the way, or because the perceiver suddenly lost consciousness or perceptual ability. It takes time to take in and process all the details of a face or a complex scene or a voice or a texture, and the mind, as we saw in the closure effect, is prone to enhance perceptions imaginatively, sometimes at the cost of accuracy.

Motion

Then there's the fact that the getaway car was speeding away at the moment the witness caught a glimpse of its occupants. Objects in motion are harder to perceive accurately than stationary things. Stand near a busy highway with a friend some evening and try to identify features of those riding in the cars as they pass; note how much easier it is to identify your companion. Difficulties arise in the converse situation, too. Try to identify people on the roadside as you speed by them in a car or train. Try to grasp the contents of a conversation in a car or boat speeding along. It isn't easy, even under otherwise good conditions. Critical thinkers should ask, therefore, whether (1) the objects of perception were in motion when perceived; (2) whether the perceiver was in motion; and (3) whether the light or sound source was in motion. An object perceived only by the light of a passing car or train is more difficult to grasp than one observed under a stable light.

Distance

Two of the witnesses that identified Nicola Sacco claimed to have seen him, not only in a moving vehicle and for just a moment, but also at a distance of over 70 feet. Hawks and other birds of prey are renowned for their distance vision, not so much human beings. Critical thinkers scrutinizing the evidence of observation will do well, therefore, to inquire at what distance an observation is made. Roughly speaking, the greater the distance the less reliable the observation.

Context and comparison

Have you ever seen a perspective-bending "Alice in Wonderland" room which is constructed such that standing at one end makes you appear to be a giant, larger than ordinary furniture and doors, while walking to the other end seems to transform you into a shrunken and tiny being. It's not you, of course, who has changed but the objects that surround you. Those surrounded by taller people and things seem short, while the same person surrounded by shorter people and smaller things seems large. An object set against a brightly colored backdrop may seem dull, while the same object set against a neutral background may seem to possess a more intense hue. The colors that surround an object, too, can make it appear to change color. An object may appear to be orange when surrounded by blue, while that same object will appear brown when surrounded by a more vivid orange. Critical thinkers, therefore, should attend to the *context* in which a perceived object is observed, especially when *comparative terms* are enlisted to describe it. If something is described as tall or short, large or small, forceful or gentle, thick or thin, blue or purple, high-pitched or low-pitched, ask about what surrounded it when it was observed. A woman's voice is likely to be high-pitched compared to a man's but lower-pitched than a child's. Ask about observations and descriptions, "compared to what?"

Availability error

A more general consideration of environment that often leads to distortion is what critical thinkers call *availability error*. It would be uncharitable (see 5.5) to say that people are often lazy about acquiring all the information they need before making judgments; but it wouldn't be improper to say that people are prone to give more weight to evidence and data that are readily available than information that may be relevant but that's hard to acquire. When people use Google to find the answer to a query, they typically only check out the first page of results. When people look into what kind of car is best to buy, they typically only ask the advice of those around them. Even scholars often neglect to consider scholarly literature written in languages they cannot read. A witness to a crime who is difficult to find might never be interviewed. Information that might take days or longer of tedious sifting through libraries, billing records, or that is available only in foreign languages might be ignored. We tend to consider only what is easily acquired, and we tend to give disproportionally greater weight to what we've already come by, even if we know other relevant information remains out there. In short, we prefer what's *available*. Beware, however, the truth may not be as readily available as error.

SEE ALSO

7.2 Cognitive Errors
8.3 Skepticism and Sensory Perception
9.4 Scientific Method
9.7 Six Criteria for Abduction

READING

E. Bruce Goldstein, *Sensation and Perception*, 9th edn (2013)
Theodore Schick & Lewis Vaughn, *How to Think about Weird Things: Critical Thinking for a New Age*, 7th edn (2013)

7.4 Background and Ignorance

It may seem odd, but there are people whose principal job is to sex baby chicks – that is, to determine whether any particular chick is male or female. You see, as one might imagine, newly born chicks generally look very much the same. Little, fuzzy, yellow, and cute – both male and female. In fact, very few people are able to examine a baby chick and easily determine its sex reliably. What's remarkable, however, about reliable chicken sexers is that they characteristically can't explain how they do it. It can take some time, too, for people to explain how they are able to identify one painting as a Picasso and another as a Braque, or one musical composition as Vivaldi but another as Scarlatti.

Access to *background information* or *background experience* explains these abilities. While at a first listen, a great deal of early eighteenth-century European music may sound similar, after acquiring sufficient experience with it one begins to detect subtleties of composition that had first been ignored. The work of early twentieth-century cubists can appear confusingly similar, too. It can be very much the same with identical twins (which, of course, is one reason they're described as identical!). While at first one may find it very difficult to distinguish one identical twin from another, after a period of time small differences between the two become more evident. That's one reason why the parents of twins rarely mix them up. Experienced physicians can sometimes make surprisingly quick diagnoses of patients upon a first presentation of their symptoms or distinguish a benign mole from a dangerous melanoma.

Critical thinkers, therefore, will do well to consider that errors may result from the judgments of people who lack background experience with some field, subject matter, or set of data. As a critical thinker assessing testimony, authority, and generally factual claims made about complex phenomena, you will do well to consider whether your sources (or you yourself) possess sufficient background information. Encountering a claim from a source lacking proper background information or experience should be a red flag (though not a reason to dismiss that claim fully) and an invitation to inquire further.

7.5 Misleading Language

In Section 5.15, we encountered question-begging sentences – sentences that include, buried within them, questionable assertions. We will also discuss the capacities of meta-narratives (10.1), of rhetorical tropes (10.2), and of voice (10.4) to advance claims. But as language can lead us to errors in almost countless ways beyond the scope of these devices, it's worth saying a word more generally about leading language.

Suspect the negative

The mere use of negative language can direct audiences to a negative conclusion. It would prove a generally poor sales technique to approach a customer saying, "You wouldn't want to buy this product, I suppose, but let me tell you about it." On the contrary, political campaigns often enlist a device known as a *push poll*. The "poll" poses as an inquiry into voter attitudes, but it's actually a device designed to shape or push those attitudes. A clue that you're being subjected to a push poll is that they often begin not with a question but with a statement. For example, a push pollster might say, "An editorial in the *St. Petersburg Sentinel* recently described the president's foreign policy as a shambles and his economic program as badly advised. In light of pervasively negative judgments by journalists and policy experts, on a scale of 1 to 10, where 10 is the worst, how badly do you think the president has performed in office?"

That's not to say that polling without leading questions is easy. In fact, wording the language of a poll so that it doesn't lead respondents to certain answers is one of the most difficult challenges of polling as a form of inquiry. Just consider how difficult it is to ask questions about the topic of abortion. Referring either to a "baby" or a "fetus" or a "person" or a "human being" or to "tissue" seems from the start to influence the response. Referring to those in armed conflict as "freedom fighters," as "rebels," as "soldiers," as "combatants," as "savages," or as "terrorists" similarly seems to call for different kinds of responses.

Implications and connotations

Attorneys, when judges and opposing counsel do their jobs properly, are generally prohibited from asking leading questions, but people in commerce, politics, academia, personal interactions, and often even in the law, despite formal prohibitions, commonly use leading language. In general critical thinkers will be sensitive to the presence of leading, tendentious, or provocative language and to the way context may magnify or inflect the language used. Researchers have found that even apparently innocuous language can lead audiences to respond differently than they otherwise would. People are, for example, likely to respond differently if they are asked about engaging in a certain activity "frequently," "occasionally," "periodically," or "often." A jury or readership might regard the same action differently if it's described as "seizing," "taking," "grabbing." A parent's conduct toward a child might be understood quite differently if it's called "paddling," "spanking," "striking," "whacking," "pounding," or "hitting." Government expenditures are notoriously judged differently by fiscal conservatives who describe them as "spending" and by fiscal liberals who speak instead of public or social "investment."

Damning by silence or understatement

Sometimes it's not only what's said but also what's not said that leads an audience to one judgment rather than another. If a letter of recommendation for a job candidate speaks a great deal about the candidate's personality and moral fiber but very little or nothing about the candidate's skills and talents relevant to the job, a critical thinker is warranted in suspecting that there's a message in that – namely, that the candidate is weak in those qualities.

Language can lead in all these and many other ways. So, as good critical thinkers, we would be wise to keep this principle in mind:

> *To test how leading a claim might be, consider alternative ways of expressing it, considering positive and negative descriptors and noting what is not said.*

Remember that language is powerful and that, as much as we use it, it uses us, too.

SEE ALSO

10.1 Meta-Narratives
10.2 Governing Tropes
10.4 Voice
10.5 Semiotics: Critically Reading Signs

READING

Jonathan E. Adler & Lance J. Rips, *Human Reasoning: Studies of Human Inference and Its Foundations* (2008)
Dariusz Galasinski, *The Language of Deception* (2002)
Malcolm Peet & David Robinson, *Leading Questions* (1992)

7.6 Standpoint and Disagreement

Consider the following scenario. Alice works as a housekeeper for the Brady family. A single, middle-aged woman from a low-income, agricultural background in Arkansas, Alice rents an apartment in one of the poorest parts of town but spends most of her days, and some of her nights, in the Brady house, where she's afforded a small room adjacent to the kitchen and laundry. The Bradys are well-off members of the professional class with Mike, the father and husband, heading an architectural firm and Carole, the wife and mother, working as an executive for a cooking oil manufacturer. Carole and Mike both have post-graduate educations from fine universities, while Alice never finished high school. Carole and Mike, generous contributors to the political party to which they belong, are friends with the governor of their state, and Mike has been recruited to run for Congress in the next election. The Bradys are white, while Alice is an undocumented Hispanic immigrant. Alice is a widow with two children. One of her children is a single mother who works at a downtown luxury hotel for a food service corporation; the other, her son, is in prison on illegal drug charges. *Standpoint theorists* (part of a movement that grew out of feminist epistemology) and some types of *social epistemologists* think that all these social and economic differences carry critical epistemological import. That is, they have important implications about any knowledge claim the Bradys or Alice might make.

For standpoint theorists, knowledge is always socially situated; in thinking critically about knowledge claims, we will do well to consider the social location or standpoint that those who advance particular claims occupy. Social location, of course, may affect access to information and to training in the procedures of inquiry and justification. Mike and Carole were raised by well-educated parents who pushed them to read and study various topics. They attended fine schools, possess enough wealth to travel and to buy books and computers; they have access to institutions that license, legitimate, certify, and otherwise validate their own knowledge claims; they circulate in social strata where certain kinds of information is also circulated.

But it's not the case that those occupying positions of status, wealth, and power possess access to all knowledge in equal measure; and it's not the case that those who occupy positions commonly thought to be of lower status, wealth, and power are denied access to all knowledge in equal measure. As the nineteenth-century philosopher G. W. F. Hegel, for example, argued in a famous passage addressing what's come to be known as the *master–slave dialectic*, those in subordinate relationships often understand certain aspects of social, and even material, reality better than the powerful, since they know both the masters' and the slaves' worlds. The masters, in contrast, know primarily only their own (see Hegel's 1807 *Phenomenology of Spirit*, Section 179 ff.).

Carpenters and home repair workers may not know the theories of chemistry and physics that universities teach, but they know the properties of wood, stone, metal, and lots of other compounds through the experience of working with them. Alice may know, and in fact is likely to know, the material details of the Brady home better than the Bradys. Moreover, because Alice lives partly among the wealthy and partly among the poor, she, unlike the Brady family, has acquired experience of both of their worlds. The Bradys have never been to her neighborhood, and like many others of their station, they have taken great care to construct lives that keep them out of "bad neighborhoods," even providing Alice with a room so traveling there isn't ever an issue. Alice and her daughter see the wealthy and powerful not only in professional contexts but at home and in relatively private moments.

Alice's testimony doesn't seem to count as much in court as that of people like the Bradys, but Alice and her son possess knowledge of the police and the judicial system unknown to Mike and Carole, who, like others of their class, are relatively insulated from judicial and correctional institutions. This has been true for the Bradys despite the fact that one of their children regularly uses illegal drugs and has even bought some from Alice's son. Alice, on the other hand, does share knowledge with Carole unknown to Mike, as both she and Carole have been subjected to sexual violence and harassment in ways Mike, like most men, has not (indeed, Carole has spoken more with Alice and other female friends about the abuse she's suffered than she has with her husband or any other male).

The mosaic of truth

Considering the different standpoints the Bradys and Alice hold may be important for critical thinkers if we are to comprehend the truth in, well, a comprehensive way. If we are to acquire a more complete understanding of the world, and if standpoint theory has a point, then it will be important to listen to the claims of diverse people occupying diverse standpoints. If knowledge requires a complete picture and an *exhaustive* integration of relevant evidence, different standpoints must be considered. Otherwise, our data is likely to be partial and biased. Truth may be thought of as a kind of mosaic, and to get the big picture, every tessera must contribute its part.

Incommensurability and deep disagreement

The idea that standpoints can be added together to complete the project of knowing may, however, be presumptuous. What if, rather than fitting together in a complementary way, standpoints clash and oppose one another? What if a consistent whole composed of them just isn't possible? Wilkie Collins's 1868 novel *The Moonstone* is composed of a set of interviews about the disappearance of an expensive gem. What is most interesting is that, though several of the interviewees were present for the same events, their testimonies about those events are incongruous. Getting all the testimony leaves the reader at a complete loss as to the actual events.

Consider also the profoundly different responses among people of European and African descent in the US after O. J. Simpson was acquitted in 1995 of murdering his ex-wife Nicole Brown Simpson, or the different reactions to the 2014 death of Michael Brown in Ferguson, Missouri. Consider the different voting patterns among men and women, or the different ways people understand the conflict in Palestine–Israel. Can these views be reconciled? Can these differences be overcome? Perhaps at least one party in all these disagreements is simply in error. Perhaps people are simply confused, ignorant, unreasonable, or led astray by the media, by their cultures, and by faulty information. But what if on some topics disagreement can be fundamental and judgments therefore incommensurable? At least since Plato, many have argued that while there may be many opinions or falsehoods, truth and knowledge are singular. Does the question of standpoint call that conception of truth and knowledge into question?

SEE ALSO

5.4 *Ad Hominem* Fallacies (circumstantial)
6.4 Inductive Statistical Reasoning (sampling: random and biased)
9.8 Bad Science (ideological science)
10.10 Feminist and Gender Critiques

READING

Miranda Fricker, *Epistemic Injustice: Power and the Ethics of Knowing* (2007)
Sandra Harding, ed., *The Feminist Standpoint Theory Reader* (2004)
David Bloor, Barry Barnes, & John Henry, *Scientific Knowledge: A Sociological Analysis* (1996)
John Searle, *The Construction of Social Reality* (1995)
Helen Longino, *Science as Social Knowledge* (1990)

8 Tools for Critical Thinking about Justification

8.1 Knowledge: The Basics

Philosopher John Pollock, in his 1986 book, *Contemporary Theories of Knowledge*, writes that the "fundamental problem of epistemology [the study of knowing]" is "that of deciding what to believe" (p. 10). Decisions about what to believe may not be the only goal of critical thinking, but they're certainly central, and whether or not belief is at stake, it is helpful for the sake of critical thinking to understand the basic principles logicians, philosophers, scientists, and others have developed to assess matters of evidence and justification. What counts as a belief is, philosophically speaking, a complicated matter, and there are many kinds of beliefs as well as a variety of related doxastic states (e.g., endorsing, assenting, swearing to, suggesting, having faith in, trusting). Philosopher Bas van Frassen, for example, in his 1980 book, *The Scientific Image*, explores the idea that one might be able to "accept" a proposition without believing it in the way that concerns skeptics. For our purposes here, however, it's enough to understand *belief* as certain way of accepting that a claim is true or false. For example, as we'll use the idea of "belief," if you believe that the Moon controls the tides, then you accept the truth in an ordinary sense of the claim that "the Moon controls the tides." If you believe that the Moon is not made of green cheese, you similarly accept the ordinary truth of the claim that "the Moon is not made of green cheese."

Now, some beliefs are justified and some are not. For many thinkers, broadly speaking, *justified* beliefs are beliefs formed or held on the basis of (a) the right number of (b) good or proper reasons (c) related in the right way logically speaking. As a child, your belief that Santa Claus exists may have seemed to be justified (your parents told you he does), but as an adult, you find that you lack good or proper reasons for believing it. What counts as a good or proper reason is controversial, but the general idea is that it indicates that a claim is or is likely to be true, or in the case of values and actions, that a value is worth holding or an action worth doing.

The Critical Thinking Toolkit, First Edition. Galen A. Foresman, Peter S. Fosl, and Jamie C. Watson.

Ordinary belief and hinge propositions

There may be something like "default" beliefs, which are beliefs you ordinarily don't justify with reasons or evidence, but which seem to be reasonable to have in your set of beliefs. For example, once you get to a certain age, you begin to see that you hold a vast trove of beliefs the origins of which you can't identify (e.g., "Santa Claus doesn't exist," "I live in Tennessee," "My mom's name is Janice," etc.). In our everyday lives, it seems unproblematic to hold them. Nevertheless, once we engage the processes of critical thinking, we want to be able to make sure our beliefs are responsibly held, and so we want to know what reasons, if any, support their truth, so we can decide how strongly to trust them. Beliefs for which we can offer no discernable reason for believing are necessarily weaker for us than those for which we can.

Here's a tricky bit. Philosophers have noted that there seem to be other beliefs about which it isn't even proper to ask whether or not they're justified. This is because these beliefs set the conditions that make justification and questions about justification possible in the first place. Twentieth-century philosopher Ludwig Wittgenstein called propositions of this sort "hinge" propositions in his posthumous book, *On Certainty* (Sections 341–343). It's not that we can't investigate everything, but investigating these hinge propositions and related beliefs doesn't really, as Wittgenstein says, "belong to the logic of our scientific investigations." Just as the logically necessary conditions for the possibility of science are not topics of inquiry within science, so the logically necessary conditions for the possibility of doubting or justifying, etc., are not matters open to doubt or justification. That means, according to this view, we need no proof, for example, that the world exists, that others exist, or that language is meaningful, since the very act of raising questions about their existence always and already shows that they do. Of course, as you might have already guessed, there remains some controversy about this.

In any case, critical thinkers commonly focus on those beliefs and claims that seem to demand good reasons, that is, those that require justification. And for many critical thinkers justification is closely connected with knowing. There are, however, a number of complexities and worries related to the connection between justification and knowledge. In this chapter, we'll explore several aspects of the relationships among the following: what is traditionally thought to count as knowledge – the idea that knowledge requires truth – what counts as justification for a belief, and whether it matters if justification results in knowledge.

Plato's definition of knowledge

The most prominent, though controversial, definition of knowledge originates in Plato's work (c. 427–347 BCE), in particular his dialogue *Theaetetus* (201d–210a).[1] There Plato writes about knowledge as a *belief* that is *true* and *justified*. In other words, three conditions must be met for knowing: (1) one must believe *p*; (2) *p* must actually be true; and (3) there must be appropriate reason or justification for believing that *p*.

Consider an example where you would ordinarily use the word "know." Presumably, you *know* your age. One of the characteristic features of knowledge is that you can ask, *how do you know it?* in a way that we expect a different sort of answer from the question of *why do you believe it?* The *how* question asks for justification, while the *why* question may not. So, in response to the question of *how* you know your age you might appeal to a wide variety of *evidence* at your disposal that supports the claim, "I am *X* years old," including the testimony of your relatives, a birth certificate (along with a calendar and a little subtraction), pictures with the date stamped on them, perhaps (unfortunately) a video, and a birth announcement in the local newspaper. Evidence must be, of course, evident, which means it must exhibit, show, or present reasons that justify.

Now, what does it mean to *know* how old you are, that is, what must the world be like for you to *know* that you are *X* years old? If it is *you* who knows when you were born, it follows that something about "you" is involved in the process or act of knowing. What part of you? We typically don't think that rocks "know" or that trees "know," so it must be something that distinguishes "you" from these sorts of objects. Similarly, it is not (only) your arm that knows, or (only) your leg – it's *you* who knows. What distinguishes "you" from your arm or your leg? Philosophers have long argued that your *mental states* identify you as you. It is difficult to say just what a "mental state" is – how it relates to the brain, body, and so on – but it is not very controversial to say that mental states are *states of conscious thought*, such as hoping, worrying, wondering, doubting, believing, loving, etc.

But not just any mental state is sufficient for knowing something. It seems you can know a claim without hoping, worrying, or doubting that it is true. Similarly, you can hope, worry, or doubt that a claim is true without knowing that it is true. You can even *believe* it without knowing that it's true. You may, for example, *believe* that there is a Santa Claus, but not *know* it – since (spoiler alert!) there is currently no Santa. The converse, however, doesn't seem to hold. It doesn't, that is, seem that you can know a claim without believing it or when disbelieving it. In most contexts related to critical thinking, it doesn't really make sense to say, "I know *p*, but I don't believe *p*" (even though sometimes we may say things like that to express how strange something is or how impossible it seems, e.g., "I know that my child is dead, but I just don't believe it."). It might also be rather odd to say that you know something without being aware of knowing it (though perhaps there are also contexts where it would make sense to say something like this).

Chisholm and belief

Believing, in any case, in most circumstances relevant to critical thinking seems to be a necessary condition for knowing. Again, believing involves giving some kind of assent to a claim, perhaps a range of kinds of assent, accepting it in some fashion (even if it isn't actually so). Epistemologist Roderick Chisholm distinguishes a special sort of believing that is required for knowledge that he characterizes as "taking it to be the case." A subject, S, believes that a proposition, *p*, is true in the sense relevant for knowledge only if *S takes it to be the case* that *p* (*Theory of Knowledge*, 3rd ed., 1989). The point here is that the sort of "believing" required for knowledge has a technical meaning and may be, therefore, much more specific than the way we may use it in ordinary speech. Therefore, we will say that for the most part "properly believing a claim" is a *necessary condition* for knowing whether that it's true – you may not know by believing, but you cannot know without it. (See 2.2 for more on necessary and sufficient conditions.)

So, while believing in the proper sense is a necessary condition for knowing a claim, it is not a *sufficient* condition. What else is needed? Often when we say we "know" a claim, we mean we are "fully convinced it is true," for example, "I just know she's cheating on him," or "I know it's going to rain." When we say things like this, we would probably admit that we could be wrong even though we don't think we are. But when philosophers talk about knowledge, they typically mean something more specific, that is, when someone knows something, they "know it to be *true*." You can be fully convinced of something that is completely false (e.g., that Leonard Nimoy is still alive, that Santa Claus exists, that 4 is the square root of 25, etc.), but it would seem strange to say you *know* that Santa Claus exists, if, in fact, he doesn't. Similarly, it would seem strange to say that you *know* "The cat is on the mat," if, in fact, the cat is *not* on the mat. What would you "know" if there is no cat or no mat, or the cat is not on the mat? Presumably, to *know* means to know that *something is the case*, that is, that *some claim is true*. Therefore, philosophers traditionally consider "truth" another necessary condition for knowing.

According to tradition, then, there are at least two necessary conditions for knowing: (a) it must be believed, and (b) it must be true. Are these all there is to knowing? In other words, are (a) and (b) *sufficient* for knowledge? If I believe that Santa Claus does not exist and he doesn't, do I *know* that he doesn't? In Plato's well-known passage from the *Theaetetus*, Plato's Socrates doesn't think so. Consider the following example.

Imagine you are a juror for a murder trial. Imagine, also, that the suspect is actually guilty – the claim, "Jack Doe killed Jill Doe," is true. In addition, imagine that no one was around when Jack did it. You listen to all the evidence and find none of it convincing. Nevertheless, you form the belief that Jack Doe is in fact guilty. Maybe you don't like the way he looks or how he's dressed, but you don't think of these as *reasons* to believe he is guilty – you just come to believe it. Now, this case meets both of the conditions we have identified: (a) you believe the claim and (b) it's true. Do you *know* that Jack Doe killed Jill Doe? It doesn't seem so. Something is missing. Your belief isn't *connected with the event* in the *right sort of way*.

In *Theaetetus*, Plato has Socrates suggest that what is missing is *evidence* or *proof*; in addition to true belief, you need some *reason* or *account* of *how* you know that Jack Doe is guilty before it would be reasonable to say you know it. If his fingerprints were found on the murder weapon, his footprints were found in the dirt near the body, his DNA were to be found on the corpse, or a witness were to testify to seeing the crime, *and you believe he is guilty on the basis of this evidence*, you would not only have a true belief, you would probably have a *justified* true belief. This information seems to be connected with the event of Jack's killing Jill in the right sort of way and to give an account or justification for your claim.

Given these considerations, there is a tradition among philosophers to say that knowing a claim requires that all three conditions be met. Individually, they are necessary, but together these three conditions are *sufficient* for your knowing a claim: (a) the claim is believed by you, (b) the claim is true, and (c) the claim is justified for you, that is, you have the right sort of evidence that it is true. You have what philosophers call a "justified true belief," and this is the traditional definition of knowledge. As you might expect with philosophers, this is not the end of the story. In 8.9, we will discuss one prominent worry about this definition and some attempts to overcome it.

SEE ALSO

1.2 Arguments
2.1 Deductive and Inductive Arguments
9.4 Scientific Method
9.7 Six Criteria for Abduction

READING

Laurence BonJour, *Epistemology: Classic Problems and Contemporary Responses* (2009)
Linda Zagzebski, *On Epistemology* (2008)
Linda Martín Alcoff, *Epistemology: The Big Questions* (1998)
Edmund Gettier, "Is Justified True Belief Knowledge?" *Analysis* 23 (1963): 121–123
Bertrand Russell, *The Problems of Philosophy* (1959), Chapter 13

8.2 Feelings as Evidence

There is little doubt that humans are *rational* animals. That's not to say that we always, or even regularly, use reason or use it terribly well, but we do have the *ability* to reason. We generally understand what reasons are, we can appeal to those reasons to answer questions about what to believe, and we can evaluate whether those reasons are good or bad. Furthermore, it seems that we are currently unique among living creatures in having come to reflect consciously on whether and how we reason. We've developed, that is, the science of logic and the philosophy of science. Critical thinking textbooks have traditionally focused on the rational dimension of human mental states – how to express claims precisely, how to organize claims into reasons and arguments, how to evaluate the strength of a reason for a claim, etc. But there is also little doubt that humans are *feeling* and *valuing* animals too and that our feelings often affect, for better or worse, our ability to reason well. We experience strong physical sensations and emotions that affect how we perceive the world, and we express ourselves in lots of ways other than rational judgments. Therefore, in order to reason most effectively, it's very important to develop some sense of how feelings (both sensations and emotions) and values (especially moral values) are related to evidence and reasons, as well as to recognize the conditions under which these help or harm our abilities to think rationally.

In this section, we'll explore the roles of feelings and values in reasoning. In the first half, we'll distinguish two types of feelings (sensory experience and emotional experience) and discuss their strengths and weaknesses in the reasoning process. In the second half, we'll discuss the nature of "value" and explore how values inform and shape reasoning.

Some important features of all types of feelings

In English, we use the word "feel" to describe a host of apparently unrelated mental states: *this table feels rough*; *I feel sad*; *that movie made me feel yucky*; *I feel guilty*. In order to have a chance at making sense of all these experiences, it will be helpful to distinguish two types of feelings: *sensory experience* and *emotional experience*.

Sensory experience refers to how the world is presented to our conscious selves: whether an object feels smooth or rough, hot or cold, whether a food tastes sweet or bitter, spicy or mild, whether light seems bright or dim, white or colored, etc. What we typically refer to as our five senses seems to be the vehicles through which the world impresses itself on us. Without the faculty of vision, we would have no conscious experience of color or light. Without the faculty of hearing, we would have no conscious experience of sound. The world *feels* a certain way to us because of how we experience it through our senses. In his book, *Mind and the World Order* (1929, 1956), the 20th-century philosopher C. I. Lewis called these conscious ways that the world feels, "qualia," deriving the term from the word "quality" in order to identify them as the effects of certain ways of perceiving the world and to distinguish them from whatever ways the world may be independently of how we perceive it.

In contrast to sensory experience, we feel emotionally. *Emotional experience* refers to our affective impressions of all those things that are brought into our perception through our senses: whether an event is satisfying or unsatisfying, joyful or sad; whether someone's behavior makes us angry or grateful; whether an occurrence makes us jealous or compassionate, melancholy or tranquil; whether observing a piece of art strikes us as poignant or banal, meaningful or trite. Our emotions are vehicles through which our minds and bodies impress upon our conscious states a reaction to the way the world affects us, as well as the way we reflect upon ourselves.

There are a number of similarities between these two types of feelings. First, both happen independently of our *wills*; we do not decide to see yellow or hear ringing or taste cinnamon, and we cannot choose whether to feel satisfaction or anger or compassion – we are passive recipients of these conscious events. We just open our eyes in the morning and the world presses in upon you. Second, both kinds of feeling happen largely independently of conscious, critical *judgments* we make about them. We must choose whether to accept some sensory experiences as veridical (truthful) and reject others. For instance, a wall may *look pink* to me, but if I have good reasons for believing there is a red light bulb shining on the wall, I can choose not to believe the wall is really pink – I know that it may not really be pink. It may, for instance, be white, but simply *appear* pink because of the red light. Similarly, consider the phenomenon known as "phantom limb." Some people who have lost an arm or a leg seem to feel pain in the limb that no longer exists. Although these people cannot help feeling these sensations, they rightly disregard them as "tricks" or "illusions" of their brains.

The same seems true of emotions. We cannot choose which emotions to have; they impress themselves on us against our wills. But we can choose not to act on certain emotions. For instance, although we may feel jealous when seeing an ex-girlfriend or boyfriend with someone else, we can recognize when we have no *right* to be jealous and suppress or ignore this emotion, so that we may choose to act kindly and generously to the couple if we meet them. Similarly, we may feel angry with a dog for chewing an expensive piece of clothing, and come to blame the dog for doing so. But we may subsequently recognize that animals have no appreciation of the value of such things and no sense of moral "ought," and therefore that "blame" is an inappropriate response. This consideration can lead us to stop blaming the dog.

To be sure, we rarely actually *choose* whether or not to accept our experiences. That is, we tend to accept them by default. Few of us see an orange wall and consciously think, "Should I trust my eyesight that this wall is orange?" And few of us see a painting we don't like and consciously think, "Do I really dislike this painting?" We unconsciously assume that our feelings, whether experiential or emotional, are reliable. Even the most extreme skeptics in history did not doubt the practical necessity of trusting our senses.[2] But it is a virtue of consciousness that we can stand back from these feelings and beliefs and ask difficult questions of them. If there are reasons for thinking we are wrong for unconsciously trusting our feelings, then it is important to know this. We may be able to improve our lives significantly by responding appropriately to the experiences we encounter.

Despite the similarities between sense experience and emotion, there are strong reasons for distinguishing them. As we have already noted, emotions are responses to, and often elicited by, sensory experiences. If it makes sense to say that one type of experience depends upon another, then logically these types are not identical. Second, the types of judgments to which each type of feeling is susceptible are quite different. While it would be appropriate to ask whether an object that appears yellow *really is* yellow (that is, whether it is *true* that the object is yellow under normal conditions or even independently of your perception of it), it would be strange to ask whether an event that makes you joyful *really is* a joy-making event. The latter is a joy-making event in virtue of the fact that it made you joyful. But the former is only *certainly* what we call yellow in your perception – you don't yet know whether it is a proper *yellow object* (or whether you are mistaken about it). The difference in the types of judgments to which each are susceptible seems to derive from differences in the way each refers to (or "picks out") the world.

Third, the content of sensory experience is about different types of reality from emotions. Experience seems to direct our attention to something *outside* of ourselves, which may or may not be presented to us accurately. We know that our senses sometimes deceive us (we have vivid dreams that we mistake for waking life, and sometimes objects seem much closer or farther than they actually are). So, it's reasonable to ask whether our sensory experiences are "true" or "accurate" or "veridical." The content of our emotions, however, seems to be about something quite different. For the most part, the content of emotions seems to refer to something *inside* of us – our reactions to particular events. Therefore, the relevant question is not whether we are *truly* feeling angry or sad – there is little denying that we are – but whether those emotions are *appropriate* responses to certain sense experiences. "Is it appropriate to be jealous?" "Is it right to feel that Samir did something wrong to me?" "Was Julie's action intentionally hurtful, or was it simply an accident?" "Is it right to hold a grudge against Juan? He said he was sorry."

The importance of distinguishing sense experience from emotion

Now that we've compared and contrasted sensation and emotion, how can this discussion inform how we think critically about truth claims? If we observe our behavior with respect to our beliefs, we can easily see that many of our beliefs are formed on the basis of *both* sense experience and emotional experience, that is, we take it that these two types of feelings constitute *evidence* of the way the world is, as somehow making truth *evident*. So, the important issues for us are (1) to identify what sort of information these two types of feeling seem to reveal to us about the world and (2) to determine whether or not they actually do so (that is, whether or not they count as *good* reasons).

SEE ALSO

5.5 Appeal to Emotions or Appeal to the Heart
7.2 Cognitive Errors
10.1 Meta-Narratives

READING

Robert Arp & Jamie Carlin Watson, *Philosophy Demystified* (2011)
Linda Zagzebski, *On Epistemology* (2009)

Robert Audi, *Epistemology: A Contemporary Introduction to the Theory of Knowledge* (1998), Chapter 1
Douglas Walton, *The Place of Emotion in Argument* (1992)

8.3 Skepticism and Sensory Experience

In the last chapter, Chapter 7, we examined some of the many ways perception can fail us in particular cases. Here we'd like to take a much larger and more philosophical view and consider questions about the veracity of sense experience in a more general way, you might say in a global way. We generally regard sense experience as the most basic source of evidence for our beliefs about the world. We believe trees exist because we have *seen* certain objects, and we have *heard* people telling us those objects should be called "trees." We believe sour foods exist because we have *tasted* certain things, and we have *heard* people telling us we should call those things "sour foods." Indeed, almost all philosophers have held that the great majority of our knowledge of the world comes to us through sense experience. But before we consider whether sense experience is a reliable source of reasons for forming beliefs, a few distinctions are in order.

First, sensation (via our five senses) need not be considered the only type of sense experience. John Locke (1632–1704) and David Hume (1711–1776), for example, distinguish the experience produced by our sense faculties (which they call "sensation") from that produced in other ways, for example, introspection and the way our minds interact with and organize our thoughts – for instance, the mental processes of believing, doubting, reasoning, intending, remembering, naming, categorizing, etc. This second type of experience (which Locke and Hume call "reflection") also seems to reveal something about the world. Introspection is sometimes distinguished from sense experience because its content is about events in our minds (information available only subjectively) rather than events outside of our minds (information that seems available objectively). For our purposes, however, we can expand the notion of sense experience to include this additional category of experience. Our conclusions about one seem to extend easily to the other, and this will simplify our discussion of the strengths and weaknesses of experience.

Second, in contrast to Hume, philosophers such as Descartes (1596–1650) and Immanuel Kant (1724–1804) have argued for certain types of concepts distinct from those we draw just from our sense experiences. Ideas such as those related to number, infinity, nothingness, and logical relationships such as identity, possibility, necessity, and contradiction seem by some accounts to be purely abstract and perhaps prior to sensory experience (philosophers often use the Latin phrase "*a priori*" to talk about our understanding of these ideas). That is, rather than drawing them simply *from* experience it may be the case that we bring them *to* experience, that we use them to organize experience in the first place, something in the way the firmware or operating system organizes data that's fed into a computer. It's a question that answering would draw us too far beyond the goals of this book but one that might come in handy when thinking critically. (See Fosl & Baggini's *The Philosopher's Toolkit* for more on the *a priori*.)

Ideas we understand …	**… through sense experience.**	**… through experience (broadly construed).**	**… through thinking abstractly**
	• Touch, taste, scent, sight, hearing	• introspection (believing, doubting, reasoning, intending, remembering, naming, categorizing), morality(?)	• number, infinity, nothingness, identity, possibility, necessity, contradiction, morality(?)[3]

The weaknesses of sense experience as evidence

On what could we rely if we couldn't rely on our sense experience to tell us about reality? Clearly, very little. Even if our logical and mathematical reasoning were distinct from sense experience, these, along with some basic language skills, could only help us formulate definitions and derive conceptual implications. But this would tell us very little about the world around us, if anything. If we couldn't depend on our senses to reveal the world outside of our minds, then we would be forced to assert things about the world purely according to appearances, perhaps pragmatically. If anyone were to ask us whether the sky is blue, or whether grass is green, or whether penicillin cures bacterial infections, the best we could say would be: *Well, it seems so, and it is useful to believe so, but I couldn't say whether those claims are in any final or absolute way true.*

Perhaps this option is more than sufficient for human life, and it may be. In fact, a group of ancient skeptics known as Pyrrhonians, named after the Greek philosopher Pyrrho of Elis (c.360–c.270 BCE), are thought to have extolled the virtues of this sort of purely practical living. The Hellenistic philosopher Sextus Empiricus (c.160–210 CE) described the Pyrrhonian idea that, if we let go of dogmatic claims about truth and reality and limit ourselves to engaging the world simply as it appears, then our lives will be much more peaceful. Pyrrhonian skeptics suspend judgment about *any* dogmatic claim about reality (e.g., the sky is really blue, grass is really green, etc.). Pyrrhonians reach this kind of suspension (what they call *epochē*) through a particular practice or discipline, namely by balancing arguments or evidence or reasons of equal strength against one another. To see how this practice works, consider an example from Sextus's *Outlines of Pyrrhonism* (Book 1, Chapter 14, Sections 40–78).

Take note of what you're seeing in front of you right now – a book, words on a page, maybe a table or the arms of a chair in your peripheral vision, whatever you see. Do you have any reason to *doubt* that these things you are seeing are *real*? Can you know that they are real and that they metaphysically are as they appear? Notice that your eyes are organized in a very particular way – according to scientists, they are made up of a series of curved lenses along with an iris and pupil that determines how much light enters the eye at any given time; that light is reflected off objects, directed through those lenses and that pupil onto the back of your eyeball, which contains an arrangement of special living cells arranged as rods and cones that separate out shapes and colors and transmits all the information carried by that particular spectrum of reflected light to your brain through your optic nerve. That's a lot of machinery.

And notice that many animals have different organs for seeing. Some have differently shaped lenses, differently colored irises, differently arranged rods and cones, and differently organized visual pathways. For example, whereas humans are built to see three basic colors, the mantis shrimp has 16 types of color receptors. Honeybees don't see red, have compound eyes, and can see ultraviolet light. The pupils of goats' eyes are rectangular. Snail eyes float around in different directions. Rattlesnakes can detect infrared light. So, the question is: which, of all these creatures with different seeing mechanisms, "sees" the world *as it is*? How could you tell? Think of how many different ways images can be "distorted" by changing one of the mechanisms of the visual system. Just press on your eyeball and watch the world move! Think about the different shapes of fun-house mirrors; think about different types of cameras that detect different wavelengths of light, such as infrared and ultraviolet; think about cataracts and astigmatism, burst blood vessels and jaundice; think about how difficult it is to see in dim lighting or under "black" lights. Think how different the world would look if we had eight eyes like a spider.

Now, recall all those reasons that support the idea that you are seeing a book in front of you. Are they still strong enough to convince you that you see it as it "really" is? You may say: "Well, sure they are, because I am looking at the world in 'normal' lighting under 'normal' conditions, with 'good' eyesight." But notice all those qualifying words. The very problem that the skeptics highlight is that *you don't know* whether what you call "normal" is anything like the "right" conditions for seeing *accurately* or whether any conditions disclose the true world. There is no observer-independent perspective from which to establish that humans normally see the world *as it is*, whereas, say, eagles and bats and infrared cameras do not.

Skeptics like Sextus Empiricus (160–210 CE) and Michel de Montaigne (1533–1592) offer a plethora of examples of how our senses are inconclusive under a variety of conditions. They claim that all this shows we can get around quite well in the world if we just let go of the idea that we have to have absolutely true beliefs about reality. We will be much happier if we stop believing in a dogmatic way altogether and adopt an attitude of "take life as it comes." We don't ignore the fact that it seems bad for us to be run over by a chariot; we just don't allow that idea to dominate our thoughts. We avoid what *seems* or *appears* bad; we pursue what *seems* good; and we lay aside claims about ultimate truth (including denials that there is ultimate truth), all the while remaining open to its possibility.

Let's assume for a moment that the skeptics are right and that we are not, it seems, justified in believing that our senses are reliable for telling us about reality except as it appears to us. Is this a weakness of sensory experience? The answer depends on your interests. In one sense, the skeptics are certainly right: our senses are not self-validating – it is *always possible* that we are in the midst of a very vivid dream or a deception of the sort depicted in the 1999 film *The Matrix*. But who cares? This is not the criterion we use for evaluating our sense experience most of the time. Most of the time, in ordinary life, we just want to be able to distinguish among experiences to which we do have access: Is this is a fake Rembrandt or an authentic one? Is this what I mean by meat or is it tofu? Is it going to rain tonight? And we can have good reasons for answering these questions *even if* we are in a vivid dream. All that is necessary is a dream or illusory world in which events occur in stable, predictable patterns – even if the content of those patterns is nothing like the real world outside of our perceptions.

But there is a deeper worry about skepticism. Sometimes, no matter how careful we are or how useful some predictable pattern of nature has been, we suddenly discover evidence that we're wrong – in some cases, seriously wrong. Recall Ptolemy's geocentric theory of the cosmos: the Earth sits unmoving at the center of the universe and "wandering stars" or "planets" revolve around the Earth in concentric crystalline spheres against a backdrop of fixed stars embedded in the outermost shell. As odd as this theory sounds to 21st-century ears, it was based firmly in the empirical evidence available at the time and was proven over and over again for hundreds of years to be useful for navigation and for predicting all sort of astronomical phenomena.

Unfortunately, it couldn't predict every motion. Ptolemy and his followers tried to account for these anomalies by adding components to the view (particularly, he added orbits onto points circling other orbits, called "epicycles"). Eventually, the theoretical baggage became too heavy, and a change was needed. Now, this sort of change – giving up obviously problematic beliefs – isn't necessarily bad. The problem is that *every new account of the heavens faces similar difficulties*: Copernicus's account replaced Ptolemy's, while later scientists such as Johannes Kepler, Tycho Brahe, and Galileo Galilei refined Copernicus's account by rejecting some of his basic assumptions. Newton collapsed these refined theories into an almost completely new set of laws of motion, and Einstein's calculations forced us to abandon even the most commonsensical aspects of Newton's theory (e.g., that space and time were uniform and separate entities). Now, quantum physics challenges the adequacy of the best-supported claims of Einstein's view. All these changes are just in the field of physics! This sort of constant rejecting, updating, and reformulating occurs in every discipline. Is there any reason to think that because these new theories are more satisfying or work better for contemporary purposes that they somehow better apprehend or represent reality? How different might our ways of thinking about the world be in five hundred more years?

The instability of theory obviously casts doubt on the total accuracy of scientific theories. But it has also led many philosophers to question even the *usefulness* of our sensory experience for justifying scientific claims. One theory may be useful given certain assumptions and aims, but completely useless on a different set of assumptions and for a different set of aims. Is there a necessary connection between what is useful and what is true? If not, then perhaps we can abandon the aspiration of acquiring a "true" theory of reality as it simply is, absolutely, in a way not relative to us. Perhaps we can forge a way of "believing" stripped of dogmatic implications about apprehending the absolute real.

The strengths of sense experience as evidence

Many philosophers are deeply unsatisfied with these skeptical arguments. They aren't content with believing only what is useful for getting around or what simply appears to be the case. They want to know what the world is *really* like, as science and metaphysical philosophy understand the term "real." Though they admit that no particular sense experience is self-validating (that is, can convey to someone that it's *certainly* and absolutely true), they argue that our capacity to *reason* can supplement our experiences and provide additional reasons for thinking that our sense experience really tells us something about reality.

We're not in a position to settle the philosophical debate about *realism* here. How, then, should we proceed? Notice that skeptics and non-skeptics alike can agree on at least two features of sense experience: it is unavoidable and it's been incredibly useful (for at least some specified aims). In addition, they can mostly agree about what sense experience is *useful for*, namely, getting around in the world (not walking in front of buses, heart surgery, sending satellites into space, etc.). Perhaps most importantly, they can agree that what it's useful for seems fairly stable. For instance, we can send a rover to the Moon using *either* Newton's *or* Einstein's formulas – we experience the same results from using these theories, and therefore, if our goal is sending rovers to the moon, sense experience is reliable for accomplishing that goal. We know what to do to make it happen, and we can often figure out what to do to fix our calculations when we don't get the exact results we want. This is, arguably, all we could ever ask sense experience to do for us.

John Locke offers a detailed and fairly intuitive account of how sense experience could convey truths about reality. Locke concludes that skepticism is just not a reasonable alternative because, even if our senses don't give us everything the dogmatic realist wants, they give us all we need. Considering the skeptic who claims we could be in an elaborate and vivid dream, Locke explains in his 1689 *Essay Concerning Human Understanding* (Book 4, Chapter 11, Section 8):

> I must desire him to consider that if all be a dream, then he doth but dream that he makes the question; and so it is not much matter that a waking man should answer him. But yet, if he pleases, he may dream that I make him this answer, that the certainty of things existing in *rerum natura* [the nature of things], when we have the testimony of our senses for it, is not only as great as our frame can attain to, but as our condition needs. For our faculties being suited not to the full extent of being, nor to a perfect, clear, comprehensive knowledge of things free from all doubt and scruple, but to the preservation of us ....

The idea is that, even though the skeptic is right that our senses are not self-verifying, they are nevertheless suited to the only purpose we really need, namely, self-preservation. Locke goes on to show why he thinks our senses are suited for this purpose:

> ... [our senses] serve to our purpose well enough, if they will but give us certain notice of those things which are convenient and inconvenient to us. For he that sees a candle burning, and hath experimented the force of its flame by putting his finger in it, will little doubt that this is something existing without him, which does him harm, and puts him to great pain: Which is assurance enough, when no man requires greater certainty to govern his actions by than what is as certain as his actions themselves.

Locke is arguing that our simple experience with a flame shows that our sense experiences help us to make the most important judgments, namely, how to correlate our behaviors with our goals. Twentieth-century advancements in science have given us an ever-expanding arsenal of such examples, including heart transplants, a map of the human genome, pharmaceuticals that relieve depression and anxiety, nanotechnology, genetically modified foods, multiple terabytes of data storage, etc. Sense experience, combined with reason and applied systematically, seems to allow us ever-greater advantages for getting around in the world – at least as it appears.

In addition, sense experience works much better than any other putative source of evidence for helping us deal with the world. Notice that problems in other fields persist unsolved. Philosophical problems such as whether we have a soul or whether we have free will, linguistic problems as to the roles of the author and context in interpreting a text, historical problems such as the influence of time on the reliability of certain types of testimony, and political problems such as whether it is better to permit citizens maximal freedom to pursue their interests or to restrict their freedoms for their own protection all endure in contemporary debate with little hope for resolution. Yet, scientific problems such as finding a cure for polio, finding a therapy for certain types of schizophrenia, building an automobile airbag, walking on the Moon, or building a device smaller than your palm that will hold 80 gigabytes of music are being checked off the list daily. New problems arise, of course, and many are solved within a few years. This suggests that scientific programs guided by sense experience are highly reliable and useful resources for navigating our way through reality.

Although there are good reasons for thinking that sense experience does not give us direct, unmediated, and comprehensive access to the reality outside our minds, there are also good reasons for relying on sense experiences as reasons for forming beliefs. As long as we do not overstate the strengths of sense experience and we cautiously guard against those factors that distort our perceptions, sense experience remains a viable and valuable source of reasons. Since emotional experience and sense experience share important features (both are unbidden and occur independently of judgment), does emotional experience share the strengths of sense experience as evidence?

SEE ALSO

7.2 Cognitive Errors
7.3 Environment and Error
10.5 Semiotics: Critically Reading Signs
10.6 Deconstruction

READING

Antonio Damasio, *Descartes' Error: Emotion, Reason, and the Human Brain* (2005)
George Lakoff & Mark Johnson, *Metaphors We Live By*, 2nd edn (2003)
Bertrand Russell, *The Problems of Philosophy* (1959), Chapter 2
Julian Baggini & Peter S. Fosl, *The Philosopher's Toolkit* (2010)

8.4 Emotions and Evidence

Many people treat emotions as if they were a source of reasons. For instance, we often hear people say, "You gotta go with your gut," or "You should always follow your heart," or "My intuition is often right." But philosophers tend to be skeptical of treating emotions this way. It is a hallmark of Immanuel Kant's moral theory that he rejects the legitimacy of any moral judgment motivated by "inclination," by which he means emotion. It is distinctive of W. K. Clifford's (1845–1879) view of responsible belief that he explicitly rejects the use of passion or wishful thinking or emotion as legitimate sources of evidence. Many skeptics about knowledge regard emotion as the *primary threat* to knowledge. As the skeptic Michel de Montaigne (1533–1592) explains in his famous essay, "An Apology for Raymond Sebond" (1580): "What we see and hear when we are transported with emotion we neither see nor hear as it is." Furthermore, many have rejected certain religious views as irrational because these views seem motivated more by fear or wishful thinking than other (supposedly more reliable) sources of evidence – Bertrand Russell, for example, in "Why I Am Not a Christian" (1927) and Sigmund Freud in *The Future of an Illusion* (also 1927). But why think emotions are unreliable or inappropriate sources of evidence? Since they're a type of feeling, similar in important ways to sense experience, why prefer sense experiences to emotions in epistemic or critical matters?

The weaknesses of emotional experience as evidence

Twentieth-century novelist and philosopher Ayn Rand (1905–1982) disparages emotional experience because it is not the sort of experience that could help us increase knowledge. In a March 6, 1974, address to the cadets at the United States Military Academy at West Point, she explains that:

> A man who is run by emotions is like a man who is run by a computer whose printouts he cannot read. He does not know whether its programming is true or false, right or wrong, whether it's set to lead him to success or destruction, whether it serves his goals or those of some evil, unknowable power.[4]

In an earlier piece, spelling out a bit more clearly *why* emotions are misleading, she writes:

> An emotion tells you nothing about reality, beyond the fact that something makes you feel something. Without a ruthlessly honest commitment to introspection – to the conceptual identification of your inner states – you will not discover what you feel, what arouses the feeling, and whether your feeling is an appropriate response to the facts of reality, or a mistaken response, or a vicious illusion produced by years of self-deception.[5]

Jean Paul Sartre (1905–1980) regarded emotions as, for the most part, an expression of magical thinking, an expression of our wish to change reality that resists us – e.g., becoming angry with a golf club is an effort to make the ball fly straight when it's hit, as if by magic. The concern seems to be that emotional experience isn't connected with reality in the same way that sense experience is. But why think this? Couldn't it be the case that emotional experience just conveys different information than sense experience?

Philosophers such as Søren Kierkegaard (1813–1855) and Martin Heidegger (1889–1876) have suggested that some emotions – e.g., angst or existential dread and boredom – do reveal important aspects of human existence. Perhaps, then, Sartre and Rand's criticisms of emotions go too far. We do not disparage mathematics just because we cannot use mathematical formulas to predict the weather. Nevertheless, to see why emotional experience might be an unreliable source of evidence, consider the following thought experiment.

Imagine sitting in a room with fifteen people and holding up a series of solid-colored placards one-by-one. Imagine that, as you hold up each placard you ask the people in the room to identify the color. Now, as long as the room has no artificial light, you would expect people to say "green" when you hold up a green placard, "red" when you hold up a red placard, and "blue" when you hold up a blue placard. To be sure, someone may be color-blind and, therefore, may not be able to distinguish blue from purple or red from green. And you may have people who disagree about the name that should be ascribed to certain colors: whether mauve or pink, indigo or navy, cobalt or lapis or lavender. But by and large, these disagreements will be limited to a predictable set, and most can be resolved by agreeing on a common language about color (for instance, I might have been taught to use the word "chartreuse" for a certain shade of bright yellow hue, whereas you might have been taught to use the word "lemon"). Thus, unless someone were drastically misinformed, we would not expect anyone seeing the orange placard to say "blue," or anyone seeing the yellow placard to say "red."

But now imagine the same scenario, except instead of asking what color each person sees, you ask how the color makes each person feel, *emotionally*. What sort of patterns might you expect their answers to take? Would holding up the red placard reliably elicit anger or sadness? Would holding up the green placard reliably elicit happiness or tranquility? (See 10.5 for a discussion of the semiotics of "red.")

It seems likely that *no* pattern would emerge – red might make one person feel sad (for instance, because of some childhood experience) while it makes another person feel happy (for instance, if it is her favorite color). We often hear the phrase "green with envy," but few people would say that green *makes them feel* envious. It is not clear that there would be much agreement at all with respect to how colors make us feel, and they may not make us feel anything at all.

As we saw in the Section 8.3, the mere fact that we humans all agree to call a certain color *blue* doesn't mean that we are right – perhaps the rods and cones in our visual systems are deluding us as a species about the nature of the world outside of our minds. But *the fact that we can agree* that some object is blue at least allows us some means by which to communicate and to reason with one another about the color of objects. If two of us testify that we saw a white man with red hair drive away in a blue car, our joint testimonies could constitute grounds for conviction if the person fitting that description had just robbed a bank. This would not be possible if we were to testify about how the man made us feel upon seeing him.

Interestingly, recent empirical evidence (based on sense experience, of course) supports this conclusion about the weakness of emotional experience. Experiments correlating judicial decisions in parole cases with food breaks found that judges typically make favorable parole recommendations about 65% of the time at the beginning of their shift, but by lunch time, this favorable percentage drops to "nearly zero," and then returns to around 65% following a food break.[6] This suggests that emotional experiences such as stress, fatigue, and hunger play a non-trivial role in decision-making. But, of course, whether a judge has eaten shouldn't have any effect on her ruling on an inmate's parole – presumably, only legal evidence, solid interpretation, and good reasoning are relevant. Therefore, emotions seem to distract decision-makers from relevant evidence.

Additional evidence suggests that negative emotions lead to an increased number of incorrect responses on conditional and deductive reasoning tasks.[7] To be sure, some psychological evidence suggests that emotions can improve reasoning in some contexts.[8] Nevertheless, all this research suggests that there are enough contexts in which emotion negatively affects reasoning that we should be aware and cautious of its influence. Whereas sense experience introduces stable features of reality into our conscious thoughts (even if we are severely deluded about the *real* features of reality), our emotions reveal information primarily about our psychological states. It is this relativity to the reality of our psychological states (rather than the reality outside our minds) that explains why some of our emotionally influenced reasoning about reality goes wrong.

The strengths of emotional experience as evidence

Despite its unreliability in many areas of our rational lives, emotional experience is not wholly without value. Hume argues that rationality – and therefore our evaluation of sensory experience – could not function without feeling:

> Mathematics, indeed, are useful in all mechanical operations, and arithmetic in almost every art and profession: but it is not of themselves they have any influence. … A merchant is desirous of knowing the sum total of his accounts with any person: why? but that he may learn what sum will have the same effects in paying his debt, and going to market … . Abstract or demonstrative reasoning, therefore, never influences any of our actions, but only … directs our judgment concerning cause and effect … .[9]

The idea is that a merchant would never be concerned to add up his accounts on the basis of reason alone. The sheer mathematical process doesn't exert any influence on his conscious mind. It is the desire for money or for the things that money can buy that motivates him to balance his accounts. Reason must be *motivated*, Hume argues, by emotion:

> It is obvious that when we have the prospect of pain or pleasure from any object, we feel a consequent emotion of aversion or propensity, and care carried to avoid or embrace what will give us this uneasiness or satisfaction. … It can never in the least concern us to know that such objects are causes, and such others effects, if both the causes and effects be indifferent to us.[10]

Notice that Hume doesn't say that experiencing pain or pleasure is an emotion, but the prospect of experiencing pain or pleasure elicits a certain value judgment from us, either a *desire* to avoid pain or a *desire* to pursue pleasure. These desires are what move us to act, and this is where reason becomes relevant. We may recognize that pain is bad and desire to avoid it, but also recognize that, say, a certain vaccine, although painful for a moment, holds the prospect of avoiding in the future a much more intense and long-lasting pain. Therefore, reason guides our emotions, but it does not originate or motivate our actions.

Hume's analysis of the role of emotion still allows us to acknowledge the importance of reason in epistemic and moral judgment, since reason may help us recognize that some emotions are inappropriate or *ir*rational (as opposed to simply *a*rational, which means irrelevant to reason). As such, we can guide our actions to avoid the consequences of following inappropriate emotions and also guide them in pursuit of the consequences of following appropriate emotions. Reason also allows us to understand the consequences of our actions. We can't, after all, effectively avoid pain and pursue pleasure unless we reason a great deal about how the world is and works. We may, therefore, acknowledge Hume's point with relative indifference: *Yes, sure, emotions motivate us to act, but reason is still necessary to make judgments about our beliefs and behavior.*[11]

In the 20th century, some philosophers became convinced that emotion plays a much larger role in our belief-forming systems than even Hume recognized. William James (1842–1910) – an American pragmatist philosopher and known widely as the "father of American psychology" – argued against the prevailing view that reason is superior to emotion.[12] He suggested, along slightly different lines than Hume, that there are some beliefs for which rational evidence is not relevant and for which emotion is the only reasonable ground for deciding to believe or disbelieve.

Consider, for example, the very decision we are trying to make right now: *Should we give priority to sensory experience or emotion?* Can sensory experience help us answer such a question? The weaknesses we've noted about emotional evidence are themselves the products of empirical (sensory) evaluation. In defending the claim that emotion isn't always an appropriate source of evidence, we appealed to empirical (sensory) evidence about the reliability of applying emotion to a particular problem. If we thus conclude that sensory experience should be given priority, it might seem that we have committed the fallacy of *begging the question* (see 5.14), that is, we have assumed the very thing we need to prove, namely, that sense experience should be given priority over emotional experience.

James considers a slightly different question but in the same vein:

> There are two ways of looking at our duty in the matter of opinion ... [1] *We must know the truth*; and [2] *we must avoid error* – there are our first and great commandments as would-be knowers; but they are not two ways of stating an identical commandment, they are two separable laws[13]

James is drawing a distinction between two approaches to the theory of knowing. One option is to *pursue truth at all costs*. This view was famous among empiricists like Locke, who was content to have a few false beliefs so long as he developed a theory that provided a good shot at important true beliefs. The alternative is to *avoid error at all costs*. This view was famous among rationalists such as Descartes, who approached knowledge from a skeptic's perspective to see what could be rationally believed after all the skeptical arguments had been given their due.

The question that James wants to press is: what evidence would be relevant for deciding among these approaches?

> [W. K.] Clifford ... exhorts us to the latter course [course #2]. Believe nothing, he tells us, keep your mind in suspense forever, rather than by closing it on insufficient evidence incur the awful risk of believing lies. You, on the other hand, may think that the risk of being in error is a very small matter when compared with the blessings of real knowledge ... .[14]

James claims that this choice is not susceptible to rational evaluation:

> I myself find it impossible to go with Clifford. We must remember that these feelings of our duty about either truth or error are in any case only expressions of our passional nature. Biologically considered, our minds are as ready to grind out

> falsehood as veracity, and he who says, "Better go without belief forever than believe a lie!" merely shows his own preponderant private horror of becoming a dupe. He may be critical of many of his desires and feelings, but this fear he slavishly obeys.[15]

Thus, even if we are suspicious of the role emotional experience plays in reasoning, we cannot completely eradicate it. If James is right, emotions are involved in our most basic assumptions about how to evaluate evidence!

Applying this conclusion to our decision as to whether to give priority to the senses or emotions, we see we are in a similar predicament. Just as James cannot decide whether to pursue truth or shun error on the basis of passionless, rational considerations, similarly, we cannot give priority to the senses over emotions solely on the basis of sensory evidence. According to James since every choice is motivated in part by emotion, we are *wrong* to believe that *we should only believe on the basis of non-emotional evidence.* We are begging the question against those who employ emotions in their reasoning processes – since we must exclude emotion (and use only sense data) to show that emotion is unreliable.

So, what's a reasoner to do? One approach is to be thoroughly pragmatic. We can apply both sensory experience and emotional experience liberally and see where each is most appropriate. We will surely see that emotions are inappropriate for mathematics and physics and that pure sensory experience is inappropriate for how to behave in interpersonal relationships. Emotions are likely inappropriate for logic and philosophical analyses of God's existence and morality, and bare sensory experience is likely inappropriate for talking someone through a traumatic experience. James would argue that this is not only the best we can do; it is all we really need.

Another option is to use our sketches of both sensory and emotional experience (that we set out at the beginning of this chapter) to help us infer the appropriate domains of each – that is, to apply *reason* independently of either sense experience or emotional experience. Hume, of course, thinks this is impossible. But notice that Hume is in no better position to dictate a starting point than we are. He can say that emotions are essential for reason, but we can see that this follows from his characterization of emotion. If a case could be made for alternative accounts of emotion and reason that do not entail his view, then we would not be committed to his conclusion.

Of course, we've already noted that we can accept Hume's point with relative indifference. Let's say that emotion does direct our reasoning processes to the questions we end up considering important. Even so, we can choose to allow reason to assist as arbiter. Doing so, we can evaluate emotional experience and sensory experience with relative, regular, and stable equanimity. If it turns out that our emotions are misleading more often than not and that our senses are reliable more often than not, then we have a good reason for giving priority to sensory experience. Apart from the extreme skeptical worries about the reliability of any of our perceptions, this is exactly what we find to be the case: sense experience seems to be more reliable than emotional experience for reasoning about the things we care most about.

Here's a quick graphical summary of the highlights from this section:

	Sensory Experience	Emotional Experience
Similarities	• **Occur independently of our wills**	
	E.g., I see pink or smell cinnamon regardless of whether I want to.	E.g., I feel jealous or happy regardless of whether I want to.
	• **Occur independently of our critical judgments about them**	
	E.g., Although the wall appears pink, I judge that it may not be pink because I know a red light is shining on the wall.	E.g., Although feelings of jealousy arise in me, I judge that I should not be jealous because I understand that I have no right to be.
Differences	• **Often elicit emotional experiences**	• **Are often elicited by sensory experiences**
	E.g., The sensation of smelling cinnamon gives me a happy feeling that I associate with childhood.	
	• **Subject to questions of accuracy**	• **Subject to questions of appropriateness**
	E.g., I can ask whether I really smell cinnamon or whether the building is really yellow.	E.g., I can ask whether it is appropriate to feel happy about losing my ink pen.
	• **Directs our attention to something outside of ourselves**	• **Directs our attention to something inside ourselves**
	E.g., If I do not sense the presence of my ink pen, I am focused on things in the world around me.	E.g., If I feel happy about losing my ink pen, I am focused on my attitudes about things in the world around me.

Tips for eliminating the negative effects of emotions

To avoid the negative effects of emotions on your reasoning, the first step is to realize that they play a role and to understand the ways in which they undermine critical thinking (such as those listed under "The weaknesses of emotional experience as evidence" earlier in this section). Here are a few more tips:

1. *Compare the question at hand with other, similar questions.* Hypothetical examples can serve as a testing ground for your inferences and conclusions. Try to construct alternative cases that are very similar to the case you're considering but that include content about which you're less emotionally invested, or about which you can be more objective. If your judgment is different about these hypothetical

cases, emotion might be affecting your judgment in the original case. But be careful: your hypothetical case must mirror your original case very closely, and it is easy to miss a relevant feature. For examples of how philosophers use these sorts of cases, see Peg Tittle, *What If… Collected Thought Experiments in Philosophy* (2004).

2. *Recognize potential biasing factors.* There has been a lot of research on the psychological factors that affect rational judgment. For instance, the order in which various cases are considered sometimes affects judgments (*ordering bias*). Be sure to account for the emotional effects of the context in which you are evaluating a case. Similarly, the way that cases are worded sometimes affects judgments (*framing bias*). Be sure to account for the way a concept is presented when evaluating a case. Watch especially for emotionally charged language, either language of "excess" (extremely, incredibly, excessively, totally, staggeringly, etc.) or language that is already infused with a judgment (deplorably, appallingly, abhorrently, irrationally, unreasonably, etc.). Further, beware of your own interest in a particular conclusion (*confirmation bias*, see 7.2). Consider getting *corroboration* or a second or even third opinion just to be sure you aren't ignoring relevant evidence to see the conclusion you most desire. And finally, be aware that the vividness or recentness of an event may lead you to draw inappropriate conclusions about the probability that it will happen again. For instance, people who know heart attack victims tend to rank their chances of having a heart attack higher than those who don't know heart attack victims. Similarly, the more prominently an event is presented in the media leads people to overestimate its uniqueness and frequency.
3. *Be aware of emotion-driven fallacies.* We've already mentioned the appeal to fear and the appeal to pity (5.5), but there are a number of other fallacies that can be motivated by emotions, including appeal to guilt (5.5), snobbery, vanity, and even celebrity (5.9). Spend some time with Chapters 5, 7, and 8 to keep abreast of some of the many ways that emotions can undermine good reasoning. Beware, in general, of the ways that emotions can lead you to ignore good evidence.

SEE ALSO

5.5 Appeal to Emotions or Appeal to the Heart
9.4 Scientific Method
9.6 Experiments and Other Tests

READING

Martha Nussbaum, *Upheavals of Thought: The Intelligence of Emotions* (2003)
Robert Nozick, "Emotions," in *The Examined Life: Philosophical Meditations* (1989)
Harry G. Frankfurt, "The Importance of What We Care About," in *The Importance of What We Care About* (1988)

8.5 Justifying Values

Values are about what we take to be especially meaningful or significant to us. Values may admit of degrees. For example, if I order steak and you bring me chicken, it seems appropriate for me to say, "This should have been steak," though this objection seems to express a pretty insignificant value. On the other hand, if I ask for change for a fifty dollar bill, and you only give me two tens, it is not only appropriate for me to say, "These bills should add up to $50," but also that "I have been *wronged*" in not getting fifty dollars. To narrow this enormous discussion, it is helpful to draw a distinction between *personal* and *interpersonal* values.

Personal values are those things we find individually valuable, and these are fairly non-controversial. If you value watching *Casablanca* more than *Titanic*, you may be upset if I turn on *Titanic*, but you won't regard me as immoral or irrational for doing so – you will simply recognize that I hold different values and preferences from you. Interpersonal values – those things we think others, perhaps everyone, should prefer – are highly controversial. How much value should be placed on human life? How much on truth telling? How much on sexual activity? Which types of sexual activity? Because interpersonal values spark the most controversy in critical thinking, in the rest of our discussion we will use "value" to mean "interpersonal value."

In addition, we will even more particularly regard interpersonal values as referring to *moral* values. There are interpersonal values other than moral values. For instance, there are cultural values that don't include moral values (e.g., holding the door for someone; shaking hands with someone when you meet; enjoying lots of personal space in social contexts; automobiles). These interpersonal values can be controversial, but they are often controversial only within their respective cultural contexts. So, for simplicity, we will focus on moral values, which in many cases seem to cut across cultural and religious boundaries more broadly.

Reasoning about values is different from reasoning about feelings and perceptions. Whereas feelings of various types impose themselves on us, the source of values is less clear. Feelings seem to tell us how the world *is*, but values seem to tell us how the world *should* be. Values are, as philosophers like to say, *normative* or *prescriptive* rather than simply *descriptive*. If I *value* my friends, then I think my friends *should* be treated a certain way. If I *value* peace, then I think people *should not* fight if possible. When we judge something to be good or bad or right or wrong, then, we are distinguishing two aspects of a state of affairs – *descriptions* (details about what *is* or might be happening) and *prescriptions* (details about what *should* or *should not* be done or be changed, irrespective of whether it actually is the case).

In addition, value language seems to work differently from perception-feeling language; it plays a different role in our language. When we use feeling language, we are trying to describe states of affairs in the world – "that is a cat; that cat is on the mat" or "I feel pleasure" – and these claims are true insofar as the states of affairs really exist – that is *really* a cat; that cat is *really* on the mat. To be sure, we can use feeling-like language to refer to states that don't exist, for example: "I wish he had arrived on time; I hope the vote passes." But these still refer descriptively to states of affairs, and we know whether the expressions are appropriate according to whether the states of affairs did or do obtain. But value language doesn't depend on any of these considerations. "He should have told the truth," implies some descriptive state of affairs that did not obtain, but this is not all that it does. What does the "should" refer to? What role is it playing in the expression? Concerns about the source of value content and the role of values in language make reasoning about values more difficult than reasoning about sensory and emotional experience.

The role of moral values in arguments

One difference in how value language works compared with feeling language is that values are often invoked in arguments in order to *motivate* you to *behave* a certain way. If you become convinced that you *shouldn't* do *X*, your conviction is not to *do X*. If you become convinced that you have an obligation to do *X*, your conviction is to *do X*. This is different from classical argument strategies that are primarily concerned with beliefs. These beliefs may have implications for behavior (e.g., if you are convinced that the claim "God exists" is true, then you may begin seeking ways to worship this being), but the primary concern is with whether the beliefs are true or false. Value reasoning in contrast is typically still about beliefs (it still uses standard argument forms), but is primarily aimed at conclusions that govern behavior.

Thus, if some people attempt to convince you, for instance, that animals have a "right to life" similar to that of humans, they are probably trying to convince you to stop eating meat or to stop supporting meat or fur industries. Similarly, if someone attempts to convince you that individuals have the sole authority over property they have obtained fairly, he may be trying to convince you to vote against what he perceives as excessive taxation or taxation for the care of others.

One difficulty with evaluating arguments for value-laden claims is identifying precisely the behavior at issue. For instance, with respect to the first example above: could someone believe that animals *may permissibly* be eaten and yet also believe that animals possess a "right to life" in a sense similar to the way humans possess that right? With respect to the second example above: given a legitimate political system, could *any* taxation be regarded as *excessive*? By what moral standard could taxation be evaluated?

Summing up, value judgments can be understood as a relationship between three things: something perceived to be valuable (the valued); someone for whom it is valuable (the valuer); and the evaluation (the value itself). For instance, Sam believes that it is good to tell the truth. But which criteria are we to appeal to when making *judgments* of value? If our senses are really reliable, the sensory data provide the criterion of perceptual judgments about the world outside our minds. But to what criteria can we appeal when making *normative* or value judgments? Just as it is with descriptive judgments in fiction (e.g., that Darth Vader wears a black cape), the fact that we can *express* normative claims doesn't mean we are expressing something *real*. So, what are we expressing when we make value judgments?

Four common views of value judgment

At least four possibilities have been widely discussed in philosophy:

(1) Normative criteria are grounded in objective reality, just like descriptions.

Moral realism is the philosophical view that morality is objectively real. The idea is that the normative grounds of a value judgment are part of objective reality that is either independent of how our minds and feelings work, or it's a universal function of how our minds interact with reality. Some *fact about reality*, in short, makes it meaningful to make judgments such as: "intentionally killing innocents is wrong" and "charity is good." By the most common accounts of philosophers who hold this view, we can access evidence for these facts either through purely abstract reasoning, through our normal experiential faculties, or through some special experiential faculty (a "moral sense").

One of the most common appeals to objective properties is the idea of excellences, perfections, or *virtues*. Traditional virtue theorists hold that there is something objective that defines the excellence of a human life, human flourishing, human physical, mental, and social well-being, and that values ought to give support to those excellences. (This is, of course, a controversial idea.) Some, such as John Locke and Thomas Paine (1737–1809), argue that *human rights* are in some sense objective, real, and independent of any given culture or society – that's what makes it, on this view, possible to judge societies and cultures. A Nazi who argued that it was an authentic expression of German culture to annihilate Jews would not, therefore, persuade those who think independently grounded human rights exist.

While the view that objective moral grounds really *exist* is a form of *metaphysical* moral realism, the position that holds that those grounds can be *known* is called *epistemological* moral realism. As a matter of critical thinking, then, it's generally not sufficient for moral realists to argue (1) that objective grounds for moral judgments exist; they must also argue (2) that those grounds can be adequately known. *Cognitivists* hold that it's meaningful to regard moral statements as true or false, that there is some moral truth or moral fact that cognition can apprehend. Many other philosophers, however, reject this view in favor of *non-cognitivism*; for them, the categories of "true" and "false" are not relevant in the way cognitivists accept. A prominent group of philosophers known as *subjectivists* commonly accept non-cognitivist positions about morality (see Section 5.2). Let's consider their view.

(2) Normative criteria are grounded in subjectivity, in our individual or collective mind/s.

This view is known as *subjectivism*. The central idea of subjectivism is that what is valuable is fully determined either by what each subject finds valuable or by a collection of valuing subjects, say those composing a culture. The grounds of normativity, for subjectivists, therefore, cannot be understood to be independent of subjectivity.

Relativism – the view that values are relative – is consistent with many versions of this position, but subjectivism *per se* does not entail relativism. From an objective point of view, no opinion about values on this model is better or worse than any other. But it doesn't follow from this that no values can be judged better or worse than any other. It means only that judgments about what values are better or worse must be made subjectively – as a matter of what is available to different subjects. Universality of value judgments is possible for subjectivists if they hold that all subjectivities share common features – e.g., capacities for moral sentiment, rationality, pleasure, pain, feeling and sympathy. On these bases, agreements can be found or created even for subjectivists that are widely shared, perhaps even universally.

Subjectivism is also, like relativism, often associated with *tolerance* (since there are no utterly objective grounds for moral decision, no one would seem to have grounds for criticizing or devaluing opposing values). But, similarly, subjectivism offers no objective grounds to prohibit criticism. After all, one's individual or subjective judgment may require the condemning or even suppressing of other values. Indeed, relativists often see fit to condemn absolutists. In short, subjectivism, like objective realism, permits criticism and universal claims, but those claims must appeal to different grounds. Critical thinkers, therefore, could inquire about the objective grounds claimed by realists (e.g., material facts, divine commands, or principles of logic) or the subjective grounds of subjectivists (e.g., feelings, sympathies, customs and habits, affiliations). It's also important to note that subjectivism is not the same as *egoism*. Egoists are actually moral realists; they hold that there is some fact of the matter about what is right and wrong, and that is the putative fact that each individual should do what's in his or her own interests.

(3) Normative criteria come from collective, but not subjective, agreements among people.

This view posits a social but also objective basis for at least some values. The idea is that normativity doesn't exist independently of human interactions. Normative criteria emerge from the arrangements or agreements people set up and enforce when they form societies. One school of this sort is known as *social contract theory* (e.g., the thought of Thomas Hobbes, 1588–1679). For an admittedly simplistic example: if citizens democratically agree to abolish slavery and workplace discrimination, these acts are on that factual basis immoral. We access this content through explicit agreements (contracts, promises) or through the implicit cultural norms. A related view, developed by philosophers such as Charles Stevenson, R. M. Hare, and Stanley Cavell, finds moral claims and values built more or less into human language. A strong case Cavell considers in his 1969 essay, "Must We Mean What We Say?" demonstrates that to make a promise obligates one no matter what one's intent or subjective feelings about it.

(4) Normative criteria are illusory (either we imagine them, mistake them for our preferences, or they are a function of the evolution of our human psychology).

This fourth view encompasses a family of views, all of which hold that our moral language doesn't do what we think it does. We use "value language" as if it refers to some authoritative rule of action (when we say, "You shouldn't do that," we expect you and anyone else in that situation not to do it), but we are mistaken in thinking this is the way moral language actually works. Some philosophers argue that we *are* referring to a rule of action, but that rule *is not authoritative* because there are no moral facts to make them true and binding. What makes a descriptive claim true is that there is some fact or state of affairs that it describes – this is how we distinguish good journalism from pseudo-journalism and fiction, for example. With moral claims, say thinkers of this persuasion, there are no states of affairs upon which we can ground our value judgment as true – they are all therefore false. This view is known as *error theory* (e.g., in the work of J. L. Mackie).

Well, that's a start. This is a brief and incomplete list. There are many theories of morality, and it would be impossible to sketch them all out here. Critically reasoning about values today, however, will likely involve inferences about moral value claims informed by one of these common perspectives. Reasoning about interpersonal values is tough, but it is not impossible. For a fuller treatment of moral reasoning, see Julian Baggini and Peter Fosl's *The Ethics Toolkit: A Compendium of Ethical Concepts and Methods*. For now, here are some tips for reasoning well about values.

Tools for reasoning about moral values

1. *Develop an understanding of basic moral theories.* Moral theories guide consistent arguments for values. Every argument for a value claim appeals to some kind of ground for normative considerations, whether *rights* or *pain* or *agreement* or something else. Philosophically speaking, moral theories appeal to something that plays an authoritative role in governing morally proper judgment. The most influential moral arguments appeal to the normative considerations defended in standard moral theories: *deontology* (that morality is about fulfilling duties despite the consequences), *consequentialism* (that morality is about producing the most desirable consequences), and *virtue ethics* (that morality is about being excellent). Thus, a grasp of these theories will help you sort through arguments that other people make, and will help you clarify and strengthen your own arguments for values.

2. *Distinguish the descriptive from the normative content of a claim.* Curiously, value disagreements often come down to disagreements about states of affairs rather than moral principles. For instance, a common claim in the abortion debate is that the "morning after" pill (which initiates a menstrual discharge that expels the embryo) is immoral because an embryo has a *right* to life from the moment of conception. It may (or may not) alter someone's moral judgment to note that, as a matter of simple fact,

"conception" may mean a variety of different things in the research community and that also as a matter of fact the embryo typically doesn't yet possess a full, unique set of human chromosomes for 7–12 days after sexual intercourse.

3. *Be aware of the most common fallacies employed in moral reasoning.* There are a number of common mistakes in reasoning about values, and recognizing these can defuse unnecessarily contentious debates rather quickly. For example, two very common fallacies in moral reasoning are the *subjectivist fallacy* (5.2) and the *appeal to unqualified authority* (5.10). Becoming skillful in identifying these and the other fallacies discussed in this book will help clarify not only your logic and your science but also your moral thinking. Indeed, the ability to recognize and defuse fallacious arguments can help facilitate good reasoning and can help avoid unnecessary disputes.

SEE ALSO

9.1 Science and the Value of Scientific Reasoning
10.8 The Frankfurt School: Culture Critique
10.9 Class Critiques
10.12 Traditionalist and Historicist Critiques

READING

Louis Pojman & James Fieser, *Ethics: Discovering Right and Wrong*, 7th edn (2011)
Jamie Carlin Watson & Robert Arp, *What's Good on TV? Understanding Ethics Through Television* (2011)
Michael Huemer, "The Lure of Radical Skepticism," in Nils Ch. Rauhut & Robert Bass, eds. *Readings on the Ultimate Questions: An Introduction to Philosophy*, 3rd edn (2010)
James Rachels, *The Elements of Moral Philosophy*, 4th ed. (2003).
Martha Nussbaum, *Upheavals of Thought: The Intelligence of Emotions* (2001)
G. E. Moore, "Proof of an External World," in G.E. Moore, *Philosophical Papers* (1962)
Bertrand Russell, *Problems of Philosophy* (1959)
Julian Baggini & Peter S. Fosl, *The Ethics Toolkit: A Compendium of Ethical Concepts and Methods*

8.6 Justification: The Basics

Returning to our discussion of knowledge and its relationship to justification, we can now ask about the nature of justification. Some philosophers talk about justification as a *property of claims* (that is, that there exists a *reason* that *p* is true irrespective of anyone's knowledge or beliefs about *p*), while others talk about it as a *property of believers* (some subject *S* has a *reason* to believe that *p*). It may be that there are objectively justified claims (first sense) – perhaps, for instance, the claim that "whatever is necessarily true (i.e., it couldn't be false) is an *epistemically good* thing to believe" (since it is *true*, and we want true beliefs). There are, however, many necessarily true claims that we have no reason to believe, either because we haven't thought about them (e.g., the result of 1,000,000,000 divided by 762,345 – mathematical truths being necessarily true) or because, even if we have thought about them, they require information to which we don't have access (e.g., the number of stars divided by the number of planets). It's intuitive to think of justification as a property of a claim because, if a claim is objectively justified, then we can be sure there exists somewhere an objective reason to believe it – and that objectivity seems to many to be a better indication of knowledge than relying only on the information to which we have access.

Justification and the problem of access

Unfortunately, we only have access to the information, well, *to which we have access*, and that information may or may not include reasons for believing that a claim is objectively justified. Therefore, for us even to know whether there's a reason to believe that a claim is objectively justified or not, we need to know whether *we* (subjectively) have any reasons for believing it. Ultimately, our evidence is our own and no one else's. Therefore, when we talk about justification, we will be talking about it as a property of believers. In a more formal way, we'll talk about justification such that: person *S* is justified in believing *p* only if *S* has good reason for believing that *p* (review 8.1 for more on definitions of justification).

The consequence of our limited information is that some people could be justified in believing that *p* while others are justified in believing that not-*p*. Now, we know that *p* and not-*p* can't both be true (on pain of contradiction), so that means at least one of them must be false. But if someone can be justified in believing falsely, why is justification a necessary condition for knowledge? How is "justified true belief" better than just "true belief" if our justifications do not always make the difference between *knowing* and *not knowing*? We will address this question below. For now, note that even this explanation of justification isn't very good; we need to fix it up a bit before moving on.

It isn't enough for *S* to believe *p* responsibly that *she has good reason to believe that p*. This is because she may also possess an equally strong reason (or even stronger reason) to believe that not-*p*. Consider the Müller-Lyer illusion below.[16] Line (a) looks to be longer than line (b), and (given that we have a reason to trust our senses) this is a reason to believe that, "Line (a) is longer than line (b)."

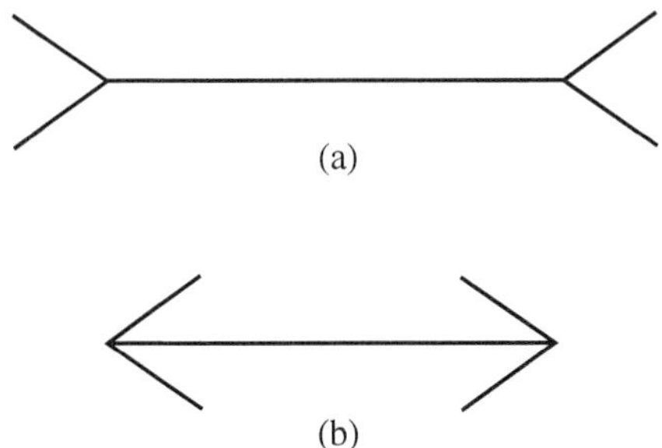

Without further information, you may be justified in believing this claim. If, however, you measure the lines with a ruler, you'll discover that they're the same length.

Now you have an equally strong (and probably stronger) reason to believe, "It is not the case that line (a) is longer than line (b)." If your reasons are equally strong for each, the responsible thing to do is what the Pyrrhonian skeptics would do, and that's suspend judgment. In order to believe one claim over the other, you'll need some evidence to break the evidential tie. Most of us, however, trust the ruler over our sense of sight. We know our eyes deceive us on a regular basis (when we're tired, when the light is dim, when we're on certain medications, etc.), but we consider a ruler to be a fairly stable and reliable indicator. Therefore, most of us would probably say that the second belief (that line (a) is *not* longer than (b)) is justified for us over the first belief.

No reasons not to believe

The Müller-Lyer illusion shows that having a justified belief that *p* requires both having a reason to believe that *p and also* having no equally strong or stronger reason for believing that not-*p*. Under most circumstances, we take this latter requirement to simply mean: I *can't think of any reason* not to believe *p*. This is the most basic way to form beliefs, and Kent Bach calls it the "taking-for-granted" (or TGF) rule:

> *(TFG) If it seems to me that p, then I infer that p, provided no reason to the contrary occurs to me.*

But while this is the way we normally do things, it isn't clear that this practice results in genuinely justified beliefs. We may, in some circumstances, have an epistemic obligation to double-check this "inability to think of reasons to the contrary."

For instance, your parents may have told you: "The tallest candidate for political office is always right." You may have never heard anything to the contrary, you may take your parents to be fairly reliable sources, and you might not be able to think of any reason not to believe this. Is this belief justified? Probably not, and if so, not very strongly. Even if your parents are fairly reliable sources about many things, they may not be reliable on this issue – perhaps they're mistaken. And just because you can't think of any reason this claim might not be true, that doesn't mean you have very much evidence. You may have never heard anything to the contrary because you've never met anyone who isn't friends with your parents (and shares the same political views). If this is your evidence pool, it's likely to be deeply biased.

Beyond a reasonable doubt

The "tallest candidate" example suggests that we should not interpret the second half of our account of justification according to the taking-for-granted rule. We need to account for the amount of evidence we actually have for a claim. Roderick Chisholm (1916–1999) refers to a version of the taking-for-granted rule as expressing a fairly weak sort of justification that he calls being "epistemically in the clear," by which he means there is a little support for *p* and no support for not-*p*.[17] In order for a belief to be justified for you, according to Chisholm, the claim has to rise to the epistemic level of *beyond reasonable doubt*. For now, we'll say that this means you've done your homework (you've actively looked for good reasons) in all those cases where it seems like you need to look for good reasons.

Obligation and permission to believe

What's the upshot of all this "homework"? What are your *responsibilities* once you've discovered a reason for thinking a claim is true? Philosophers such as W. K. Clifford have argued that if a claim is justified for you, you are *obligated* to believe it – you are violating an *epistemic duty* if you don't believe it. Others argue that justification makes claims "permissible" for you to believe. You can take them or leave them, but if they're justified, you're violating no epistemic duty in believing them. Similarly, if a belief is unjustified, you are permitted not to believe it; you are not violating an epistemic duty in refusing to believe them.

Of course, in both cases, it would be "irrational" for you to believe something contrary to what the evidence permits, or even in excess of what the evidence permits. As David Hume prescribed in Section 10 of his *Enquiry concerning Human Understanding* (1748):

> ... in our reasonings concerning matter of fact, there are all imaginable degrees of assurance, from the highest certainty to the lowest species of moral evidence. ... *A wise man, therefore, proportions his belief to the evidence*. (Our emphasis.)

For instance, if the claim, "Evolution is the best explanation for biodiversity," is justified for you, then it is at least permissible for you to accept it. (Note that for some it isn't clear that it would be *irrational* not to accept it, and note that for others it would be obligatory to believe it.) It's *not*, however, permissible for you (on this view) to believe that (1) "evolution is *not* the best explanation for biodiversity" or for that matter that (2) "it is absolutely certain that evolution is the best explanation for biodiversity that could ever and will ever be given." The evidence doesn't make *this* belief permissible in (1) the first instance because it's *contrary to the evidence* and in (2) the second because it *surpasses the evidence*. In short form, for many purposes when thinking critically:

1. *Don't adopt beliefs contrary to what evidence justifies.*
2. *Don't adopt beliefs that surpass what the evidence justifies.*

This discussion also suggests the following "minimal" account of justification:

> *S is justified in believing p if and only if for any claim, p, if S has evidence, E, that p is true and lacks evidence equal to or stronger than E that not-p, S is permitted to believe p.*

This is not an uncontroversial account, and in particular it risks being too broad, as some philosophers have argued that some beliefs – e.g., that the world exists – don't require justification because they are prior conditions for the possibility of any justification at all. They are, according to some, *basic* beliefs or *hinge* propositions (see 8.1). Moreover, some beliefs – for example that my spouse loves me, that my friend is trustworthy – often surpass the evidence in a strict sense. There is much that we take on trust or as a matter of faith in life and much of it would be wrong to subject to rigorous testing. But our evidence requirement (the *only* if, as we saw in 2.2) is a place to begin critical thinking. In the remainder of this chapter, we'll explain the value of this view for critical thinking and offer an account of the relationship between evidence and justification. We'll end the chapter with some tips for determining whether a claim is justified for you.

SEE ALSO

8.3 Skepticism and Sensory Experience
9.1 Science and the Value of Scientific Reasoning
9.7 Six Criteria for Abduction

READING

Trent Dougherty, ed., *Evidentialism and its Discontents* (2011)
Thomas Kelly, "Evidence: Fundamental Concepts and the Phenomenal Conception," *Philosophy Compass* 3.5 (2008): 933–955
Robert Audi, *Epistemology: A Contemporary Introduction*, 3rd edn (2010), "Introduction."
Laurence BonJour & Ernest Sosa, *Epistemic Justification: Internalism vs. Externalism, Foundations vs. Virtues* (2003)
Kent Bach, "A Rationale for Reliabilism," *The Monist* 68.2 (1985): 246–263

8.7 Truth and Responsible Belief

If knowledge is justified true belief, and if our account of justification turns out to be adequate, then we have one obvious reason for regarding justification as valuable: it helps us to gain what best seems to be *knowledge*. If our evidence is connected with the world or connects us with the world in the right sort of way, then we are, it seems, more likely to possess true beliefs about the world than false ones.

A second reason to value justification is that it helps us form *responsible beliefs*. Justification depends on evidence that some claims are true.[18] Justification plays this role whether we are trying to obtain knowledge or simply trying to form responsible beliefs. That is, justification allows us to distinguish between beliefs we think are good or proper to hold (responsible beliefs) and beliefs we think are not good or proper to hold (irresponsible beliefs). For instance, the evidence you obtain from looking both ways before crossing a street allows you to make a more *practically effective* decision about whether to cross than, say, reading tea leaves, checking your horoscope, or hoping the street is clear of traffic. In this sense, you might say that looking both ways is a *more responsible* way of forming a belief about the street than any of these other methods. Why do we say more *responsible*? Responsibly formed beliefs seem true in relation to the events and outcomes about which we care, as opposed to irresponsibly formed beliefs. In this case, looking both ways is more responsible to our personal well-being.

Why is responsibility relevant to belief?

Imagine you want to walk due south. It would be more responsible to rely on a compass for evidence about due south than a goose's flight direction in winter. Why? We have other evidence that (1) not all geese fly south in winter, (2) geese can fly directions other than due south, even in winter, and (3) geese are more likely to be wrong than a compass. Thus, practically, it would seem that relying on a goose's flight direction is less responsible to ourselves and to anyone dependent upon the right outcome of our decision than a compass. Though this example may be a bit out of the ordinary, we make similar judgments about the value of evidence every day: we choose one news network over another; we choose one web site over another; we choose one professor to ask over another if we have questions about a difficult text, etc.

Responsibility without truth

Notice, moreover, that we would make these judgments regardless of whether such claims as, "The street is clear of traffic" and "The compass says due south is this way," are true or whether they are made under deceptive conditions. To see why, recall our discussion of skepticism from 8.3 (especially the section, "The weaknesses of sense experience as evidence"). Imagine you are in a world that is completely the fabrication of some malicious entity that's out to deceive you (think of Descartes's evil demon, or, if you're familiar with the film *The Matrix* (1999), imagine you're in a Matrix-type world without knowing it). In a situation of that sort, none of your beliefs about what you perceive with your senses are true. Everything you see, hear, touch, taste, and smell around you is the fabrication of a powerful deceiver – your perceptions are illusory, and most of your beliefs are false.[19] Nevertheless, even in this completely fabricated world, there are more and less responsible beliefs. There is better and worse evidence about whether to cross the street, about the direction of due south, about which professors to rely on when asking certain questions, etc. Now, since evidence plays this same role regardless of whether we're forming *true, responsible beliefs* or *merely responsible (but false) beliefs*, and since justification depends on the role that evidence plays in our belief-forming system, justification is valuable both for knowing (in those worlds where we are not systematically deceived) and for forming responsible beliefs (in all worlds). That's an important consideration for critical thinkers to keep in mind, even if you don't take the red pill and follow Alice down the rabbit hole.

SEE ALSO

8.5 Justifying Values
9.7 Six Criteria for Abduction
9.8 Bad Science

READING

Linda Zagzebski, *On Epistemology* (2008), Chapter 6
Cora Diamond, "Truth: Defenders, Debunkers, Despisers," in *Commitment in Reflection*, Leona Toker, ed. (1994), 195–222
Roderick Chisholm, *Theory of Knowledge* (1966), Chapter 1

8.8 How Does Justification Work?

In general, we evaluate a person's degree of rationality according to how much evidence she or he has for those beliefs. For instance, imagine you're feeling ill, and you want to know what disease you have. You ask your friend, Paul, who recently had similar symptoms, and Paul says, "I went to a doctor, and he said I had *X*." Although this seems like a good reason to believe you have *X*, there are many mitigating factors: you're relying on Paul's understanding and explanation of your symptoms; Paul's understanding of his own symptoms; that Paul is competent to determine that you have roughly the same symptoms he had; Paul's inference that his physician's advice about his own symptoms applies to your symptoms; Paul's physician's expertise, etc. With all of this in mind, you ask your friend, Ann, who is herself a physician, for a second opinion. Imagine that Ann says, you have *Y*, not *X*. This seems like a good reason to believe you have *Y*, and what's more, it seems like a better reason to believe you have *Y* than that you have *X*. But *why*? There are still many mitigating factors. So, what makes evidence *evidence*? And what makes one piece of evidence *better* than another?

Claims as evidence

Evidence can take the form of a *claim*, *experience*, or *event*, and is often a highly complex combination of the three. For instance, the claim: "That woman's hat is yellow," is evidence for the claim, "That woman has a hat." Why? In this case, the first claim logically implies the second, even if the first isn't true. There is a logical relationship between the claims; the content of the second is *implied* by (or, perhaps more strongly, is *entailed* by)[20] the content of the first. And this is true regardless of whether you have any reason to believe either of them, and regardless of whether either is true. So, if you have any reason to believe "That woman's hat is yellow," you also have a reason to believe "That woman has a hat." This sort of implication holds also in the following examples:

"That is a bachelor" entails, "That is a man."
"That is a barrister" entails, "That is a lawyer."
"I was sitting at the bar" entails, "I was sitting."
"There are no round-squares" entails "That is not a round-square" (for any "that"!)

Just as in our hat example, if you have a reason to believe any of the former claims, you also have a reason to believe the latter claims. This doesn't mean you will believe the latter claims – they may never cross your mind. But once you *recognize* the logical entailment, you have evidence that they are true.

Of course, logical entailment is a pretty sparse sort of evidence; it is difficult to determine much about the world around you on this evidence alone. But now imagine that you *see* a woman with a yellow hat. On the basis of this experience you can come to believe, "That woman's hat is yellow." Your experience of the woman's hat is evidence for this belief. What's more, your logical ability to separate *hat*-ness from *yellow*-ness allows you to talk about (and form a belief about) the hat irrespective of its color. So, your seeing a woman with a yellow hat is a reason to believe the woman has a yellow hat, and combined with your logical ability, you have a reason to believe, "That woman has a hat." Your experience takes this logical relationship from the realm of pure concepts and connects it with the world around you.

Experience as evidence

It's not a trivial fact that conscious human perceptual experiences operate as evidence. If perceptions were simply brute images, it would be difficult to regard them as "evidence" in any meaningful sense. We would be little more than sophisticated video cameras – we could capture data, and perhaps there is some mechanism that would turn what we capture into behavior, but we wouldn't understand the significance of that data. As it is, there is this odd feature of our perceptions that they make certain claims *seem to be true*. When I look out my window, *my seeing* a car pass makes it *seem to me* that a car is passing; I now have a *reason* to believe that the claim, "a car is passing," is *true*. And this perceptual seeming is different from our logical seemings (such as that "X is a bachelor" entails that "X is a man"). Our "perceptual seemings" (apparently) take us out into the world around us; they apparently tell us something about reality. Seeing is in part judging, and as many philosophers such as Edmund Husserl have argued, all seeing is seeing *as*.

We cannot deny this evidential role of perceptual experience, but we should be cautious of it. It's important to have tools for deciding whether or not to accept a perceptual seeming as true or when to reject it. Recall from 8.3 our discussion of the role of sense experiences in our epistemic lives – we ordinarily believe that our senses are generally reliable. And even if we're wrong, even if we fully admit the possibility that we are deceived by Descartes's evil demon or perhaps something else imagined by a skeptic, it still *seems* or *appears* to us that our senses are revealing something meaningfully called "real" or "true," even if not perhaps in the senses in which metaphysicians use the term: if I see a tree in front of me, it *seems true to me* that there is a tree in front of me; if I hear a train whistle, it *seems true to me* that a train whistle is blowing. And although I could be wrong, this does nothing to weaken the *seeming* that these experiences are experiences of something real.

Notice that we experienced the same state when considering the logical relationships above: it *seems* to us as if being a bachelor entails being a man, and that being a barrister entails being a lawyer. This *seeming* remains even when we recall that we make mistakes in reasoning. If it didn't seem that way to us (perhaps we don't know the meaning of the word "barrister"), we would not "*see*" the logical relationship between them (in some metaphorical, intellectual sense of *see*), and therefore, we would not regard the former claim as evidence for the latter.

What these examples suggest is that (a) there is something about the state of *seeming to me* that is essential to evidence and that (b) evidence is distinct from truth. This means that something's seeming like *X* to me (whether logical or experiential) doesn't entail that I believe that something is *X*. As we discussed in 8.2, a wall may seem to me to be red, but if I know that a red light bulb was recently installed above the wall, I can suspend judgment about the color of the wall (it may be white and simply seem red because of the bulb). Therefore, experiential evidence that *X* is logically distinct from concluding that *X* is so. Whether such evidence *should lead me to form the conclusion* that *X* is so is an additional question we will consider below. Of course, the question naturally arises: if *seeming to me* isn't a necessary marker of truth, why call it *evidence*? There are two reasons.

First, seeming is a cognitive state that we just can't do without. There's no seeming-independent conscious state from which to begin our investigations. Every conscious state involves a seeming of some sort. To be sure, some seemings are better than others; we saw in 8.2 that emotions seem less reliable than sense experience. Nevertheless, even to come to believe that one source of evidence is more or less reliable than another, we must depend on one of them *seeming to us* to be more or less reliable. We cannot escape seemings as a starting-point for evaluating truth.

And second, some seemings are foundational for all other evidential evaluations, namely, those that involve "seeming to be true." We must rely on seemings-to-be-true when we read news reports, evaluate scientific data, or remember where we left our keys. And these seemings-to-be-true are ours and ours alone, as epistemologist

Alvin Plantinga notes, "I must do the best I can, according to my own lights. (Who else's?)."

SEE ALSO

6.8 Mill's Five Methods
9.6 Experiments and Other Tests
9.5 Unfalsifiability and Falsification Resistance

READING

Thomas Kelly, "Evidence," *The Stanford Encyclopedia of Philosophy*, Edward N. Zalta, ed. (Fall 2008)
Bertrand Russell, *The Problems of Philosophy* (1959), Chapter 14
Edmund Husserl, *Ideas: General Introduction to Phenomenology* (1931)

8.9 A Problem for Responsible Belief

This tradition of relying on our seemings to help us form, evaluate, reject, and maintain beliefs is known as *internalism*, and there are some serious concerns about it. Just as our seemings can be mistaken, and thus there can be reasons to resist believing them, so the beliefs we form on the basis of seemings can be mistaken. Roderick Chisholm explains in the 3rd edition of his *Theory of Knowledge* (1989): "According to this traditional conception of 'internal' epistemic justification, there is no *logical* connection between epistemic justification and truth. A belief may be internally justified and yet be *false*." Skepticism, therefore, for internalists remains on the scene as a legitimate option.

Some philosophers find this state of affairs unsatisfactory. Chisholm notes, "This consequence is not acceptable to the externalist. The externalist feels that an adequate account of epistemic justification should exhibit *some* logical connection between epistemic justification and truth." (To be clear, these philosophers tend to be externalists *because* they don't find the internalist lack of a logical connection acceptable; they are not externalists who happen to find it unacceptable.) Nevertheless, internalism seems for some thinkers to be the best we can do, if we cannot get outside of our heads to determine whether our evidence connects us with the world in the way we think it does. If we could check our connection with the world, skepticism wouldn't be a problem. It is also important to realize that our inability to get outside ourselves need not necessarily lead to skepticism or nihilism – we can make good use of our seemings to get around in the world, for example, to send spaceships to the outer solar system, to construct artificial hearts, and to write computer code that allows us to record and edit language (as I am doing with this text) with minimal, unconscious effort.

Despite this intuitive case for internalism, externalists have powerful arguments for an alternative account of justification, one that focuses on the connection between our beliefs and the world independent of our seemings and, indeed, to whatever justifications we have access. There is a very obvious reason philosophers would be motivated to pursue this sort of project. If justification is supposed to help us obtain knowledge, then whatever justifies our beliefs in an objective sense *should* be connected with the world in a particular way, namely in a way that makes them true, a way philosophers like to call *truth-conducive*. The world may do this indirectly, through a variety of *processes* that produce output beliefs that are more likely true than not, or it may do so directly, through a *causal chain* between the world and our beliefs. To appreciate the externalist understanding of justification and knowledge, let's briefly review one of the most influential versions of externalism called *process reliabilism*.

Gettier cases

In order to possess knowledge, we must be justified in our beliefs, but it seems that not just any justification will do. In 1948, Bertrand Russell proposed three examples that suggest that good evidence (even the best possible evidence!) cannot guarantee that we *know* the claims supported by that evidence.[21] In his 1948 book, *Human Knowledge: Its Scope and Its Limits*, Russell writes:

> There is the man who looks at a clock which is not going, though he thinks it is, and who happens to look at it at the moment when it is right; this man acquires a true belief as to the time of day, but cannot be said to have knowledge. There is the man who believes, truly, that the last name of the Prime Minister in 1906 began with a B, but believes this because he believes that Balfour was Prime Minister then, whereas in fact it was Campbell-Bannerman. There is the lucky optimist who, having bought a ticket for the lottery, has an unshakeable conviction that he will win, and, being lucky, does win. Such instances can be multiplied indefinitely, and show that you cannot claim to have known merely because you turned out to be right. (p. 140)[22]

In this case, the man in the example (a) believes that it is, say, noon; (b) it is true that it is noon; and (c) the man has a really good reason for believing it is noon (clocks are generally reliable). Unfortunately, it's just luck that this man has a true belief – the clock (in this case) isn't a *reliable* indicator of time. In 1963, Edmund Gettier made this style of example famous, and contemporary versions are called "Gettier cases."

These cases have convinced most philosophers that a revised account of knowledge is needed. Knowledge must be justified true belief *plus an anti-Gettier condition*. What might an anti-Gettier condition look like? One suggestion has become exceptionally popular: such a condition makes sure that evidence is connected with the world in the right sort of way. Consider a famous example from Alvin Goldman, who in his influential 1976 article, "Discrimination and Perceptual Knowledge," writes:

> Henry is driving in the countryside with his son. For the boy's edification Henry identifies various objects on the landscape as they come into view. 'That's a cow,' says Henry, 'That's a tractor,' 'That's a silo,' 'That's a barn,' etc. Henry has no doubt about the identity of these objects; in particular, he has no doubt that the last-mentioned object is a barn, which indeed it is. ... Suppose we are told that, unknown to Henry, the district he has just entered is full of papier-mâché facsimiles of barns. These facsimiles look from the road exactly like barns, but are really just façades .... Having just entered the district, Henry has not encountered any facsimiles; the object he sees is a genuine barn. But if the object on that site were a facsimile, Henry would mistake it for a barn.

Before we get the information that Henry is in fake-barn country, Goldman says most of us would be comfortable saying that Henry *knows* he sees a barn. But after we find out that Henry is in fake-barn country (unbeknownst to Henry), we would be much less likely to ascribe knowledge to Henry. As with Gettier cases, it is just a matter of luck that Henry picked out a real barn (rather than a facsimile) to form a belief about. Because of this Goldman suggests that the relevant anti-Gettier requirement is that beliefs should be connected up with the world in a reliable way, that is, *justified* beliefs are beliefs formed by *reliable processes*. In fact, Goldman ditches the notion that we must have *internal access* to the conditions that justify us – regardless of whether Henry has access to evidence that he is in fake-barn country, he is justified or unjustified by his reliability at picking out real barns over fake ones; since that reliability is low in fake-barn country (Henry can't tell the façades from the real barns), Henry isn't justified in saying, "That is a barn," while he is in fake-barn country. Because of this, we will discuss a third type of evidence (in addition to the two we've explored as *claims* and *experience*).

Processes and probabilities as justification

If by "justification" all we mean is that our beliefs are formed in such a way that they are appropriately connected with the world in a way that secures the truth of those beliefs, then it may be that we are justified in believing some propositions even without having any discernible (that is, directly accessible) evidence, that is, *without any seemings*. It is possible, some philosophers suggest, that we come to hold beliefs by means whose reliability we are not in a position to assess, but which are, nevertheless, reliable producers of true beliefs (where "reliable" means they produce more true beliefs than false, even if, every now and then, they produce a false belief). These means can be divided into roughly two categories: *processes* and *probabilities*. (See 6.4 and 6.5 for more on statistics and probabilities.)

According to some philosophers, the processes that produce beliefs in us (which may or may not have a causal relationship to the world) have a *reliability indicator*, a kind of reliable *criterion* of truth. If the reliability indicator reveals that a belief-producing process produces more true beliefs than false, then that process is a *justifier* for the beliefs it produces. Goldman, in one of his formulations of externalism, puts it this way in a 1980 paper: "beliefs are justified if and only if they are produced by [relatively] reliable belief-forming processes." According to this sort of externalist account, beliefs are justified if they are produced by a process that gets it right most of the time.

Let's say you have two processes in your brain that produce beliefs: *A* and *B*. Process *A* produces beliefs at a rate of 97% accuracy – if *A* produced your belief, it is, more likely than not, true. *B*, on the other hand, produces beliefs at a rate of only 30% reliability – if *B* produced your belief, it is, more likely than not, false. Now, these processes are at work regardless of what phenomenal experiences (or what we have called *seemings*) you are having – that is, regardless of what evidence you have. *A* may correspond to your five senses, or it may not. *B* may correspond to poorly chosen heuristics (e.g., recent memories are more likely to be true than distant ones, people with beards are less trustworthy than people without), or it may not. There may be phenomenological correlates and there may not. This seems to show, then, for reliabilists that whether or not a proposition *seems true* to you, given experience or logic, is irrelevant to your justification for believing that proposition. After all, both processes *A* and *B* yield seemings that *seem* true, but they are not equally reliable.

Varieties of externalism

There are a number of formulations of externalism about justification, all of which address particular problems. Our goal here is not to survey all these theories, but to help you navigate some important issues in critical thinking. So, we'll just say two things about externalist theories of justification relevant for thinking critically.

First, externalists make an important point for the study of knowledge. If our evidence actually renders any of our beliefs about the external world *knowledge*, then it must have a non-trivial connection or relationship with that world. Our evidence must reliably transmit information about the world to our cognitive faculties, and it must underwrite doxastic acceptance (or belief) of propositions expressing that information. This suggests that externalism is almost certainly true of knowledge (at least knowledge of anything outside of our minds). Knowledge of that sort requires that features of our cognitive states or claims are connected with the world, and, unfortunately – here's the rub – we have little to no access to this connection. To be slightly more precise: we don't know whether we have access to this connection. This is because skeptical worries remain present it seems for every conscious mental state (see 8.3 on the strengths and weaknesses of experience). This has led some philosophers to be *externalists about knowledge* while maintaining *internalism about justification* – we are justified in holding a wide range of beliefs, but only those that are externally connected with the world in the right sort of way constitute knowledge.

Second, however, we cannot ignore the criticism Paul K. Moser advances against externalist theories of justification in his 1989 paper, "A Defense of *Empirical Justification*":

> Epistemic externalism ... allows that a person, S, can be justified in believing a proposition, P, even if S is completely unaware, and has never been aware, of the evidence that justifies P, i.e., the evidence that makes P highly likely to be true. (p. 209)

This may not be a damning criticism – many externalists would accept it as a natural consequence of their view. The problem for us here is that the project of critical thinking involves learning how consciously to manage our beliefs; we want to be responsible, rational believers. As Roderick Chisholm says, "Our *purpose* in raising [epistemic] questions is to correct and improve our own epistemic situation" (*Theory of Knowledge*, 1989: p. 1). We would add, our purpose in critical thinking is in large measure to improve our doxastic situation. Now, what all this may mean is that we, critical thinkers, aren't just interested in "justification." If the only plausible account of justification turns out to be external, then justification must not be the only matter we're talking about. Perhaps we should say we are interested principally, then, in "responsible" belief, or other responsible forms of assent.

In any case, the distinctions between justification and knowledge and internalism and externalism are important to keep in mind for two reasons. First, they help us to be very cautious about what we claim to *know*. Knowledge is very difficult to obtain, and so we should be concerned, first and foremost, with evidence and what access we have to it.

- *Does my evidence make it rational to believe* p*?*
- *Do I have any evidence that counts against* p*?*
- *If so, is my evidence for* p *stronger than my evidence against* p*?*

Second, these distinctions remind us that many disagreements arise from using words differently. It may be that we don't actually substantively disagree with someone, even though the dispute at hand centers on words we are both using (albeit, unknown to us, in different ways); and so, we need to be especially careful to define our terms with one another. If someone disagrees with how you are using the word "evidence" or "justification," in some cases you can simply stipulate your definitions of "evidence" or "justification" so that the conversation stays on topic and the content under discussion is clearer (see 2.4).

So, how can you tell when something is a "seeming" that amounts to evidence sufficient for justification or when it's *just* an ungrounded claim or *just* a meaningless datum? Making this discernment is one of the trickiest and most difficult tasks of critical thinking; and it requires a good deal of energy and practice. In what follows, we will suggest some tips for identifying and evaluating evidence. Applying these tips in the real world takes patience, so we encourage you to bear with it.

SEE ALSO

8.6 Justification: The Basics
8.8 How Does Justification Work?
9.4 Scientific Method
9.6 Experiments and Other Tests

READING

Alvin Goldman, "Reliabilism," *The Stanford Encyclopedia of Philosophy*, Edward N. Zalta, ed. (2011)

John L. Pollock & Joseph Cruz, *Contemporary Theories of Knowledge*, 2nd edn (1999), Chapter 4

Paul K. Moser, "A Defense of Empirical Justification," *Philosophical Studies* 56.2 (1989): 209–215

Alvin I. Goldman, "The Internalist Conception of Justification," *Midwest Studies in Philosophy* 5, P. French, T. Uehling & H. Wettstein, eds. (1980): 27–51

Alvin I. Goldman, "What Is Justified Belief?" *Justification and Knowledge*, George Pappas, ed. (1979): 1–23

Alvin I. Goldman, "Discrimination and Perceptual Knowledge," *The Journal of Philosophy* 73.20 (1976): 771–791

8.10 Evidence: Weak and Strong

Our discussion in 8.9 suggests that the relevant sense of evidence and justification for critical thinking, anyway, if not perhaps for pure epistemology, is internal rather than external. In order to take responsibility for your claims, you must have access to the means of determining the accuracy of doxastic and epistemic commitments; and all accuracy-evaluating conditions are internal. All of the evidence we discuss, then, will take the form of claims and experience.[23]

Direct and indirect evidence

Claims and experience as evidence can be divided into roughly two distinct categories: *direct* and *indirect*. Direct evidence is evidence to which you have direct access, that is, there is nothing mediating your access to information that constitutes evidence. This is evidence that often seems, by itself, a reason to believe that *p*. For example, seeing with one's own eyes that *The hat is yellow*, hearing that *The song is loud*, feeling that *The surface is rough*, and seeing intellectually that $2 + 2 = 4$ all constitute direct evidence for the truth of claims expressing those seemings. The most common examples of direct evidence include *sensory experience* and logical and mathematical *intuition* (or what's sometimes called *intellectual intuition*).

Indirect evidence is evidence to which you have mediated access, that is, something besides the information that would be evidence conveys or transmits this information to you. The most obvious example of indirect evidence is testimony. There is a difference between *seeing that p* (direct evidence) and *someone's testifying that they saw that p* (indirect evidence). The latter seems (if you trust the witness), given everything you know about the process that produced it, a reason to believe that *p*. For example, someone's testifying that, "The hat is yellow," a calculator's report that, "2 + 2 = 4," experimental results that, "Drug *X* relieves pain" all constitute indirect evidence that those claims are true.

Experimental results may be the least easily understood as indirect on this list, since we regard science as providing pretty secure evidence about the world. Not all experimental evidence is indirect, but in any case it's important to note that whether evidence is direct or indirect, evidence for a claim doesn't affect how securely or strongly it justifies beliefs. Experimental results about motion using instruments to measure that motion are much more secure evidence for claims about motion than our personal experiences of motion or our pre-theoretical intuitions about motion, despite the fact that the former is indirect evidence and both the latter are types of direct evidence. Experimental results are indirect because the evidence they convey is mediated by a number of factors.

Consider the claim, "Acetaminophen relieves pain," along with some experiments aimed at determining whether or not this is true. Your personal experience of acetaminophen's relieving pain is evidence that it is true, but it's very weak evidence. You didn't directly see or hear or feel the acetaminophen relieving the pain – once you put the pill in your mouth and swallowed, it was out of your direct access. And so, the fact that your pain was relieved may have been a result of the acetaminophen or any number of other factors (pains regularly go away without medication). To get strong evidence about acetaminophen's relationship to pain in the human body, we need to test it on a lot of different sorts of humans under a variety of conditions. In none of these cases will we directly experience acetaminophen's relieving pain, but a set of data showing that people who take acetaminophen are significantly more likely to experience relief from pain than those who don't would be strong indirect evidence that it's true.

The distinction between direct and indirect evidence is important to critical thinkers for two reasons. First:

> *Some types of claims are more appropriately evaluated with direct evidence, and some are more appropriately evaluated with indirect evidence.*

For example, in relation to a belief about whether a car is pulling out in front of you, direct evidence is more appropriate. For determining how much alcohol you can drink without negatively affecting your health, indirect evidence is more appropriate. But second, and more importantly:

> *Different types of evidence can go wrong (can fail to justify our beliefs), and they can go wrong in several ways.*

Direct evidence, even when appropriate, can fail because our mechanisms of apprehension fail. Indirect evidence, even when appropriate, also has a number of vulnerabilities independent of our subjective evaluation: the appropriateness of the instruments we choose to gather the data; the reliability of our instruments for collecting data; our reliability at determining whether the data we've gathered is really relevant to the claim we're interested in.

We saw some of the various particular ways indirect evidence can go wrong in Chapters 6 and 7 on inductive reasoning. Now, let's take a broader view and consider when something should even count as evidence and when it shouldn't. Most of what we read and write about is based on the testimony of others, often "experts" in a field, so we'll start with some examples of testimonial evidence. We'll take an even harder look at this in Chapter 9 on science.

Testimony as evidence

When an expert testifies that some claim, *p*, is true, there is some presumption that the expert is right (see 5.10 on unqualified authority for more on this). Who's in a better position to evaluate the relevant evidence than an expert? We live a lot of our lives by expert testimony: the weather forecaster says it will rain; the economist says we're heading for a recession; the physician says you have high blood pressure; your personal trainer says you should be consuming more protein; etc. While we regard expert testimony as, in general, *good enough* for many of our beliefs, we must recognize that this sort of justification is very weak. Why? Because experts often disagree. One weather forecaster says it will rain, while another is skeptical. One economist says we're heading for a recession, but another disagrees. One physician says you have high blood pressure, another says you're fine for your age. So, for *strongly justified* beliefs (or "well-justified" beliefs), especially those concerning matters of serious importance, we need to go a step further – we need to *check the experts themselves.* You may be perfectly rational in accepting the weather forecaster's prediction – not much rides on it (perhaps at worst you may carry an umbrella you don't need). But when a physician says your blood pressure is too high, there's too much at stake to rely simply on one judgment. For strong justification, we need to double-check even the experts.

There is a worry about saying we need to double-check the experts. Some might say: *So, I need to become a physician to evaluate the physician's claim? Then, I would have to become an accountant to double-check my accountant, and a lawyer to double-check my lawyer.* We certainly don't mean that. There are strategies for testing an expert. The most common is the *second opinion*. Testing your physician's claim against the claims of another physician or other reputable sources is good strategy for determining the reliability of the testimony without having to become a medical professional yourself. But in addition to getting a second opinion, knowing *why* the expert arrived at the judgment he or she did is important (although, sometimes you won't understand all the reasons). For instance, if your physician says your blood pressure is high *relative to the national average of everyone*, then it might be consistent for another physician to say you are fine *for your age*.

Strong enough evidence?

How might we tell whether a piece of evidence (whether ours or an expert's) is strong enough? There are measures of evidential strength. You can measure it (1) relative to the evidence for or against that particular claim, and you can measure it (2) relative to the evidence for or against competing claims. We'll explain these in order.

First, as a useful definition, a piece of evidence is *strong* if it makes the belief seem more likely to be true than not. This is easier to determine when the evidence is quantitative rather than qualitative. For instance, evidence for a 51% chance of rain is strong evidence, though evidence for a 90% chance is stronger. If the wall seems red to you, then if you have no evidence to the contrary, that is, no evidence that would override this evidence, then you have a strong reason for believing the wall is red.

On the other hand, if you remember the weather forecaster saying there is a 90% chance of rain, and a stranger in a coffee shop says she remembers the chance is only 20%, you will have to determine how reliable your memory is relative to the stranger's memory and testimony. The stranger probably has no reason to lie, and your memory is not infallible. Of course, her memory isn't infallible, either. In this sort of case, you will have to determine for yourself whether you still have a strong reason to believe it will rain or whether you should suspend judgment (Is your memory vivid on the subject? Did you discuss the forecast at the time so that your memory might be more reliable?). If you choose on reflection to believe that it will rain, because of the *disagreement among sources* you will probably want to mitigate the degree to which you regard yourself as justified, some percentage less than 90%.

Both of these pieces of evidence (your memories of the forecaster and the stranger) are about the claim at hand: the likelihood that it will rain. But in some cases, competing hypotheses are not mutually exhaustive in this way. For instance, consider the evidence that Darwin's theory of evolution best explains biodiversity. In reality, there isn't just one formulation and interpretation of this theory. There are several, each of which has a different probability. Indeed, among all the theories explaining biodiversity, some are competing hypotheses (a divine being's creative action is the best explanation of biodiversity vs. non-theistic naturalistic explanations), but some are not. Technically, some of these hypotheses aren't mutually exclusive because both could possibly be true (a divine being could have created Darwinian processes), and both could be false (there is some other theory *X*, that's neither Darwinism nor creationism and that's the actual reason for biodiversity).

Given the many, many possibilities for how biodiversity came about, and given that no one actually observed the long history of biodiversity, the probability that any one of them is true is very low. (And note, for the record, that *any* one-time event is incredibly improbable – it occurred, to our knowledge, only once! So, we have little idea what conditions make that event probable relative to another. This is particularly frustrating for philosophers of religion who discuss miracles, which are, by definition, rare events if they occur at all.) With cases like this, then, we evaluate the strength of evidence not according to whether it makes the hypothesis seem more likely to be true than false, but according to whether the evidence seems to make it more likely to be true than any *competing* hypotheses. It's worth restating this as a principle:

> *Evidence should be judged strong or weak not only according to whether it makes the hypothesis seem more likely to be true than false, but also according to whether it makes the hypothesis seem more likely to be true than any competing hypotheses.*

Those who defend a contemporary version of Darwinian evolution do not, properly speaking, argue that it's highly likely given the evidence, but that it is more likely to be true than any current competing hypotheses for explaining biodiversity. So, even if the probability that Darwinism is true is 1.5%, as long as every competing hypothesis is <1.5%, there is relatively stronger evidence for Darwinism than there is for any of its competitors.[24]

Suppressed evidence fallacy

Having good evidence that a claim is true is not all there is to good reasoning. We also have to take reasonable care that there isn't evidence that is equally strong (or stronger) against that claim. For example, think about those people who say, "Every time I wash my car, it rains." If you ask them to prove that, they may be able to cite a number of instances where it did in fact rain after they washed their cars. That is some evidence that their claim is true. But this is not all the evidence that is needed. Are there *any* instances where they washed their cars and it didn't rain? Did they mention those? Can they remember any? If so, how many times did this happen relative to the times it did rain? This is a version of suppressed evidence called the *base rate fallacy* – the base rate of occurrence of "rain after car washing" must be evaluated against its counterinstances, "no rain after car washing" (see 6.5). Similarly, there are people who say to their romantic partners, "You never agree with anything I say!" If asked to cite instances, these angry people might be able to cite instances, but in doing so, they conveniently leave out the times when the partner did agree. This could result from one or more different reasoning errors. It could be that someone only remembers the instances that support their claim (*availability error*, see 7.3), or it could be that someone only recognizes the cases that support their claim as legitimate evidence (*confirmation bias*, see 7.2).

Regardless of why countervailing evidence is left out, reasoning that excludes it is rationally incomplete. Positive evidence alone is not enough to establish the truth of a claim; we need (to the best of our abilities) to consult the total evidence set.

The tendency to ignore relevant evidence is also called "cherry picking." When politicians cite their opponents' various failures, they do not compare them to their successes. Since everyone makes mistakes, knowing that someone makes mistakes is not very informative (though, admittedly, sometimes the gravity of the mistakes matters). But notice that book endorsements do not include critical reviews and movie trailers never cite critics who do not like the movie. This suggests that we must be careful when considering even scientific-sounding evidence, by asking questions like: Was this the only study conducted (see 9.7)? If not, what are the results of other studies (9.6)? If so, is the study likely to be representative (was the sample large enough, was the population diverse enough; see 6.4)?

Four tips for recognizing "good" evidence

When encountering claims and arguments appealing to evidence, good critical thinkers, then, will assess the quality of that evidence. Here are a few tips for how to proceed.

1. *Check the Source.* Attempt to determine where your evidence comes from. Does it come from an academic, scholarly source at a reputable university or institution? Is the source likely to be biased? What reasons do you have for trusting the source? Have the data gatherers used the best available methods for gathering this sort of data?
2. *Check the Context.* Attempt to determine how and in what context the source's claims are being used. A claim about teachers' unions is not necessarily apropos to claims about other types of unions. Also, a claim made in haste may not represent a considered judgment on a subject, even if made by an expert. And check the meaning of the terms used: a claim made about socialism just after World War II may not be relevant for criticizing contemporary forms of socialism.
3. *Consider its Degree of Certainty, Self-evidence, and Necessity.* Some claims and evidence enjoy the luxury of seeming necessarily or self-evidently true. Logical and mathematical truths often enjoy this status. In these cases, you need not consider the source or the context so carefully – the evidence is right in front of you. When someone makes the argument that, "It's raining, and if it's raining, then the sidewalks are wet; so, we can conclude that the sidewalks are wet," you need not ask about the person's credentials to see that the argument is a good one (see 4.2). If

a claim or argument seems self-evident or necessarily true, recognize that it's to be evaluated differently from other types of claims.

4. *Corroborate.* Are the claims corroborated by reputable sources? Pew Research Center, the National Institutes of Health, the German National Academy of Sciences, and the Royal Society are well-respected sources of evidence, and so claims gain significant support when corroborated by results they report. But is anyone else doing similar research? How often has such research been conducted? Can you corroborate their results by appealing to other sources? Is there disconfirming evidence? The more corroboration you have, the stronger your belief's justification will be. The more disconfirming evidence, the weaker your belief's justification. Remember, single experiments often reveal idiosyncratic results. This is why our personal (anecdotal) experiences do not amount to evidence sufficient for generalizing to beliefs about everyone. Seeking corroboration also helps to avoid the suppressed evidence fallacy (8.10 and 9.7).

Knowing full well the follies of secondary sources, even Wikipedia progenitor, Jimmy Wales, warns students from committing the all-too-common act of citing an encyclopedia, writing, "Citing an encyclopedia for an academic paper at the university level is not appropriate – you aren't 12 years old any more, it's time to step up your game and do research in original sources." In true Wikipedia style, the online encyclopedia has an entire page dedicated to Wikipedia hoaxes, such as Gaius Flavius Antoninus, the supposed assassin of Julius Caesar (shhh, don't tell Shakespeare).

Evidence: A few examples

Because evidence is so important to rationality, let's take a look at a few examples of evidence as it's used in a variety of fields. We distinguish here examples of "weaker evidence" and "stronger evidence," and we explain why each falls into the category it does. (By "weaker," we simply mean, weaker than it could be; it may not be as weak as it could possibly be. Similarly, by "stronger," we mean *fairly* strong; it may not be as strong as it could possibly be.) For each example, imagine you come across the sentence or passage used as evidence in something you are reading. Don't get distracted by the citations. They're simply examples of what you might find in an article or book.

Example 1 *Public Policy*

Weaker Evidence: "Moe (2011) argues that, 'unions collectively bargain'" (345).

Who is Moe? Is Moe an expert in this field? Knowing the type of publication in which Moe is published would help us with this: if this is from a blog or popular book, we would have less reason to trust it than if it were from an academic book or peer-reviewed academic journal. This is indirect, testimonial evidence twice removed. Moe says it, and then someone else says that Moe says it. Is the person citing Moe using

Moe's claim correctly and in context? This is "weaker" evidence because, even if Moe is an expert in this field, we have no idea why Moe is making this claim or whether Moe or the citer is reliable. If you were using this in a paper, you would want to explain what reason Moe has for this claim (see below).

Stronger Evidence: "Terry M. Moe (2011) of the Hoover Institution at Stanford University found that teachers unions use collective bargaining to limit the power of administrators over them: 'In the 2009 New York school district negotiations, the AFT [the American Federation of Teachers – a union] conceded to allow administrators to conduct in-classroom observations and evaluations of teachers; but the observations had to be announced *a priori* and the results could not be made available to parents and could not be used in deciding teacher promotion or demotion'" (46).

This is indirect, testimonial evidence, but it is not twice removed. We don't have to rely on the author's claim that Moe argues that unions collectively bargain; we have been given Moe's reasons through quotation. We can still ask whether the author of this piece is interpreting Moe accurately and in context. If we think so, we must then decide for ourselves whether this constitutes a reason to believe that unions engage in collective bargaining. This still isn't great evidence: we don't know how good Moe's sources are and this is only one instance of collective bargaining, which doesn't seem to be strong enough to make the general claim that, "unions collectively bargain." Also, does this meet the conditions of "collective bargaining"? What does it mean to bargain *collectively*? If we disagree with Moe's definition, we may disagree with his conclusion.

Example 2 *Public Policy*

Weaker Evidence: "Moe (2011) states, 'unions spend an enormous amount of money on political campaigns'" (46).

Again, who is Moe? Is Moe an expert in this field? In what context does Moe say this? Does he mean *all* unions do this? Knowing the type of publication in which Moe is published would help us with this: if this were from a blog or popular book, we would have less reason to rely on it than if it were from an academic book or peer-reviewed academic journal. Also, why does Moe make this claim? Even if Moe is an expert in his field, why exactly should we believe him? This is another case of indirect, testimonial evidence twice removed. This claim needs to be filled out with an argument.

Stronger Evidence: "The Hoover Institution's Terry M. Moe (2011) found that teachers' unions provide a higher proportion of campaign money to Democrats than to

Republicans: 'In the 2008 election cycle, the AFT [American Federation of Teachers] gave over 32 million dollars to Democratic campaigns for school board members, representatives and senators in the state of California as opposed to 3.2 million dollars to Republicans running for similar offices" (547). This is better than the first evidence because we have some data to evaluate. We don't know Moe's data-gathering methods, so we still don't have strong evidence that unions favor Democrats over Republicans or which unions we should be thinking about (this author only lists one type). Also, this is only one campaign in one state; this isn't enough information to justify the more general claim that, in general, teachers' unions give in higher proportions to Democrats.

Example 3 *Philosophy*

Weaker Evidence: "Arp and Watson (2011) argue that true belief isn't sufficient for 'knowledge'" (53).

Now that we have a little practice considering evidence, we can start abbreviating the process with a list of concerns:

- *What is the source? Is it academic or popular?*
- *What is the context? Is the author using Arp and Watson correctly?*
- *What is the argument? Why should we believe this?*
- *What do the authors mean by "true belief" and "knowledge"?*

Stronger Evidence: "Arp and Watson (2011: 53) show that true belief isn't sufficient for 'knowledge' with a brief thought experiment. If you were on a jury and you suddenly (for no apparent reason) came to believe that the defendant was guilty, and it happens to be true that he is guilty, you would have a true belief that the defendant is guilty. Since, however, you didn't have any good evidence for believing this, it doesn't seem proper to say you *know* he's guilty."

- *What's the source? Is it academic or popular?*
- *What is the context? Is the author using Arp and Watson correctly?*
- *Now we know why Arp and Watson believe it, but is their argument convincing to us?*
- *Is any alternative possible? Is it possible to have knowledge without "justification"?*

Example 4 *Philosophy*

Weaker Evidence: "Jesse Prinz (2008: 191) says that philosophical 'intuition' is best characterized as 'an introspective memory retrieval process.'"

Let's assume that Prinz is a respected philosopher, that we know this, and that this claim is from an academic publication. Let's also assume that the author isn't using the claim out of context. Is this a reason to believe Prinz's claim? Well, he's an expert in the field, so we have a presumption that he knows what he's talking about. But we don't know *why* he thinks this claim is true, so our reason for believing him is still pretty weak. A summary of the actual argument would be helpful.

> *Stronger Evidence*: "CUNY Professor of Philosophy Jesse Prinz (2008: 191) says that philosophical 'intuition' is best characterized as 'an introspective memory retrieval process.' He says this because in order to 'discover what our intuitions are' we must 'introspect.' And when we introspect, we are engaging in 'sensory observation once removed' because our introspected beliefs are 'memories of ordinary objects experienced in life.' Together, these imply that intuition involves introspection about memories."

This example is a little more sophisticated. Let's assume, again, that Prinz is an expert, that we know this, that this is an academic publication, and that the author is using him correctly and in context. Here we are given *his* reasons for thinking that intuition is an introspective memory retrieval process, but are these *good* reasons? To know whether they are, we need to know more about the terms he's using.

If by "intuition" he just means "introspection," then he's probably right. Anyone who disagrees with him is just using the term "intuition" differently. But if he thinks everyone should use "intuition" this way, he needs to give some reason for thinking *that*. As it turns out, many philosophers use the term "intuition" in ways vastly different from this; instead, they argue that intuition is analogous to direct sensory experience – it is a direct source of evidence about concepts and relations among ideas, not an indirect source of evidence about memories. So this evidence is stronger than the previous evidence, but Prinz's conclusions are irrelevant for people who define their terms differently from the way Prinz defines them.

SEE ALSO

8.6 Justification: The Basics
6.3 Fallacies about Causation
9.4 Scientific Method

READING

Peter Achinstein, *The Concept of Evidence* (1983)
W. V. O. Quine, "Two Dogmas of Empiricism," *Philosophical Review* 60 (1951): 20–43
A. J. Ayer, *Language, Truth, and Logic* (1936)
Rudolf Carnap, *The Logical Structure of the World* (1928)
David Hume, "Of Miracles," *Enquiry Concerning Human Understanding* (1748), Section 10

8.11 Justification: Conclusions

It would be great if all, or even the great majority, of our responsible beliefs turned out to be true – really great! Unfortunately, skeptical possibilities (evil genius arguments, Matrix-type scenarios, etc.), Gettier problems, as well as a myriad of other problems (e.g., those related to "heuristics and biases") show that we seem to have no way of finally determining when our beliefs relate us to the world in the right way, or at least the way required for proper knowledge. Since our beliefs about the process are formed only as part of the process, we cannot get outside of these processes to check. Despite this, justification is supposed to connect our beliefs to the world in the right sort of way (regardless of whether we are aware of this connection). This raises the question: What should we conclude about the role of justification in our critical thinking strategies? Two considerations leave ample room for optimism.

First, we have no choice but to rely on the best justification procedures the human mind has so far (it seems by its own lights) been able to determine – the very sort we've collected in this book. However reliable or unreliable our directly accessible evidence-evaluating processes are, we are, it seems, stuck with them – at least for now. It seems probably not true that we are in an illusionary world courtesy of a Cartesian demon or a *Matrix*, but there are lots of reasons to doubt that our beliefs meet all the conditions for knowledge. Nevertheless, if we want to get around in the world, we must make use of the tools we have, and those tools have been pretty handy for curing polio, building spaceships, constructing skyscrapers, and designing information systems that allow us to talk instantly with people anywhere on the planet (or the Moon, for that matter!).

Second, the success of science suggests that things aren't as bad as they seem. We know scientists don't have infallible access to truth about the world (they seem to have been wrong more than they've been right – just think of all the failed scientific theories: Ptolemy's universe, Newtonian physics, Euclidean geometry, the phlogiston theory of fire, the caloric theory of heat, etc.). Still, the success of science in helping to make our world a safer, more comfortable, and more productive place is quite astonishing. Think of the vast improvements in the quality of life that has resulted from scientific investigation and the enlarged capacity to trade with one another. We've designed ships to take us across the ocean, through the air, and into space in just a handful of generations. We've designed fast, inexpensive cars, cheap clothing, disposable diapers, and sterilized operating and delivery rooms to increase our comfort and reduce our suffering. When we think of a problem, we often think of a way to solve it. This suggests that our evidence-gathering procedures are pretty good for helping us form responsible beliefs (see 9.1).

Exercises and study questions

1. Explain the three conditions for "knowledge" according to the traditional account of knowledge. Use examples to explain your answer.

2. Why isn't "having a good reason to believe *p*" sufficient as an account of justification?
3. What is one drawback to Kent Bach's "taking-for-granted" rule? Can you think of any other drawbacks?
4. Why is justification valuable for critical thinking?
5. In your own words, explain three sources of evidence.
6. What is a "Gettier case," and what sort of objection does it raise for the value of justification?
7. Briefly explain Goldman's "fake barn" case in your own words. What problem does it raise for the "internalist" about justification?
8. What is one problem with relying on expert testimony as evidence? Can you think of any others?
9. What are two measures of evidential strength? Explain your answers.
10. What is the difference between direct and indirect evidence? How might this distinction help us think more effectively about evidence?

SEE ALSO

9.1 Science and the Value of Scientific Reasoning
9.2 The Purview of Science
9.8 Bad Science
10.5 Semiotics: Critically Reading Signs

READING

Ted Poston, "Internalism and Externalism in Epistemology," *Internet Encyclopedia of Philosophy* (2014)

George Pappas, "Internalist vs. Externalist Conceptions of Epistemic Justification," *Stanford Encyclopedia of Philosophy* (2005)

Theodore Schick, Jr. & Lewis Vaughn, *How to Think About Weird Things: Critical Thinking for a New Age*, 7th edn (2013)

NOTES

1. Whether or not Plato actually held this view is controversial. Writing in dialogue form, Plato uses his character Socrates to outline this view. Historically, it is difficult to tell what either Plato or Socrates actually believed, since Plato's depiction may not be entirely accurate.
2. In his defense of skepticism, Hellenistic philosopher Sextus Empiricus writes: we "do not overthrow the affective sense impressions which induce our assent involuntarily; and these impressions are the 'appearances.' And when we question whether the underlying object is such as it appears, we grant the fact that it appears, and our doubt does not concern the

appearance itself but the account given of that appearance ... ." (*Outlines of Pyrrhonism*, 2nd century, CE: Book 1, Chapter 10, Section 19). Similarly, despite his skeptical conclusions about what we can know, Scottish philosopher David Hume notes that the utter rejection of beliefs cannot be maintained outside of intense philosophy: "Most fortunately it happens, that since Reason is incapable of dispelling these clouds, Nature herself suffices to that purpose, and cures me of this philosophical melancholy and delirium, either by relaxing this bent of mind, or by some avocation, and lively impression of my senses, which obliterate all these chimeras. I dine, I play a game of backgammon, I converse, and am merry with my friends. And when, after three or four hours' amusement, I would return to these speculations, they appear so cold, and strained, and ridiculous, that I cannot find in my heart to enter into them any farther" (*A Treatise of Human Nature* [1739], Book 1, Part 4, Section 7, paragraph 9).

3. Philosophers disagree about whether and the extent to which moral and even mathematical thinking is an experiential (empirical) or non-experiential matter, so we put a question mark here to note this disagreement.
4. "Philosophy: Who Needs It," in *Philosophy: Who Needs It* (1982), 7.
5. "Philosophical Detection," in *Philosophy: Who Needs It* (1982), 20. Originally published in *The Ayn Rand Letter*, vol. 3, no. 9 (Jan. 28, 1974).
6. Shai Danziger, Jonathan Levav, and Liora Avnaim-Pesso, "Extraneous Factors in Judicial Decisions," *Proceedings of the National Academy of Sciences* (2011), Early Edition 1–4, www.pnas.org/cgi/doi/10.1073/pnas.1018033108.
7. Isabelle Blanchette, "The Effect of Emotion on Interpretation and Logic in a Conditional Reasoning Task," *Memory and Cognition*, 34.5 (July, 2006): 1112–1125; Blanchette, Isabelle and Joanna Leese, "The Effect of Negative Emotion on Deductive Reasoning: Examining the Contribution of Physiological Arousal," *Experimental Psychology* 58.3 (2011): 235–246; Baba Shiv et al., "Investment Behavior and the Negative Side of Emotion," *Psychological Science* 16.6 (2005): 435–439.
8. Cf. Antonio Damasio, *Descartes's Error: Emotion, Reason, and the Human Brain* (1994).
9. *A Treatise of Human Nature* (1739), Book 2, Part 3, Section 3, Paragraph 2.
10. *A Treatise of Human Nature* (1739), Book 2, Part 3, Section 3, Paragraph 2.
11. Hume is a bit cagy here. It isn't obvious that he would grant that reason is *superior* to emotion even in the sense we have identified. For Hume reason and emotion seem to have the same source (nature) and purpose (usefulness, pleasantness, and durability for self and others). In his 1751 work, *An Enquiry Concerning the Principles of Morals*, he argues that the only difference between "superstition" and "justice" is that the former is useless to a society and the latter is necessary for the well-being of humankind – and, of course, what is regarded as useless and necessary differs from society to society. He says, for instance: as "justice evidently tends to promote public utility, ... the sentiment of justice is either derived from our reflecting on that tendency or, like hunger, thirst, and other appetites, resentment, love of life, attachment to offspring, and other passions, arises from a simple original instinct in the human breast, which nature has implanted for like salutary purposes" (Section 3, Part II, Charles W. Hendel, ed. [1957], 31–32). Nevertheless, his analysis leaves him open to the conclusion that reason is useful for directing emotions in a way beneficial for society.
12. William James, "The Will to Believe," in *Essays in Pragmatism*, Alburey Castell, ed. (1968).
13. William James, "The Will to Believe," in *Essays in Pragmatism*, Alburey Castell, ed. (1968), 99.

14. William James, "The Will to Believe," in *Essays in Pragmatism*, Alburey Castell, ed. (1968), 100.
15. William James, "The Will to Believe," in *Essays in Pragmatism*, Alburey Castell, ed. (1968), 100.
16. The Müller-Lyer illusion was first published in 1889, by Franz Carl Müller-Lyer, a German psychologist and sociologist, in his book, *Optische Urteilstäuschungen* ("Optical Errors in Judgment").
17. Chisholm's version goes like this: "If S accepts h and if not-h is not probable in relation to the set of propositions that are probable for S, then h is epistemically in the clear for S"; "In Defense of Empirical Justification," *Philosophical Studies* 56 (1989): 64. Chisholm's version is a bit different than Bach's; Chisholm assumes S already believes h, whereas Bach's rule is a reason for S to adopt the belief that h. The "little bit of support" comes from Chisholm's account of "probable" beliefs, part of which involves accepting a belief. So, if you already hold a belief, then that "tends to make [that belief] probable," but not "probable for S," since we don't know whether S has sufficient reason for maintaining the belief. Chisholm's account is very complicated and we will refer only to the clearer pieces of it in this chapter.
18. This is a bit controversial. A prominent group of philosophers regards a subject's access to evidence as irrelevant to justification. We will discuss this access condition and the view that denies it (known as "externalism") in more detail below.
19. We say "most" of your beliefs because, following Descartes who argued along these lines in his famous *Meditations on First Philosophy* (1641), it's at least probably the case that some beliefs couldn't be held unless they were true, for example, "I am thinking, therefore, I exist," and necessary truths such as, "Everything is self-identical."
20. There is some ambiguity in the use of "entailment" among philosophers. Some use "entails" synonymously with "logically implies," as in the case that, "That object is red" logically implies "That object is colored." Some philosophers, however (e.g., Roderick Chisholm), reserve "entail" for cases where a person understands the relationship between the claims (he calls this "doxastic entailment"). Whereas one claim can logically entail another without anyone's recognizing it (e.g., if X is greater than 5, then X is greater than the square root of 25), doxastic entailment involves logical entailment *plus* understanding. According to Chisholm, a person cannot understand the claim, "That man is a bachelor" without understanding that, "That man is unmarried." Since our account of justification will require a person to have access to the evidence that justifies a belief, we will use entailment in Chisholm's *doxastic* sense. See Baggini & Fosl, *The Philosopher's Toolkit* Section 4.8 on entailment and implication.
21. In 1906, Alexius Meinong offered a similar set of examples. It isn't clear who offered the earliest version of these examples that are now known as "Gettier" cases.
22. In this remark and others, Bertrand Russell is probably the first to recognize and construct a Gettier-style counterexample to the claim that justified true belief is knowledge. Apparently, however, neither Russell nor the broader philosophical community recognized the significance of this sort of example at the time (see *Human Knowledge: Its Scope and its Limits*, Section D under Part II, Chapter 11; "Fact, Belief, Truth, Knowledge," 140ff.).
23. It is important that we construe "experience" broadly to mean "phenomenal experience" of a wide variety of kinds. For instance, memories and introspection do not fit neatly with perceptual experiences such as seeings and hearings. In addition, the seemings involved in mathematical and logical inferences, while phenomenological, are very different from memories, introspection, and perceptual experiences.

24. For our math-minded readers, we should note that we are referring to "epistemic probabilities" here, and not "objective probabilities." The objective probability that biodiversity occurred the way it did (whatever way that is) is 100% – it occurred that way and no other. But the epistemic probability is a measure of how likely some *theory* of how biodiversity seems to have come about *given our current body of evidence about* biodiversity.

9 Tools for Critical Thinking about Science

9.1 Science and the Value of Scientific Reasoning

It may seem strange to ask about of the value of scientific reasoning. Most people regard it as something like the gold standard of rationality, the best that humans can do in thinking about the world, our most obviously important conduit for knowledge and truth. The evidence for this view seems all around us.

Useful, durable, and pleasant goods

Science has altered the human world immensely by underwriting technologies that have produced all kinds of devices that have made human life easier, longer, and – one supposes – more pleasant. One need only, perhaps, think of dentistry to drive the point home. Dental practices – when they were practiced at all – in the medieval, ancient, and prehistoric worlds were dreadfully different from those people enjoy today. Without anesthetics, analgesics, high-speed drills, x-rays, fillings, antibiotics, or even a rudimentary understanding of germs, the treatment of simple cavities could be a torturous, life-threatening affair – assuming, of course, they had any way of diagnosing tooth decay in the first place. Similarly, reductions in infant and maternal mortality rates associated with childbirth offer another compelling example of the value of science, and one could go on: from agriculture, to transportation, to communication networks, to medicine, to public health, to entertainment, to military power, to rocketing a group of men beyond Earth's atmosphere, placing them on the Moon, and returning them safely to Earth. All these and more, science has made possible through the theories that have underwritten the development and invention of countless technologies now commonplace in human life. One of early modernity's most important philosophers and promoters of science, Francis Bacon (1561–1626), famously remarked that "knowledge is power," *scientia est potentia*. Our experience as beneficiaries of five

The Critical Thinking Toolkit, First Edition. Galen A. Foresman, Peter S. Fosl, and Jamie C. Watson.

centuries of scientific inquiry since Bacon wrote those words is strong evidence for his claim.

An agreement engine

Besides the useful technologies science has made possible, one of the most valuable qualities of scientific reasoning has been its power to compel human agreement. Disagreement, for example, characterized scientific inquiry over the past few decades as to whether or not a certain kind of particle exists, a particle University of Edinburgh physicist Peter Higgs and his team thought might help explain why material things possess "mass." So basic and important would this particle be to the fabric of reality, if it existed, that it was dubbed informally the "God particle." Controversies about the existence of the "God" particle, however, now seem to have been quelled, because inferences based upon a number of experimental findings have pointed in the affirmative to the reality of the particle, now a bit more formally called the "Higgs boson."

In contrast, a debate called the *filioque* (Latin for "of the son") controversy has occupied Christians for nearly eighteen centuries, dividing the eastern and western Christian churches, and it's still unresolved. It concerns the nature of the Trinity, the Christian doctrine that there are three persons in one God. This difficult idea was the crux of many theological disputes in the early church. Roughly speaking, the *filioque* question has been about whether God-the-Son proceeds from only God-the-Father (as the eastern churches hold) or both the God-the-Father and God-the-Holy-Spirit (as those in the west maintain). For all the energy expended on this argument, it has resulted in little agreement. In part, that's because the methods of thinking used to adjudicate the issue are simply not as powerful in producing agreement as those in the sciences – even though they might be extremely powerful for other purposes. While one of the two positions may be right, no resolution is expected in the *filioque* controversy, as people on both sides seem to have conceded a limited capacity in theological argument to produce any consensus in this issue. In short, while inquiries in natural science about the God particle have proven decidable (after an arduous application of scientific reasoning), questions about certain doctrines in theology remain indeterminate.

A path to knowledge

Of course, science is often regarded as valuable for more than just the *useful* technologies it has produced and the *agreement* in beliefs it has generated. Science is also highly valued simply as the best means for human beings to make *epistemic* gains – that is, to *know* the world and us. The word "science," after all, derives from the Latin *scientia*, meaning knowledge. If anything is able to disclose the real nature of the world and us within it, modern science seems, to many, to be the best candidate for doing so. Now, of course, not all agree. Some have argued that while the sciences achieve some measure of epistemic gain, there is much they do not (and cannot) apprehend. These critics hold that there are other modes of understanding ourselves and the rest of the world that yield human self-understanding that extends beyond the capacities of science. Those who support this view often cite examples such as art and aesthetic experience, literature and poetry, as well as religion. Good critical thinkers would be wise to consider whether or not there's something to the critics' claim.

SEE ALSO

8.2 Feelings as Evidence
8.3 Skepticism and Sensory Experience
10.1 Meta-Narratives

READING

Robert M. Hazen & James Trefil, *Science Matters* (2009)
American Association for the Advancement of Science, *Benchmarks for Science Literacy* (1994)
Henri Poincaré, *The Value of Science* (1905)

9.2 The Purview of Science

Given the success of physics in deciding claims about the existence of the Higgs boson, one might raise the question, then, as to why the nature of the Trinity isn't simply examined scientifically. The response is typically that it just isn't a scientific topic. But then, what's a proper sort of topic for scientific inquiry? If, after all, scientific reasoning is so powerful in its capacity to produce agreement, why can't we use it to bring agreement to unsettled disputes more generally, including theological disputes? How are these disputes not the purview of science?

It's interesting to raise the question of just how far empirical science can go in answering questions about the world. Many thinkers, in fact, are devoted to the idea that the methods of science can help answer all kinds of questions not typically considered scientific. For others, however, it seems unlikely that empirical science possesses the capacity to settle questions such as the *filioque* controversy simply because reflective scrutiny has, merely as a matter of experience, found it difficult and perhaps even impossible to do so. Theological questions seem to be, for a variety of reasons we'll consider, beyond the scope of empirical inquiry, and so it seems clear that science as both a matter of theory and practice has its limits. The question of precisely what those limits are, however, continues to engage philosophers and scientists alike, and certainly good critical thinkers will raise questions about whether or not science is suitable for addressing the objects of inquiry in various controversies.

The limits of empiricism

One reason empirical science seems unlikely to settle religious disputes is due in large part to the fact that the data it uses are, well, *empirical.* The empirical nature of scientific data is itself a limiting factor for science. The word "empirical" is drawn from the ancient Greek word *empeiria* for experience, and the sort of experience from which science draws its data must possess specific attributes.

For starters, the kind of experience to which science appeals must be *objective* in the sense of being *shareable.* We all share observations of the Moon. If not directly *shareable*, experiences relevant to science must at least connect to experience *shareable* by others with normally functioning cognitive capacities in definable, regular ways. The shared experience of a dog's yelping gives others data on the basis of which they can conclude that it is in pain. On the other hand, experiences that are entirely private and not connected to observable behavior or events would be problematic for any sort of empirical inquiry. Experiences like that, if there are such experiences, just can't be investigated with scientific methods. (Might religious experiences be of that sort, and thereby count as experiences beyond the scope of science?)

Now, empirical science deals with unobservable things all the time – for example, magnetic fields, light and other electromagnetic spectra (such as X-rays) that are beyond the range of human vision, as well entities such as quarks and neutrinos and photons that are just too tiny and fast for human beings to observe. Science is able to investigate questions about those *unobservables*, however, because they are related to things we *can* observe in uniform and specifiable ways that we describe as natural laws. So, while no human beings can see X-rays themselves, we *can* see the regular effects they produce on sensitive photographic plates. While pain experiences are *subjective*, and in a sense *private*, they are connected to behavior and physical phenomena that normal human beings can observe, as in the stimulation of C-fibers and A-delta fibers in the brain, or in just crying out.

What is and what ought to be

Can empirical science settle moral questions or aesthetic disputes (see 5.19)? Biologists seem to be figuring out the way our evolutionary history has contributed to making moral life possible, and they are also starting to explain why natural, human moral life has possessed the general features that have characterized it. But as David Hume argued, there is a conceptual distinction between saying *what is the case* and *what ought to be the case.* So, while evolutionary theory may explain why humans have developed *what is the case* about us physically and psychologically, it is not fully possible for biologists to determine *what ought to be* the case about our conduct in a moral way. It wasn't a biological change in human beings that ended racial segregation or slavery or monarchy.

From this point of view, even if it were possible to know all the factual truths about the world, there would still be something left over. Knowing all the facts about the world would still not answer whether or not it was *right* to drop atomic bombs on Hiroshima and Nagasaki. Biological science can tell us that the racist claims that informed the early modern enslavement of Africans are false, but biology cannot tell us whether slavery is *wrong*. Biology may come to tell us when fetuses become capable of experiencing pain, but it cannot tell us whether abortion is *morally permissible*. Science cannot tell you whether it's ever morally right to lie, whether to divorce your spouse, under what circumstances lethal force is right, whether one is obligated to give to the poor, etc. Similar concerns apply to science and politics. Can science settle the Palestine–Israel conflict? It seems unlikely, though it may contribute information important for settling it.

What about aesthetics? Perhaps science will be able to explain what makes it possible for us to have experiences of beauty, ugliness, sublimity, gracefulness, and other aesthetic matters. Moreover, empirical psychology and science are likely to be able to tell us something about the kinds of properties that human beings have and continue to find aesthetically valuable. But, as the Prussian philosopher Immanuel Kant argues, the fact that we criticize artistic judgments shows that it's not enough to show simply *what is the case* about what in general people find beautiful; we also think that others *ought* to share in certain aesthetic judgments, that people ought to find beautiful some of what we find beautiful, and that they are missing something if they don't. This suggests that, while science may explain what happens in our bodies and brains when we make aesthetic judgments, it's not likely able to settle the question of whether or not Elvis Presley was the greatest singer of all time, or whether or not the Parthenon or the Willendorf Venus is beautiful, whether the Nymph of the Luo River or the Bonumpak murals are great artwork, or whether Michelangelo was a better artist than Thomas Kinkade.

Different kinds of science

Curiously, one reason we continue to ask questions about the limits of scientific reasoning is that it is very difficult, perhaps impossible, to *define* scientific reasoning. In part that's because there is no single kind of science, and different sciences employ different methods.

Branches of science

Perhaps the most substantial distinction among the sciences is between those we call "natural" and others we call "social." (Some also distinguish between those such as chemistry that are centrally "empirical" or grounded in observation and those, such as mathematics and logic, that are "formal" and based largely in deductive reasoning using more abstract concepts.)

Central to the distinction between natural and social science is the question of whether human conduct can be understood in the same terms as the rest of the (natural) world. Are human "reasons" different from physical "causes" such that conventional causal explanations are insufficient in the social sciences? Must people's intentions be considered in order to understand their conduct, and do "intentions" or "freedom" make human and meteorological behavior different in kind? You might say that the big question (the metaphysical question, perhaps) behind all this is whether human beings are continuous or discontinuous with the natural world generally? If continuous, could one argue that since humans are one species of primates among others, social science isn't really different from natural science, that ultimately it's just a branch of primatology?

Even among the natural empirical sciences there are differences. The methods of biology are not identical to the methods of astronomy or subatomic particle physics or the methods of psychology or bacteriology or the methods of entomology. So, when thinking about "science" and "scientific method," it may be relevant to ask "which science" and "which method"?

Evolving science

Of course, the sciences have changed very much throughout history and in different parts of the world. One might even say they have *evolved.* Alchemy as a science employed methods specific to it but that are no longer regarded as properly scientific. So did astrology, phrenology, and inquiries that came to be known as forms of "natural magic."

Aristotelian science of ancient and medieval times involved figuring out – using deduction, intellectual intuition, and observation – the different qualities that define natural kinds of things (bears, wolves, oaks, swans, stones, etc.), more particularly the properties that *differentiate* them in *essential* ways from others. Aristotelians inquired not only into the metaphysical categories of the world but also into four different kinds of "causes" (*aitia*) that determine the changes that take place in the world. Aristotelian scientists worked to distinguish as causes (1) the *material* of things (e.g., the clay brick of a building) from (2) the *forms* it takes (a house), what (3) *moves* or brings it into that state (the builders), and (4) the *end* or *final* purpose it realizes (a place to inhabit in private life).

Modern physical science has largely eliminated consideration of two of those Aristotelian *aitia*: ends or "final causes" and metaphysical forms or "formal causes" (2 and 4 above). Instead modern physical science explains natural phenomena in terms of modern variants of the other two Aristotelian causes (1 and 3): modern ideas of matter for Aristotelian "material causes" and the physical processes and forces that initiate particular changes for the Aristotelian "moving cause." Investigation of

Aristotle's metaphysical *forms* (formal causes) of ultimate reality has been transformed by modern thinkers into the investigation of conceptual and linguistic *categories* of analysis as well as the *formulations* of natural *laws*. Modern biology, for example, labors to develop useful species concepts; and many sciences remain concerned with formulating the definitions and specific distinguishing properties of different types of phenomena – all quite successfully without Aristotelian metaphysics.

Different kinds of nature

Not only has scientific method changed over time, but our ideas about what composes "nature" have, too. For Aristotelians, the sky (or the celestial realm) was a profoundly different kind of order from the Earth and its inhabitants (the terrestrial). The celestial order was thought to be composed of a different kind of matter and to behave according to different principles. For example, Aristotelians thought that the surfaces of celestial objects were perfectly smooth, that they were everlasting objects, and that they could only move in circles. Galileo in Italy disproved the smoothness thesis when he observed craters on the Moon through a telescope. Danish Tycho Brahe's observation of a nova, or new star, in 1572 suggested that the eternity thesis was incorrect. German Johannes Kepler, working in Prague, disproved the circularity thesis when he explained how planets move in elliptical orbits. Aristotelians also thought that natural objects were self-moving and in fact often moved because of a kind of internal urge to reach their ends. Alchemical nature, similarly, is full of affinities and repugnancies. Platonists believed in a *spiritus mundi* or "world soul" that animates the natural universe. Stoics believed the natural world operates according to fate and providence. Vitalists believed that living matter was qualitatively different from non-living matter. While nature itself may have remained fundamentally the same, our views about it certainly have not. Nor should we expect them to cease changing.

Even in recent times, our views of the dynamics and composition of the natural world have undergone remarkable and profound change. As recently as 2014, a single World Wildlife Federation report catalogued 367 *newly discovered* species in Southeast Asia. Not many decades ago, the idea that the principal constituent of the universe is a kind of "dark" or invisible matter and that everything is pervaded by a "dark energy" driving the accelerating expansion of the universe was all but unknown. The theory that the universe started with a "big bang" was only first advanced formally in 1927. The first scientific paper published arguing for the existence of black holes appeared only in 1958. Besides the Higgs boson, many subatomic particles have only recently been discovered, not to mention matter's twin, anti-matter. Scientists have increasingly warmed even to the idea that ours may be only one of many universes, that we inhabit just one component or iteration of a "multiverse." And, of course, as recently as the early twentieth century, Einstein advanced his extraordinary theories of relativity.

Different cultures, different sciences?

Science, of course, or what might loosely be called science, as well as "nature" as it's conceived, has varied by culture. If you've ever visited Chichen Itza, Mexico, or the Jantar Mantar in Jaipur, India, or read about the celestial observations of the Dogon of Mali, you'll know that the Maya, ancient Indians, and pre-colonial Africans, as well as many others, practiced astronomy, often according to different theories of physics and different methods of calculation. Chinese and Indian forms of medicine operate on different theories of how the body and disease work, appealing to powers such as *chi* or the deep elemental qualities of different types of people. The Romans used a different numbering system.

Might it be reasonable, then, to speak of ancient science, Chinese science, Indian science, Egyptian science, etc., in addition to modern empirical and formal sciences, each with its own methods and standards for justification and explanation? If it is, then, upon recognizing that the methods defining science have been diverse and have changed over time and place, it seems a fair inductive inference to think that we should expect that the content, scope, and methods of science will continue to change. Might science be as different five hundred years from now as current science is from that of the Renaissance?

The boundaries of nature

The characters in the 1984 film *Ghostbusters* employed ghost detectors, but there may be reasons to think of that sort of device as impossible. It all depends upon your definition of *supernatural.* Divine beings and otherwise supernatural things, whether or not they exist, are by definition different in kind from those of the natural order. One implication of angels, souls, and demons existing beyond the possibilities of natural observation might be that they bear no well-defined or law-like relationships to what is naturally observable. It's true that people attribute to them regularities of a sort – cold in their presence, behavior similar to the sort we attribute to human emotions such as anger or grief. To that extent we might think of them as partially natural beings. But unless those sorts of phenomena are sufficiently regular and law-like, it may be a fair bet to think that while people can build photon detectors, ghost detectors won't be coming onto the market soon.

This suggests that it may be meaningful to speak of boundaries to nature. Some questions about what "nature" includes and excludes, therefore, reside on the boundary distinguishing metaphysics from science. Are there minds or forms of consciousness distinct from body? Do the terms "person" and "self" refer to something natural or part of nature? Do sets and numbers and other mathematical "objects" in some sense exist? Are they part of nature? What about logical relations and formal principles such as equality, identity, negation, and difference? Have the laws of nature changed over time, and are they uniform across the universe? Are there other forms of life different from those we recognize? Is the distinction between what's living and non-living meaningful? What is time, and do the past and future exist, perhaps as dimensions of an unchanging space–time continuum? Must time only move forward? How many spatial dimensions exist? How complete is our periodic table? Can anything move faster than light? Is there "nothingness" or even just purely empty space? What's inside a black hole, and are there worm holes?

So, like scientific methods of investigation and reasoning, "nature" as we conceive it has hardly been static, and what counts as "the natural world" is still a matter of investigation and conceptual controversy. As this chapter unfolds, we'll examine some of the most important features of scientific reasoning that have been settled upon over centuries of scrutiny and with them ideas about the natural world. We don't claim to present an exhaustive account or one that will endure forever, but each characteristic of scientific reasoning and the natural world that we consider is the product of philosophers' and other theorists' considerable critical reflection upon what makes for solid reasoning about the dynamics of natural and social phenomena, and each has proven widely influential. Understanding the sciences and corresponding ideas of nature helps critical thinkers assess not only sound science but also pseudo-science and just plain bad science.

Critiques of science

Before we leave this topic, however, there's another dimension of science good critical thinkers should consider. In our next chapter we'll examine some powerful social-political and philosophical critiques that may be brought to bear against not so much the epistemological capacities of science but, rather, its cultural impact. To the extent that science has been connected to technological ways of thinking, some critics have argued that science has altered for the worse the way we conceive and act in relation to the (rest of the) natural world and the living things that inhabit it. One of the founders of modern, empirical scientific method, the English philosopher Francis Bacon, for example, described scientific laboratories as torture chambers and described nature as a woman whom – presumably, male – scientists would coerce to give up her secrets (to be fair, Bacon also said that nature to be commanded must be obeyed). Another key figure in the formation of early modern scientific theory, René Descartes (1596–1650), promoted his new science by promising it would make us "masters and possessors of nature."

In response to the kind of attitude Bacon, Descartes *et alia* established, philosophers such as Martin Heidegger (1889–1976) have argued that an excessively technologically focused way of viewing the world has led us to regard nature simply as a reserve of resources for humans to use, conquer, own, and exploit (see 10.13, Ecological Critiques). Frankfurt School philosophers (see 10.8, The Frankfurt School: Culture Critique) have found in the "instrumental" forms of reasoning associated with modern science the tendency to use and misuse other humans reductively, in merely instrumental ways, to see others in ways simply related to the functions they serve, principally in the modern economy. People themselves, in the technological way of thinking modern science has cultivated, become in the minds of some critics little more than physical tools. Then, of course, there's the way natural science is often related to metaphysical forms of naturalism, which deny that anything exists beyond the natural order. Could this kind of thinking be blind to other dimensions of human existence? In an old saying: "Not everything that counts can be counted, and not everything that can be counted counts."

SEE ALSO

10.8 The Frankfurt School: Culture Critique
10.10 Feminist and Gender Critiques
10.13 Ecological Critiques

READING

Thomas Kuhn, *The Structure of Scientific Revolutions: 50th Anniversary Edition* (2012)
Timothy McGrew, Marc Alspector-Kelly, Fritz Allhoff, *Philosophy of Science: An Historical Anthology* (2009)
Samir Okasha, *Philosophy of Science: A Very Short Introduction* (2002).
Russell Shorto, *Descartes' Bones: A Skeletal History of the Conflict Between Faith and Reason* (2008)

9.3 Varieties of Possibility and Impossibility

One common charge against the use of evolutionary theory in biology is offered by Joseph Mastropaolo in his 1999 article, "Evolution is Biologically Impossible." Now, claiming that something is impossible is a pretty strong criticism. It's not only to say that something is not true but also that it is not *possibly* true or that it *cannot* be true. Possibility claims can be complex, too, and logicians have developed special *modal logics* to deal with issues of possibility and necessity. There are, in fact, lots of claims that are false but nevertheless possible. For example, it's possible that the Earth has two moons. It's possible that Omaha, Nebraska will become the capital of the United States. (It may be *improbable* that the US capital be moved to Omaha, but there seems little reason to say it's *impossible*.) It's possible that pigs will develop wings.

Good critical thinkers, however, will prick up their ears when they run across the words "possible" or "impossible," because those terms are used in many different ways. Indeed, corresponding to different kinds of scientific reasoning and different ways of thinking about the world are different kinds of possibility and impossibility. Typically, what's possible or impossible is defined by a set of rules, laws, or defining concepts or principles. In chess, for example, it's possible to move the bishop diagonally, but not horizontally. That's what the rules of chess say. It is, of course, physically possible to move the bishop horizontally. Doing so violates the rules of chess, but not the rules of physics. It's also not possible, but in a different sense of possibility, to score a touchdown in chess or to draw a straight flush in football. What it means to play those games doesn't allow for those possibilities. Let's consider, then, some of the principal forms of possibility and impossibility relevant to critical thinkers.

Logical possibility

What's logically possible is what is permitted by the laws of logic, most importantly, the law of non-contradiction. To assert a contradiction is, as we have seen, to simultaneously assert both *p* and not-*p*, where *p* is a statement that means exactly the same thing in both assertions. For most purposes, then, anything is logically possible that's not self-contradictory or that doesn't entail a contradiction. (This last bit is the difficult part, as it's not always immediately obvious what does and does not entail a contradiction.) Logical possibility is the broadest kind of possibility because, as we'll see, there are many, many things that are logically possible but impossible in other senses.

Related to logical possibility is mathematical possibility. What's mathematically impossible is what violates the principles and defining concepts of mathematics. So, for example, it's mathematically impossible in the set of real numbers for 2 to be less than negative 2; it's impossible that $1 + 1 = 5$ in standard arithmetic. Now, it's true that some philosophers have tried to reduce other forms of possibility/impossibility to just logical possibility/impossibility. For example, mathematician-philosophers Bertrand Russell and Alfred North Whitehead tried to define mathematics simply as a branch of logic. They were, however, unsuccessful. In any case, if Mastropaolo thinks evolution is impossible in a logical or mathematical sense then he thinks it violates the law of non-contradiction or some other mathematical or logical law.

Physical possibility

What is physically possible is what is consistent with the laws of physics, and what is physically impossible violates the laws of nature. So, while it's not logically impossible for a pig to fly without wings (there's no logical contradiction in it), its doing so would violate the laws of physics as we know them. It's impossible to defy the law of gravity by levitating as an act of will, and it's impossible to defy the law of entropy by moving from lower energy states to higher energy states (for example, for cold water to heat up) without the input of additional energy. So, the set of physical possibilities is smaller than the set of logical possibilities.

Now, critical thinkers will also want to be aware that the sets of what are thought of as physical possibilities and impossibilities are more likely to change than those that are logical. Why? Because logical laws are pretty well settled, while those of physics have proven more subject to revision. Descartes and Newton changed what were thought to be the principles of physics in fairly radical ways. Einstein, Bohr, and other recent physicists didn't exactly overthrow Newton's laws, but they did show that Newton's laws work best with middle-sized objects but poorly with tiny, fast things and objects of tremendous mass. Evolutionary theory itself has been under revision, and like the phenomena it explains, it is likely to evolve more over time.

Other types of possibility

There are, of course, many other types of impossibility. Some behaviors might be thought to be *psychologically impossible*, for example not to be emotionally affected by the death of a beloved parent or child or not to break down psychologically after repeated waterboarding. Paying off the US national debt would be *financially impossible* if using any one individual's wealth. "Sophie's choice," in which a mother was forced to choose which of her two children to turn over to be murdered by the Nazis, might be described as a *morally impossible* situation. It might have been *militarily impossible* for the Spartans holding the pass at Thermopylae to have prevailed over the Persians. You get the idea.

To assess, as a critical thinker, a claim to possibility or impossibility, you must first understand the context that determines what's possible and impossible. Criticizing a claim to possibility or impossibility may require showing that an arguer has misused the context, or it may require criticizing the context itself. It will require remembering, too, that what's impossible in one sense may be perfectly possible in another sense. So, either defending or criticizing the possibility of evolution will require thoroughly understanding the relevant principles of chemistry, physics, biology, logic, or mathematics. It's a degree of understanding, alas, that few possess.

SEE ALSO

4.1 Propositional vs. Categorical Logics
8.1 Knowledge: The Basics
9.2 The Purview of Science

READING

Theodore Schick & Lewis Vaughn, *How to Think about Weird Things: Critical Thinking for a New Age*, 7th edn (2013)
Michael Jubien, *Possibility* (2009)
Samir Okasha, *Philosophy of Science: A Very Short Introduction* (2002)
Timothy Williamson, *Knowledge and Its Limits* (2000)
M. J. Cresswell & G. E. Hughes, *A New Introduction to Modal Logic* (1996)
Brian F. Chellas, *Modal Logic: An Introduction* (1980)

9.4 Scientific Method

When you look at the development of early modern science, it quickly becomes clear that at the heart of the new enterprise was method. Dissatisfaction with ancient and medieval forms of inquiry set early modern philosophers on a quest for the right method, the best set of procedures to apprehend the truth. So, Francis Bacon undertook what he called a *Great Instauration* (1620) to reform the sciences. Central to that project was the development of a new scientific method with the *New Organon* (1620), or a new set of conceptual tools for inquiry. Around the same time, Galileo set out seminal scientific ideals in both his theoretical and experimental work. Descartes's first major publication appeared just a bit later, and the title says it all: *Discourse on the Method of Rightly Conducting One's Reason and of Seeking Truth in the Sciences* (1637).

Philosophical inquiries into new methods for investigation seemed wildly successful, as indeed a raft of new natural and social sciences developed over the following centuries. In another sense, however, they were unsuccessful – if success means finding the one true method. Today there is no single scientific method, and perhaps, as Paul Feyerabend has argued in his book *Against Method* (1975), the only methodological principle that unites all those who call themselves scientists is that they call themselves scientists! The procedures of inquiry among theoretical physicists are different from those among experimental physicists, and the methods of psychology and sociology are different from those of primatology, ornithology, and astronomy. Still, we might for the sake of our purposes here posit a few general, widely shared principles of scientific method that will be useful for critical thinkers to consider.

Causal explanation

One of the deep metaphysical questions about social science and how it differs from natural science is whether or not social science is distinct because its subject matter (the thought and behavior of human beings) cannot be fully understood in causal terms. That is, some argue that social science is fundamentally different from natural science because human beings are in some sense free or independent of the causal order. Theorists such as Michael Oakeshott, for example, have argued (*On Human Conduct*, 1975) that human conduct cannot be understood without considering the intentions, goals, and purposes chosen by human agents. Human beings, according to this view, are not fully subject to causal explanations. It is a difficult question to decide and one not likely to be decided soon.

In any case, we might say that as far as possible, scientific method attempts to give a causal explanation for some phenomenon (in technical terms usually called the *explanandum* – it's what's "dum" and so needs explanation; see 1.2). To say that a phenomenon is subject to causal explanation is to say that it's part of a *regular order* of causes and effects (see 6.3 and 6.8). That means that whenever the "cause" is in place, the "effect" will always follow and follow in the same, uniform way – unless some other causal system interferes with it. As the philosopher David Lewis argues, a causal relation is such that, all other things being equal, if the cause had not occurred, the effect would not have occurred, at least not precisely as it did occur. So, for example, adding a gram of caesium or any alkali metal to an open cup of water under normal terrestrial conditions will always lead to a kind of explosion with exactly the same amount of energy released each time. (If you've never seen what happens when caesium encounters water, check out an online video. It's pretty spectacular.) A scientific explanation, then, is an account of the cause or causes that produced some outcome – it is to give an *explanans* for an *explanandum*.

Sometimes the "laws" formulated to describe causal relationships are stated as rough approximations. So, in economics, Engel's law states that as income rises, the proportion of income people spend on food falls (and so reductions in the proportion spent on food are an indicator of improved standards of living). Scientific method, however, typically demands that explanations are quantified more precisely. Engel's law, for example, can be formulated more precisely by establishing a numeric coefficient based upon the ratio of food expenditure to income.

This imperative of method to quantify in precise terms means that the kinds of causal sequences science determines are just the sort that *can* be quantitatively measured and formulated in mathematical relationships. This practice is exceedingly powerful. So, in physics $p = mv$ (momentum equals mass times velocity) and $E = mc^2$ (energy equals mass times the speed of light squared). In chemistry, the combined gas law may be expressed as, $PV/T = k$, where pressure multiplied by volume then divided by temperature equals an established constant (k). You can use this law, for instance, to explain the drop in temperature encountered when climbing up a mountain, for example, by the drop in air pressure at higher altitudes. Similarly, this law explains why balloons expand when the air inside them is heated.

Understanding this about scientific method gives critical thinkers a way of criticizing supposedly scientific explanations. Are the laws to which scientists appeal in the explanation adequate to the task? Do they really describe the universal and regular causal sequences of the world? Might other laws do the job better? Have scientists identified the right causes in their explanation? Can everything be explained this way? Some critical thinkers point to quantification as marking a limit to scientific thinking. The critics hold that not everything in the world can be quantified – beauty, for example, or human motives. Is there anything that can't be explained by quantified causal explanations?

Observation

Empirical scientific method is also committed to empiricism, in the sense that scientific claims must be grounded in observation. Not just any observation may count as the sort proper to underwrite scientific claims. The observations with which science is concerned must be the kind any normal human observer can make and that are therefore open to confirmation by others. When the kid in M. Night Shyamalan's 1999 film *The Sixth Sense* says, "I see dead people," he makes a claim that, by itself, cannot be considered a good scientific observation. His unshared personal experience, even if true, isn't enough to count as useful to the procedures of testing employed by science. Unless implications and predictions can be drawn from his perceptions for observations we all can make (for example, the video he plays to the group gathered after the murdered child's funeral), his observations don't quite rise to the level of scientific data.

But when the unobserved or the strictly private and personal does connect with matters of shared observation in regular, law-like ways, it *can* become a topic of scientific investigation. That is to say, science can investigate not only what is *actually* observed but can also make claims about what is *unobserved* and even *unobservable.* In fact, it does so all the time. While ghosts may not meet the conditions for scientific investigation, science does make meaningful claims about magnetic fields and electromagnetic spectra (such as X-rays) that are beyond the range of human observation, such as dark matter. No one today can observe Alexander the Great, microwaves, the beginning of the universe, or the microscopic Higgs boson, and yet claims are commonly made about Alexander's military campaigns and about the big bang, about microwaves, neutrinos and other subatomic particles. That's because claims about those unobservable entities are associated in precise ways with observations that can be currently made and shared.

Science relates *unobservables* to things *observable* in uniform and specifiable ways, typically using precisely formulated natural laws to make the connections. So, while we can't see X-rays themselves, we *can* see the regular effects they produce, and the relationship between X-rays and those effects can be described by physical law. Inscriptions and ancient texts give observable evidence about the existence of Alexander. Observable changes in instruments or sensitive materials (e.g., food in a microwave oven) can allow us to detect invisible electromagnetic radiation as well as the presence or absence of entities such as Higgs bosons. Microwave detectors, in fact, unlike ghost detectors, have provided us with observations consistent with just the sort of leftover radiation that big bang theory predicts we should find.

When engaging matters in a scientific way, critical thinkers ought to ask questions about what observable evidence there is for or against some position. Is there observable evidence, for example, for the different categories of persons and life-forces (*doshas*) used by Ayurvedic medicine? Is there observable data beyond what placebo effects would predict for claims about various pharmaceutical products such as antidepressants? What observable evidence is there for the effectiveness of homeopathic remedies or for the existence of black holes or dark matter? What kind of empirical evidence supports claims about evolution or about climate change, about ghosts or alien visitations?

Verification and falsification

Observation, in short, plays a crucial role in deciding whether or not some claim or *hypothesis* is true. Observations are used scientifically either to "verify" (prove the truth) or "falsify" (prove the falsehood) of a *hypothesis* (see 9.5). Some argue that these terms are too strong because science is always changing and adapting; what is scientifically "true" at one point in time may become "false" at another. Because of the fluid nature of science, some prefer the terms "confirmation" (evidence that a hypothesis is true) and "disconfirmation" (evidence that a hypothesis is false); we can have this sort of evidence regardless of whether the hypothesis is true or false. Either way, in scientific practice, good hypotheses must be crafted so that they are *testable* (see 9.7). There is, however, a logical issue that figures into the practices of both verification and falsification that will be helpful for you to understand when thinking critically about scientific reasoning.

Consider the logic of verification. We might understand verification to work this way: *If the hypothesis is true, then the predicted result of the experiment takes place.*

True hypothesis → Prediction comes about

For example: *if the hypothesis that caesium reacts with water is true, then this piece of caesium explodes when placed in this water.* This seems right given our immediate intuitions about experiments. But if we think of verification this way, it's technically possible for the conditional to be true where the caesium explodes while the hypothesis is nevertheless false. (That is, the hypothetical as a whole can be true even if the antecedent – the hypothesis – is false and the consequent true, as you'll recall from the discussion of the truth conditions for conditionals in Sections 2.2 and 4.1.) For example, it might be the case that caesium explodes when it is exposed to light refracted by water and not by the water itself. If that were the case, this logic would yield something like a false positive verification. (Again, this is why some prefer the term "confirmation" over "verification," though this still doesn't help us to find the lurking variable until we conduct more experiments.)

The water-refraction alternative hypothesis is, of course, false (we just made it up), and it can be shown to be so by conducting the experiment again in the dark. Nevertheless, philosophers of science worry that there may always be hidden possibilities that might lead to false positive conclusions if the logic of verification in science is conceived this way. Some skeptical philosophers have argued that this means that verification can never be absolutely conclusive – or, in technical terms, that *crucial experiments* (or experiments that are final and definitive) are not possible.

So, perhaps the logic will work better if we think of verification instead this way, using the converse of our first formulation: *If the predicted result of the experiment takes place, then the hypothesis is true.*

Prediction comes about → Hypothesis true

In other words, reconsidered, we might think of our caesium test this way: *If this caesium explodes when placed in this water, then the hypothesis that caesium reacts with water is true.*

This seems to capture much of what we intuitively think of as an experiment. But technically, as you might have already figured out given what we explained in

Chapter 4, under this way of thinking we'll get a true conditional even if the caesium doesn't explode; and that seems just inconsistent with what verification should show. So, positive results work to prove a hypothesis under this conception, but negative results leave the validity of the hypothesis at least undetermined.

The best way to think of verification from a logical point of view seems to be in terms of a biconditional (see 2.2), such that whenever the test turns out positive, the hypothesis is confirmed and whenever the test results are negative, the hypothesis is falsified or disconfirmed.

Hypothesis is true ↔ Prediction occurs

This formulation seems to capture what we're after, but it's hardly perfect.

We encountered in Chapter 7 a variety of practical and theoretical problems with observation and therefore experimentation. There is also, however, a logical problem with verification rooted in the very logical properties of scientific laws. No general or universal scientific claim, and that includes all scientific laws, is fully verifiable simply because we can't normally test every instance of the law's operation across the currently existing universe. Of course, unless time machines become a reality, we can never test its application in the past and in the future. As Hume argued in his 1739 *A Treatise of Human Nature*, we have no ultimate reason to conclude that the future will resemble the past and no reason to conclude finally that causal regularities will continue in the same way they have so far. We have no conclusive reason, in Hume's words, to believe "*that instances, of which we have had no experience must resemble those, of which we have had experience, and that the course of nature continues always uniformly the same*" (Book 1, Part 3, Section, 6, Paragraph 4). What some philosophers have called the Principle of the Uniformity of Nature (or, affectionately, the PUN) seems, in other words, to be something like an assumption. We cannot check to see whether each and every piece of caesium that has ever existed, now exists, or will ever exist reacts with water in the same way or whether all light travels, has traveled, and will travel at the same velocity. So, we simply can't fully verify the hypothesis that it does.

Worries like these have led some to conceive of science as a process of *falsification* rather than verification. Falsification, indeed, works very well for the general and universal claims commonly investigated by science. We can easily falsify the claim that "all light travels at 100 m/sec" by conducting a test that shows an example of it traveling at another speed. We can falsify the claim that "All swans are white," simply by finding just one black (or non-white) swan. As we saw in 3.4, A-claims are contradicted by O-claims; and E-claims are contradicted by I-claims.

So, falsification shows us what is false. In this way, as the philosopher of science Karl Popper argues, science works like natural selection in biological evolution, eliminating maladaptive hypotheses through falsification. There's something disappointing about this thought, at least for those who think science finally settles questions. Falsification doesn't prove anything to be *true*. Although we can easily disprove it, we cannot fully prove that "*all* light in space travels at 299,792,458 meters per second" – as modern physics holds. This way of thinking about scientific method renders science methodologically *open* in a sense – which for those who don't require final answers is actually one of the best things about science. Unlike religious dogma, science always stands open for more testing to be done and always allows the possibility that new testing will falsify what has so far passed our scrutiny. Now, in practice, many scientists would say they're engaged with a combination of falsification and verification, accepting the limits of doing so. But in light of the logical complexities of verification and falsification, it seems reasonable to say that to the extent scientific inquiry proves anything, it does so *only in provisional ways*. Even the central idea in physics that nothing travels faster than light has been challenged (albeit still unsuccessfully) by recent experimental findings regarding neutrinos. Those who think that in modern science anything has been proven once and for all just don't understand science.

Paradigms: normal and revolutionary science

There's more, however, to thinking critically about scientific inquiry than these logical concerns about experimentation. Empiricism, inductive generalization, deduction, verification, falsification, and basic logic are not by themselves enough to engage scientific matters in a properly reflective and critical way, not by a long shot. Thomas Kuhn and others have argued that scientific observations and claims must be interpreted against a conceptual background he calls "paradigms." Others have used ideas of "conceptual systems" or "web of beliefs" or even just language and culture to express similar ideas. The basic idea for these thinkers is that facts or observations are not understood in isolation but only within a larger network of ideas. As Ludwig Wittgenstein remarked in his *Philosophical Investigations* (Section 199), "To understand a sentence means to understand a language."

Observations and data must be interpreted. And so, for example, within a paradigm where the Earth is understood to be still, the Sun is seen to "rise" and "move across" the sky. From a paradigm where the Earth is rotating, even though the observations remain the same, it's not the Sun that rises but the Earth that's turning the viewer toward the face of the Sun. In some paradigms, militants are "freedom fighters," while in others they may be "terrorists." The conduct of some women appears pushy and irritating from within a sexist paradigm, while from another point of view the same conduct may appear strong and confident. According to economic mercantilists, the establishment of monopolies or closed colonial markets was an advance in a country's economic standing, while free market theorists see closed markets as diminishing economic well-being. Because this view argues that the parts of a scientific theory (its terms and formulae) can only be understood against a wider background, it is sometimes called *holism*.

Paradigms, of course, change – as for example the Ptolemaic geocentric paradigm gave way to the Copernican paradigm. Observations do play a role in that, but philosophers of science have learned that the shift is also important in conceptual ways. For the most part, we fit observations into the existing paradigms in which we think and live. Kuhn calls that fitting process, "normal science." But sometimes observations don't quite fit, or it becomes difficult to make them fit – just as it became difficult to fit the observed motion of all the planets and comets into the Ptolemaic mode. When that happens, a new conceptual paradigm may be produced that supplants the old. Kuhn calls this, "revolutionary science." Good critical thinkers, then, when faced with people's reports about the observations they make, will do well to consider what paradigms inform those reports about observations. You may also critically think about how a given paradigm might be criticized, challenged, or destabilized to advance a revolutionary change in paradigms. Even our most fundamental conceptual networks might be revolutionized. Some logicians have, in fact, actually proposed what are called *paraconsistent* logics that have revised the principle of non-contradiction, the most basic principle of reason, as well as the way logic refuses inconsistencies. Those who accept *dialetheism* in logic even say that some contradictions are true! Galileo's *Discourse Concerning Two World Systems* (1632) effectively helped destabilize the Ptolemaic view. Adam Smith's *The Wealth of Nations* (1776) helped undermine the mercantile paradigm in economics. Simone de Beauvoir's *The Second Sex* (1949) has contributed to the destabilization of patriarchy. These three texts have all been, therefore, conceptually revolutionary. Might new revolutions be initiated today?

SEE ALSO

8.1 Knowledge: The Basics
8.6 Justification: The Basics
9.6 Experiments and Other Tests

READING

Hugh G. Gauch, *Scientific Method in Brief* (2012)
Stephen S. Carey, *A Beginner's Guide to Scientific Method* (2011)
Stephen Gimbel, *Exploring Scientific Method: A New Approach to Teaching Scientific Method* (2011)

9.5 Unfalsifiability and Falsification Resistance

People rarely like being proven wrong. Sometimes people have not only invested their egos into their claims, they have also puts years of their lives and a great deal of their wealth into them. As a result, on a purely psychological level, people resist their claims being falsified. In addition, however, it turns out that it's surprisingly easy to resist falsification.

Ad hoc hypotheses and the fallacy of unfalsifiability

Also known as *death by a thousand qualifications*, the fallacy of *unfalsifiability* occurs when an arguer keeps changing his or her definition of a term, concept, or worldview in an *ad hoc* manner in order to avoid criticism. *Ad hoc* changes are additions or changes made solely for the purpose of protecting a term, concept, or worldview from counterexample or critique.[1]

Imagine Sarah says to you: "There is an elephant in this room." And you say, I don't see an elephant." Sarah might respond, "Oh, it's an invisible elephant." You could try to say, "Well, I don't smell it; elephants are smelly," but Sarah could simply say, "Invisible elephants don't smell." And you might get up and walk around and say, "Well, I'm walking all around the room, and I don't feel or bump into an elephant." But even then, Sarah, convinced there is an elephant in the room, could say, "You don't understand; it's an *insensible* elephant. But it's there." At this point, you would probably feel exasperated. Sarah has so qualified her "elephant" that there's *no* criterion by which to prove her wrong. Her claim that there's an elephant in the room is simply unfalsifiable. But, of course, the fact that Sarah can do this doesn't mean there are good reasons to believe her claim.

Upon first encountering this fallacy, you might think it isn't fallacious at all. After all, *if there is no way to prove that a claim is false, surely it must be true!* That's a very tempting line of thought. Falsifiability (the capacity for a claim to be falsified) is, as we've seen, an important feature of well-supported claims. We have a better idea of how to support a claim adequately if we know what sort of evidence could *dis*prove it, that is, if we know what to expect if it isn't true. This is clear in empirical cases. We have evidence that the drug ibuprofen reduces pain, but we know what to expect if this were to be false: pain would consistently not diminish even after taking ibuprofen. But even putatively necessary claims, like those of mathematic and logic, have falsifiability conditions, even if those conditions could never be met. We tend to think that $2 + 2 = 4$ is necessarily true because the axioms of arithmetic entail it. But if it turns out that rejecting one of these axioms makes more sense in light of other mathematical claims, we could discover a proof for the claim that $2 + 2 \neq 4$. So we know what it would take to disprove $2 + 2 = 4$ even if we don't think those conditions could ever occur.

Consider another example of unfalsifiability. Imagine Trayvon says, "Senator Jones's policy is the most effective policy to reduce homelessness." We can imagine Sarah challenging Trayvon's claim by presenting data that similar policies have failed to reduce homelessness adequately: "That policy was tried in Dallas, and it didn't work." In response, Trayvon might say, "Well, Dallas has a different demographic; it's likely to be more effective here." Sarah might then discover that a similar policy didn't work in a place with a similar demographic, but Trayvon could respond: "The problem wasn't the policy; it was the implementation. The state didn't put enough money in the right place." We can now begin to suspect that Trayvon isn't really open to the possibility that the policy is ineffective. He has a tendency to qualify all counterevidence so that it doesn't affect his opinion of the policy. If he just doesn't allow that some evidence would falsify his claim about the effectiveness of the policy, he is committing the fallacy of unfalsifiability.

Falsification and holism: hypothesis vs. theory

We encountered *holism* in 9.4, the idea argued by thinkers such as W. V. O. Quine and Pierre Duhem that we don't engage claims singly but rather against a background of other claims that form a kind of whole and that are assumed to be true. So, when we use analyses of light spectra from faraway stars to determine the composition of those stars, we assume the background claim that the correlations between light and various elements that we observe on Earth also hold in faraway galaxies. People can therefore resist apparently falsifying data by instead arguing that the data must actually undermine one of the background assumptions rather than the claim they wish to protect from falsification. For example, when a car or train travels past us blowing its horn, we hear the pitch of the sound drop. That drop is called the Doppler effect. Light declines in energy when emitted from objects traveling away from us, too, shifting toward the red end of the light spectrum. That "red shift" of the galaxies around us indicates to many astronomers that the universe is expanding. Someone holding that the universe is not expanding might resist the falsification implicit in this finding by suggesting that light behaves differently in other parts of the galaxy. It's not that the galaxies are moving away from us, it's that the light they emit operates differently.

The "no true Scotsman" fallacy

Philosopher Anthony Flew identified a fallacy related to falsification resistance in his 1975 book, *Thinking about Thinking*. He recounted the story of a man called Hamish who read about a horrible murder in England in the newspaper. Hamish exclaimed that, paraphrasing Flew, "No Scotsman would commit such a crime!" only to be informed by his companion about a similar crime having recently been committed by a Scottish man in Aberdeen. Against this apparently falsifying evidence, Hamish simply retorted, "No *true* Scotsman would do such a thing." The fallacy is often committed by those who wish to defend some beloved group. Jews, Christians, and Muslims have each been accused of committing atrocities motivated by their religion only to have members of those groups respond that, "No *true* Jew/Christian/Muslim would behave that way."

Legitimate uses of unfalsifiability and resistance to falsifiability?

There seem to be no epistemically legitimate uses of unfalsifiability; even necessarily true claims have conditions under which they would be false. But there are cases that can seem as though they are being treated as unfalsifiable but aren't. Consider the hypothetical conversation between Trayvon and Sarah over Senator Jones's policy to reduce homelessness. Social science research is fraught with difficulties because social situations cannot be replicated in a laboratory. We can always criticize such a study by arguing that the study has a selection bias, or a sampling bias, or that the wrong statistical measurements were used to calculate the results, etc. (see 6.4). Because of this, a researcher can always defend his or her conclusions by noting that those conclusions are valid *given the limitations of social science methodology*. This isn't quite the same as unfalsifiability, but it is close. Social science researchers still owe us an account of how additional research could confirm or disconfirm their conclusions. Any one study may be problematic, but comparing similar studies with similar information might be informative. Nevertheless, if someone has an easy answer for any particular criticism you have, take the time to ask what sort of evidence would count against the claim at issue.

Examples of fallacious unfalsifiability

1. The following is Anthony Flew's telling of John Wisdom's "Gardener Parable," from Flew's article, "Theology and Falsification" (1968): "Once upon a time two explorers came upon a clearing in the jungle. In the clearing were growing many flowers and many weeds. One explorer says, 'Some gardener must tend this plot.' The other disagrees, 'There is no gardener.' So they pitch their tents and set a watch. No gardener is ever seen. 'But perhaps he is an invisible gardener.' So they set up a barbed-wire fence. They electrify it. They patrol with bloodhounds. (For they remember how H. G. Wells's *The Invisible Man* could be both smelt and touched though he could not be seen.) But no shrieks ever suggest that some intruder has received a shock. No movements of the wire ever betray an invisible climber. The bloodhounds never give cry. Yet still the Believer is not convinced. 'But there is a gardener, invisible, intangible, insensible, to electric shocks, a gardener who has no scent and makes no sound, a gardener who comes secretly to look after the garden which he loves.' At last the Sceptic despairs, 'But what remains of your original assertion? Just how does what you call an invisible, intangible, eternally elusive gardener differ from an imaginary gardener or even from no gardener at all'?"
2. "I am convinced that there is extraterrestrial intelligence somewhere in the universe far beyond the reach of any technology we will ever have. And, of course, they wouldn't care to contact a puny, little species like ours."
3. "The attacks on the World Trade Center on 9/11 were part of a huge government conspiracy. But we'll never be able to hold those responsible to account because they are too good at hiding the evidence. They have all the resources necessary for eliminating any hint of a connection between the US and those plane crashes. They get away clean, and the whole world is duped! Except me, of course. I know the truth."

4. The following is another version of John Wisdom's "Gardener Parable" from Carl Sagan's book, *The Demon-Haunted World* (1996): "A fire-breathing dragon lives in my garage" … "Show me," you say. I lead you to my garage. You look inside and see a ladder, empty paint cans, an old tricycle – but no dragon. "Where's the dragon?" you ask. "Oh, she's right here," I reply, waving vaguely. "I neglected to mention that she's an invisible dragon." You propose spreading flour on the floor of the garage to capture the dragon's footprints. "Good idea," I say, "but this dragon floats in the air." Then you'll use an infrared sensor to detect the invisible fire. "Good idea, but the invisible fire is also heatless." You'll spray-paint the dragon and make her visible. "Good idea, but she's an incorporeal dragon and the paint won't stick." And so on. I counter every physical test you propose with a special explanation of why it won't work.
5. Every time I snap my fingers the entire universe doubles in size, and I mean everything, so there's nothing to compare the now double-sized universe with the original universe. But I tell you, it's true.

9.6 Experiments and Other Tests

Testing is often one of the features of modern science hailed as rendering it superior to other forms of inquiry and other ways human beings advance claims about the world. Indeed, testing is crucial to empirical science. So, if empirical testing is so important to scientific methods, what is testing? Here are a few dimensions of testing critical thinkers ought to keep in mind when evaluating scientific (and non-scientific) claims.

Controls and variables

One of the most important requirements of a scientific test is to isolate the factor that is to be tested. Consider the following hypothesis: *higher levels of carbon dioxide in the atmosphere will result in higher atmospheric temperatures.* To test this, an experimenter must be able to isolate carbon dioxide levels and vary them independently of other variables. So far as possible, all potentially relevant factors should be kept the same except the CO_2 levels (the factor that's being tested). To do this, we might acquire two samples of atmosphere that are exactly the same in composition, volume, pressure, container, and the amount of sunlight to which each is exposed. We could, at that point, take an initial reading of temperature in each sample. Then we might add carbon dioxide to one sample while leaving the other unchanged. We would then take subsequent readings of temperature, comparing the samples to see if temperature changes with the addition of carbon dioxide. If the temperature rises, the hypothesis is confirmed (or at least not yet falsified). (See 6.8 and Mill's Method of Concomitant Variation.)

In this experiment, the temperature is called the *dependent variable*. It's the component of the experiment that we expect to be changed by altering the factor upon which we hypothesize it depends (the CO_2). Our hypothesis says that the temperature of the sample will change because it's dependent upon CO_2 levels. CO_2 is, in contrast, the *independent variable*. It is the factor changed by the experimenter and is not contingent or dependent upon the dependent variable (if it is, our experiment won't tell us anything new about our hypothesis). It must, of course, be independent.

This type of experiment is called a "controlled" experiment because the independent variable is varied while many other factors are held fixed. The sample where no independent variables are varied is called the *control group*. The sample in which the independent variable is varied is called the *experimental group*. To test the effectiveness of a new medicine in a controlled way, therefore, an experimenter would need two groups of patients that are alike in every way except that one receives the claimed medicine to be tested (the experimental group) and one does not (the control group). Constructing a controlled experiment isn't easy – though, as you can probably see, it's much easier to conduct controlled experiments in laboratories than in the outside world. Indeed, constructing controlled experiments is one of the principal reasons laboratories exist. Moreover, it's very difficult to conduct controlled experiments on people, given the tremendous variety among human beings. Putting together samples that are exactly the same and remain exactly the same except for a single factor is simply a tall order and is one reason science is so difficult.

Epidemiological studies

People are difficult to get into the laboratory, and they don't always comply with the rules of controlled experiment. It would be immoral to force them to stay there or to be treated in ways likely to harm them (forcing them to smoke or experience tragedy). So, in studying people it's often desirable just to examine the way they live in the world. You've probably heard about studies finding that eating low fat diets containing fish, garlic, and olive oil are good for your heart. For the most part, this wasn't discerned through controlled laboratory studies but by examining what people actually eat all over the world. Researchers noticed that large groups of people with high olive oil, low fat, and high fish consumption, such as the Japanese and those living in the Mediterranean, experience lower rates of heart disease than groups with different kinds of diets.

In these cases, people have already experienced the independent variable; to see whether this variable is correlated with the outcome we hypothesize, we compare these groups with people who haven't experienced the independent variable. This backward-looking type of study is called an *epidemiological* or *retrospective* study.

Epidemiological studies are not as strong as experiments with more controls for isolating specific causal factors, and so it's quite possible that the lower rates of heart disease among fish- and olive oil-eating populations are the result of something else (a lurking variable). Perhaps it's just a matter of genetics. The findings of epidemiological studies, however, are a good place to start looking for hypotheses that can be tested in labs or at least in more controlled conditions. What changes might occur if some testable population of, say, Scots moved to a Mediterranean diet? Sometimes, of course, epidemiological studies offer the best that's possible given the constraints of morality and human conduct.

Personal experience and case studies

Upon visiting a health food store, Peter met a clerk who swore that eating shark cartilage had cured his cancer. How did the clerk know? It was his personal experience, he said. He took the shark cartilage, and his cancer went into remission. We greet stories like this frequently in life. Typically, personal experience, however, is not taken to be adequate proof of very much, scientifically speaking. There are lots of reasons for this. For one thing, we are subject to many kinds of biases and cognitive distortions (the subject of Chapter 7). We deceive ourselves, we see what we want to see, and we miss a lot in experience. It's also just very difficult to sort out all the different factors that may contribute to an event, and especially a medical cure. The human body is complex, and we live in environments where we are exposed to thousands of different compounds daily. The body of the clerk with whom Peter spoke may have healed itself (spontaneous or natural remission happens in a remarkably high number of cancers). There may have been some compound in his environment that helped cure him. The original diagnosis may have been in error. On a more formal level, a sample of one is much too small on the basis of which to draw conclusions as general as "shark cartilage cures cancer." As we saw in 6.4, samples to be tested must be of an adequate size, randomized, stratified, perhaps studied in longitudinal ways (across long periods of time) – and, of course, the outcomes produced by experimental samples must be contrasted with control groups. Experiments, ideally, should be repeated, too.

Strictly speaking, even the personal experiences of physicians with their patients are not adequate as the bases of scientific conclusions. Such one-off experiences are called *anecdotal evidence*, and we cannot rationally infer from one or two instances something about whole populations. Physicians are highly skilled in the arts of diagnosis. They must be deeply informed about anatomy and the many ailments to which people are subject, as well as the many ways those ailments present themselves in different people. But physicians are subject to just the same biases and distortions as the rest of us. Having done what many of us cannot and produced an accurate diagnosis, a physician should not attempt to do on the basis of personal experience alone what only research scientists are competent to do – namely conclude what treatments are most effective for that illness. A physician's prescription should be evidence based – that is, based upon the findings of controlled, repeated scientific experiments – so far as possible. Physicians' and other healthcare givers' experiences with treatments are called, when recorded and organized, "case studies." Case studies, like personal experiences and epidemiological studies, are good starting points for developing hypotheses to test in rigorous, scientific ways. And recently there has even been increasing pressure to think of case studies as a weaker but still important kind of testing. But nothing beats a controlled scientific experiment to decide questions about matters of fact.

Blinding and double blinding

It may sound strange to suggest that good science sometimes requires blinding people, even in a metaphorical sense. After all, science is normally taken to help us see the world more clearly. But blinding is often regarded as necessary when experiments involve human beings. It's an admission that human subjectivity and beliefs may have some effect upon perception.

"Blinding" involves keeping human subjects of an experiment in the dark, so to speak, about whether or not they have been subjected to the factor being tested, or whether they are part of the control group. As an example, Teri has agreed to take part in an experiment testing a new analgesic medicine. Upon coming down with a headache, Teri takes the pill that had been distributed by the experiment staff and then gives a report on its effectiveness. Teri, like the other participants in the experiment, knows she's in an experiment, but she doesn't know whether the pill she received is the medicine or a dose of sugar. She is, in a sense, blind to what she has received. That's important because of what researchers call the *placebo effect*. The placebo effect occurs when people report a positive result from a medicine they believe they have received even when they have not really received it – that is, even when they have received only a placebo. The effect is related to *wishful thinking* (see 7.2). People wish for the medicines prescribed them to be effective. That wish can affect the way people interpret what they feel subjectively. (Some critics think that the placebo effect accounts for much more of the positive regard for the drugs prescribed for mental illness than is commonly understood.)

Blinding does not eliminate wishful thinking, but the procedure makes it possible for testers to factor it out of experimental results. When the results come in, rather than simply count positive outcomes, experimenters only need look for whether or not there is a significant difference between the results of the subjects who received the placebo and the subjects who really received the tested factor. This, of course, assumes the placebo effect and wishful thinking are distributed evenly across the experimental population.

Another form of blinding is called "double blinding." In double blinding, both the subject and the person administering the factor are kept in the dark about who's received the experimental therapy and who's received only a sugar pill or salt water. That's because the body language, facial expressions, and tone of voice of the person administering the therapy might give away the truth to patients. You may have heard, for example, about the famous case of "Clever Hans." Hans was a horse whose owner (and many others) was convinced could do basic arithmetic. But as it turned out, careful observation discovered that the owner was making quite unconscious facial gestures that Hans was correctly interpreting. Hans would stroke out the answer with his hoof, pawing one, two, three, etc., until the answer to the math problem was reached.

But when the answer was reached the owner would physically react, raising his eyebrows, widening his eyes, leaning forward, etc. Hans would stop pawing there and receive a welcome reward – perhaps a sugar cube! Sometimes people are as smart as horses, and researchers need to protect their experiments from the sorts of errors the reading of body language can introduce.

In vitro studies

One thing case studies and epidemiological studies have going for them, however, is that they deal with people as they live in the world. Labs are artificial environments – necessarily so. And as such they may miss something of the synergies and interfering, magnifying, intersecting causal networks that compose the world and that produce the phenomena in which scientists are interested. So, some therapies that work in the lab may be stifled by factors in play out in the world. Popular household cleaners may react with, say, anti-cancer drugs.

Experiments done in the lab are, therefore, often done "*in vitro*" (from the Latin for "in glass") – that is, in petri dishes, test tubes, vials, and beakers – in isolation from the hundreds of thousands of compounds that compose the human body and its normal environment. The strength of *in vitro* studies is that scientists can bracket out the possible influence of those other potential factors and isolate the independent variable. The weakness, however, is that a drug that effectively diminishes the activity of cancer cells in a petri dish may not do so in the human body precisely because of the way it interacts with those many other factors in the real world – and vice versa. *In vitro* studies may, therefore, seem a good place to start, but remember that a drug that doesn't work "in the glass," so to speak, might actually work in a living body because of those same unknown but crucial interactions. In cases like that, *in vitro* experiments may actually mask a drug's beneficial effects.

Non-human animal studies

Similar problems (and advantages) arise with studies conducted on non-human animals such as rats and mice. It's a lot easier to work with mice, and since most people don't mind mice dying in the course of studies the way they'd object to human mortality, rats and mice can be subjected to various compounds and treatments we would find immoral (and illegal) to administer to people. But the very thing that has made it permissible to conduct experiments on non-humans also raises questions about the scientific value of studies involving them – namely, that non-humans are different from humans. As any veterinarian will tell you, drugs that may be effective in treating diseases afflicting mice may be ineffective in treating even the same disease in human beings. And, vice versa, treatments that fail in non-humans may succeed in humans. Aspirin can be toxic to cats, for example, and chocolate in substantial quantities is toxic for dogs. Researchers using non-humans must be very careful, therefore, that the sorts of biochemical mechanisms they examine are, in fact, sufficiently similar across species and that no intervening factors are at play in one subject species but not in others.

There are, moreover, continuing controversies about the moral propriety of experimenting on living non-humans, too, even in cases where it's scientifically valuable to use them. Good critical thinkers will consider that issue. Remember that Nazi experiments on their prisoners did yield real scientific results, but it doesn't for that reason make those experiments or others like them morally permissible. A number of European countries (Netherlands, Austria, Sweden, the UK, Germany) and New Zealand have banned the use of "great apes" or, more precisely, family *hominidae* (chimpanzees and bonobos, gorillas, orang-utans) as well as humans in various forms of experimentation. The United States seems to be reducing the scope of its use of non-humans in experimental contexts, as well. The US National Institutes for Health (NIH), for example, announced in 2013 its decision to comply with the recommendations of the Institute of Medicine (IoM) and dramatically reduce its use of primates in scientific studies. Science is a human practice like any other, and human practices are governed by moral considerations. What counts as moral and immoral scientific practice, as well as what counts as strong and weak science, is a complex and rich subject with which critical thinkers should remain engaged.

SEE ALSO

8.1 Knowledge: The Basics
8.6 Justification: The Basics
9.7 Six Criteria for Abduction

READING

John Wright, *Explaining Science's Success* (2014)
Hans Radder, *The Philosophy of Scientific Experimentation* (2003)
Samir Okasha, *Philosophy of Science: A Very Short Introduction* (2002)

9.7 Six Criteria for Abduction

Abduction? No, we're not talking about kidnapping but, rather, an important set of considerations for deciding among multiple possible explanations. The term "abduction" was coined first by the philosopher Charles Sanders Peirce (1839–1914) for this kind of thinking. Because the word "abduction" seems so odd, people often just call these procedures *inference to the best explanation*. They have been developed because, contrary to what many people believe, evidence and scientific data don't always point to a single explanation.

Consider, for example, the serious illness called AIDS. AIDS is a "syndrome" or a collection of symptoms and conditions. The scientific community has so far settled on an infectious virus, HIV, as the explanation for the emergence of that syndrome. But other explanations are possible. Consider, for example, that some have explained the disease as a punishment by God for human sin, in particular the sin of homosexual sex. Consider, too, that rather than causing the disease, HIV might just be part of the AIDS syndrome such that HIV infection might itself be the result of a deeper common cause (see 6.3). Perhaps people's chakras or humors are out of balance. Perhaps there is a still unknown biological condition that produces illness. Perhaps some evil scientist or the CIA has developed a machine that can strike people down with this syndrome from a great distance. How is one to decide? One's immediate instinct is to appeal to the empirical evidence. But what if it's the case, as French physicist Pierre Duhem and US philosopher W. V. O. Quine have argued, that no matter how much evidence we amass there will always be possible alternative explanations. In part for reasons we saw in 9.4 and 9.5, Duhem and Quine argue that no body of evidence can fully determine our truth claims.

Don't worry, though. In the face of the limits of empirical evidence to decide among possible explanations, inquirers have developed a number of criteria you can use to decide what is the "best" explanation available. There remains some controversy about what standards are relevant, but the following set reflects a large consensus of thinkers.

1. *Predictive Power.* Explanations that offer greater predictive power are better than those that offer less. The HIV theory seems to be a better predictor of who will contract AIDS than the theory of divine punishment, since there is a much tighter correlation between HIV infection and AIDS than there seems to be between "sin" and AIDS. The evil scientist theory of AIDS doesn't even seem to allow for prediction at all, since we are unable to observe the operations of either the machine or the evil scientist. Untreated HIV infection, in fact, seems closer than any other explanation to describing a *nearly sufficient* and *necessary condition* for contracting AIDS. That is, if one contracts HIV, then in the absence of treatment one faces a rather high likelihood of AIDS; and if one has AIDS, then it is almost certain that one is infected with HIV. (You can see a bit more here about why the logical considerations of sufficient and necessary conditions we explored in 2.2 are so important.)
2. *Scope.* Theories that cover more phenomena are preferred to those that are less comprehensive. So, Einstein's physics is thought to be stronger than Newton's because it explains physical phenomena at large, medium, and subatomic scales at any speed, while Newton's theories don't seem to be able to explain the behavior of very massive or very tiny and very fast things at all. Similarly, the HIV explanation of AIDS is part of the more comprehensive germ theory of disease, a theory that has been able to explain an enormous variety of human illnesses. One might, of course, hold that all disease, or perception of disease, flows from divine or supernatural causes, as perhaps Christian Scientists do. That

would be an explanation of pretty large scope. But for most, the divine punishment theory of disease is limited in its scope to a relatively restricted number of afflictions.

3. *Coherence with Established Fact.* We've already seen in our discussion of "paradigms" that sometimes claims and hypotheses that do not fit with current science – e.g., Galileo's conclusions – end up later being accepted as true. In general, however, what fits with established fact and theory is preferable to what does not. Science often assumes that the order of reality or nature is coherent, systematic, and logically consistent. If that's true, then a patchwork of incompatible theories to explain the world isn't desirable. Better to work toward a comprehensive science where various sectors of explanation all fit together to compose one great, consistent, and unified theory of the world. The HIV theory seems to fit better than others with what people have discovered about other similar diseases – namely, that viruses or bacteria cause them. The evil scientist theory and the divine punishment theory fit less well.
4. *Repeatability.* Science, as we've seen, relies on various forms of testing. All things being equal, theories confirmed through tests that are repeated and repeatable are preferable to those that are not. One might even say as a general principle that: "A single test does not a fact establish." Single experiments have found correlations between prayer and recovery. Repeated and multiple tests have produced inconsistent results. The relatively tight correlation between HIV infection and AIDS, however, has been observed over and over.
5. *Simplicity.* This criterion is often associated with medieval philosopher William of Ockham (1288–1347) and the principle known as "Ockham's Razor." For our purposes, the idea is that the best explanation is the simplest. By simplicity, we mean the fewest kinds of causal factors (whether physical or metaphysical) or the fewest unproven theoretical commitments. So, the HIV theory of AIDS implies at most the existence of the natural, biological world. The divine punishment theory implies the existence of that world plus the existence of God. The former theory is therefore simpler.

   Simplicity, however, may also apply even to the positing of entities within a given metaphysical framework. So, the evil genius argument requires adding to the world technologies that have been so far unknown, while the HIV theory requires no additions.

   Of course, the weakness of this standard can be seen in the thought that the world just might not be a simple place. As a matter of characterizing good explanation, then, we might better think of the simplicity standard as one of caution, as a caveat. Ockham's principle requires not that one should never add complications to an explanatory theory but only that one should not do so unless it's rationally necessary or there's some other compelling scientific reason to do so. In other words, keep theories simple and limited until the evidence compels you do otherwise. When thinking critically, look for excesses in a theory under scrutiny. What can it deal without? Are there other, simpler theories that might explain the phenomena just as well? When Napoleon asked Simon Laplace (1749–1827) why his book on celestial mechanics did not refer to God, the scientist did not answer with the metaphysical claim that God does not exist. Instead, appealing to the principle of explanatory simplicity, Laplace is reported to have simply said, "*je n'ai pas eu besoin de cette hypothèse*" ("I had no need of that hypothesis").

6. *Fruitfulness*. Theories are more "fruitful" when they make possible more hypotheses to test and when they encourage more testing. The germ theory of infection has made possible immense fields of scientific research into microbiology, biochemistry, and pharmaceuticals. The divine punishment theory has opened up fewer possibilities for testing. Yes, it's possible to test whether refraining from sinning changes one's likelihood of being afflicted with AIDS, but the HIV theory in contrast leads to vastly more avenues of investigation into the biological and natural worlds. Moreover, the HIV theory not only opens the possibility of new lines of inquiry, it encourages them. The divine punishment theory, however, instead resists additional testing and encourages what we've seen is called "falsification resistance." While the emergence of AIDS in populations that don't engage in homosexual sex and its control among homosexuals by practicing safe gay sex might be seen to falsify the idea that AIDS is a punishment for sin, those committed to the punishment theory readily find ways to explain the falsification away. Perhaps God accomplished His objectives already; perhaps God created HIV as a warning of the sort of thing that would be coming in the afterlife. Perhaps everyone who contracts AIDS deserves it, but not only for homosexuality. The facility with which explanations that appeal to the divine evade falsification renders them difficult and perhaps impossible to assess in scientific ways. That resistance to falsification may be something important for critical thinkers to remember about religious controversies.

SEE ALSO

6.3 Fallacies about Causation
9.4 Scientific Method
9.6 Experiments and Other Tests

READING

Douglas Walton, *Abductive Reasoning* (2014)
Mark Battersby, *Is that a Fact? A Field Guide to Statistical and Scientific Information*, revised edn (2013)
Atocha Aliseda, *Abductive Reasoning: Logic Investigations into Discovery and Explanation* (2006)
Peter Lipton, *The Inference to Best Explanation* (2004)

9.8 Bad Science

The terms "junk science," "pseudo-science," and "fringe science" are more and less pejorative. They suggest that whatever is named by the term is not strong, solid, or authentic science.

Junk science

The label "junk science" suggests that the supposed science in question is flawed or distorted because of ideological, financial, or otherwise political interests, etc. Findings claiming to show that human activity is causing the Earth to warm and the climate to change have been attacked as "junk science." The critics charge that climate scientists have skewed their findings in order to advance an environmental, political, and economic agenda as well as to secure both grant money and institutional status. In 2011, Pennsylvania senator Rick Santorum, for example, proclaimed on the Rush Limbaugh radio show, "It's just an excuse for more government control of your life.... And I've never ... accepted the junk science behind the whole narrative." Of course, defenders of climate change sometimes argue that financial and political interests in the fossil fuel industries motivate critics of anthropogenic (i.e., human-caused) climate change. Supporters of the theory of anthropogenic climate warming have, for example, suggested that the work of Harvard-Smithsonian scientist Willie Soon, which suggests that the Sun is the principal cause of climate change, may be junk of this sort because his studies have been largely funded by the energy industry (see 5.4 on the *ad hominem* circumstantial fallacy).

Pseudo-science

The term "pseudo-science" is less politically charged and points to claims and theories that claim to be scientific but actually are not. Those claims fail to be properly scientific, however, typically not because of the distorting influence of money and power but rather because they are not well grounded in scientific procedures. Often what is today called pseudo-science comprises fields of inquiry that in the past presented themselves sincerely as new and real sciences but were then later jettisoned by the scientific community.

Consider a few examples. Phrenologists claimed to be able to discern psychological and moral propensities of people by examining the bumps on their heads. Eugenicists and racial biologists argued that controlled human breeding and the cultivation of racial "purity" could eliminate all kinds of social problems, including poverty and crime. Mesmerists, following the theories of Franz Mesmer (1734–1815), manipulated their hands around patients to alter energy fields and to affect their patients through hypnotic-like suggestion. Practitioners of therapies grounded in theories about

Animal Magnetism, a spinoff of Mesmer's theories, believed that people are pervaded by magnetic fields the manipulation of which with magnets can produce healthful effects. Scientists devoted to the therapy developed by Austrian farmer Vincent Priessnitz (1799–1851) and called by him "hydropathy" maintained that immersing patients in cold water improved their mental as well as physical health. All of these practices were candidates for genuine science, but the results of testing and scrutiny of their methods and concepts disconfirmed them. Ayurvedic therapies, homeopathy, and Chinese Traditional Medicine have often been characterized as pseudo-scientific, too, for similar reasons.

Fringe science

You may be familiar with the television show *Fringe*, in which a special division of the FBI uses exotic scientific ideas to solve crime. And, indeed, "fringe" science often sits on that vague boundary separating science fiction and fantasy and New Age superstition from authentic science. While fields such as phrenology and racial biology arose and were discarded, other scientific theories that at first appeared strange and even bizarre have moved from the "fringe" (or extreme minority positions) to the center, often only after overcoming substantial opposition. The heliocentric views of Copernicus are perhaps the most stunning example of this kind of shift. But views related to "dark matter," black holes, and the multiverse (i.e., the idea that ours is just one of many universes) have also moved from fringe to center. Ideas like "worm holes," cosmic strings, time travel, telekinesis, artificial life, and using intention to change causal systems remain today at the fringe, but who knows where they'll stand tomorrow? That some science is called "fringe" indicates both its apparent strangeness and the small degree to which it has so far been accepted. Calling a science fringe, however, does not directly imply that it is flawed. At its most critical, it implies only that it's suspect. The critic who calls a form of science "fringe" implicitly allows that in the future it may well no longer be so.

Good critical thinkers will approach these characterizations of theories with care and will understand that both science and critics of science can be influenced by politics and money. Critical thinkers will also appreciate that those who doubted Galileo later to their chagrin understood that what is today diminished as fringe may someday be accepted as sound. Critical thinkers, however, will also be careful to remember that there's been a lot of bad and pseudo-science foisted upon the world. Scrutiny and reflective vigilance can separate the bad from the good, but it takes care, diligence, and sometimes even courage to do so.

Ideological science

There is some question as to whether science can be free of ideology, but whether or not it can be, it's clear that sometimes ideology produces bad science. *Racial science* is perhaps the best example of the problems ideology can wreak in science. The racist background beliefs of scientists arguably affected the way many scientists interpreted anatomy and social data well into the twentieth century, perhaps still today. Nazi scientists offered physical evidence for the inferiority of Jews, and Anglo-American scientists offered empirical proof of the inferiority of "negroes." Feminist critics have found sexist language and biased inferences in biological research. In 1927, as a result of scientific arguments influenced by the ideology of social Darwinism, the US Supreme Court (*Buck v. Bell*) authorized compulsory sterilization programs in rural Virginia and elsewhere. Most of the sterilization efforts were directed at poor white women as people deemed biologically and socially inferior or "unfit" – though others, e.g., Native American women, were sterilized, as well. *Tens of thousands* of otherwise healthy people were for eugenics reasons sterilized in the US (the largest number in California), and the US programs became a model for those in Nazi Germany, where through the influence of the ideology of Aryan supremacy forced sterilization was expanded.

SEE ALSO

9.2 The Purview of Science
9.7 Six Criteria for Abduction
10.10 Feminist and Gender Critiques
10.11 Critiques of Race and Racism
10.13 Ecological Critiques

READING

Kevin R. Grazier, ed., *Fringe Science: Parallel Universes, White Tulips, and Mad Scientists* (2011)
Lynne McTaggart, *The Intention Experiment* (2008)
Steven J. Milloy, *Junk Science Judo* (2001)
Arthur Wrobel, *Pseudo-Science and Society in Nineteenth-Century America* (1987)

NOTE

1. The phrase "*ad hoc*" does not have this negative connotation in every context. In Latin, it means "to this," or, more smoothly, "for this" or "for the purpose." It is often used to describe committees that are formed to serve a single, short-term purpose, such as a hiring committee. After someone has been hired for a position, the *ad hoc* hiring committee will be dissolved. The alternative to the *ad hoc* committee is the *standing* committee, which is ongoing and may serve a number of purposes, for instance, a hospitality committee.

10 Tools from Rhetoric, Critical Theory, and Politics

10.1 Meta-Narratives

Here's a story about a student named Asli. Asli works her way through a critical thinking text and improves her ways of thinking, talking, writing, and living in general. She starts off lonely, rather poor, and not terribly critical in the way she goes about things. But by the time she's finished the book, she's acquired an exciting new set of concepts and skills that lead her to engage in a critical way with everything from the news to Hollywood films to her university assignments. She flourishes, becomes wealthy, respected, admired, popular, powerful, and immortal, capable of traversing and even manipulating space and time by mere act of will.

Despite its rather implausible ending, one might say that the story here is of the sort that has guided the writing and publication of this book. The story, as Aristotle says of all good stories, has a sequential beginning, middle, and end, ordering particular events and investing them with meaning. But stories aren't just about particular people or events (this isn't just the story of Asli the critical thinker). They also possess general forms and features that resonate through our cultures. Philosopher and critic Jean-François Lyotard (1924–1998) articulated important ways to think about the stories that order and invest meaning in our culture. In his explosive 1979 book, *The Post-Modern Condition*, he called these "meta-narratives" or "grand narratives."

Stories that govern stories plus a whole lot more

"Meta-" is a prefix deriving from ancient Greek, and it means "beyond," "across," "throughout," or "of a higher order." The term "metaphysics," as it's typically used in philosophy, is concerned with the concepts that underwrite all of physics: all that physics assumes about the nature of reality and all that composes the most general, basic, and pervasive dimensions of physics. So, while physicists might be

The Critical Thinking Toolkit, First Edition. Galen A. Foresman, Peter S. Fosl, and Jamie C. Watson.

concerned with the particular laws governing the causal interactions of specific beings, metaphysicians are concerned with being, time, causation, and lawfulness themselves.

According to Lyotard, the modern world has been ordered by one very general meta-narrative – the story of reason progressively overcoming myth. As a meta-narrative or grand narrative, this story informs and structures many of the stories we use to make sense of our lives. Our lives as knowers are ordered by the story of science progressively overcoming ignorance and superstition by disclosing the true features of reality. As a result, our political lives gain meaning as part of the story of our progressively and rationally overcoming oppressive customs and traditions through various kinds of liberation – e.g., ending slavery, extending the franchise to women, legitimizing unions, learning to tolerate different religions, expanding the institutions of marriage, and so on. You know the story.

Governing, varying, and disintegrating narratives

How is all this related to critical thinking? Well, for one thing, meta-narratives not only give us templates to structure and lend meaning to our lives; they also govern us in practice by ordering people's values, conduct, and judgments. For this reason, some refer to meta-narratives as "master-narratives," and as critical thinkers we ought to assess whether or not the "masters" that govern us do so well: whether they ought to be sustained, or whether we ought to dismantle or deconstruct them and replace them with something else (or nothing at all). Thinkers belonging to what's called the Frankfurt School (see 10.8) along with various postmodern and post-structuralist critics have argued, in fact, that modern conceptions of reason have led to all kinds of undesirable practices and events – from the rise of the National Socialism to racism and cultural imperialism. Lyotard himself argued that the attempt to impose a way of thinking and acting upon others who don't order their lives through it lies at the heart of injustice. Partly as a result, post-modernity is characterized by the disintegration of not only the modern meta-narrative but of all of them.

Thinking critically, then, can involve scrutinizing meta-narratives. First, figure out just what meta-narratives are in play, and then assess what sort of posture to take toward them – subversive, sustaining, or otherwise. Lyotard identified the modern meta-narrative of *progressive rationality*, but we'd like to suggest you consider a few others.

Fall and Return: Christianity and communism (as well as the work of philosophers as diverse as Hume and Wittgenstein) share in what might be called a narrative of fall and return, of first losing something important, then finding oneself in a dark, diminished, or negative condition, and then finally achieving a kind of redemption or restoration. The story here isn't from "lower to higher" but from high to low and then back to high. A wound is inflicted and then healed, leaving one perhaps even better off. An evil emerges but is then vanquished. This form typifies many hero tales, like the American story of World War II.

Gain and Loss . . . and Gain? This meta-narrative first finds things improving but then becoming worse, perhaps much worse. Environmentalists often enlist this kind of narrative to describe modernity and industrialization. The ancient tragedy of Oedipus follows this pattern, as does the story of Icarus. In this pattern first there is an upward trajectory, but then things go downhill very badly. What follows the ending, or rather closing, is left open. The story feels unfinished in important ways. Will their final decisions lead to gain or loss? It's a form characteristic of cautionary tales and tragedies.

There are many other meta-narratives, too: adversity and triumph; suspicion and disclosure; pollution and purification; integration and disintegration – most variants and recombinants of others. Of course, meta-narratives sometimes overlap and reinforce one another. Sometimes they clash and conflict, perhaps more so as time goes on. It's going to take capable critical thinkers not only to identify and untangle the meta-narratives governing our world but also to plumb their effects and their value. Is it possible for the world to be meaningful without meta-narratives? What meta-narrative governs the story of meta-narratives itself? If everything is governed by a meta-narrative, is there any place left for justified belief or knowledge? If meta-narratives leave no room for justification or knowledge, is this a reason to be suspicious of justification and knowledge, or is it a reason to be suspicious of the idea that meta-narratives govern our language? If they do leave room for justification and knowledge, how might we know?

Exercises and study questions

1. What is the meta-narrative of the *Star Wars* saga? How does it compare to the meta-narrative of modernity as Lyotard understands it?
2. Compare the meta-narratives of *Dr. Who* and *Star Trek*.
3. What is the meta-narrative of post-War Europe in the discourse of contemporary popular culture?
4. What is the meta-narrative of Africa in Europe and North America? Can you find any indication that Africans have a different meta-narrative of Africa?
5. Compare the meta-narratives governing ecological and economic discourses.
6. Compare the meta-narrative of *Moby Dick* and modern industrial society.
7. What is the meta-narrative of Augustine's *Confessions*? Compare that meta-narrative with Rousseau's *Confessions*, Montaigne's *Essays*, and Ralph Ellison's *Invisible Man*.

SEE ALSO

10.2 Governing Tropes
10.3 The Medium is the Message
10.5 Semiotics: Critically Reading Signs

READING

Sandra Baringer, *The Metanarratives of Suspicion in Late Twentieth-Century America* (2004)
John Stephens & Robyn McCallum, *Retelling Stories, Framing Culture: Traditional Story and Metanarratives in Children's Literature* (1998)
Jean-François Lyotard, *The Post-Modern Condition: A Report on Knowledge* [1979], trans. Geoff Bennington and Brian Massumi (1984)

10.2 Governing Tropes

"Fidel Castro is the Josef Stalin of the Caribbean."
"Capitalism is a jungle."
"It was a come-to-Jesus moment for everyone in the office."

Thinking critically involves thinking logically and having at one's disposal the capacity for analyzing the validity and soundness (or strength and cogency) of arguments and explanations. Critical thinking, however, also comprises knowledge of rhetorical thinking, including the capacity to discern and assess the rhetorical and poetic devices used to advance ideas and conclusions.

Meta-narratives are rhetorical instruments that guide the direction of people's thought, language, and conduct toward specific endpoints. But meta-narratives aren't the only kind of rhetorical instruments at work in (and on) our lives. Others are commonly known as poetic or rhetorical tropes, especially when they recur in a text. When they are centrally important to the meaning or objectives of a text, they may be thought of as "governing tropes." The word "trope" derives from the Greek *tropos* or "turning," and tropes may be thought of as figures of speech that are used to turn thinking in specific, often calculated ways. The following are some of the most important.

Simile, analogy, metaphor, and allegory

Simile

A text enlists a simile when it simply maintains that something is "like" or similar to something else – that *X* is like *Y*. Nothing is, of course, exactly like anything else (otherwise they wouldn't be different things). So, when two or more things are claimed to be "like" one another, a critical thinker should ask: *in what sense are they similar and does this similarity really hold?* But the critical thinker should also ask: *in what sense(s) are these things different, and why has this simile been selected?* Typically, similes are used to clarify or illuminate an idea, for example, "When the sauce is properly prepared, it will have a consistency very much like that of molasses."

Analogy

Analogies, like similes, hold that things are like one another in specific ways – but pointedly so, typically not just to clarify an idea, as a simple simile might, but also to advance a claim, even in service of an inference leading to the conclusion of some argument. For example, a text might characterize an opponent's strategy as analogous to the Maginot Line, arguing that therefore one can get around it (without meaning that the strategy is actually an expensive but ineffective French military fortification). Logicians often speak of drawing conclusions this way as "arguments from analogy." Arguments from analogy can be challenged by either (1) disputing the similarities upon which the analogy turns – or by (2) claiming that various differences override the similarities. (See 6.2.)

Metaphor

Metaphors expose particular properties of the topic under consideration by applying names or attributive words and concepts in unusual contexts, contexts where they don't, in a literal sense, apply. For example, one might speak of pinpointing (itself a metaphor) the linchpin (another) of an argument. Of course, what's been identified isn't an actual steel pin inserted through the end of an axle to secure a wheel but instead an idea, premise, or principle that's crucial to the argument under consideration.

Allegory

Allegories are images – verbal, visual, or musical – usually of a narrative sort, that symbolically portray or suggest something beyond themselves, often something unmentioned or not named directly, and often with some moral content. Plato's cave is a famous allegory of the philosopher's acquisition of wisdom and his or her relationship to non-philosophers. George Orwell's *Animal Farm* is an allegory of the rise and degeneration of modern Marxist-Stalinist governments. The British Union Jack flag presents an allegory of the United Kingdom – English, Scottish, and Irish – united and interwoven. The "Conference of the Birds," the poems of Rumi, and the "Song of Solomon" present allegories of the soul's love and longing for God.

Metonymy and synecdoche

Metonymy

The word "metonymy" is of Greek derivation and means "a change of name." Metonymy works by designating something by a term usually applied to one of its attributes or something associated with it. A monarch is often referred to as "the crown." That weapons are called "arms" stems from metonymic usage.

A related trope, *antonomasia*, uses proper and figurative names to guide an attribution. The founding political figures of the US are often, for example, called founding "fathers" to cultivate affection and respect for them, just as Mustafa Kemal is called "Ataturk" or "father Turk." Someone might be called intelligent by calling him or her an "Einstein." Someone who's betrayed another's trust might be called a "Judas."

Synecdoche

The word "synecdoche" derives from the Greek for simultaneous understanding, and a synecdoche, sometimes thought of as a specific kind of metonymy, is a rhetorical trope that designates a whole by one of its parts or vice versa. A police officer might be referred to as "the law," for example. One might call a steer a "head" of cattle (even though there's more to the animal than a head). The US financial sector is often just called, "Wall Street," even though it is far more extensive. A bodyguard might be referred to as "the muscle." You get the idea. Strong critical thinkers will be sensitive to the poetic and rhetorical tropes at work in any text they confront, how they may bias or lead readers, thereby turning their thinking and acting in one direction or another.

It's important to recognize these tropes as tropes because that way we will be less likely to confuse them with testable descriptions of reality. Plato was skeptical of artists because their use of metaphor and allegory was more likely to mislead people about the nature of reality than to help them understand it. Tropes reveal important features of reality, but not in precise, logical ways. Much interpretation and clarification is required before we can draw strong inferences from them.

Exercises and study questions

1. What tropes govern your national anthem?
2. What are the implications of the use of the word, "Father," in relation to God? Would it be different to use "mother" or some other trope?
3. What tropes are at work in the *Terminator* films? In the *Twilight* books and films?
4. Interpret the tropes used by L. Frank Baum in his 1900 novel, *The Wonderful Wizard of Oz*, and by the filmmakers who produced the 1939 film based on it?
5. What tropes inform *The Yellow Wallpaper*?
6. *The Lord of the Rings* books and films, like Walter Scott's *Ivanhoe*, are said to employ tropes that speak to popular English understandings of the Anglo-Saxon past. How so, and why do those texts continue to attract readers today? Do their tropes somehow connect with or illuminate contemporary life? Compare tropes of *The Lord of the Rings* and *King Lear* in this regard.
7. What tropes inform various super hero comics such as *Batman*, *Superman*, *Avengers*, and *X-Men*?

8. What are some of the most important tropes evident in Plato's work? The Cave, the Ladder of Love, the Chariot of the Soul, the Myth of Er, Atlantis, etc.
9. Do the tropes of *Beowulf* still resonate with contemporary culture? Compare Beowulf with the Dude in *The Big Lebowski* as a hero through the tropes usually associated with heroes.
10. What do characters in *The Canterbury Tales* symbolize? What allegories are at work in those stories? Compare the allegories of *The Canterbury Tales* with those of Dante's *Divine Comedy* or Dostoevsky's *The Brothers Karamazov*.
11. How might John's Apocalypse or the story of the Exodus or the Hijrah be read through poetic and rhetorical tropes?
12. What tropes inform the novel *Huckleberry Finn*? Compare them to those of the *Odyssey*, the *Harry Potter* series, or *Heart of Darkness* and the film, *Apocalypse Now*.

SEE ALSO

8.2 Feelings as Evidence
10.1 Meta-Narratives
10.3 The Medium is the Message
10.5 Semiotics: Critically Reading Signs

READING

Zoltan Kovecses, *Metaphor: A Practical Introduction* (2010)
William M. Keith & Christian O. Lundberg, *The Essential Guide to Rhetoric* (2008)
Mardy Grothe, *I Never Metaphor I Didn't Like* (2008)
George Lakoff & Mark Johnson, *Metaphors We Live By* (2003)
Edward P. J. Corbett & Robert J. Connors, *Classical Rhetoric for the Modern Student* (1999)
Donald Rice, *Rhetorical Poetics* (1983)

10.3 The Medium is the Message

Ideas, thoughts, and texts are, one might variously say, presented or carried or communicated not only through arguments and poetic tropes. They are conveyed by various media – by paintings, drawings, television, cinema, printed texts, song, braille, digital texts, telegraphs, smart phones, and SMS devices.

One might be tempted to think that the various media that transmit meaning are distinct and irrelevant to the ideas and arguments in play, but critical thinkers like Marshall McLuhan have thought otherwise. His famous 1967 book *The Medium is the Massage* (a pun on his famous declaration, "the medium is the message"), published with Quentin Fiore, argues that the medium advances very powerful messages of its own, in some ways messages more important than the overt content.

Cinematic films offer a common example. In the first place it seems perhaps wrong to call this form of media *films* anymore, since so many are produced via digital media and not with film at all. And many of us have become sensitive to changes in expression that have become possible through digital media – not only the tiny recording devices that make films like *Paranormal Activity* and *The Blair Witch Project* possible, but also the powerful CGI (computer generated imagery) of *Avatar*, *Inside Out*, *Tomorrowland*, and *Inception* (a film self-consciously about how the architects of images can change one's ideas). Films are, moreover, edited with cascades of jump cuts and move along in compressed and high-speed ways compared to books. All this, McLuhan argues, alters the way we inhabit space, time, and ourselves.

Beyond McLuhan's analysis, telephones, e-mail, video-conferencing, more so than trains and airplanes, have changed the way we relate to one another in friendships, sexually, as families, in education, and in commercial ways. Our ideas of privacy, of public spaces, of our own personalities have been altered by media, too. Think about how differently relationships among people at a distance unfolded in the past via written letters or via only oral communication. Think of how differently a bowl of fruit is portrayed in a tapestry, in a painting, in a photograph, in a film, and on a computer screen. Think about how different it is to communicate with a friend on the phone, via text messages, via Skype or FaceTime, face to face, through writing with a pencil, or through messages sent by friends.

To gain a handle on all this, philosopher Jacques Lacan used the analogy of the way people sometimes represent themselves not directly but through agents and lawyers. What are the implications, however, if we can't communicate directly but must always enlist some kind of medium (from voice, to writing, to print, to photos, etc.)?

Understanding the ineluctable and actually inescapable quality of media, critical thinkers must engage questions of how the medium affects any message, both in obvious and not so obvious ways. One important way to parse out the effects of a medium is to conduct thought experiments in which the same content is expressed in different ways. For example, take the very sad SPCA (Society for the Prevention of Cruelty to Animals) commercials that show images of abused animals in the context of very sad music. The heart-wrenching medium is supposed to convince you to give to the SPCA. Imagine now, that we change the medium; instead of the sad music and images, someone simply writes that many domestic animals are abused and that the SPCA can help alleviate their suffering. It turns out that the content is the same. This means, in this case, the medium is *not* the message, though the medium helps to motivate people to act a certain way (if they are not aware, perhaps, of the fallacy of appeal to emotion). Alternatively, consider the patriotic feelings that accompany the playing of a national anthem. Though the words are usually about obscure events long past, and not particularly inspiring in themselves, the inspirational content is very much the combination of words and music in a particular historical-sociological context.

Exercises and study questions

1. How have modern communications media affected the human self and human relations?
2. If "the medium is the message," what is the message of Facebook?
3. How did the advent of writing affect human life? How is communication by writing different from voice and other forms of communication?
4. What political effects do various media have in our world?
5. What does it say about human beings that we have developed just the current forms of communication and not others? What modes of communication have been abandoned?
6. Are people who refuse certain modes of communication, for example mobile phones, onto something?

SEE ALSO

10.2 Governing Tropes
10.5 Semiotics: Critically Reading Signs
10.8 The Frankfurt School: Culture Critique

READING

Marshall McLuhan & Quentin Fiore, with illustrations by Shepard Fairey, *The Media is the Massage: An Inventory of Effects* (2005/1967)
Marshall McLuhan, *Understanding Media: Extensions of Man*, critical edition edited by W. Terrence Gordon (2003)

10.4 Voice

Country music legend Johnny Cash, as an old man, recorded a remarkable cover of the Nine Inch Nails rock song, "Hurt." The lyrics are the same, but the voice is entirely different; and that change in voice produces a deep alteration in the meaning of the song. Different meanings emerge from the voice of an older man, from the voice of a country musician, and from a voice that is slower, gentler, sadder, a bit frailer and more experienced, though more exhausted, too. Think about the different meanings the US national anthem, "The Star-Spangled Banner," conveyed when Jimi Hendrix played it.

Parents and teachers can often be overheard admonishing children to use their "indoor voices," reminding us not only that certain kinds of voice are appropriate and inappropriate in different places, times, and circumstances but also reminding us who is the boss. A joke told by an African American comedian about African Americans might take on an utterly different valence if told by an American politician of northern European descent for similar reasons but in different ways.

In short, voice matters. It obviously matters in these contexts, but it matters in contexts of critical thinking, too, though voice as an important element of critical thinking is often under-appreciated.

Vocalized words, of course, can be distinguished from written words in the sense in which the spoken voice is different from writing. So, it can be important to consider whether a given text was first spoken, sung, or written to understand the meanings it has generated and acquired. Martin Luther King Jr.'s famous 1963 "I Have a Dream" speech comes across rather differently, and with much less force, when read on paper rather than spoken aloud. Song lyrics often come across differently when simply read, as do poems. Spoken voices also inflect meanings differently in recordings as opposed to live performances, as any concert-goer will tell you. Think about how differently a marriage proposal might come off when done in person as compared to left on a phone message or delivered as an SMS text or by a third party.

But one can certainly speak of the voice with which something has been written, too. Authors commonly understand what Aristotle wrote in his book on *Rhetoric*: "All people are willing to listen to speeches that harmonize with their own character" (1390a16). More broadly, authors consciously and unconsciously craft the voice of the text they produce in ways related to its meaning, its argument, and its power.

As you read and think critically about a text, ask yourself questions like this: Is the voice of the text authoritative? Is it sincere or ironic? Is it singular or plural? Is it authentic? Whom does this voice think it's addressing? Is the voice reliable and honest, or does it err and dissemble? Does the voice expose or hide the author? Does the voice condescend to its audience, does it address the audience as peers, or does it cloy and flatter? Is it sarcastic? Is it angry, hopeful, bored? Is the voice of the text posturing? Is the voice that of a fictive character or the author's authentic self (assuming that distinction is meaningful)? Is the voice vulnerable or confident, decisive or wishy-washy? Is it positioning itself in a contest or competitive way against some adversary? Is it only showing part of what the author knows or intends? Is there something the voice wishes it could say but can't? Does it express any desires or longings? Must one read between the lines, and has the author offered us a nudge-nudge, wink-wink, suggesting that we should do so? Does the voice have an agenda – conscious or unconscious? Is the voice gendered, does it seem male or female or queer? Does it seem culturally or historically located? Does it speak from a certain racial or class position? We could go on, but you get the point.

The voice of texts often changes between the beginning and the end, and it often does so as a matter of the author's design. For example, David Hume's famous book *A Treatise of Human Nature* (1739) begins with a bold voice, but by the end of Book I the voice of the text is in despair. Why? What does the text mean to convey with this alteration of voice? The *Treatise* also begins with a curious remark, a quote from the Roman historian Tacitus that says: "Seldom are men blessed with times in which they may think what they like, and say what they think." For many interpreters, given the time and place the book was written, Hume's remark comes off as ironic, indicating that in fact he does not, in the text that follows, say everything he thinks. In a complicated text like this, then, critical thinkers have to consider not only what the voice says but also what it's not saying?

One might take shuddering notice of Oscar Wilde's acerbic remark, "Irony is wasted on the stupid." Sometimes, indeed, it's wasted on the smart, as well. As a critical thinker, instead follow Henry James's more positive remark, "Try to be someone on whom nothing is lost."

Exercises and study questions

1. Compare the voice in *Catcher in the Rye* with that of *The Color Purple.*
2. Compare the voice of *The Phenomenology of Spirit* with that of *Thus Spake Zarathustra.*
3. How do the voices in Handel's *Messiah* affect the meaning of the Scriptural passages the piece uses?
4. Compare a speech delivered by Adolf Hitler in the film, *Triumph of the Will*, to a speech by a more recent head of state.
5. Compare the voice of Abraham Lincoln's "Gettysburg Address" to that of Matthew Arnold's poem, "Dover Beach."
6. Compare the voice of one of Shakespeare's sonnets to that of Sappho's poem, "Come Here to Me from Crete."
7. Compare the voice of Hildegard of Bingen's "O viridissima virga" to Beyoncé's "Single Ladies (Put a Ring on It)."
8. Compare the voice of Karl Marx's *Communist Manifesto* to Edmund Burke's *Reflections on the Revolution in France* and to Emma Goldman's "Anarchy: What it Really Stands For."
9. Compare the voice of Mary Wollstonecraft's *A Vindication of the Rights of Woman* to Thomas Paine's *Rights of Man* and to Franz Fanon's *The Wretched of the Earth.*

SEE ALSO

8.4 Emotions and Evidence
10.6 Deconstruction
10.11 Critiques of Race and Racism

READING

Theresa Enos, ed., *Encyclopedia of Rhetoric and Composition* (2013)
Howard Kahane & Nancy Cavender, *Logic and Contemporary Rhetoric* (1997)
C. Jan Swearingen, *Rhetoric and Irony* (1991)

10.5 Semiotics: Critically Reading Signs

At the end of the Coen brothers' 2007 Academy Award-winning film, *No Country for Old Men*, we see the villain, Anton Chigurh, leaving the home of Carla Jean Moss, a woman with whom he's just had a confrontation. The audience knows he has gone there to kill Carla Jean, but the woman offered him a plea for her life, and the film cuts away to her front porch before the audience sees whether he accepts or refuses that plea. Chigurh casually ambles out onto the front porch as if to enjoy the sunny day. Almost offhandedly, he raises first one foot, then the other, to check to see whether there's anything on the bottom of his shoe. It's a telling sign that Chigurh has in fact killed Carla Jean.

It's a sign because it doesn't directly show Chigurh's having killed her. Signs point beyond themselves. They tell us about what is not immediately apparent or present in them. Just as an "Exit" sign points beyond itself to an exit, doorway, or passage, Chigurh's gesture points back beyond the front porch to what has just transpired in the house.

Signs are associated with symbols, and symbols, since they also point or refer beyond themselves, are sometimes thought of as a type of sign. Symbols, however, have the distinctive quality of somehow embodying or making incarnate what they symbolize. So, the word, "Women," on a door in a restaurant is likely to signify the entrance to a toilet designated for female use. A simplified, cutout shape of a human figure wearing a dress fixed to a door in a public space, however, since it visually resembles a woman, instead symbolizes the same thing.

Peirce and Saussure

Various models for the way signs work have been developed by semioticians over the years. Two of the most prominent are the triadic model of Charles Sanders Peirce (1839–1914) and the dyadic model of Ferdinand de Saussure (1857–1913). The study of signs or "semiotics" became prominent, especially among critical thinkers involved in what's come to be known as "cultural studies," through the work of Roland Barthes (1915–1980), Umberto Eco (1932–2016), Julia Kristeva (b. 1941), and Stuart Hall (1932–2014).

For Peirce, signification has three elements: (1) the *sign* itself, (2) the *object* to which it refers, and (3) the *interpretant* who interprets the sign. What's important for critical thinkers to understand in Peirce's model is that signs do not interpret themselves. They must be interpreted or read by people; and, of course, different people read signs differently. A good critical thinker will therefore be attentive to the different ways different interpretants are likely to interpret signs, yes, differently.

Of virgins, ghosts, and cuckolds

People, for example, interpret the color red in many different ways. In M. Night Shyamalan's 1999 film *The Sixth Sense*, red is used to signify the presence of ghosts.

If you ever see a prominent red object in the film, you can bet a ghost is around. For many Chinese people, red represents good luck, and so Chinese doors are often painted red, and traditionally Chinese brides wear red wedding gowns. A red wedding gown among Westerners, however, would generally be unthinkable as red, especially in a dress, in the west commonly signifies sexual availability, even profligacy. Westerners prefer white wedding dresses because they signify sexual purity. White in China can signify death. In religious art, red can signify the blood of martyrs or the Christ, or at bullfights it can signify the anger and violence of the struggle. A Washington State agricultural official with a business delegation in China found out the hard way about the significance of color when he handed out green caps to his hosts only to find none would wear them. He was politely informed that the color green in China signifies being a cuckold. British soccer/football fans know the importance of not wearing the wrong color in the wrong space, as do people in Northern Ireland attending a political march. The wrong color can sometimes provoke a violent response.

Mention of contexts (which means *with-texts*, texts alongside the text) raises what Saussure emphasizes. Saussure's model is apparently simpler than Peirce's, since on its surface it's just "signifiers" and the "signified." The "signifier" for Saussure, however, isn't precisely the material sign (the physical thing hanging on the women's room door); it's the way in which the material object or sound or text is received by someone. And the "signified" isn't the material object to which one of Peirce's signs points but, rather, the idea or concept connected to that signifier.

What's important for critical thinkers to consider from a Saussurian point of departure is that the relationship between signifiers and the concepts that are signified by them isn't isolated. Rather signifiers operate in a vast network of other signifiers, in contrast to which they are differentiated and distinguished. So, to understand any particular signifier (for example, the word "women") is to understand the perhaps vast surrounding network of other signifiers – the network of signs that compose restaurants, homes, schools, epic poems, action movies, university text books, plays, seductions, weddings, dances, etc. No sign is an island.

The semiological problem

The way Saussure looks at it, our whole world is a text composed of various signifiers; or rather everything in the human world is a signifier. And, so, everything must be read and interpreted by positioning each signifier within the network that gives it meaning. One of the ways, then, that Saussure's semiotics can be useful for critical thinkers is as a reminder that to understand any given sign, one must read the context or network in which signifiers gain significance.

What may be even more important, however, is that critical thinkers must also consider alternative networks of significance that might inform a given sign. So, President George W. Bush got into a little trouble when he described his response to the 9/11 attacks as a "crusade" – since the word "crusade" figures into the network of meanings in the Middle East in a different way from the way it finds meaning among people in the United States. In the Middle East, "crusade" signifies an attack by the Christian West on the Muslim Middle East in order to regain sovereignty. For many in the US, however, the word signifies simply a project motivated by strong moral convictions. Western apologists dismissed the incident as simply a thoughtless misstep on the part of President Bush, but an additional semiotic analysis might give an oblique kind of acknowledgment to the critics' concerns. As a political figure with strong allegiances to evangelical Christians in the US, President Bush's use of the word might be read as an expression of his embracing a religious as well as moral crusade in some sense after all.

By opening up new ways of reading signs and signifiers, by considering alternative ways different interpretants and networks of signs might inflect the meaning of a sign, critical thinking with semiotics might open up as many questions as it answers; and there may be no definite end to those questions. All semiotic thinking, then, is an expression of what's often called, following Saussure, the "semiological problem." Peirce seemed to think there were some kind of natural constraints the objects of the world place on signs, but for Saussure and those who follow him, the problem we face as critical thinkers, even as human beings, is that there doesn't seem to be a single, natural, definite relationship between signs and what they signify.

Signs must always be read, and they must be read with sensitivity, with an understanding of contexts, of background, of the kinds of interpretants involved; but we must understand, nevertheless, that alternative readings will always be possible. That we live in a world we experience as a field of signs means that becoming skilled semioticians is not only a necessary condition for critical thinking but also an endless task.

Exercises and study questions

1. Conduct a semiotic analysis of the battle flag of the Army of Northern Virginia, commonly called the Confederate flag. How might Peirce-styled and Saussure-styled analyses differ? Be sure to attend to issues of race, states' rights, the saltire, regional or sectional identity, and both Civil War and post-Civil War politics. Why might it seem strange for people to fly both the Confederate and the US flags together? Why not strange? How might the controversy over the meaning of the flag be understood as a semiological problem?
2. Use semiotics to interpret Scotland's Rosslyn Chapel. Compare your analysis with the way Dan Brown interpreted it in *The Da Vinci Code*.
3. Assess the semiotics of Mozart's opera, *The Magic Flute*, or Pink Floyd's *The Wall*.
4. Conduct a semiotic analysis of the currency you use.
5. How might semiotic analyses illuminate the issues and controversies related to consent and rape? What are the semiotics of sexual assault, rough but permissible sex, and sado-masochistic sex?
6. What semiotic effect might the rise of LGBTQ identities have on gender?

7. Use semiotics to interpret Anne Sexton's poem, "45 Mercy Street." Does Peter Gabriel's song "Mercy Street" change the meaning of the poem's signs?
8. Write a semiotic analysis of the *Vanity Fair* magazine cover introducing Caitlyn Jenner (formerly Bruce Jenner) to the world.

SEE ALSO

8.4 Emotions and Evidence
10.1 Meta-Narratives
10.2 Governing Tropes

READING

Roland Barthes, *Mythologies: The Complete Edition, in a New Translation*, trans. by Richard Howard & Annette Lavers (2012)
Daniel Chandler, *Semiotics: The Basics*, 2nd edition (2007)
Winifried Nöth, *Handbook of Semiotics* (1995)
Charles Sanders Peirce, *Semiotics and Significs*, Charles Hardwick, ed. (1977)
Ferdinand de Saussure, *Course in General Linguistics* [1916], trans. by W. Baskin (1977)

10.6 Deconstruction

One of the most popular terms in critical thinking today is "deconstruction." Its use has become so broad that it often seems like a synonym for criticism. But "deconstruction" has a more precise definition, one rooted in the work of French philosopher Jacques Derrida (1930–2004).

In books like *Of Grammatology* (1967), Derrida radicalized the thought of German phenomenologist Martin Heidegger (1889–1976), who wished to perform a "*Destruktion*" or "raid" on the Western metaphysical tradition. Derrida argued against the Western tradition of meaning as "presence." As far back as Parmenides (who argued that being is only "what is"), Western philosophers have tended to focus on what is simply and directly "present" to the regarding mind. Whether this is the presence of an observation, sensory evidence, the self-evidence of logical principles such that idea that contradictions are always false, the idea of the "real presence" of the Catholic Eucharist, or the superiority of direct speaking over the written word as a form of communication, what is present – and ideally purely present – seems to be what matters most.

But is this really the right way to think about meaning? Philosophers like G. W. F. Hegel (1770–1831), Edmund Husserl (1859–1938), and Ferdinand de Saussure

(1857–1913) argued that "what-is" can only appear in relation to "what-is not." So, X can only be understood in contrast to, or as the negation of, or against a background horizon of what X is not (that is, not-X). Derrida took that a step farther by arguing that "what is" can't ever be fully present, that in every attempt to pin down or define meaning, it escapes, exceeds, or slips away from what we posit. Moreover, a text will undermine itself and bring inverse meanings to bear against the very assertion it attempts to make. Proof of a sort for this can be found in the way that resources for the subversion of its own apparent message can be found in each text itself. (Part of the fun of deconstruction is to look for those self-subverting dimensions of texts.) So, for example, literary critic Paul de Man argued that the liberal ideal of free speech is only possible to the extent that speech is denied – sometimes hate speech, or disruptive speech, or unconventional, uncivil, crazy, or irrelevant speech.

Critique of presence

Derrida called Western philosophy's proclivity to privilege presence its *logocentrism*, and critical thinking can therefore employ deconstruction either (1) to criticize logocentric readings of texts or (2) to find the ways a text undermines logocentric readings of itself. How is it that someone's freedom depends upon someone else's enslavement, how is someone's wealth possible only on the condition of someone else's impoverishment, how does the telling of one truth become possible only on condition of another lie?

One might also try to show how some value or attempted meaning that a text tries to convey in fact fails. How does a superficially just resolution in a narrative fail to achieve the justice to which it makes claim, how does the truth finally escape the revelation the text pretends to convey, how does a text's claim to clarity and definition remain muddy, ambiguous, and equivocal – not only in spite of itself but because of itself?

Undermining binaries

The undermining and redefining of differences formulated as binaries is also associated with deconstruction. As we saw in 10.5, for Saussure, meaning is made possible through differences, often binaries defined by differences. So, thinking critically about a text that hinges on a binary of male/female, good/evil, city/country, sane/insane, etc., involves identifying the differences and binaries that structure the text and then challenging them, optimally even from within the text itself. Challenging differences and binaries, however, cannot be made in the name of a fundamental unity, oneness, wholeness, or completeness, because difference is inescapable. The event of challenging and criticizing itself becomes the goal of critical thinking.

Any given structure of differences undermines itself, since according to deconstruction no structure can be whole or complete or consistent or unified, and so the critical thinker interrogates and searches a text looking for the ways it falls apart. In its falling apart, however, the text also opens itself to new meanings and new insights. One might, for example, challenge the attributes identified by gender differences by looking for ways the characters of a text define and defy the binary. One might interrogate a text to see how despite its own apparent assertions to the contrary its criminals are just, its powerful weak, its appeals to freedom and equality actually ways of suppressing diversity and liberty, its cosmopolitan figures actually provincial, and so on.

Typically among the binaries through which a text is constructed, one is dominant or privileged. How does the text subvert, invert, or in any way resist that domination and privilege? How is the slave the master? How does the slave owner's power undermine itself? In L. Frank Baum's parable of political economy, *The Wonderful Wizard of Oz* (1900), and its famous 1939 Hollywood film adaptation, the witch seems clearly "presented" as the villain in a good-witch/bad-witch binary, but that position becomes muddied by the reading of Baum's story in Gregory Maguire's 1995 book and Stephen Schwartz's Broadway adaptation, *Wicked* (2003), which figures Elphaba the witch as an empathetic and even heroic character.

On the other hand, it's important not simply to assert the secondary member of a binary as dominant and privileged. The task of deconstruction is not to simply invert one putatively present logocentric order with another, with its inverse. The inverse, too, is to be subject to deconstruction. Mary Shelley's 1818 novel, *Frankenstein*, for example, presents its sympathetic monster as an allegory critical of both the monster/human binary and the hatred and exclusion of the working class by the upper and educated classes. But that inversion is itself just a new logocentric assertion that destabilizes itself in its retributive, murderous anti-heroic hero. New logocentrisms and new binaries of domination always supplant the old, but the task is to destabilize every presented structure.

The politics of deconstruction

In one sense deconstruction is not political, as its work is to deconstruct political orders, orders that logocentrically pretend to present justice, fairness, freedom, goodness, or some other meaning. In another way, however, deconstruction is deeply political, and indeed Derrida seems to have realized more of the political import of his work as he grew older. Deconstruction becomes political not only in the dismantling of oppressive binaries. It enacts a task of ongoing and perpetual criticism. Critical thinking with deconstructive procedures, then, is just the ongoing task of politics, the prying open of new spaces or possibility, new ways to play and reconfigure our lives, new ways to wriggle out of the structures that confine and define us, not in favor of an endpoint or heaven or utopia but in favor of an ongoing process of resisting, criticizing, and deconstructing.

Exercises and study questions

1. How does the binary of "good guys" and "bad guys" deconstruct itself in John Ford's classic western, *The Searchers*?
2. How are ideals of freedom and equality not so? Deconstruct particular texts in answering this question.
3. How can Achilles as hero be deconstructed within the text of the *Iliad*?
4. How does *Animal Farm* deconstruct the socialist ideal of equality? How does *Animal Farm* deconstruct itself?
5. In groups of two, have one partner select a text that has a clear meaning and then ask the other partner to deconstruct the text by showing how in the very way the text asserts that meaning it undermines or resists or subverts it. Then ask the first partner to deconstruct the second partner's deconstruction. See how long one can continue in this play of construction and deconstruction. Reverse roles and repeat. Ask why one partner is first and the other second. How might the binaries of teacher/student, critic/criticized, construction/deconstruction themselves be deconstructed?

SEE ALSO

6.4 Emotions and Evidence
9.1 Meta-Narratives
9.2 Governing Tropes
9.4 Voice
10.7 Foucault's Critique of Power

READING

Gert J. J. Biesta & Geert Jan J. M. Stams, "Critical Thinking and the Question of Critique," *Studies in Philosophy and Education* 20 (2001): 57–74
Jacques Derrida, *Of Grammatology* [1967], trans. Gayatri Chakravorty Spivak (1998)
Jacques Derrida, *Margins of Philosophy* [1972], trans. Alan Bass (1984)
Jacques Derrida, *Writing and Difference* [1967], trans. Alan Bass (1980)

10.7 Foucault's Critique of Power

No book on critical thinking would be complete without discussing the ideas of one of the most influential philosophers, historians, and social theorists of the past 40 years, Michel Foucault (1926–1984). Foucault opened up entirely new lines of critique by calling attention to the multifarious ways that power is exerted in our world. Foucault argues that people exercise power in many ways, but especially important among the world's instruments of power are what he calls "discursive practices," the way ideas and theories are practiced. In many cases, the most important question for critical thinkers pursuing lines of Foucauldian critique is not whether some theory or concept is true but, rather, how is it used in the exercise of power.

Archeological method

Among Foucault's earliest approaches to understanding the organization of ideas and practices was what he called "archeological." In texts like *Madness and Civilization* (1961), *The Birth of the Clinic* (1963), *The Order of Things* (1966), and *The Archaeology of Knowledge* (1969), Foucault undertook to excavate the functions of words and ideas, not by situating them in historical streams stretching back across time but instead by exposing how they fit into shale-like layers of thinking and acting (sometimes called "discursive formations" or *epistemes*) that order people lives and thinking of a given time. So, using archeological method, to understand an idea requires not so much understanding its historical origins and development but, rather, figuring out how it functions in the structural grammar of ideas that pervades the entire sedimentary layer of a specific episteme.

According to this approach, the biological, economic, social, and physical ideas of a historical episteme may be expected to be more similar to each other than to ideas within any disciplines of the same or related names from earlier times. For example, through the concept of "madness," seventeenth- and eighteenth-century social formations laying claim to "rationality" and "reason" excluded those who didn't fit into them. Women's practices of midwifery, for example, were excluded from childbirth because they were not thought to be scientifically rational. In the nineteenth century, when another episteme had taken hold, the concept of "madness" was deployed against those who did not adhere to norms of bourgeois society, such as the unusually sexually active.

Genealogical method

In *Discipline and Punish* (1975), Foucault examined concepts and practices in a more diachronic way, showing for example how the concepts clustering around "criminality" and the techniques of managing those called "criminal" have changed over time. In tracing out the history of a concept, its changes, and the purposes behind them, Foucault develops what Friedrich Nietzsche called a "genealogical" method – a method Nietzsche used to criticize the concepts and practices of Christian morality in his book, *The Genealogy of Morals* (1887). The genealogical method aims to uncover the trivial, petty, arbitrary, and sometimes nasty purposes of what it investigates – the "dirty origins" of things. While, for example, many have seen changes in the criminal justice system as efforts to become more humane, Foucault argues that those changes have, rather, been organized around sharpening new, more effective techniques of social control. Along similar lines, he later undertook a genealogy of concepts and practices of sexuality in his *History of Sexuality* (1976, 1984). If we were to examine throughout history the motives, purposes and struggles that determined the origin and development of apparently innocent and even widely admired concepts, institutions and practices, would we find objectionable devices for control, manipulation and oppression?

Microphysics of power and biopower

Unlike other forms of social critique, however (such as Marxism and psychoanalysis), Foucault maintains that there is no single, comprehensive system of social order (like capitalism or patriarchy). Rather, Foucault argues that there are many, many different power systems interweaving and operating simultaneously, not always in consistent ways. Hence he himself eschews developing a single complete system of social and conceptual dynamics, instead calling his project a *microphysics of power.*

Among the most important ways power has been formed and exercised in modernity, however, has been via what Foucault calls *biopower*, exercised through the modern nation state for the sake of disciplining, controlling, and cultivating the bodies of groups of citizens so that they as populations remain healthy and available and also conduct themselves in ways needed by modern capitalism.

Among the most famous objects of Foucault's scrutiny was philosopher Jeremy Bentham's plan for a modern prison called a "panopticon." (One was actually built in 1926 and put into use in Cuba – the Presidio Modelo prison.) The panopticon has no cells with bars. It exercises power through constant surveillance (and the threat of violence if one is seen behaving badly). More precisely, it works by *convincing* inmates that they are always under surveillance, by internalizing that belief. As a result, those subject to panoptics come to discipline themselves.

Normalization

Another powerful tool of Foucauldian critical thinking is the idea of *normalization.* Foucault argues that in its manifestations of order power seeks to diminish the range of human possibility by privileging certain beliefs and practices as "normal." Hence sexual practices, family structures, religions, ways of speaking and acting that differ from the "normal" are called "deviant" and are through various oppressive techniques quashed, reducing individuals to the "docile bodies" needed to serve modern industrial and post-industrial society.

Foucault, then, offers us a number of powerful additions to our toolkit. When assessing a theory, idea or practice, Foucault enjoins us to ask ourselves what devices for exercising power might be lurking there – for power is subtle. He also cautions us not to rely on any single system of critique – for power faces us in many different guises, using many different techniques. Implicitly, Foucault also challenges us to abandon the fantasy that we can escape relationships pervaded by the exercise of power.

Exercises and study questions

1. How might concepts and institutions of family, woman, school, father, beauty, virtue, or truth serve as instruments of social order and control? Whom do they oppress or exclude or diminish in power and how?
2. What kind of power is exercised through the discursive practices of "critical thinking" itself?
3. How many kinds of social power can you name?
4. In what sort of episteme do we live today? What common grammar structures the "knowledges" and practices of knowledge operant today?
5. How might what is thought of as more "humane" today exhibit instead just more successful formations of power?
6. Do CCTV, electronic records of our credit and debit purchases, "rewards" or "loyalty" cards, social media, mobile phones, and government surveillance exert a "panoptic" effect on society?
7. How does state surveillance of electronic communications affect and effect power?
8. Name some pairs of practices that are normal and abnormal. Do any of these pairings exhibit an exercise of diminishment that you might prefer to resist? Are any ways that power is exercised through the idea of the "normal" or the "healthy" defensible? Which? Why? Could we abandon the idea of normalcy entirely, or would doing so be impossible?

SEE ALSO

9.9 Class Critiques
10.10 Feminist and Gender Critiques
10.12 Traditionalist and Historicist Critiques

READING

Gary Gutting, ed., *The Cambridge Companion to Foucault* (2005)
Judith Butler, "What is Critique? An Essay on Foucault's Virtue" in *The Political: Readings in Continental Philosophy*, David Ingram, ed. (2002), 212–226
Paul Rabinow, ed., *The Essential Works of Michel Foucault* (2000)
Michel Foucault, "What is Critique?" in *The Politics of Truth*, Sylvère Lotringer & Lysa Hochroth, eds. (1997)
David Hoy, ed., *Foucault: A Critical Reader* (1991)

10.8 The Frankfurt School: Culture Critique

To try to understand war and oppression people often examine governments and government officials, financial interests, and explicit political ideologies. So, to understand the Iraq War, analysts often consider the political ideas of President George W. Bush, characteristics of US policy, the strategic power struggles playing out among the world's great powers, national interests such as security in the wake of the 9/11 attacks, economic interests in oil and weaponry, and more. Interpreters may even consider explicit cultural ideas related to war – for example, xenophobia and religious intolerance, a militant gun culture and the relatively recent conquest and struggles with its frontiers, ideas of American exceptionalism and preeminence, etc.

But what if the sources of war and oppression are far more pervasive in a society? What if they are rooted in the most ordinary aspects of daily life, in consumer goods, in films, music and other media, manufacturing processes, and in consumer-industrial-commercial culture generally? Critical thinking in the form of "culture critique" developed by Frankfurt School philosophers such as Walter Benjamin (1892–1940), Theodor Adorno (1903–1969), and Herbert Marcuse (1898–1979) undertakes to investigate just these questions. Influenced by the massive outburst of industrialized violence in World War I and then the horribly oppressive totalitarian systems that emerged with World War II, the Frankfurt School (so-called because of its origins in the Institute for Social Research at Goethe University in Frankfurt) synthesized elements culled from a host of disciplines – including Marxism, Freudian psychoanalysis, philosophy, art, and even modern physics – in developing their new forms of critical thinking.

Lipstick is ideology

Theodor Adorno famously declared that objects such as lipstick are themselves ideological. He didn't only mean by that what feminist critics and others have argued – that the norms of female beauty (e.g., social demands on women to wear lipstick) can be harmful and oppressive. He meant that in the shiny, plastic, refined, obviously mass-produced object called lipstick, it is clear that the object is manufactured and sold through large-scale, highly regulated, modern, capitalist, industrial processes. The slick, smooth, sexy, polished, and glossy qualities of the stick of lipstick, repeated in the millions of lipsticks that have been sold, themselves announce the backstory of homogenized mass production through offices, roads, shipping, wage labor, industrial-technological industry, advertising, shopping malls, women's magazines, electricity, fossil fuels, and fashion institutions that inform the object and make it possible. More importantly, the socially accepted desirability of the cylinder of lipstick turns around to legitimate and make acceptable, even desirable, all that stands behind it. Lipstick, in short, legitimates modern capitalist society in general and creates appetites for it. To desire something is to desire the social relations that produce the object of desire, that produce the desirability of the object. Critical thinkers, therefore, must work to understand the ideologies that inform the everyday objects that surround us and the networks of desire in which both those objects and we are immersed.

Makers who are made

The critique runs even deeper, however. It's not just that those objects and cultural artifacts legitimate all that make them possible. It's that they shape us, and they shape us in ways that lead often to oppressive and violent conduct. It's not just that we desire a manufactured object like lipstick and the system behind it but also that our desire is itself manufactured. Our desires are not antecedent to the social order in which we live, and they are not independent from it. It's not just that lipsticks are themselves mass produced, homogeneous, repeated, and regularized through modern capital and culture but that we are, too. The processes that churn out mass-produced consumer goods also mass produce consumers – mass produce us. The discipline that it takes to work and consume and even participate in manufactured enjoyments (films, amusement parks, computer games) requires disciplined and regularized people; and that regularization prepares people to accept the disciplined and organized systems of war, policing, and control characteristic of totalitarianism, etc. The adulation that people are cultivated to express toward celebrities prepares them to adore state leaders.

The Dialectic of Enlightenment

Perhaps one of the Frankfurt School's most trenchant critical claims is that the rationality we've inherited from the eighteenth-century Enlightenment is not (only) a force for liberty, equality, and community but (also) ultimately the source of concentration death camps and other forms of oppression that characterize more recent history. Modern rationality becomes increasingly "instrumental," and it transforms us all into mere instruments, disposable in service to other ends. It demands the subjection of the world (including others and non-humans in the world) to its demands for utility, efficiency, and technological power. Are totalitarianism and cultural imperialism, then, the antithesis of modern reason or its natural result?

Exercises and study questions

1. How can one use Frankfurt School-style forms of critical thinking to think critically about mobile phones and social media?
2. How might the very form and material properties of Hollywood blockbuster films, especially those that heavily employ computer graphics technologies, be criticized from a Frankfurt School perspective?

3. Did the role of technology and modern industrial practices make the Holocaust different from mass killings in the ancient world, for example, Alexander's destruction of Tyre or the Roman destruction of Carthage?
4. In what way is air conditioning ideology?
5. How might a Frankfurt School analysis connect popular music, fast food, slaughterhouses, and forest clear cutting?

SEE ALSO

10.9 Class Critiques
10.10 Feminist and Gender Critiques
10.13 Ecological Critiques

READING

Jeffrey T. Nealon & Caren Irr, *Rethinking the Frankfurt School: Alternative Legacies of Cultural Critique* (2002)

Stephen Eric Bronner & Douglas MacKay Kellner, eds., *Critical Theory and Society: A Reader* (1989)

Andrew Arato & Eike Gebhardt, eds., *The Essential Frankfurt School Reader* (1978)

10.9 Class Critiques

One of the most important tools of critical thinking is what we'd like to call "class critique." By this we mean criticizing texts, theories, artwork, practices, etc. on the basis of the ways in which they serve or subvert class hierarchy or class struggle.

Classical Marxism: superstructure and substructure

There are a variety of prominent forms of class critique. Perhaps the classic formulation of this critical tool is to be found in the work of German philosophers Karl Marx (1818–1883) and Friedrich Engels (1820–1895). Most philosophers before Marx and Engels held that philosophy and other elements of human culture develop through the action of the thoughts, ideas, and intentions of individuals, independently of the economic order in which they were produced. Marx and Engels challenged this idea, arguing instead that a society's "mode of production" (e.g., feudalism or capitalism) acts as a kind of *substructure* that determines the attributes of the cultural *superstructure* built upon it.

For Marx and Engels it is not the dynamics of ideas that determine social arrangements (a view Marx attributed to Hegel); it's the dynamics of the economic base that determine our ideas. A bit more bluntly, if you want to understand some text, etc., figure out how it supports or undermines the mode of production in which it was written and in which it's read. For example, the US Civil War, which Marx covered as a journalist, was not from a classical Marxist perspective fought to end chattel slavery but rather to clear the way for a profit-generating system based on wages – wage-slavery. Similarly, a Marxist might argue that US racial segregation ended not because of the political savvy and clever arguments of activists such as Rev. Dr. Martin Luther King, Jr., but because ending it served the interests of capitalism. This strict, traditional reading of Marx, however, has largely given way, even among Marxists. Another version of class critique in the work of Antonio Gramsci (1891–1937) rejects the classical Marxist thesis that this determination is one-directional, arguing instead that the culture reciprocally affects the economic substructure, too.

It's the class hierarchy, stupid

Another prominent class-based form of criticism is rooted in the anarchist rather than the Marxist tradition. While Marxists root class struggle and the many forms of oppression in the fundamental division between those who own or control the means of production and those who work the means of production, for anarchists economic domination is not basic. Rather, domination *per se*, in any form, is the problem. American anarchist Emma Goldman (1896–1940), for example, objected to the hierarchies created not only by private capital but also by government and by religion. Other anarchists have objected to the hierarchies of patriarchy, of racism, of humans over non-human animals, and of Western culture over non-Western societies. This leads to an important difference in prescriptions: while Marxists accept a positive and important role for the state in creating a post-capitalist society, anarchists do not.

Exploitation, alienation, and class struggle

Two of the most powerful tools class-based forms of criticism have developed are the concepts of "exploitation" and "alienation." *Exploitation* has a fairly precise meaning in Marxist analyses. It's the expropriation of wealth from workers who ought to own that wealth, principally because they have produced it through their labor. *Alienation* is a complex and less precise idea, but the nub of it is that certain social orders stifle, damage, and deform human beings, preventing people from developing and flourishing in the ways that are best for them. Humans exist today not in the best ways they can but instead in a diminished state – alienated from others, from the natural world, from their work, and even from their true selves.

Marxists understand the Protestant Reformation, for example, not fundamentally as a theological innovation but as a change in thinking demanded by the newly burgeoning capitalist institutions of Europe. Because capitalism needed to break the communal, local ties characteristic of feudalism, it developed new conceptual superstructures that emphasized individuality and personal conscience over communal, feudal church authority. This atomized way of living is alienating to people, and alienation is painful. Of course, feudalism entailed its own forms of alienation, and in the Middle Ages religion was used to justify the divine right of royals and aristocrats to rule and expropriate from the poor. That kind of domination and exploitation is alienating, too, and in both cases pain marks the potential for rebellion. So, Marx explains, religion has also functioned as a tool to dull the wounding the alienated endure. Religion is, says Marx in his 1844 *Contributions to a Critique of Hegel's Philosophy of Right*: "the sigh of the oppressed creature, the heart of a heartless world, and the soul of soulless conditions. It is the *opium* of the people." It is the work of critical thinking, then, from a Marxist perspective to expose the ways that texts and social arrangements exploit and diminish us, the ways we are alienated, and how we respond to that alienation – either by coping, resisting, masking, or profiting from it.

False consciousness

Class-based criticism, therefore, often works to expose and explain what Marxists call *false consciousness*, the false and misleading ideas foisted upon the exploited and dominated to convince them to support the very order that oppresses them. One common target of false consciousness criticism is the set of liberal political and economic rights -with examples such as free speech and the free market. The exploited often take solace in the understanding that even if they are weak and poorly compensated, they at least compete on a level playing field and enjoy precisely the same freedoms as the ruling class in political action and the marketplace. Marxists criticize this view, maintaining that these rights were developed for the ruling class and are effectively enjoyed only by that class. Perhaps most importantly, liberal rights and freedoms mask the real power imbalances that determine social outcomes.

Criticizing class critique

The importance of class critique is that, historically, it has influenced a great deal of political rhetoric and social policy. And since rhetoric and policy affect all of us, we have an interest in asking hard questions about whatever influences them. For instance, is society actually structured the way Marxists critics claim? Should we accept Marx's definition of "exploitation"? Can wages compensate or eliminate what Marxists call "alienated" labor? Have workers' lives improved under capitalism? If so, how much of that improvement can be attributed to capital investment and how much to labor? How much to class struggle through, say, strikes, and how much through market forces? Is there any empirical evidence to suggest that socialism or communism would improve people's lives or, instead, make people worse off? The empirical facts matter for Marxism, so we can at least in part test it for accuracy.

Exercises and study questions

1. In what way does Christopher Nolan's *Batman* trilogy of films help serve or subvert the interests of capital? Is his film *Inception* about false consciousness?
2. In what way does "race" figure into the class struggle? How did ending legal segregation serve the interests of capital?
3. How does religion help manipulate and exploit subordinate classes, relieve their suffering, or blunt their resistance?
4. Develop a class-based analysis of the Iraq War.
5. What are the principal forms of class struggle today?
6. In what ways has the exploitation and alienation of people changed since the mid-nineteenth century? How has globalization affected exploitation and alienation?
7. What are some of the hierarchies that exist in today's society? Are they good and justifiable or wrong and exploitive?
8. Can a class-based critique be made of the Internet and social media?
9. Is religion still the "opium of the people"? Or can religion also promote positive social change, even revolution? Give a class analysis of militant religious movements.
10. How from a Marxist point of view are racism and sexism and ecological harm related to class oppression?

SEE ALSO

10.7 Foucault's Critique of Power: Microphysics of power and biopower
10.8 The Frankfurt School: Culture Critique
10.10 Feminist and Gender Critiques

READING

Peter Marshall, *Demanding the Impossible: A History of Anarchism* (2010)
Peter Singer, *Marx: A Very Short Introduction* (2001)
Emma Goldman, "Anarchism: What it Really Stands For" (1910)
Karl Marx & Friedrich Engels, *Manifesto of the Communist Party* (1848)
Karl Marx, *Theses on Feuerbach* (1845)
Friedrich Engels, *The Peasant War in Germany* (1850)

10.10 Feminist and Gender Critiques

German athlete Dora Ratjen placed fourth in the 1936 Olympic high jump competition and took the gold medal in the 1938 European championship, but three years later Ratjen was arrested and the medal returned. Her name was changed to Heinrich. Why? Because Ratjen was determined not to be female. For a variety of reasons, social and physical, however, many have argued that it was also wrong to call Ratjen "male." Perhaps Ratjen's trouble wasn't fraud, or an error made by her parents and childhood physicians at all. Perhaps the difficulties Ratjen faced were cultural and conceptual; perhaps they were rooted in the very ideas and practices of the ways we think about gender?

Among the most important ideas around which human life is organized are those of gender and sex. The roles and rules of social conduct, the distribution of wealth and power, psychological and political identity, protocols and manners, as well as many other dimensions of life are determined or inflected by ideas of male and female, man and woman, girl and boy, heterosexual and homosexual, feminine and masculine. So, critical thinking about texts, institutions, and practices must include criticism of matters of sex and gender.

It used to be the case that people made what they thought was a clear distinction between "sex" and "gender." "Sex" was biological and had to do with the behavior and physical structures of animals and plants that reproduced, well, sexually, ultimately through the combination of DNA from what biologists call a "male" and a "female." "Gender" was cultural and had to do with the social roles, styles, manners, and customs contingently associated with the biological reality. Today, however, theorists have become reluctant to make that distinction, at least in a clean way. For one thing, the biological concepts themselves have been, upon closer examination, found to be less clearly separable from other cultural ideas. And, moreover, the biological binary has become problematic insofar as the world seems less clearly divided along two well-demarcated sex lines.

Some creatures are biologically intersexed, exhibiting biological traits associated with both sexes, and that in a variety of ways – some snails and worms, and spotted hyenas, for example. Humans with Klinefelter syndrome possess XXY chromosomes (whereas most humans called "male" possess XY and most called "female" possess XX chromosomes). Some living things shift sex from male to female and from sexual to asexual forms of reproduction. Aphids are female for most of their lives but sometimes shift to being male, so they can reproduce asexually or sexually. Bluebanded goby fish and Amborella shrubs shift back and forth between female and male, and Australian bearded dragon lizards can shift sex when temperature changes. And, of course, different species bear and raise young in many different ways. Male seahorses are just one species where childcare is not the job of females.

Understanding the problematic dimensions of a simple binary and of forcing people into it, today people like Ratjen often prefer to be called "genderqueer," exhibiting the physical structures and other traits (e.g., dress, ornament, and speech) associated with both sexes – or neither.

These distinctions become relevant because we often treat one another differently based on how we perceive one another sexually. Religious convictions may make us critical of some sexual orientations or even biological conditions. Political convictions may bias us against certain groups before we fully understand what is at issue. Even the structure of our daily lives might make it difficult for some people to pursue their interests. Consider that the workday is typically 8am to 5pm, while school runs from 8am to 3pm. This means that the primary caregiver of a child either cannot work or must make arrangements for childcare between 3pm and 5pm. If, as has traditionally been the case, the primary caregiver is female, then the very structure of the workday excludes more women than men from the workplace.

Politics and gender

Thinking critically about the gendered dimensions of a social institution or practice will involve asking how it is organized. Are different roles or practices associated with one gender or another? If so, how are those roles enforced? Are resources, power, privilege, wealth, credibility, and stature distributed in gendered ways? In what way do participants enact their roles and perform their gender in these institutions? What is it to be a proper "man" or "woman" in these conditions? What rules and standards govern gendered conduct? Who is excluded?

Some critical thinkers scrutinize and then decide that some practice or institution is gendered and properly so. Others thinking critically about these matters, however, adopt a subversive or restive posture. Can questions or ideas or forms of conduct be formulated that interrupt or challenge or subvert the gendered dimensions of an organization, a theory, a ritual, a culture, a practice? Can androgyny, cross-dressing, role reversals, rule transgressions, body modifications, linguistic alterations, diversified sexual practices, carefully chosen social improprieties, etc., "jam" or obstruct the operation of oppressive gendered norms and cultures, especially those that are patriarchal and hetero-normative?

The practice of "queering" is to do just that with "hetero-normativity." Hetero-normativity is the privileging of heterosexual norms, values, and identities while excluding what is non-heterosexual – e.g., lesbian, gay, bi-sexual, asexual, or queer (though these categories and terms are themselves somewhat in flux). To open a space for transgender people of whatever sexuality, some have begun to add the prefix "cis" (from the Latin for "on this side" of) to the terms male and female, establishing *cisgender* such that those who retain and who are publicly acknowledged by the gender they have been assigned at birth are *cisgender*, principally *cis male* and *cis female*, while those who have transitioned to another gender are *trans male* and *trans female* (where "trans" is drawn from the Latin for "across" to) – though of course this may establish another binary.

Critical thinking about gender can involve thinking about what sorts of concepts and conduct can "queer" or interrupt or open new spaces of self-understanding, identity, and behavior beyond those defined by the gendered ways of being, thinking, and doing that currently exist. Would it be possible to eliminate gender entirely from society and just consider each human being without gender? Can there be more than two genders such as the "berdache" or Native American "two-spirit"? If so, is there a limit to how many genders, or can people define their own gender in perhaps a countless variety of ways? What practices of sexuality are to be identified, permitted, and excluded? How best should the fluidity and dynamism of gender and sexuality be acknowledged? How much does nature and biology determine or restrict an individual's or society's gender and sexual divisions?

That all sounds pretty abstract. So, let's consider a few examples and critical questions that might be used to illuminate them. In a given organization (say a family or a business or a school), what roles do men and women and genderqueer people play? Do men hold more or different kinds of power? Are compensation rates equal, vacation time, and parental leave? Are women expected to be the primary caregivers of children, the sick, and the elderly? Are men discouraged from that role? Are men allowed to show emotion, and do they show emotion, besides anger? How are those who are not heterosexual but rather transgender treated? How are toilets and other private spaces arranged? Why do women wear certain kinds of clothing but men others? Are women sexualized, subjected to sexual violence, or harassed in ways men are not? Are men subject to violence and punishment in ways women are not? Are women and men expected to behave differently in different situations? Are standards of evaluation different for the different genders? Are work assignments different? Are forms and modes of speech different? What practices reinforce standard forms of gender? Is one gender given greater credibility, regarded as more knowledgeable, more rational, more responsible, more capable, better suited to some roles than others? Are one gender's opinions and judgments treated differently?

In one of the Western tradition's first philosophical arguments for gender equality, Plato wrote in Book V of the *Republic* that both men and women are fit to serve as philosopher-kings and -queens of his ideal society because being male or female, while relevant to other functions, is irrelevant to ruling. The idea that males and females are politically equal has gained serious acceptance in the West, especially since Mary Wollstonecraft (1759–1797) and John Stuart Mill (1806–1873) started defending women's rights in the 1700s and 1800s. Indeed, the idea that biological differences ought to make no difference in most contexts is a commonplace in liberal societies. Nevertheless, in many cases gender and sexuality continue to prove complicated, undesirably restrictive, and otherwise problematic for people. The goal of critical thinking in relation to these problems is to clarify and to structure thinking about these issues, perhaps especially in those areas where obstacles or exclusions persist, in order to help eliminate those that are improper and wrong. The very act of critical questioning, too, may open up new possibilities for gendered and sexual ways of thinking and acting.

It's certainly not always true that gender is irrelevant in life. The fact that maternity wards cater exclusively to women is not discriminatory against men any more than the fact that children's hospitals cater exclusively to children is not discriminatory against adults. It remains important in medical research and healthcare to distinguish male and female human beings. In these cases, gender matters. But there have been challenges to the idea that mothers receive paid maternity leave while fathers do not. In response, some companies and countries such as Iceland and Norway now extend paid parental leave to fathers. When, then, is gender and sexuality properly considered in making moral, political, economic, etc. judgments and when not?

Feminist critique

Feminism has developed a spectrum of critical approaches. It's impossible to cover them all here, but we might say that in contrast to queering and jamming gender, feminism focuses more specifically on subverting "patriarchy" or more broadly what feminist thinker bell hooks (1952–) has called "sexist oppression." Patriarchy can be defined roughly as the domination of women by men (and of some younger men by some older men). Defining feminism, hooks writes in her 1984 essay, "Feminism: A Movement to End Sexist Oppression":

> Its aim is not to benefit solely any specific group of women, any particular race or class of women. It does not privilege women over men. It has the power to transform in a meaningful way all our lives .... Feminism as a movement to end sexist oppression directs our attention to systems of domination and the inter-relatedness of sex, race, and class oppression.... The foundation of future feminist struggle must be solidly based on a recognition of the need to eradicate the underlying cultural basis and causes of sexism and other forms of group oppression.

So, thinking critically about a text will involve considering questions such as: In what ways does this text reinforce or resist patriarchy? How are women and girls depicted here? Do they have a voice? Is violence against women eroticized or made somehow a pleasing spectacle? Is force and violence the solution to problems? Do the actions of females in the text express agency? How are their desires understood? Are sexual double standards invoked? How are parenting and childcare depicted? Do evaluative concepts determined by patriarchy, such as "honor" or "beauty," control or punish women? What relationships of power between men and women are valorized or undermined? Who controls the wealth? How are reason and feeling, authority and passivity, command and nurture, civilization and nature related to male and female in the text? What norms of gender govern any expression related to divinity or the sacred? Feminist philosophers have argued that even some of our most basic philosophical (and other) categories are inflected in sexist ways – e.g., good/evil, truth/opinion, science/superstition, public/private, freedom/oppression. Indeed, perhaps these binaries, as binaries, are themselves patriarchal.

While the driving motivation of the feminist movement is political and moral equality, the strategies for achieving that equality fall on a continuum between two endpoints. Some feminists have emphasized *equality* and argued that women are just as capable as men and can do what they can do, whether it involves physical labor, academic scholarship, or corporate or political leadership. The danger of this approach is that, if the social structure really is patriarchal, by simply placing women in these roles without reforming them we may be embracing patriarchal social structures as socially and politically correct. Others, emphasizing difference, have argued that women are distinct from men, perhaps essentially so, rejecting the norms of abstract thinking, reason, and careerism as patriarchal. The danger of this option is that at the extreme it can define males and females as virtual aliens, unable to find common ground even on something as basic as logic. Perhaps a middle ground might be found between these two poles, highlighting the fact that, while men and women share much in common, women possess capacities and dispositions that are both distinctly feminine and important for understanding reality, even though they've been devalued and excluded from too much of life.

For critical thinkers, the important question here is how we might discern whether a feminist critique is accurate. Are binaries such as good/evil, truth/opinion as they're commonly understood gendered? How might we know? If we argue against moral and epistemological binaries, are we simultaneously implying that women do not or cannot think or act like men – and vice versa? What are the indicators of patriarchal structures? In what ways might society look different if it did not have these structures? How might we start moving away from a power imbalance between genders? Can men be involved in the process without reinforcing that power imbalance? The ability to test claims through the tools set out in this volume sets the critical thinker apart from those who succumb merely to the rhetoric of the loudest voices.

Text and gender

To be clear, we don't mean just texts on mobile phones and social media, but "text" in the sense of something read and interpreted: feminist and gender critics have raised important questions about whether the form of texts itself exhibits masculinist and heteronormative biases. To think critically about patriarchy and gender consider questions such as: Does the text speak in a male or binary voice? Does it take a male gaze upon the world and upon women? Does it assert a single, authoritative truth and move to a single definitive climax, or does it express multiple perspectives and a polyclimactic structure? Are moral judgments determined by moral principles, or do they emerge from networks of personal relationships, as psychologist Carol Gilligan famously suggested is more commonly female?

In general, to use this tool, ask how the text, practice, or institution under scrutiny is informed or inflected by concepts related to gender and sex such as male and female, masculine and feminine, heterosexual and queer, perhaps regardless of the intent of its authors or those participating or enacting the practice.

Exercises and study questions

1. What would have been the best way to handle the Dora/Heinrich Ratjen case? Should M to F trans women be allowed to compete in athletic contests against cis women? Should sport be organized by the gender binary at all? Perhaps some sports but not others?
2. If someone possesses physical structures typically associated with one sex or gender but self-identifies as another, what if anything is the best way of thinking or acting in relation to that person? Does context make a difference: primary school, university, employer, prison, military, or toilets?
3. Can the gender binary be disrupted or subverted? Partially or totally? If so, why and how? If not, why not?
4. Is patriarchy the best way to describe existing gender relations?
5. In what sense might governments be described as patriarchal?
6. Are the Abrahamic religions patriarchal? If so, are they intrinsically or just accidentally patriarchal?
7. Is family typically patriarchal today? If so, how can it be altered to become less so?
8. Are contemporary forms of paid employment patriarchal? If so, how can they be altered to become less so? Should there be paid paternity as well as maternity leave?
9. Are males intrinsically more violent than females? Is masculinity more violent than femininity? How is violence differently practiced and experienced among the different sexes/genders?

SEE ALSO

10.9 Class Critiques
10.8 The Frankfurt School: Culture Critique
10.5 Semiotics: Critically Reading Signs

READING

Anne Fausto-Sterling, *Sex/Gender: Biology in a Social World* (2012)
Cordelia Fine, *Delusions of Gender: How Our Minds, Society, and Neurosexism Create Difference* (2011)
Miranda Fricker & Jennifer Hornsby, eds., *The Cambridge Companion to Feminism in Philosophy* (2000)
Bell Hooks, *Feminism is for Everybody* (2000)
Rosemarie Putnam Tong, *Feminist Thought: A More Comprehensive Introduction*, 3rd edn (2008)

10.11 Critiques of Race and Racism

There's little dispute that modern history has been racialized, that people have been classed according to concepts of "race," and that the ideology of "racism" has been used to organize various social institutions, practices, and distributions of goods. There is less agreement, however, about exactly what race and racism is. Racism may be *overt* or *explicit*, evident in overt statements and intentional acts of racial discrimination, abuse, or violence. South African apartheid institutions, US Jim Crow segregation laws, and the French *code noir*, as well as lynchings and the burning of crosses by the Ku Klux Klan, exemplify overt and explicit racism. Racism, however, may also be *covert* and people may be influenced by *implicit bias*, even without the conscious intent or understanding of those who engage in racist practices. That may be the case, according to some, because of the *systematic* and pervasive character of racism – that is, the way racism pervades the very structures and organized systems of our societies, our languages, our customs, our conceptual schemes, and our dominant institutions so that they may function to produce racist effects even without people (any longer) consciously intending them to do so. There are a variety of critiques that thinkers have developed to confront race and racism. Critical thinkers today will be well advised to gain facility with them.

Scientific critique of race

One way of thinking critically about race has been to subvert or deconstruct the very idea of it by showing that sound scientific inquiry actually falsifies or resists the concept. Although race was until recently accepted and cultivated by scientific authorities, contemporary biologists have scrutinized race and largely shown that the *scientific racism* of the eighteenth, nineteenth, and early twentieth centuries is not well grounded in the empirical data or otherwise in scientific theory. The concept of "race" doesn't illuminate biological facts. Instead it obscures and distorts them. So, racialized biological claims are false or, at best, misleading. Call this the *scientific critique of race.* You might say that while the natural and social sciences failed in the past by falling for the ideologies of racism, the sciences have also redeemed themselves by self-critically overcoming and falsifying racist ideas. The sciences are vulnerable to *ideological science* (see 9.8), but they are also well equipped for self-correction.

Liberal critique of race

Another way of criticizing racialized practices, ideas, and institutions is by arguing that they conflict with our most cherished moral and political ideals – often ancient religious precepts or modern political ideals of human equality. Race may not adequately express biological facts, but it certainly expresses social reality. One might call criticisms of racialized social reality based on the liberal ideal that all people are equal and should be treated equally as individuals the *liberal critique* of race. US Supreme Court justice John Marshall Harlan, from the once segregated and former slave state of Kentucky, articulated a liberal criticism of race when he argued in his dissent to the 1896 Supreme Court ruling in *Plessy v. Ferguson* that:

> Our constitution is colorblind, and neither knows nor tolerates classes among citizens. In respect of civil rights, all citizens are equal before the law. The humblest is the peer of the most powerful . . . . The arbitrary separation of citizens on the basis of race, while they are on a public highway, is a badge of servitude wholly inconsistent with the civil freedom and the equality before the law established by the Constitution. It cannot be justified upon any legal grounds.

Racism, according to this way of thinking, is a failure to live up to social-political ideals. It's a shortcoming and a corruption of modern republican government and democratic egalitarianism. Martin Luther King, Jr., and others involved in the US Civil Rights movement are often, along these lines, credited with helping the US live up to its own political principles, with helping the nation to understand that the existence of slavery and legalized racial segregation represented inconsistencies and imperfections of US political aspirations.

Marxist critique of race

Marxist theorists have argued that racism, while inconsistent with liberalism, is not inconsistent with the economic system that underwrites both race and liberal ideals for the purpose of advancing and sustaining itself – namely capitalism. As South African anti-apartheid activist and University of Cape Town professor Jack Simons argued, racism is a "special form of colonialism," and modern colonialism, according to Marxists, was a project of capitalism. While, for liberals, racism can be confronted independently of a critique of capitalism (and very probably *should* be confronted independently of a critique of capitalism), according to Marxists, doing so can only prove insufficient to the task because race and class are inextricably intertwined.

For Marxists, ideologies of race exist because they make it possible to divide the working class against itself and thereby inhibit workers from uniting against capitalism. Race convinces white labor that even if it's exploited, it can be contented at least with the understanding that it's better off than the workers of other racial groups. Rather than making demands upon capital, white labor in that way can be made principally to fear and to expend its energies resisting the gains of racial minorities. Race also gives a social legitimation to the exploitation of racialized groups. It was permissible to enslave some people or to drive others into horribly exploitative sweatshop, railroad, or agricultural work because their "race" legitimated it; and those racialized as non-white expanded and contracted as it suited the demands of capital. Race, for Marxists, is a tool that capitalism uses (1) to undermine the solidarity and unified demands of the proletariat and (2) to justify exploitative labor practices. Call this the *Marxist critique of race.*

Critical race theory

There's another radical approach to the criticism of race in modern society, however, a more recent approach called *critical race theory* that began with the work of a number of legal theorists, in particular Derek Bell (1930–2011). There are several critiques developed by this movement that critical thinkers about race will find useful.

1. *Race is intrinsic and central.* Critical race theorists argue that race and racial discrimination are not aberrations, imperfections, inconsistencies, or distortions of otherwise noble and fine political ideals but rather that race is intrinsic to modern US and European cultures and institutions. Racism, by this account, then, doesn't represent a failure of those ideals but actually the social arrangement proper to them. Racism, in short, is normal in contemporary Western society. Criticizing modern racism requires, then, criticizing not only the failure of people to live up to dominant ideals but instead the ideals themselves.

2. *Race is principally a social rather than biological matter.* Critical race theorists agree with those advancing scientific critiques that concepts of race are not well grounded biologically. They emphasize, in addition, even more broadly than Marxists, that although race poses as biological it arose for social-political-economic reasons and has been frequently reconfigured for social-political-economic purposes. English common law was inverted, for example, in colonial Virginia in 1662 so that children would follow in slave status and race from the condition of the mother (appealing to the Roman principle of *partus sequitur ventrem*) rather than the father. (This made it possible for male slaveholders in Virginia to produce more slaves simply by impregnating the women they owned.) The Irish were configured as a non-white race, when it suited. In some circumstances, "one drop" of "black" blood (a single ancestor at any point) was enough to define someone as black. Racial position was defined elsewhere by who sat at which table. As a result, critical thinkers will do well to understand that "race" is not a single concept but a family of concepts that applies differently to different groups and even differently to what seems to be the same group across time and space. Blackness is not an essence or a trans-historical singularity but, rather, a complex, variegated, and often inconsistent network of ideas and practices.

3. *Race has epistemic implications.* Race, according to critical race theorists, produces epistemic standpoints of the sort we addressed in 7.6 when we discussed social-political standpoints and their implications. Critical thinkers, therefore, might wonder whether or not knowledge claims about social reality can be complete and objective without including the judgments of groups marginalized or excluded on the

basis of race. One might even consider whether standpoint critique prevents epistemic agreement about social facts, perhaps because of the effects of *white privilege* – e.g., whether the police treat whites and non-whites equally. Critical race theorists are suspicious, even resistant, to the idea that race can today be transcended and that a strictly neutral view of social reality is under current conditions possible – at least without considering the racial standpoints of the claims being entered. Criticism of race cannot itself be "colorblind" but instead must employ race itself as a category of critical analysis.

SEE ALSO

9.8 Bad Science
10.9 Class Critiques
10.8 The Frankfurt School: Culture Critique

READING

Michael Omi, *Racial Formation in the United States* (2014)
Richard Delgado & Jean Stefancic, *Critical Race Theory: The Cutting Edge* (2013)
Richard Delgado & Jean Stefancic, *Critical Race Theory: An Introduction*, 2nd edition (2012)
Ali Rattansi, *Racism: A Very Short Introduction* (2007)
George M. Fredrickson, *Racism: A Short History* (2003)

10.12 Traditionalist and Historicist Critiques

A few days after the September 11, 2011, attacks on New York and the Pentagon, President Bush characterized the response the US government was about to undertake as a "crusade." It was a choice of words critically received in Europe and across the Middle East, largely because the president seemed to have forgotten the provocative historical meaning the word "crusade" carries, especially for those whose ancestors were on the receiving end of the Crusades. (See 10.5.)

Some forms of critical thinking turn upon considerations of logic, evidence, and the justification of knowledge claims. Other forms of critical thinking turn upon ethical and political considerations of justice, power, oppression, liberty, and liberation. Still others advance criticisms using what might be called "conditions of meaning." We've seen that critical thinking about meaning can employ critical lenses that focus on matters of semiotics (that is, signs, signifiers, and reference), voice, perspective, and poetic tropes. Traditionalist and historicist forms of critical thinking also consider condition of meaning, but in a different way. One might say that these approaches criticize forms of forgetfulness.

A history of thinking about history

The German philosopher Martin Heidegger (1889–1976) described human beings as "thrown" (*geworfen*) into a world not of their own making. Unlike stones, which simply exist across "time" (*Zeit*) unconsciously, human beings are "temporal" (*gezeitlich*) and "historical" (*geschichtlich*), thrown into a world in which we must define our present and project ourselves into the future in relation to the world's history. Heidegger was certainly not the first philosopher to have noticed this. In the nineteenth century, German thinkers like G. W. F. Hegel (1770–1831) as well as, later, British thinkers like F. H. Bradley (1846–1924) and R. G. Collingwood (1889–1943) speculated about the importance of history in human life. Earlier Europeans like Giambattista Vico (1668–1744) and David Hume (1711–1776) were also sensitive to the way in which human life is deeply and essentially historical.

Among the historical dimensions of human existence one might identify specific, customary lines of meaning and practice called *traditions*. Traditions may be relatively unreflective – such as the traditions of speech and ornament. Or they may be more consciously developed – such as the traditions of theology. Tradition has also, of course, been very important among Asian thinkers. Confucius (551–479 BCE), for example, rooted virtues of *li* (proper conduct) and *jen* (benevolence) in an appreciation of traditions and customs.

Views from nowhere

An important line of criticism argues that many texts and theories are flawed because they pretend to have transcended or escaped history, custom, habit, and tradition. Critics like Michel de Montaigne, Edmund Burke, Karl Marx, Michael Oakeshott, and more recently Chantal Mouffe advance, in various ways, this sort of criticism. They point out the way many speciously claim to have achieved, usually through what poses as reason, some sort of transcendence beyond, independence from, and authority over customs, opinions, and traditions. They pretend to have achieved a God's-eye, absolute point of view on reality, a view Benedict Spinoza (1632–1677) called approvingly "a view from eternity" (*sub species aeternitatis*) and Thomas Nagel, by contrast, called critically "a view from nowhere."

Nagel's point is well taken, for how is it possible for a text, a writer, a speaker, a theorist, etc. to become independent of history, culture, custom, and tradition if humans are inescapably historical, cultural, and customary beings? The concepts people use, the languages they speak, the architecture and disposition of their feelings, their attitudes, beliefs, and habits are informed by history and tradition – ethical concepts, beliefs, feelings, and habits among them. Isn't it specious, then, to pretend to be a "citizen of the world," as some stoics and other cosmopolitan thinkers claim to be? Isn't it presumptuous to argue, as early liberals like Thomas Paine and Thomas Jefferson did (and many liberals since), that they have discovered universal human rights that apply to all people at all times and in all cultures? Can anyone make claims about what is just, beautiful, right, and true for all times and places? (Curiously, however, some traditionalist critics, e.g., Frithjof Schuon (1907–1998), argue that an appreciation of the deep traditions from which modern society has departed can actually reconnect us with the divine.)

The harm in forgetting

One might think critically, then, about a text by considering whether and how it pretends to demonstrate an ahistorical point of view, or at least how it positions itself in relation to what is traditional or customary. The text's shortcoming, however, may be more than an issue of pretended knowing. It may be existential, since sometimes a practice or set of ideas may even wrongly threaten another culture or tradition by not honoring its history. Criticism might, for example, be brought to bear against prohibitions of African or Appalachian or First People's speech patterns as "improper" or "ungrammatical." Or, for another example, perhaps critics might wish to challenge the way some practices of gender, marriage, religion, cuisine, and healthcare have been judged inferior when they have sprung from other, unfamiliar traditions.

The importance of careful listening

All this is not to say that tradition is always good or that change is impossible. People aren't stuck in the past, and traditions are not strictly speaking always conservative. There are, after all, traditions of resistance and rebellion, even, as we'd like to emphasize, traditions of criticism. And we don't mean to argue for a strict relativism that holds it's impossible for people with different histories and cultures to communicate with one another or even to criticize one another meaningfully and properly. Histories and cultures are not hermetically sealed but move within and across one another like currents interweaving and intermixing in the sea. There are long traditions of inter-cultural exchange and meaningful critique. Sometimes, in fact, the most trenchant criticisms come from those who possess critical distance from a tradition. Mahatma Gandhi, for example, effectively criticized British colonial traditions when he responded to an English reporter who asked him what he thought of Western civilization with the retort: "I think it would be a good idea." Gandhi himself appealed to Indian traditions of weaving one's own clothing and spinning one's own thread to guide and sustain his independence movement.

Attending to history and tradition implies thinking and writing sensitively. It means that one must listen hard and carefully to others, paying attention to the different histories that inform their ways of thinking and doing. It also means taking care not to speak and write as if from a transcendent point of view, outside of any historical location. It's not wrong, intrinsically, to speak for others, especially others who cannot speak for themselves, but one must do so carefully and without the claim to transcendent authority.

Careful attention to history does not ensure tranquility. Sometimes understanding something's history results in seeing how dangerous and intolerable it is – for example, the long history of anti-Semitic demagoguery. If one is to criticize historically rooted practices, however, one will do well to consider instruments of criticism grown in the right soil of history, custom, and tradition. To present meaningful forms of criticism, persuasion, and argument one must speak in recognizably meaningful ways, one must sympathize with others' customs and habits of feeling and reasoning, and one must attend carefully to the deep historical resonance ideas, symbols, words, and images carry for people. Doing all this requires understanding and appreciating people's histories, others' and your own. It's no easy task, but good critical thinking requires it.

Exercises and study questions

1. Is consumerist and capitalist society anti-traditional?
2. How might traditionalist and historicist criticism address the question of whether or not to prohibit polygamy, arranged marriage, or child marriage?
3. How might practices of female genital cutting be well or poorly defended or criticized in light of traditionalist and historicist criticisms?
4. Is it meaningful to characterize natural science and deductive logic as Western?
5. Are human rights properly described as universal?
6. How might historicist and traditionalist criticism be brought to bear on controversies about the purchase and sale of lands inhabited by tribal peoples?
7. Is there a way using traditionalist and historicist forms of critique to resolve the conflict between Muslim traditional religious practices of *hijab* and French Republican political traditions of *laïcité*?
8. Is reason contrary to tradition?

SEE ALSO

9.2 The Purview of Science
10.7 Foucault's Critique of Power
10.8 The Frankfurt School: Culture Critique

READING

Emmanuel Chukwudi Eze, *On Reason: Rationality in a World of Cultural Conflict and Racism* (2008)

Maria Rosa Menocal, *The Ornament of the World: How Muslims, Jews, and Christians Created a Culture of Tolerance in Medieval Spain* (2003)

Georgia Warnke, *Gadamer: Hermeneutics, Tradition, and Reason* (1987)

Michael Oakeshott, *Rationalism in Politics and Other Essays* (1962)
Edmund Burke, *Reflections on the Revolution in France* (1790)

10.13 Ecological Critiques

It may seem a strange question, but is the acquisition of a refrigerator, air conditioner, or clothes dryer a sign of becoming better or worse off? In terms of immediate creature comforts, the answer seems obvious, but considered from an ecological perspective things become less clear. People have become increasingly aware of the substantial impact that human activity has had on the Earth's biosphere, and that impact has in many ways been negative (see 9.2). Thinking critically today, therefore, must involve thinking about the ecological dimensions of human ideas, institutions, and practices.

Consumption and pollution

One of the most important environmental considerations critical thinking can raise is that of resource consumption. When examining a practice or theory, raise questions about how many resources are likely to be consumed in its realization. Will the building of a road through a forested area lead to the consumption of more land and energy as travelers and commercial interests grow up along the roadside and the adjacent areas? Should individual homeownership be encouraged given that individual, detached homes use more land and energy resources than row houses, apartments, and condominium blocks? What sorts of foods are the least resource intensive to produce? Can we find forms of entertainment that don't require electricity? How much water and cropland does beef production require, and can that be changed? Is that the most efficient means of food production? In general, how can we change our institutions, ideas, and practices so our lives consume less of the world? Are market systems more ecologically responsible than non-market or socialized economies?

When one listens to policy makers and analysts speak about the economy, it's nearly always about growth. But since growth is generally correlated with growing resource consumption, is, say, GDP growth really a good measure of economic progress? Should, under the present ecological circumstances, economic growth be encouraged at all? Isn't there enough wealth already and the problem just that it's poorly distributed? Why don't policy makers consult an environmental well-being index such as the GGEI (the Global Green Economy Index) along with (or instead of) standard economic indexes that ignore the environmental effects of economic activity?

Consumption has risen with wealth increases in many societies. More wealth means more consumption. And so it has become an ecologically relevant question to ask whether too much wealth is ecologically acceptable. Consumption has also risen, as population theorist Thomas Malthus (1766–1834) argued, albeit inaccurately, it would with population. How much population is too much? Has the Earth already exceeded its ecologically sustainable carrying capacity? Should we be working to reduce human population? Is it responsible to have more than one child? How do contemporary practices and ideas help encourage and justify expanding human populations?

Since the processes that consume resources always produce effluents, it's important that critical thinkers also consider pollution. Climate change has been in part driven by the release of carbon compounds into the air, but these compounds are just one form of pollution among, unfortunately, many others. The land, air, and seas have been polluted by all kinds of effluent: plastics (the vast extent of which has only recently been understood), carcinogens, sewage, ozone-eroding agents, pharmaceutical products, pesticides, fertilizers, radiation, and even artificial light and sound that can disrupt plant and animal life. Can food be grown and raised with less effluent and less soil erosion? Should plastic food packaging be eliminated? Should we continue to eat food shipped across such enormous distances? Are there ways to cool and warm and illuminate living spaces that require less energy? Are personal automobiles and trips for pleasure that require air travel justifiable when both release so much carbon?

Ecological justice

"Cancer Alley" is a stretch of the Mississippi River between Baton Rouge and New Orleans that has experienced extraordinarily high cancer rates, apparently as a result of pollution. Perhaps unsurprisingly, the area is poor and populated predominantly by people of African descent. Cancer Alley and the many places in the world like it raise one of the most important social-political dimensions of ecological thinking – namely, how the negative environmental effects of modern life are distributed. Environmental impacts are not equally distributed to all people. Often environmental effects have a disproportionately negative impact upon minority populations. Sometimes there are greater environmental impacts upon one gender or another. As it has been in Cancer Alley, pollution has a greater and disproportionate impact upon the poor than the rich. Rising sea levels resulting from global warming, for example, are likely to affect the poor more adversely. The poor, also, are often housed in areas with little greenery or exposure to wildlife. In short, critically thinking about environmental impacts will involve asking about who will bear those impacts the most.

Who should pay to stop and remedy the effects of pollution, especially the pollution that's caused climate change, is an important question of ecological justice. Some argue that those countries that have been most responsible for the problem over the preceding centuries, the United States and the countries of Western Europe, should pay most of the cost. Others have argued that the cost should include developing and more recently developed countries, such as China.

Non-human life

Of course, those impacts are often biggest upon non-human populations of plants and animals. For many people, human beings enjoy a kind of privileged position. We are, in this view, categorically more important than the members of other species. Some have even argued that non-human living things have no moral standing whatsoever – that moral considerations do not apply to non-humans, so that humans may use them in whatever ways we choose. But are these justifiable positions? Ecological thinkers have challenged the idea of human privilege. They've criticized both the idea (1) that non-humans have no moral standing and (2) that humans possess a superior standing. Philosopher Peter Singer, one of those critics, coined the term *speciesism* to describe the unjustified belief in human superiority, just as "racism" and "sexism" are used to criticize unjustified beliefs and practices associated with racial and gender superiority.

Thinking critically about a text or practice along these lines might raise questions about how it affects non-human animals and what implicit or explicit statements of human superiority or privilege the text advances. Historian Lynn White, Jr. has, for example, argued that the Bible has enabled ideas of human superiority in the passages from Genesis that speak about God's creating "man" in "His" image and giving human beings "dominion" over the rest of the natural world, as well as in instructing humans to "subdue" the natural world. So in the Bible's Book of Genesis 1:26–28 you'll find:

> And God said, Let us make man in our image, after our likeness: and let them have dominion over the fish of the sea, and over the fowl of the air, and over the cattle, and over all the earth, and over every creeping thing that creepeth upon the earth. So God created man in his own image, in the image of God created he him; male and female created he them. And God blessed them, and God said unto them, Be fruitful, and multiply, and replenish the earth, and subdue it: and have dominion over the fish of the sea, and over the fowl of the air, and over every living thing that moveth upon the earth.

Others have argued that this passage has been inflected by translation and that ideas of "stewardship" and "creation" offer a strong environmental basis for environmental responsibility. What qualities of any text might reinforce or legitimate undesirable ecological conduct?

Critical thinkers ought also to ask whether a particular practice will cause suffering or disruption to non-human life. Must we eat non-human animals, and is veganism the only responsible dietary option, at least for those in economically wealthy societies? Can we eliminate leather? Is it possible to conduct medical research without laboratory testing on non-human animals? Is laboratory testing on non-human animals good science? Do non-humans possess certain rights to territory/habitat that limit human property rights – such as rights to limit building upon and altering the landscape? Are zoos morally justifiable? Circuses? Domestic pets? Why is zoophilia prohibited? Should military practices take non-humans and their habitats into account (for example, in targeting considerations and as casualties)? What disanalogies might be found between speciesism, sexism, and racism?

Exercises and study questions

1. Examine from an ecological perspective some form of human entertainment – e.g., amusement parks, fireworks, hunting.
2. Should non-humans possess moral standing? If non-humans possess moral standing, should it be equal to that of humans? Why or why not?
3. How might we assess the performance of our economies in ecological ways? What criteria of performance might be used instead of or in addition to GDP, equities and commodities market values, and employment rates?
4. Are there ecological injustices taking place in or near your home? What policy changes might affect ecological injustices?
5. How ought the world deal with massive population growth? With climate change?
6. Who should pay the costs associated with remedying climate change caused by human activities?

SEE ALSO

10.7 Foucault's Critique of Power
10.9 Class Critiques
10.10 Feminist and Gender Critiques
10.11 Critiques of Race and Racism

READING

Peter Singer, *Animal Liberation: The Definitive Classic of the Animal Movement* [1975], (2009)
Michael Pollan, *The Omnivore's Dilemma* (2007)
Joni Adamson, Mei Mei Evans, & Rachel Stein, eds., *The Environmental Justice Reader: Politics, Poetics, and Pedagogy* (2002)

Appendix: Recommended Web Sites

1. *Bad Science Blog* (www.badscience.net), Ben Goldacre's critical blog about questionable science in the news and elsewhere.
2. *Critical Theory Blog* (www.critical-theory.com), an accessible blog of critical news and application.
3. *The Critical Thinking Community* (www.criticalthinking.org), a professional organization devoted to advancing, defining, and refining critical thinking.
4. *Glossary of Rhetorical Terms* (mcl.as.uky.edu/glossary-rhetorical-terms), a helpful resource in understanding rhetorical and poetic tropes from the University of Kentucky Department of Classics.
5. *Fallacy Files* (www.fallacyfiles.org), Gary N. Curtis's extensive and informative collection, explication, and taxonomy of logical fallacies.
6. *Informal Logic* (www.informallogic.ca), an Open Access academic journal devoted to scholarly inquiry into matters of informal reasoning.
7. *Internet Encyclopedia of Philosophy* (www.iep.utm.edu), an accessible, clear, and informative collection of entries, many relevant to critical thinking; see especially its collection of fallacies.
8. *Rationally Speaking* (rationallyspeaking.blogspot.com), Massimo Pigliucci's site about scientific reasoning.
9. *Silva Rhetoricae* (rhetoric.byu.edu), an online guide to terms and topics in ancient and Renaissance rhetoric from Gideon Burton of Brigham Young University.
10. *The Skeptic's Dictionary* (skepdic.com), a great resource not only for logic and perception theory but also for debunking pseudo-science.
11. *Stanford Encyclopedia of Philosophy* (plato.stanford.edu), an extraordinary collection of substantial articles on a vast spectrum of topics in philosophy and critical theory, including many of those addressed by this book.
12. *Wikipedia* (wikipedia.org), a helpful resource on many topics in critical thinking.

The Critical Thinking Toolkit, First Edition. Galen A. Foresman, Peter S. Fosl, and Jamie C. Watson.

Index

The Critical Thinking Toolkit, First Edition. Galen A. Foresman, Peter S. Fosl, and Jamie C. Watson.

Terms
eristics 12
enthymemes 14
indicators 14

argument vs explanations 12
critical thinking '2-step' process 32
steelmaning 163
inductive reason and causal inquiry 166

* argument as bridge 19

analogy as inductive argument 168

* how to evaluate analogies 169

confounding of hidden variable
- in inductive argument 173

* types of causes 175

fallacies

appeal to origins
- genetic fallacy 112
begging the question 143
- rhetorical use of 143
question begging sentences
- politics 144

fallacy of composition 146
is-ought fallacy 150
* hasty generalization 161

Statistical reasoning

inductive generalizations 177
normal distribution 180
* base rate fallacy 182

* Mill's methods